Building on her seminal contribution to social theory in *Culture and agency*, Margaret Archer develops here her morphogenetic approach, applying it to the problem of structure and agency. Since structure and agency constitute different levels of stratified social reality, each possesses distinctive emergent properties which are real and causally efficacious but irreducible to one another. The problem, therefore, is shown to be how to link the two rather than conflate them, as has been common practice – whether in upwards conflation (by the aggregation of individual acts), downwards conflation (through the structural orchestration of agents), or, more recently, in central conflation which holds the two to be mutually constitutive and thus precludes any examination of their interplay by eliding them.

Realist social theory: the morphogenetic approach thus not only rejects Methodological Individualism and Holism, but argues that the debate between them has been replaced by a new one between elisionary theorizing (such as Giddens' structuration theory) and emergentist theories bases on a realist ontology of the social world. The morphogenetic approach is the sociological complement of transcendental realism, and together they provide a basis for non-conflationary theorizing which is also of direct utility to the practising social analyst.

Realist social theory: the morphogenetic approach

Realist social theory:
the morphogenetic approach

Margaret S. Archer

University of Warwick

CAMBRIDGE
UNIVERSITY PRESS

Published by the Press Syndicate of the University of Cambridge
The Pitt Building, Trumpington Street, Cambridge CB2 1RP
40 West 20th Street, New York, NY 10011-4211, USA
10 Stamford Road, Oakleigh, Melbourne 3166, Australia

First published 1995

A catalogue record for this book is available from the British Library

Library of Congress cataloguing in publication data

Archer, Margaret Scotford.
Realist social theory : the morphogenetic approach / Margaret S.
Archer.
        p.   cm.
ISBN 0 521 48176 7. – ISBN 0 521 48442 1 (pbk.)
1. Sociology – Philosophy.   2. Social structure.   3. Realism.
I. Title.
HM24.A722   1995
301'.01–dc20   94-45174   CIP

ISBN 0 521 48176 7 hardback

ISBN 0 521 48442 1 paperback

Transferred to digital printing 2003

To my husband
Andrew
Thank you

Contents

Figures

Acknowledgements

I am grateful to many people for their different kinds of help and support whilst this text was being written. However, my particular thanks are due to Roy Bhaskar for his generous encouragement and incitement to boldness, which included persuading me to give the book this title. Various sections and chapters benefited greatly from benign criticism by Martin Hollis, Peter Manicas, William Outhwaite and Roger Trigg. None is responsible for the final contents, though I hope they are not inclined to disown them altogether.

1   The vexatious fact of society

Social reality is unlike any other because of its human constitution. It is different from natural reality whose defining feature is self-subsistence: for its existence does not depend upon us, a fact which is not compromised by our human ability to intervene in the world of nature and change it. Society is more different still from transcendental reality, where divinity is both self-subsistent and unalterable at our behest; qualities which are not contravened by responsiveness to human intercession. The nascent 'social sciences' had to confront this entity, society, and deal conceptually with its three unique characteristics.

Firstly, that it is inseparable from its human components because the very existence of society depends in some way upon our activities. Secondly, that society is characteristically transformable; it has no immutable form or even preferred state. It is like nothing but itself, and what precisely it is like at any time depends upon human doings and their consequences. Thirdly, however, neither are we immutable as social agents, for what we are and what we do as social beings are also affected by the society in which we live and by our very efforts to transform it.

Necessarily then, the problem of the relationship between individual and society was *the* central sociological problem from the beginning. The vexatious task of understanding the linkage between 'structure and agency' will always retain this centrality because it derives from what society intrinsically is. Nor is this problem confined to those explicitly studying society, for each human being is confronted by it every day of their social life. An inescapable part of our inescapably social condition is to be aware of its constraints, sanctions and restrictions on our ambitions – be they for good or for evil. Equally, we acknowledge certain social blessings such as medication, transportation and education: without their enablements our lives and hopes would both be vastly more circumscribed. At the same time, an inalienable part of our human condition is the feeling of freedom: we are 'sovereign artificers' responsible for our own destinies, and capable of re-making our social environment to befit human habitation. This book begins by accepting that such ambivalence in the daily experience of ordinary people is fully authentic. Its authenticity does not derive from viewing subjective experiences as self-veridical. By themselves, the strength of our feelings is never a guarantee of their veracity: our certitudes are poor guides to certainty. Instead, this ambivalence is a real and defining feature of a human being who is also a social being. We *are* simultaneously free and constrained and we *also* have some awareness of it. The former derives from the nature of social reality; the latter from human nature's reflexivity. Together they generate an authentic (if imperfect) reflection upon the human condition in society. It is therefore the credo of this book that the adequacy of social theorizing fundamentally turns on its ability to recognize and reconcile these *two aspects* of lived social reality.

Thus we would betray ourselves, as well as our readers, by offering any form of social scient*ism* with 'laws' which are held to be unaffected by the uses and abuses we make of our freedoms, for this renders moral responsibility meaningless, political action worthless and self-reflection pointless. Equally, we delude one another by the pretence that society is simply what we choose to make it and make of it, now or in any generation, for generically 'society' is that which nobody wants in exactly the form they find it and yet it resists both individual and collective efforts at transformation – not necessarily by remaining unchanged but altering to become something else which still conforms to no one's ideal.

From the beginning, however, betrayal and delusion have been common practice when approaching the vexatious fact of society and its human constitution. The earliest attempts to conceptualize this unique entity produced two divergent social ontologies which, in changing guises, have been with us ever since. Both evade the encounter with the vexatious ambivalence of social reality. They can be epitomized as the 'science of society' versus the 'study of wo/man' : if the former denies the significance of society's human constitution, the latter nullifies the importance of what is, has been, and will be constituted as society in the process of human interaction. The former is a denial that the real powers of human beings are indispensable to making society what it is. The latter withholds real powers from society by reducing its properties to the projects of its makers. Both thus endorse epiphenomenalism, by holding respectively that agency or structure are inert and dependent variables. In this way they turn the vexatious into something tractable, but only by evading the uniqueness of social reality and treating it as something other than itself – by making it exclusively super-ordinate to people or utterly subordinate to them.

Furthermore, what society is held to be also affects how it is studied. Thus one of the central theses of this book is that any given social ontology has implications for the explanatory methodology which is (and in consistency can be) endorsed. This connection could not have been clearer in the works of the founding fathers. We need to remain equally clear that this is a necessary linkage – and to uphold it. The tripartite link between ontology, methodology and practical social theory is the *leitmotif* of this whole text.

Thus early protagonists of the 'Science of Society' began from an uncompromising ontological position which stated that there was indeed a Social Whole whose *sui generis* properties constituted the object of study. Thus, for Comte, 'Society is no more decomposable into individuals than a geometrical surface is into lines, or a line into points'.[1] Similarly for Durkheim: 'Whenever certain elements combine, and thereby produce, by the fact of their combination, new phenomena, it is plain that these new phenomena reside not in the original elements but in the totality formed by their union'.[2] Here 'Society' denoted a totality which is not reducible and this therefore meant that the explanatory programme must be anti-reductionist in nature. Hence, the methodological injunction to explain one 'social fact' only by reference to another 'social fact'. Correct explanations could not be reductionist, that is, cast in terms of individual psychology *because* the nature of social reality is held to be such that the necessary concepts could never be statements about individual people, whether for purposes of description or explanation. Consequently, practical social theories were advanced in exclusively holistic terms (explaining suicide rates by degrees of social integration) and without reference to individual human motivation. This then was a direct and early statement of what I term 'Downwards Conflation'[3] in social theorizing, where the 'solution' to the problem of structure and agency consists in rendering the latter epiphenomenal. Individuals are held to be 'indeterminate material' which is unilaterally moulded by society, whose holistic properties have complete monopoly over causation, and which therefore operate in a unilateral and downward manner. The contrary standpoint is represented by Individualism.

Those who conceived of their task as the 'study of wo/man' insisted that social reality consisted of nothing but individuals and their activities. Thus for J. S. Mill, 'Men in a state of society are still men. Their actions and passions are obedient to the laws of individual human nature. Men are not, when brought together, converted into another kind of substance with different properties, as hydrogen and oxygen are different from

---

[1] A. Comte, *Système de politique positive*, L. Mathias, Paris, 1951, vol. II, p. 181.
[2] E. Durkheim, *The Rules of Sociological Method*, Free Press, New York, 1962, p. xlvii.
[3] See Margaret S. Archer, *Culture and Agency*, Cambridge University Press, Cambridge, 1989, ch. 2.

water'.[4] Similarly for Weber, references to collectivities like the family, state or army are 'only a certain kind of development of actual or possible actions of individual persons'.[5] Having defined social reality individualistically, it followed for both thinkers that explanations of it must be in terms of individuals. Hence for Mill, 'The effects produced in social phenomena by any complex set of circumstances amount precisely to the sum of the effects of the circumstances taken singly'.[6] If society is an aggregate, then however complex, it can be understood only by a process of disaggregation, and explanation therefore consists in reduction. For Weber too, though collectivities like business corporations may look like non-people, since they are made up of nothing else then they 'must be treated solely as the resultants and modes of organization of the particular acts of individual persons'.[7] Since an aggregate is the resultant of its components, this means that in practical social theorizing we are presented with 'Upwards Conflation'. The solution to the problem of structure and agency is again epiphenomenal, but this time it is the social structure which is passive, a mere aggregate consequence of individual activities, which is incapable of acting back to influence individual people. Thus, people are held to monopolize causal power which therefore operates in a one-way, upwards direction.

Already in *stating* the manner in which early social analysts confronted society, it has not been possible to do so without touching upon three different aspects which are intrinsic to *any* solution offered. Since the purpose of this book is to proffer a particular kind of solution and one which is intended to be of use to those engaged in substantive social analysis, it is crucial to be clear about the three necessary components – ontology, methodology, and practical social theory – and their interconnections. I have already stated one basic thesis, namely that the social ontology adopted has implications for the explanatory methodology endorsed and indicated how this was the case at the start of the discipline. However, it is equally the case that the methodology employed has ramifications for the nature of practical social theorizing – and in the two early paradigms this led paradigmatically to opposite versions of conflationary theory.

I believe we should never be satisfied with these forms of conflationary theorizing, which either deny people all freedom because of their involvement in society or leave their freedom completely untrammelled by their social involvements. The fact that neither Durkheim nor Weber managed

[4] J. S. Mill, *A System of Logic Ratiocintive and Inductive*, People's Editions, London, 1884, p. 573.
[5] Max Weber, *The Theory of Social and Economic Organization*, Free Press, New York, 1964 (orig. 1922) p. 102.   [6] Mill, *System*, p. 583.   [7] Weber, *Theory*, p. 101.

to hold consistently to his own explanatory injunctions when conducting practical social analyses might have induced some reflection upon the adequacies of their methodological charters and ontological commitments. However, the nineteenth-century parting of the ways between the 'science of society' and the 'study of wo/man' passed, virtually unaltered, into the twentieth-century debate between Holism and Individualism in the philosophy of 'social science'. And there it continued to reproduce the deficiencies of both downwards and upwards conflation in practical social theorizing by re-endorsing much the same explanatory methodologies and social ontologies as had traditionally been advanced.

Both are deficient and have been regularly criticized, but the current state of the art still harbours them, together with numerous variants and claimants to the status of 'alternatives'. Because of this, commentators regularly used to signal 'crisis', whereas postmodernists now celebrate 'fragmentation' in social theory. My principal contention is that we cannot extricate ourselves from this theoretical morass without recognizing the tripartite connections between ontology, methodology and practical social theory and ensuring consistency between them. There have, however, been two different responses to the present situation whose consequences are instructive. On the one hand, some have been tempted to uncouple practical social theory from its underpinnings, to survey the array of perspectives, and suggest an eclectic pragmatism in order to have the best of all worlds. Such 'perspectivism' simultaneously denies that there are serious underlying reasons for theoretical variety and slides via instrumentalism into a marriage of inconsistent premises. On the other hand, some social theorists have returned to work exclusively on the re-conceptualization of social reality. As such they may be playing a useful role in the division of sociological labour, but if they suggest that their ontological exertions suffice, the theoretical enterprise simply cannot be resumed on this unfinished basis. The practical analyst of society needs to know not only *what social reality is*, but also *how to begin to explain it*, before addressing the particular problem under investigation. In short, methodology, broadly conceived of as an explanatory programme, is the necessary link between social ontology and practical theory.

This is what this book is intended to supply, an explanatory methodology which is indeed pivotal, called the morphogenetic approach. (The 'morpho' element is an acknowledgement that society has no pre-set form or preferred state: the 'genetic' part is a recognition that it takes its shape from, and is formed by, agents, originating from the intended and unintended consequences of their activities.) In order to play its part in the chain 'ontology – methodology – practical social theory', such an explanatory framework has to be firmly anchored at both ends.

Firstly, this means that it has to be consistently embedded in an adequate social ontology. Yet I have already begun to intimate that the study of society got off on the wrong footing in both the Individualist and Holist conceptions of reality, and in so far as these do still remain as very serious contenders, it will be necessary to break with both. Secondly, the morphogenetic approach is meant to be of practical utility for analysts of society. In itself, of course, an explanatory framework neither explains, nor purports to explain, anything. Nevertheless, it performs a regulatory role, for though many substantive theories may be compatible with it, this is not the case for all, and an explanatory methodology therefore encourages theorizing in one direction whilst discouraging it in others. The primary regulative function which the morphogenetic framework seeks to assume is one which refuses to countenance *any form of conflationary theorizing* at the practical level.

Although frequent references will be made to its substantive applications (usually drawn from my own work on education and culture), what other practitioners would make of it is left to their discretion in relation to their own substantive problems. Instead, the major concern of this book is with the link between this explanatory methodology and social ontology, precisely because existing combinations are found wanting in themselves and also guilty of fostering conflation between structure and agency, which is then registered at the level of practical theorizing.

Traditions of conflation

Generically, conflation in social theory represents one-dimensional theorizing. As in the old 'individual versus society' debate or its later expression as the 'structure and agency' problem, traditional conflationists were those who saw this as a matter of taking sides and who could come down with great conviction on one or the other. Their common denominator was this readiness to choose and consequently to repudiate sociological dualism where the different 'sides' refer to different elements of social reality, which possess different properties and powers. In contradistinction, the *interplay and interconnection* of these properties and powers form the central concern of non-conflationary theorizing, whose hallmark is the recognition that the two have to be related rather than conflated. Instead, classical conflationists always advance some device which reduces one to the other, thus depriving the two of independent properties, capable of exerting autonomous influences, which would automatically defy one-dimensional theorizing. The most generic traditional device was epiphenomenalism through upwards or downwards reduction, although the precise mechanism employed showed some variation – aggregation/disaggregation, composition/decomposition, or the homologies of miniaturization/magnification.

Traditionally, too, the major divide which theorists have sought to overcome in these ways has been labelled differently in various schools of thought and countries. Although there are differences in nuances, I regard the fundamental issues raised by those debates variously named 'individual and society', 'voluntarism and determinism', 'structure and agency' or 'the micro- versus macro-' as being fundamentally identical. Instead of attempting to see these as standing in some ascending order of complexity (*contra* Layder[8]), I regard their differential accentuation as little more than historical and comparative variations on the same theme. In particular, discussion in the UK has consistently concentrated upon the 'problem of structure and agency', whilst in the USA the pre-occupation has been with 'the problem of scope',[9] which has now resurfaced, re-named as the 'micro-macro link'.[10] However, nomenclature should not mislead us for, as Jeffrey Alexander emphasizes, these are versions of exactly the same debate: 'The perennial conflict between individualistic and collectivist theories has been re-worked as a conflict between micro-sociology and macro-sociology.'[11]

Here the parallel form of conflationary theorizing takes the form of the displacement of scope which 'is committed whenever a theorist assumes, without further ado, that theoretical schemes or models worked out on the basis of macro-sociological considerations fit micro-sociological interpretations, or vice versa'.[12] In the downwards conflationary version, a homology was asserted between the societal system and the small group which was held to constitute a miniaturized version of the former because orchestrated by the same central value system. Hence the one-dimensionality of Parsons' processes for analysing 'any system of action' whatever its scope. Since to him 'there are continuities all the way from two-person interaction to the USA as a social system', it follows that 'we can translate back and forth between large scale social systems and small groups'.[13] This licence to start wherever one wants and to move 'back and forth' with ease depends upon the validity of the homological premiss,

[8] Derek Layder, *Understanding Social Theory*, Sage, London, 1994, p. 3.
[9] Helmut Wagner, 'Displacement of scope: a problem of the relationship between small-scale and large-scale sociological theories', *American Journal of Sociology*, 1964, 69:6.
[10] Jeffrey Alexander, Bernhard Giesen, Richard Munch and Neil Smelser (eds.), *The Micro-Macro Link*, University of California Press, Berkeley, 1987. 'In the last debate the discipline of sociology resusitated an old dilemma in a new form – a form, unfortunately, that has done little to resolve the dilemma itself.' Alexander, 'Action and its environments', p. 289.   [11] Alexander, 'Action and its environments'.
[12] Wagner, 'Displacement of scope', p. 583.
[13] T. Parsons, 'The social system: a general theory of action', in R. R. Grinker (ed.), *Toward a Unified Theory of Human Behavior*, Basic Books, New York, 1956, pp. 190.

namely that the same properties (no more, no less, and no different) are indeed found throughout society.

The upward conflationary version simply made the opposite homological assumption, i.e. that society is simply the small group writ large. This led interpretative sociologists in particular to place a 'big etc.' against their microscopic expositions and to hold out the expectation that explanation of the social system could be arrived at by a process of accretion. This aggregative ethnographic programme depended upon the validity of exactly the same homological premiss about there being no more, no less and no different properties characterizing different levels of society.[14] This central premiss will be challenged in every chapter of the present work.

The final and most important similarity between these parallel debates in the UK and the USA was their firm rooting in empiricism. The conviction that social theory must confine itself to observables, since the perceptual criterion was held to be the only guarantor of reality, provided British individualists with their trump card (for who could doubt the existence of flesh-and-blood people) and the collectivists with their stumbling block (since how could they validate the existence of any property unless they could translate it into a series of observational statements about people). The American debate was even more unabashed in its positivism, since its defining terms, the 'micro-' and the 'macro-' necessarily dealt only with an observable property, that is *size*.

Since I have maintained that it was one and the same debate going on either side of the Atlantic, then I seriously want to question whether 'the main story'[15] in American social theory or anywhere else should be about size *per se*. In fact, to disassociate the United States' version of the debate from this empirical observable feature is paralleled by the more comprehensive task of disassociating the British debate from empiricism altogether. In other words, it is my view that only by rejecting the terms of these traditional debates and completely revising them on a different ontological basis can we get away from one dimensional conflationary theorizing and replace it by theories of the interdependence and interplay between different kinds of social properties.

Thus in the American debate there is a substantial consensus, that I seek to challenge, which unequivocally considers the problem of how to relate the micro and the macro as being about how to forge a linkage between social units of different *sizes*. Thus Munch and Smelser,[16]

---

[14] For a more extended discussion of these points, see, Margaret S. Archer, 'The problems of scope in the sociology of education', *International Review of Sociology*, 1987, ns 1: 83–99.   [15] Layder, *Social Theory*, p. 2f.

[16] Richard Munch and Neil Smelser, 'Relating the micro and macro', in Alexander et al. (eds.), *The Micro-Macro Link*, pp. 356–7.

reviewing the field in 1987, produced seven different definitions of the terms 'micro' and 'macro', which (with the exception of Peter Blau) all firmly associated the former with the small scale and the latter with the large scale. In other words, despite their differences, Layder's recent fomulation would generally be accepted as uncontroversial by them. 'Micro analysis or "microsociology"' concentrates on the more personal and immediate aspects of social interaction in daily life. Another way of saying this is that it focuses on actual face-to-face encounters between people. Macro analysis or "macrosociology" focuses on the larger-scale more general features of society such as organizations, institutions and culture.'[17] Instead, this seems to me highly controversial, and to represent a tradition with which social theory should break. It needs to be replaced by an emphasis upon the incidence of emergent properties which delineate different strata – an emphasis which does not assume that observable differences in the size of groups automatically means that they constitute distinct levels of social reality.

Although no one would deny that empirically there are big and small units in society, this does not necessarily mean that they possess properties whose linkage presents any particular problems. That is, the real 'aspects' or 'features' of social reality are not by definition tied to the *size* of interacting elements (the *site* of the encounter, or for that matter, the *sentiment* accompanying interaction). Thus, I am in complete agreement with Alexander's statement 'that this equation of micro with individual is extremely misleading, as indeed, is the attempt to find any specific size correlation with the micro/macro difference. There can be no empirical referents for micro or macro as such. They are analytical contrasts, suggesting emergent levels within empirical units, not antagonistic empirical units themselves.'[18] In the same way, I want to maintain that 'micro' and 'macro' are *relational* terms meaning that a given stratum can be 'micro' to another and 'macro' to a third etc. What justifies the differentiation of strata and thus use of the terms 'micro' and 'macro' to characterize their relationship is the existence of *emergent properties* pertaining to the latter but not to the former, even if they were elaborated from it. But this has nothing to do with size, site or sentiment.

Emergent properties are *relational*, arising out of combination (e.g. the division of labour from which high productivity emerges), where the latter is capable of reacting back on the former (e.g. producing monotonous work), has its own causal powers (e.g. the differential wealth of nations), which are causally irreducible to the powers of its components (individual workers). This signals the *stratified nature of social reality* where different strata possess different emergent properties and powers.

---

[17] Layder, *Social Theory*, p. 1.   [18] Alexander, 'Action and its environments', p. 290.

However, the key points in this connection are that emergent strata constitute (a) the crucial entities in need of linking by explaining how their causal powers originate and operate, but (b) that such strata do not neatly map onto empirical units of any particular magnitude. Indeed, whether they coincide with the 'big' or the 'small' is contingent and thus there cannot be a 'micro'-'macro' problem which is defined exclusively by the relative size of social units.

Thus in the course of this book, frequent references will be made to 'the societal'. Each time, this has a concrete referent – particular emergent properties belonging to a specific society at a given time. Both the referent and the properties are real, they have full ontological status, but what do they have to do with 'the big'? The society in question may be small, tribal and work on a face-to-face basis. Nor do they have anything to do with what is, relatively, 'the biggest' at some point in time. We may well wish to refer to certain societal properties of Britain (the 'macro' unit for a particular investigation) which is an acknowledged part of bigger entities, like Europe, developed societies, or the English speaking world. We would do so if we wanted to explain, for example, the role of the 'Falklands factor' in recent elections and in so doing we would also incidentally be acknowledging that people who go in for it take their nationalism far from 'impersonally', and that the 'site' of neo-colonialism may be far distant.

Similarly the existence of small-scale interpersonal encounters does not make these into a sociological category, much less if this is on the presumption that they are somehow immune to 'factors' belonging to other strata of social reality, possessed of some much greater freedom for internal self-determination and presumed to be inconsequential for the system of which they are part. To the social realist there is no 'isolated' micro world – no *lebsenswelt* 'insulated' from the socio-cultural system in the sense of being unconditioned by it, nor a hermetically sealed domain whose day-to-day doings are guaranteed to be of no systemic 'import'.

On the contrary, the entrance and exit doors of the life world are permanently open and the understanding of its conditions, course and consequences are predicated upon acknowledging this. For example, small-scale interactions between teachers and pupils do not just happen in classrooms but within educational systems, and those between landlords and tenants are not in-house affairs but take place on the housing market. Both pupils and teachers, for instance, bring in with them different degrees of bargaining power (cultural capital as expertise) that is resources with which they were endowed in wider society by virtue of family, class, gender and ethnicity. Equally, the definition of instruction which they literally encounter in schools is not one which can freely be negotiated *in situ* but is determined outside the classroom, and, at least partially, outside the educational system altogether.

Thus one of the biggest deviations in the 1970s sociology of education (which had its parallels in other specialisms) was not the determination to study those neglected educational processes and practices taking place within, but the methodological decision that this could be done by shutting the classroom door and bolting the school gates because everything needed to explain what went on within was found inside the small enclosure. Yet closure is always a misleading metaphor which conceals the *impact* of external systemic and social properties and also the *import* of internal 'micropolitics' for reproduction and change of the social and the systemic. For on the one hand, both teachers and pupils are enmeshed in broader *socio-cultural relations* which they carry with them into the classroom, and whose first affect is which type of school class they enter! Once there, teachers and pupils cannot freely negotiate the relationships they jointly will, given the impact of curricular controls, public examinations and the job market. On the other hand, classroom interaction is *never* without systemic *import*, whether this works for reproduction or for transformation.

Construed in this manner, then, the crucial linkage to make and to maintain is not between the 'micro' and the 'macro', conceived of as the small and interpersonal in contrast to the large and impersonal, but rather between the 'social' and the 'systemic'. In other words systemic properties are always the ('macro') *context* confronted by ('micro') social interaction, whilst social activities between people ('micro') represent the *environment* in which the ('macro') features of systems are either reproduced or transformed. But in neither the structural nor the cultural domains is this necessarily to talk about the big in relation to the small: for emergent properties can figure at all 'levels'. Yet since they only arise from and work through social interaction, then this crucial interplay requires examination at any level.

Two implications follow from this. Firstly, that the central theoretical task is one of linking two *qualitatively* different aspects of society (the 'social' and the 'systemic', or if preferred 'action' and its 'environment') rather than two quantitatively *different* features, the big and the small or macro and micro. The main point here is that qualitative differences defy linkage by aggregation, homology or in short by conflation. Instead, it is a matter of theorizing their mutual impact and import – which need not be reciprocal. (This accounts for why it is necessary to deal with the positive feedback producing morphogenesis and to distinguish it from the negative feedback reinforcing morphostasis). As Alexander puts the task of linking action and its environments, 'The collective environments of action simultaneously inspire and confine it. If I have conceptualized action correctly, these environments will be seen as its products; if I can conceptualize the environments correctly, action will be seen as their result.'[19] Although in general agreement, I would prefer to talk about conditional influences in order to avoid the deterministic overtones of the above.

The second implication is that if the misleading preoccupation with *size* is abandoned, then the linkages which need forging to account for the vexatious fact of society are those between the 'people' and the 'parts' of social reality, or as Lockwood[20] put it, between 'social' and 'system' integration, that is, how orderly or conflictual social relations (properties of people) mesh with congruent or incongruent systemic relations (properties of parts of society). In short, we come back full circle to the one problem of 'structure and agency'. Consequently it is necessary to return to the debate which traditionally underpinned it – between individualism and collectivism – for that is where the root divide is grounded. No apologies are made for revisiting this 1950s terrain, although I will try to review it in the sparest terms. Instead, my apologia is that unless individualism and collectivism are uprooted, reinspected and rejected once and for all, because of their radical ontological and methodological deficiencies, then social theory will remain bogged down in the fallacy of conflation and practical social analysis will remain shackled to the unworkable explanatory programmes represented by upward and downward conflationism.

The purpose and the plan of the book

The overriding aim is to come to terms with the vexatious fact of society and its human constitution which it is held cannot be achieved through any form of conflation of these two components. However, 'coming to terms' means two related things – ontological and methodological. For the aim of the social theorist is two-fold. On the one hand, the task is to explicate in what general terms 'society' should be conceptualized. Since theories are propositions containing concepts and since all concepts have their referents (pick out features held to belong to social reality), then there can be no social theory without an accompanying social ontology (implicit or explicit). On the other hand, the point of theory is practical. It is never an end in itself but a tool for the working social analyst which gives explanatory purchase on substantive social problems, through

---

[19] Alexander, 'Action and its environments', p. 303.
[20] David Lockwood, 'Social integration and system integration', in G. K. Zollschan and H. W. Hirsch, *Explorations in Social Change*, Houghton Mifflin, Boston 1964.

supplying the terms or framework for their investigation. Thus my aim
cannot be to advance some abstract account of the vexatious fact of society
which solves a theoretical problem (how to avoid conflationary formulations) but one which remains at such a high level of abstraction that it is of
no assistance to those who are vexed by some particular aspect of it.
Although books may be written in this way, I want to sustain the point
that what social reality is held to be cannot but influence how society is
studied. In other words, there is always a connection between social
ontology and explanatory methodology (however covert and however
unhelpful). The final section of the introduction is devoted to justifying
the proposition that this is a necessary and a two-way linkage.

In the next chapter, I seek to demonstrate the consistency of these two
within both Individualism and Collectivism. It follows from this that we
are still trapped in the *conjoint* ontological/methodological terms set by
this traditional debate – with the unacceptable consequence that upward
and downward conflation are perpetuated in social theory. Chapter 3
argues that it is therefore only by rejecting the terms of the traditional
debate and replacing both their ontologies and methodologies that a basis
can be developed for non-conflationary theorizing. However, this chapter
also begins to show that rejection does not mean replacement by a new
consensus but rather the re-opening of another debate about how to link
structure and agency. It outlines the (now) four different positions
systematically. It follows that the burden of choice has not been removed
from contemporary practitioners nor in replacing the terms of the
traditional debate has conflationism disappeared from social theorizing.
    On the contrary, there is now a parting of the ways between those who
seek to *transcend* the duality of structure and agency in one conceptual
move by considering the two as being mutually constitutive and necessarily linked to form a duality – such that agents cannot act without drawing
upon structural properties whose own existence depends upon their
instantiation by agents. This core notion of structure as the simultaneous
medium and outcome of action is central to Giddens's structuration
theory. Chapter 4 analyzes how this leads directly to central conflation in
social theory – as a relatively new variant, though an idealist version of it
can be found in the social constructionism of Berger and Luckmann.[21]
Although superior in many ways to its predecessors, it none the less shares
the problematic nature of all forms of conflationary theory. In this case,
the difficulty is not that of ephiphenomenalism (that is of either structure

---

[21] P. Berger and T. Luckmann, *The Social Construction of Reality*, Doubleday-Anchor,
New York, 1967. See also the comments upon this model by Roy Bhaskar, *The Possibility
of Naturalism*, Harvester, Hemel Hempstead, 1989, p. 32f.

or agency being dependent, inert and therefore causally uninfluential) but that endorsement of their mutual constitution precludes examination of their interplay, of the effects of one upon the other and of any statement about their relative contribution to stability and change at any given time.

Conversely social realism which accentuates the importance of emergent properties at the levels of both agency and structure, but considers these as proper to the strata in question and therefore *distinct* from each other and *irreducible* to one another, replaces the terms of the traditional debate with entirely new ones. Irreducibility means that the different strata are *separable* by definition precisely because of the properties and powers which only belong to each of them and whose emergence from one another justifies their differentiation as strata at all. Three *differentia specifica* are denoted by the concept of emergence:

> Properties and powers of some strata are anterior to those of others precisely because the latter emerge from the former over time, for emergence takes time since it derives from interaction and its consequences which necessarily occur in time;

> Once emergence has taken place the powers and properties defining and distinguishing strata have relative autonomy from one another;

> Such autonomous properties exert independent causal influences in their own right and it is the identification of these causal powers at work which validates their existence, for they may indeed be non-observables.

Chapter 5 is devoted to spelling out the ontological distinctiveness of social realism and clearly distinguishing it from the ontology of praxis endorsed by proponents of the mutual constitution of structure and agency. Unfortunately, because both realists and structurationists have both rejected the terms of the old debate between Individualism and Collectivism, there has been an over-hasty tendency to assume their mutual convergence and to lump them together as *an* alternative to the positions taken in the traditional debate. Instead, the crucial point is that we are now confronted by two new and competing social ontologists.

Moreover, these ontological differences bear out the conviction that what social reality is held to be serves to regulate *how* we are enjoined to study it. Because it is based four square upon the notion of emergent properties the methodological implications of social realism are quite different from the explanatory framework advanced by structurationists because the latter explicitly reject emergence itself. Quite simply, if the different strata possess different properties and powers and structure and agency *inter alia* are deemed to be distinctive strata for this very reason, then examining their interplay becomes crucial. When applied to structure and agency, the realist social ontology *entails* the exploration of those features of both which are prior or posterior to one another and of which causal influences are exerted by one stratum on the other, and vice versa, by virtue of these independent properties and powers. The 'people' in society and the 'parts' of society are not different aspects of the same thing but are radically different in kind. This being so, then social realism implies a methodology based upon analytical dualism, where explanation of why things social are so and not otherwise depends upon an account of how the properties and powers of the 'people' causally intertwine with those of the 'parts'. Analytical dualism means emphasizing linkages by unpacking what was referred to earlier as the 'impact' and 'import' of and between different strata. This focal concern with *interplay* is what distinguishes the emergentist from the non-emergentist whose preoccupation is with *interpenetration*. The cognate terms of the latter, such as instantiation and mutual constitution, all involve compacting strata rather than disentangling them, hence resulting in central conflation at the level of practical social theorizing.

It is the social realists' insistence upon ontological emergence which introduces analytical dualism as its methodological complement and which eventually culminates in the only form of non-conflationary theorizing to develop to date. The centrality of analytical dualism to social realism is laid out in chapter 6. However, generalised explanatory programmes, necessary as they are and necessarily related as they be to their underlying ontology, are not the end of the story. There is a final element needed if theory is to be of utility to the working analyst of society – and this is practical social theory itself. Analytical dualism is the guiding methodological principle underpinning non-conflationary theorizing but the injunction to examine the interplay between the 'parts and the people', the 'social and the systemic', 'structure and agency', or 'action and its environments', although indispensable is also incomplete. The social analyst needs practical guide-lines as well as good principles, s/he requires explicit sociological guidance about how to approach the problem in hand in addition to philosophical assurance that they are taking the right basic approach.

Here the morphogenetic/morphostatic framework is put forward as the practical complement of social realism because it supplies a genuine method of conceptualizing how the interplay between structure and agency can actually be analyzed over time and space. It is based on two basic propositions:

(i) That structure necessarily pre-dates the action(s) leading to its reproduction or transformation;

(ii) That structural elaboration necessarily post-dates the action sequences which gave rise to it.

As embodiments of analytical dualism, both are opposed to conflation since what is pivotal are the conditional and generative mechanisms operating *between* structure and agency. This would be a logical impossibility were the two to be conflated (in any manner or direction). Thus the last three chapters are devoted to the morphogenetic cycle and the three phases which are involved – structural conditioning → social interaction → structural elaboration, and their direct parallels for culture and for agency itself. The morphogenetic approach is thus presented as the practical methodological embodiment of the realist social ontology, the two together representing a distinctive alternative to both the upward and downward conflationary theorizing of the old debate and to the central conflation with which many now seek to replace it. It constitutes a distinctive linkage between social ontology, explanatory methodology and practical social theorising. The remainder of this chapter will argue the unavoidability of such a tripartite linkage, how it was indeed consistently advanced and defended within the traditional terms of the debate – but also how these terms were inadequate and thus how the linkages between them were correspondingly both unacceptable and also unworkable. Their rejection was merited and overdue: the central question today is whether they should be replaced by a novel version of conflationary theorizing or whether the future of fruitful social theory lies in developing the neglected option of non-conflation. The purpose of this book is to give justification for endorsing the non-conflationary option – both in principle and in practice.

Social ontology and explanatory methodology: the need for consistency

In any field of study, the nature of what exists cannot be unrelated to how it is studied. This is a strong realist statement, which I endorse, but cannot explore here. Instead, I want to examine the more modest proposition that what *is held* to exist must influence considerations about how it should be explained. In other words, what social reality is deemed to consist of (and what is deemed non-existent) do affect how its explanation is approached.

It is certainly not being maintained that the relationship between the two is one of logical implication. This cannot be the case. For it must remain possible to uphold the existence of something which need never enter our explanations (a deity indifferent to Creation), or that some things exist socially which carry no particular implications about how we should study them or what importance should be assigned to them in explanations. For example, because both pleasure and pain are undeniably part of our social lot, this does not entail that all social action must be explained as the pursuit of pleasure and the avoidance of pain. This requires a justification of the connection, which Utilitarians would adduce and others would find unconvincing on the grounds that there is significantly more to social life than that.

Nevertheless, the social ontology endorsed does play a powerful *regulatory* role *vis-à-vis* the explanatory methodology for the basic reason that it conceptualizes social reality in certain terms, thus identifying what there is to be explained and also ruling out explanations in terms of entities or properties which are deemed non-existent. Conversely, regulation is mutual, for what is held to exist cannot remain immune from what is really, actually or factually found to be the case. Such consistency is a general requirement and it usually requires continuous two-way adjustments between ontology and methodology to achieve and to sustain it as such.

Of course, the achievement of consistency is no guarantee against error, as will be argued of both the Individualist and Collectivist programmes. Nevertheless, consistency is a necessary pre-condition, and to establish this now is to define one of the conditions which those seeking to replace both Individualism and Collectivism must meet when advancing alternative social ontologies and associated methodological programmes. For whatever their defects, both Individualism/Methodological Individualism and Collectivism/Methodological Collectivism provide clear illustrations of two programmes whose respective advocates both strove for internal consistency and were well aware of the reasons why this was necessary. These reasons can be broken down into three, which are binding on all who study 'the social', but examining them also serves to introduce the distinctive ways in which Individualists and Collectivists responded, thus setting the terms of the debate between them.

Description and explanation: the ties that bind them

The most fundamental consideration is that description and explanation are not discrete from one another and therefore we cannot be dealing with separate debates about the two. What social reality is held to *be* also *is* that which we seek to explain. It is denoted as being such and such by virtue of the concepts used to describe it and their use is inescapable since all knowledge is conceptually formed. There is no direct access to the 'hard facts' of social life, at least for the vast majority of us who cannot subscribe to the discredited doctrine of immaculate perception. By describing it in particular terms we are in fact conceptually denoting that which is to be explained. In other words, our ontological concepts serve to define the explanandum, and different social ontologies describe social reality in different ways, as is the case with Individualists and Collectivists. Necessarily this circumscribes the explanans to such statements as could potentially explain social reality *as it has been defined* by each of them.

Now it might be objected that nobody disagrees that in social reality there are both individuals (X) and groups (Y), nor that there are attributes of groups (Y^1), such as efficiency and power, which are not just the sum of individual properties, nor even that there are some attributes of groups (Y^2) (like organization, stability or cohesiveness) which cannot be properties of people. This of course is the case: the crux of the matter, however, is not whether groups exist but what constitutes them. In other words, how should they properly be described? Here the Individualist insists that anything about groups and their properties (Y, Y^1, $Y^{2'}$) can be eliminated by redefining them in terms of people (X, $X^{1'}$) and that such re-description is a matter of necessity because if our concepts do not denote something about people, then to what else can they meaningfully refer? The answer given was – only a reified entity (as if there were no alternative response).

Consequently, to the individualist, however much longhand it takes to produce the acceptable re-description (of say, group stability, in terms of members' preferences for remaining together), it must be possible in principle and accomplished in practice. Here the Collectivist counters that an activity like withdrawing money from a bank account cannot be described (and there description and explanation are the self-same process of making an activity intelligible) without reference to 'group concepts' such as 'banking' or 'legal tender', since the rules of deposit accounts are internal to the concept of cashing a cheque. Try to eliminate the former and mis-description results in the misunderstanding that anyone will hand over money when presented with a written slip of paper. The Individualist responds that this presents no great problem because the referents of these 'group concepts' can be redefined or 'translated' into statements about what the individuals involved are doing; a banking institution can be descriptively reduced to the activities of people engaged in it. In turn the Collectivist dissents because descriptions of these activities will necessitate the introduction of other non-individual concepts, like the role of the cashier, which again invokes the notion of 'banking' because patterns of action themselves are unintelligible without it (e.g. to understand why cashiers don't hand out money at parties).[22]

---

[22] Maurice Mandelbaum, 'Societal facts', in John O'Neill (ed.), *Modes of Individualism and Collectivism*, Heinemann, London, 1973, p. 225.

In other words, the significance of the concepts employed to *describe* reality also circumscribe those which can legitimately be entertained as *explaining* it. This is most obvious in cases like the above where explanation *consists* in identification, that is something becomes intelligible to us through correct description. In that case, far from being separate, the descriptive and explanatory processes are identical. Indeed, in the methodological tradition stemming from Dithey to Winch, this is held to be the appropriate mode of explanation in social analysis. Yet whether we believe that we have finished the job of explaining by (descriptive) identification or are only just beginning it, there is no way in which the process of description can be omitted and the concepts deemed appropriate for this task always circumscribe those which can then consistently be allowed to explain it.

Since the Individualist describes society as constituted by individuals (their dispositions, relations, beliefs, etc.) and nothing else, then some types of explanations, that is those employing concepts inconsistent with the above, are automatically ruled out. Since 'group properties', which are synonymous with holistic entities to the Individualist, have been descriptively defined out of existence, they cannot re-enter through the methodological door in order to explain social life. Consequently, explanations as well as descriptions must be in terms of X and not Y (individual properties and not group properties) otherwise what is at best a shorthand construct (Y) or at worst a reified entity, is being assigned real causal power which properly can only belong to that which really is real, that is to individuals (Xs and Xs in combination).

Here the Collectivist re-asserts that since adequate descriptions of social life cannot be given without references to irreducibly social 'remainders' (i.e. we cannot eradicate 'banking' and 'role of cashier' from an intelligible description of cashing cheques), then these indispensable descriptive terms can, and usually must, *also* figure in our explanations. Collectivists then use the fact that it is impossible to give descriptions in purely individual terms to challenge the Individualists' assertion that the only admissible form of *explanation* is one framed in terms of 'individual dispositions'. For the Collectivist argues, these too cannot be identified without invoking the social context and to do so entails using concepts which are again irreducibly social. Thus Gellner maintains that as 'a matter of causal fact, our dispositions are not independent of the social context in which they occur; but they are not even independent logically, for they cannot be described without references to their social context'[23] (i.e. we cannot identify the dispositions of 'voters' without referring to

---

[23] Ernest Gellner, 'Holism versus individualism', in May Brodbeck (ed.), *Readings in the Philosophy of the Social Sciences*, Macmillan, New York, 1971, p. 267.

'elections', of 'soldiers' without 'armies', or of 'bank tellers' without banks).

Although it is possible of course to advance individual predicates of a non-social kind, such as those pertaining to human beings as material objects (genetic-make up), or ones which whilst pre-supposing consciousness still pre-suppose nothing about any feature of society (aggression or gratification), no theorist could seriously entertain the prospect of explaining social complexity in its entirety on the basis of predicates which we share with the animals.[24]

For on this basis we can neither explain that which distinguishes human society from animal society (the explanandum) and the explanans itself, the individual, would simultaneously have been mis-described by confining personal qualities to the properties of animals, thus omitting that which is uniquely characteristic of people. Hence Bhaskar concludes critically that 'the real problem appears to be not so much that of how one could give an individualistic explanation of social behaviour, but that of how one could ever give a non-social (i.e. strictly individualistic) explanation of individual, at least characteristically human, behaviour! For the predicates designating properties special to persons all pre-suppose a social context for their employment. A tribesman implies a tribe, the cashing of a cheque a banking system. Explanation, whether by subsumption under general law, adversion to motives or rules, or redescription (identification), always invoke irreducibly social predicates.'[25]

In short, explanation cannot proceed without prior description, yet what something is defined as being through the concepts which describe it determines what exactly is to be explained, which necessarily circumscribes the explanatory project.

Ontology as conceptual regulation

Social ontologies perform a yet stronger regulatory role, for they govern *those concepts which are deemed admissible* in explanation as in description. Precepts for proper concept formation come from the social ontology which is endorsed, as this logically *determines* the type of descriptive concepts which can be employed.[26] Of course, for the Individualist which

---

[24] See Steven Lukes, 'Methodological individualism reconsidered', *British Journal of Sociology*, 1968, 19:2. Lukes also mentions a third type of predicate, where explanation is in terms of social behaviour which, whilst involving some minimal social reference, is unspecific as to any particular form of group or institution. He sees no reason why explanations should be confined to such (pp. 124–6).

[25] Bhaskar, *Naturalism*, p. 28.

[26] May Brodbeck, 'Methodological individualisms: definition and reduction', in Brodbeck (ed.), *Readings*. Here it is argued that descriptive individualism 'is required by the logic of concept formation within the individualistic, empiricist framework' (p. 301).

particular concepts are chosen is not determined: all that is logically required is that they must be individualistic and what is prohibited is the attribution of non-observable properties to equally non-observable group entities in any acceptable description of social life. This, in turn, *regulates* what kinds of concepts can consistently appear in the explanatory methodology. Because the ontology contains judgements about the 'ultimate constituents' (and non-constituents) of social reality, it thus governs what sorts of concepts may properly be countenanced for any purpose whatsoever.

Thus Watkins, as an Individualist, is explicit about how ontology carries-over to influence explanation because the 'metaphysically impregnated part of methodology' seeks to establish the appropriate material (as opposed to formal) requirements 'which the *contents* of the premises of an explanatory theory in a particular field ought to satisfy. These requirements may be called regulative principles'.[27] Significantly, he expands on this to the effect that 'Fundamental differences in the subject-matters of different sciences – differences to which formal methodological rules are impervious – ought, presumably, to be reflected in the regulative principles appropriate to each science'. In other words, our subject matter, social reality, ought to regulate how we explain it. The fact that there is disagreement over what really exists socially does nothing to undermine Watkins's point that the ontology *held* by different students of society, their different conceptions of social reality, will indeed regulate how they try to explain it – in different ways. To regulate is not to dictate: there can be lively debate about the most useful concepts to employ within a given view of what social reality is, but equally that view of what exists (and thus constitutes our subject matter) does serve to rule out certain concepts from explanations, just as atheists cannot attribute their well being to divine providence.

The actual debate between Individualists and Collectivists provides the clearest illustration of the regulative role that ontology performs for methodology. In the following instances a major protagonist from each side begins with an uncompromising statement about the 'ultimate constituents' of social reality and then proceeds immediately to state the terms in which it should be studied. Thus for Individualism, Watkins states that 'the ultimate constituents of the social world are individual people who act more or less appropriately in the light of their dispositions and understanding of their situation. Every complex social situation, institution or event is the result of a particular configuration of individuals, their dispositions, situations, beliefs, and physical resources and

---

[27] J. W. N. Watkins, 'Methodoligical individualism and social tendencies', in Brodbeck (ed.), *Readings*, p. 269.

environment. There may be unfinished or half-way explanations of large scale social phenomena (say, inflation) in terms of other large-scale phenomena (say, full employment); but we shall not have arrived at rock-bottom explanations of such large-scale phenomena until we have deduced an account of them from statements about the dispositions, beliefs, resources and inter-relations of individuals'.[28] On the other hand, Mandelbaum draws just as tight a link between the Collectivist ontology, the concepts which can be used to refer to social reality and which also explain it: 'If it be the case, as I wish to claim, that societal facts are as ultimate as are psychological facts, then those concepts which are used to refer to the forms of organization of a society cannot be reduced without remainder to concepts which only refer to the thoughts and actions of specific individuals.' His explanatory aim is then 'to show that one cannot understand the actions of human beings as members of a society unless one assumes that there is a group of facts which I shall term "societal facts".'[29]

Here, ontological considerations are used not merely to justify a congruent methodological stand-point, but actively regulate the associated explanatory programmes. For both Individualists and Collectivists, what society is held to be made to be made up of serves to monitor the concepts which can properly be used to describe it and which in turn may legitimately figure in explanatory statements. No explanation is acceptable to either camp if it contains terms whose referents misconstrue the nature of social reality as they see it – whether such misconstruction is due to sins of conceptual omission or commission. Ontology, I am arguing, acts as both gatekeeper and bouncer for methodology.

Certainly the ontological question, 'what constitutes social reality?' is different from the question asked about methodology, 'does it work?'. However, in the Individualist/Collectivist and Methodological Individualist/Methodological Collectivist debates, the nexus between the two is so tight that the stern voice of Individualistic ontology asserts that its own explanatory programme, containing only concepts referring to individuals, 'must work in principle'. Equally it insists that its opponents' explanations deal in unacceptable terms (reified entities, social substances or unreduced group properties) and therefore must be rejected out of hand *because* of this. Even when the latter appear to work, they are only 'half-way explanations' which cannot become complete or 'rock bottom' until the group concepts they contain have been reduced to individual terms. In parallel, the Collectivists' ontological commitment to irreducible social properties leads them to assert that individualist explanations

[28] Watkins, 'Methodological individualism', pp. 270–1.
[29] Mandelbaum, 'Societal facts', p. 223f.

must fail in principle because of what they leave out (reference to the social context) and that where they do appear to work in practice this is because such necessary references have been smuggled in by incorporating them into the individual (belief systems become the individuals' beliefs, resource distributions are disaggregated into people's wealth, the situation confronted becomes a person's problem etc.). On the whole, Collectivists tend to be less ontologically strident, given the holistic skeleton in the family cupboard, and generally respond by using their explanatory successes to boost confidence and strengthen their ontological foothold. This constitutes the third reason why the two debates (the ontological and the methodological), far from being separate, are in a relationship of mutual regulation.

Explanation and ontological revision

Since the nature of social reality, like any other for once, is a matter of fact which is independent of the prior commitments of any theorists about what exists, then if and when an incongruous method of explanation gives evidence of working, or the congruent methodological programme breaks down in practice, this should result in a reinspection of those commitments themselves. What we think social reality is cannot be a separate matter from what we find it to be. The reciprocal regulation which I am arguing obtains between ontology and methodology is one which obviously has to work in both directions. Thus when a Collectivist explanation, containing 'group variables' seems to be powerful, or even unavoidable (containing irreducible references to social entities like 'banking'), then methodology has raised a question for ontology. What is at issue is the ontological status of the entities denoted by the collective terms.

Collectivists were shyly tentative about drawing robust ontological conclusions from the frequent success of their explanatory programme. Gellner went as far as to contend that 'if something (a) is a causal factor (b) cannot be reduced, then in some sense it "really and independently exists".'[30] What is being suggested here is that a causal criterion of existence is acceptable, rather than always and only employing the perceptual criterion (observability) as entrenched in empiricist Individualism. To have pressed home this argument and extracted its full ontological value (given it was first advanced in 1956), needed not only a complete break with empiricist assumptions, positivistic prescriptions and the underlying Humean notion of causality, but also an articulated

[30] Gellner, 'Holism versus individualism', p. 256.

alternative. In its absence, the furthest Gellner went was the cautious assertion that factors which were causally efficacious and also irreducible had a real and independent existence 'in some sense'.[31] He was completely correct, but unable to substantiate it without a philosophy of social science which warranted unobservable concepts, employed a causal criterion to establish their reality and departed from the constant conjuncture model of causality. This of course begged the whole question of 'in what sense?'. By using the phrase at all, did he imply that 'social properties' existed in a different sense from 'individual properties' and if so was this precisely the sense which anti-Holists had been so concerned to eradicate, namely the imputation of a reified existence to insubstantial concepts? (Retrospectively it seems certain that the phase indicated only an inability to be any clearer until much more work had been done on the causal criterion of existence and the whole empiricist framework challenged.) As matters stood, the Collectivist method of explanation had indeed reinforced the Collectivist ontology, but this was stated in such a tentative manner that it only served to keep the already converted going. Collectivists could expect no converts, precisely because they had failed to give a clear answer as to the ontological status of the entities denoted by collective terms.

Even if Individualists did not acknowledge the implications of successful Collectivist explanations (or the significance of being unable to eliminate all 'societal' concepts from explanation) for what 'really and independently exists', nevertheless the frequent failure of their own methodological programme should have been a cause for ontological concern. In practice, their own reductionist programme hinged on the development of 'composition laws'. Here reduction consists in advancing explanatory statements made up of nothing apart from propositions about individual dispositions together with a specification of how people's behaviour differs according to the membership and size of the group in which they are participating. This specification means establishing a series of relevant empirical generalizations, the composition laws, which would then enable the computation of complex situations involving more people from simpler ones involving the behaviour of smaller numbers. Provided all concepts (like a hierarchical group) are *defined* in individualistic terms (some people having authority over others) and the composition laws are known, then reduction can take place and complex group behaviour can be explained in terms of the behaviour of individuals in groups. At least this is what the methodological programme promises, but

---

[31] Gellner could only conclude that a 'full clarification of these issues would probably be possible only if we were clear about what is meant by causation in social contexts' ('Holism versus individualism', p. 261).

since composition laws are no more than empirical generalizations, the possibility of their breakdown cannot be excluded and in fact is more common than cases in which reduction has been accomplished.

However, the Methodological Individualist is not arguing that satisfactory means for achieving reduction *have* been found, or even that promising solutions are in sight, but only that *in principle* such reduction is possible. Yet such a 'principle' cannot serve as the basis for practical methodological injunctions of this kind. Whether or not there are composition laws cannot be decided 'in principle' on logical grounds, it is a matter of fact[32] – and one which poses problems for the Individualists' prior ontological commitment. For those instances where the reductionist explanatory programme breaks down, especially given their frequency, actually call for a re-evaluation of the social ontology which led to the expectation that it would (let alone must) work. There is an ontological problem not just because the definition of what exists, and therefore can legitimately be conceptualized, has produced a methodology whose concepts and laws cannot cope with the whole of social reality, but also because of what happens when such an explanation fails. In these cases, where all concepts have been defined individualistically but the composition laws break down at some level of complexity, then it has to be admitted that a new factor has come into play at that point. Its inclusion is necessary for successful explanation and this thus constitutes a case of 'explanatory emergence'. Whether or not the emergent factor, which now has to be incorporated if the explanation is to work, happens to look innocuously individualistic (like 'fear of large groups', which makes the difference between small talkative seminars and the silence which ensues when the same people are asked to comment during a lecture), the fact remains that it has come into play and is identifiable *only* in the new context of the lecture itself.

In 'some sense', but undeniably one which is indispensable for explanation, the lecture group is having an effect independent of its membership – and this despite the fact that it can indeed be described in individualistic terms (i.e. the people present and what they do). Such frequent methodological findings (cases again of causal efficacy) should have raised some ontological disquiet, for clearly there are 'things at work' beyond individuals and their interpersonal relations or combi-

---

[32] A. MacIntyre, 'On the relevance of the philosophy of the social sciences', *British Journal of Sociology*, 1969, 20: 2. 'Nothing but the progress of scientific enquiry in the formulation of scientific theories can decide whether individual properties are always to be explained by reference to social properties, or social by reference to individual, or sometimes one and sometimes the other. As mutually exclusive theses both methodological individualism and holism are attempts to legislate *a priori* about the future progress of the human sciences' (p. 225).

nations which leads to the question of *their ontological status* and whether it is compatible with an individualist conception of social reality.

In short, the practical results of the explanatory programmes associated with Methodological Collectivism and Individualism (relative success and failure respectively) called for ontological re-examination on each side. Instead, the Collectivists remained unduly tentative, settling for their explanatory variables existing 'in a sense', without pursuing the causal criterion of reality to confirm their ontological status as real and independent. On the other hand, the Individualists remained so committed to their ontological principle (that the ultimate constituents of social life were nothing but people), they remained deaf to their own methodological findings that something beside 'other people' was at work in society. Since both proved reluctant to go back to the ontological drawing board and revise their views of social reality in the light of knowledge about it, then stalemate ensued.

Conclusion

It was in this context of deadlock that the suggestion was advanced that two separate debates were being compacted together, unnecessarily and unhelpfully, in the confrontation between Individualists and Collectivists. The first, it was claimed, concerned the terms used to describe society and was therefore a matter of their meaning and whether their referents were logically meaningful. The other, it was held, was a matter of fact since it dealt with explanation and concerned the possibility or impossibility of reducing all explanatory predicates to individual terms – something upon which logic cannot arbitrate. One point of insisting upon this separation was to offer the terms of a truce between the two standpoints which got them (and us) out of stalemate. However, if the two debates are genuinely separate then it is possible to decide the descriptive debate in favour of the Individualists or the Collectivists and the explanatory debate the other way round. Effectively this is what the peace treaty first put forward by Brodbeck did, since it can be summed up in the formula 'descriptive individualism plus explanatory emergence'. Individualism was handed the honours in the descriptive debate: '*In principle*, of course', even when dealing with vague and open terms like the Reformation, 'all such concepts must be definable in terms of individual behaviour' (though in practice it was conceded that we often cannot do it).[33] Collectivism, however, had rather the better of the explanatory

---

[33] Brodbeck, 'Methodological individualisms' p. 286.

confrontation. Hence, to the peace-makers, 'Emergence at the level of explanation should be carefully distinguished from what we earlier called descriptive emergence. The latter phrase refers to the occurrence of a property of groups, like the so-called group mind, which is not definable in terms of the individuals making up the groups. Explanatory emergence, however, refers to laws of group behaviour, which, *even though their terms are defined as they should be*, are still not derivable from the laws, including whatever composition laws there are about individual behaviour. This is *in fact* the case at present'.[34] Thus Brodbeck considers it profitable to continue exploring these laws applying to social complexes, that is, to pursue the Collectivist explanatory programme – always hoping that the connections established will then suggest suitable modes of reduction.

There are, it seems to me, profound objections to this procedure for ending the stalemate. To begin with, although Brodbeck herself is advocating a particular compromise position, it is premissed on the separateness of 'the two debates' and if this is really the case, then one could end up adopting either kind of ontology and then endorsing either type of methodology or vice versa. Even though Sztompka has shown that some combinations are unlikely, neither are they impossible.[35] Yet the whole point of this introduction has been to argue that although the relationship between ontology and methodology is not so close as logical implication, it is still a tight one of *mutual* regulation.

In summary, the reasons for this are firstly that we are not dealing with discrete activities where description and explanation are concerned, and cannot be because explanation requires identification of what is to be explained, which the descriptive terms supply. Thus the same corpus of concepts is used in both and links them together. Secondly, in general and avowedly in this debate, different ontologies furnish different 'regulative principles' about the methodology appropriate to do the explaining. Negative regulation is unavoidable, for you cannot develop a method to explain that which is held not to exist. Positive regulation conditions how it is permissible to go about explanation and enunciates principles about the form of methodology to be adopted. However, adequate explanations can end up a long way from their ontological starting point and this may introduce another form of regulation, which operates in reverse, by calling for revision of the original conception of reality. Thirdly, then, methods of explanation, their workings and findings, successes and

---

[34] Brodbeck, 'Methodological individualisms', p. 301.
[35] Piotr Sztompka, *Sociological Dilemmas*, Academic Press, New York, 1979, ch. 3.

failures, also have reciprocal ontological implications because pre-conceptions about the nature of social reality cannot be immune from discoveries about it. In both Individualism and Collectivism, the latter should have prompted revisions of very different kinds in the ontological commitments of their advocates – but did not do so.

One of the implications of the stalemate reached between Individualism and Collectivism was that one had to swallow them whole (ontology and methodology together), or not at all, yet there was nothing else on offer. The corresponding attraction of the proposed truce was that of mixed medicine – or a half dose. Here lies my practical objection to it. Once social analysts have been assured that ontology and methodology are separate issues, why should they not conclude that they can merely select the methodology which pragmatically seems most useful to them (thus sliding rapidly into instrumentalism), because if ontology is a separate concern, then it need to be no concern of theirs. Equally, once social theorists have been persuaded of the separation, what prevents an exclusive preoccupation with ontological matters, disregarding their practical utility and effectively disavowing that acquiring knowledge about the world does and should affect conceptions of social reality? This is a recipe for theoretical sterility. An ontology without a methodology is deaf and dumb; a methodology without an ontology is blind. Only if the two do go hand in hand can we avoid a discipline in which the deaf and the blind lead in different directions, both of which end in cul-de-sacs. Brodbeck herself is most careful not to fall into this trap, but what does 'separatism' do other than to set it for others?

Ironically, the peace treaty was intended to have exactly the reverse effect for the impetus behind it was that the practising social theorist needed not only an acceptable social ontology but also the most powerful explanatory methods available. This is the very last thing I would contest. Equally I am fully convinced that neither Individualism/Methodological Individualism nor Collectivism/Methodological Collectivism can meet these two requirements. Yet because I am maintaining that ontology and methodology are not separate matters, I am still committed to saying they must be swallowed whole or not at all: since I am also arguing that neither of them meets the basic requirements, my conclusion has to be 'don't drink'. This caution against drinking and driving has to be justified by showing that neither position does or can meet the two requirements (ontological rectitude and explanatory power) and thus cannot take us where we need to go. The justification itself will consist in showing that it is empiricism which bedevils both standpoints. This is the force behind my injunction to abstinence rather than temperance where

Individualism and Collectivism are concerned, and my final objection to Brodbeck's temperate compromise is that it too is unashamedly empiricist.[36]

Only with the demise of the view that all knowledge is obtained from human sense experience, did 'individuals' (because alone capable of experiencing) lose their automatic primacy and could non-observable features of society avoid the question mark hanging over their existence (because incapable of being experienced as sense data). Eventually this enabled the terms in which society was conceptualized and explained to be reformulated, and those in which Individualism and Collectivism had cast them to be rejected.

Yet as always there are ties that bind ontology and methodology together and these need to be ones which are internally consistent and *also* provide a working basis for practical social theorising. Thus the main question to ask about the standpoints which later made a bid to replace both Individualism and Collectivism is how far they succeeded in both tasks. However, to understand the impetus behind replacing the two traditional approaches we need to appreciate *how* Individualism and Collectivism failed and *why* neither could supply the practical social theorist with an adequate conception of either 'structure' and 'agency' or provide a satisfactory programme for explaining the linkages between them.

I began by endorsing the authenticity of the human experience that we are both free and constrained, considering the touchstone of adequate social theorizing to be how well it captures these insights. However, there is no contradiction in upholding this lay outlook as authentic whilst denying the empiricist view that all knowledge is obtained from human experience. For fundamentally, the lay reflection on the human condition in society is not itself empiricist. Those ambivalent feelings of freedom and constraint of ours derive from what we are as people and how we tacitly understand our social context. Yet lay reflections on ourselves and our society are never restricted to sense-data or the supposed 'hard facts' it yields – for much of the time we think and act in terms of 'group properties' like elections, interest rates, theories and

---

[36] Obviously, since I reject the premises upon which this compromise is based (separatism), and the epistemological terms in which it is advanced (empiricism), there is little point in providing a more detailed critique. However, in fairness to Brodbeck it should be noted that her 1973 article 'On the philosophy of the social sciences', in O'Neill (ed.), *Modes of Individualism and Collectivism*, marks a shift towards realism compared with the naked empiricism of the 1968 paper, which is also re-printed in this collection. On the other hand, the author herself failed to signal this move towards embracing a much more relational ontology.

beliefs. On the contrary, and therefore the main reason why empiricism must be deficient, we ourselves as reflective beings are not empiricists: we would not be recognizable as people if we were, nor capable of recognizing enough of our social context to live competently within it if we tried to be.

Part I

The problems of structure and agency: four alternative solutions

2   Individualism versus Collectivism: querying the terms of the debate

Since my argument is that neither Individualism nor Collectivism can furnish the basis for adequate social theorizing, it is necessary to show why. Specifically this means examining the reasons which make their conceptions of structure, of agency and of the relations between them, unacceptable – and thus revisiting the well-trodden ground of this debate. In short, the very terms of the confrontation between Individualists and Collectivists have to be queried before we can appreciate their growing rejection and *what* they have been replaced by – in the case of those who have recently sought to redefine the terms of the traditional debate.

To develop these points it will prove impossible not to move forwards and backwards between ontological and methodological considerations, precisely because these issues are not distinct and no protagonist of either standpoint ever approached them as if they were other than inextricably intertwined. What is of the greatest importance is to disengage *how* the Individualist and Collectivist conceptions of social reality contained equally deficient concepts of both structure and agency and how correspondingly their two explanatory programmes served to block an examination of the interplay *between* structure and agency since what they had in common mandated epiphenomenalism in social theorizing. In the heritage of Individualism it was 'structure' which became the inert and dependent element, whilst Collectivism fostered instead the subordination or neglect of 'agency', thus respectively perpetuating the two forms of social theorizing which I have termed the fallacies of 'upwards conflation' and 'downwards conflation'.[1]

However, none of these connections is understandable unless Individualism and Collectivism are placed against the back-cloth of empiricism which contextualized the formulation of both standpoints and exerted stringent constraints on the nature of their confrontation. In many ways the scenery was the most important player in this particular drama. What it represented was crucial, but no more so than what it was

---

[1] See Margaret S. Archer, *Culture and Agency*, Cambridge University Press, Cambridge, 1989, chs. 2 and 3.

33

intended to occlude – the spectre of reification – a phantom which empiricism exorcized from this opera along with much else which was far from phantasmagoric. Empiricism fundamentally stood for an approach where descriptions and explanations alike were confined to observable entities, while the attribution of causality was thus restricted to the level of observable events, meaning that the aim of sociology was the discovery of observed regularities (a typically Humean quest for constant conjunctions). As such it gave enormous ontological security to the Individualists for whom the ultimate constituents of the social world were individual people and who therefore insisted that the social context should be reduced to refer to nothing but 'other people', for purposes of both description and explanation. Hence the supposedly manifest observability of 'people' fostered a confident self-righteousness in the Individualist camp. By contrast, if meeting the requirements of empiricism made Individualists over-confident, it reduced Collectivists to extreme over-wariness. They were constrained to be tentative about their trafficking in non-observables, to confine their dealings with them to translatable terms which could just evade empiricist stricture, and were discouraged from undertaking any bold ontological revision which would have spelt a full-frontal confrontation with empiricism itself. Both viewpoints have attracted subsequent criticism, but one thing empiricism served to explain is why, at the time their protagonists took their stands on different ground. For the challenges emanating from the Individualist camp were couched consistently in ontological terms, whilst the counter-blast from the Collectivists was predominantly methodological, focusing upon the explanatory incompleteness of their adversaries' best efforts (and providing another illustration of the inseparability of these two debates).

METHODOLOGICAL INDIVIDUALISM

Individualism's individual

The defects of Individualism and its explanatory programme derive directly from empiricism. This marks and mars both the concepts which are used to conceptualize the 'individual' and 'social structure', as well as the links between them, since the same concepts are employed to account for their relationship. The cornerstone of the entire enterprise is the 'individual' as such, and the confidence that this secures it on firm foundations is itself earthed in the twin empiricist assumptions that (a) talk about 'individuals' is unproblematic because their existence is incontestable, and (b) that by confining serious conversation (concepts, theories and laws) to them, the dangers of hypostatization can never threaten, unlike loose talk about groups, institutions and society, which, if taken seriously, heads straight towards reification. Both points are summed up in Hayek's statement that no collective term ever designates 'definite things in the sense of stable collections of sense attributes'.[2] The corollary, for the Individualist is that thanks to the perceptual criterion of existence can we be sure all references to 'individuals' do denote real and definite things.

Yet even within its own terms, the perceptual criterion does nothing to render the 'individual' unproblematic in this manner for, as has often been remarked, facts about individuals are not necessarily more observable nor easier to understand than facts about social organization (the motives of the criminal versus the proceedings of the criminal court).[3] Perceptual sense-data secure the 'individual' only as a visible *organism*, yet it is precisely the non-observable things about people (their dispositions) which constitute the basis of the Individualist account. However, if these latter are to be identified, as they must be, then Individualism cannot work within strict empiricist terms, for the identification of many dispositions is only possible if the social context is invoked to make sense of them (the most diffuse disposition to vote pre-supposes some notion of an election; the intention to 'vote Conservative' is predicated upon there actually being a Conservative Party for which to vote).

However, the Individualist is committed to social atomism, that is to the claim that the important things about people can indeed be identified independently of their social context. Here is the real difficulty of this procedure, for both description and explanation, namely that it presumes it is possible to isolate more elementary dispositions 'as they are prior to their manifestations in a social context. The real oddity of the reductionist case is that it seems to preclude *a priori* the possibility of human dispositions being the dependent variable in an historical explanation – when in fact they often or always are.'[4] There are only two ways of rebutting this objection. The first would be to maintain that there are indeed such pre-social elementary dispositions (genetically inscribed). But even if there are, 'no one has yet provided any plausible reason for supposing that, e.g. (logically) pre-social drives uniquely determine the social context or that this context is irrelevant to their operations'.[5] The only alternative way out which could simultaneously (i) allow the

[2] F. A. Hayek, 'Scientism and the study of society', in John O'Neill (ed.), *Modes of Individualism and Collectivism*, Heinemann, London, 1973, p. 36f.
[3] Steven Lukes, 'Methodological individualism reconsidered', *British Journal of Sociology*, 1968 19: 2, p. 122.
[4] Ernest Gellner, 'Holism versus individualism', in May Brodbeck (ed.), *Readings in the Philosophy of the Social Sciences*, Macmillan, New York, 1968, p. 260.
[5] Lukes, 'Methodological individualism', p. 126.

inclusion of contextual influences which cannot be kept out, whilst (ii) remaining faithful to individualism, is by construing the social context as itself made up of nothing but 'other people'. In that case it can then enter descriptions and explanations innocently as interpersonal influences such as socialization and enculturation.[6] This is the path followed and what has to be queried is the resulting social ontology – one in which the ultimate constituents of social reality are held to be 'socialized individuals' (the Individualist concept of 'agency') and the only other element to exist socially is 'interpersonal relations' (the Individualist concept of 'social structure').

The ontological security of the Individualist rests on the empiricist conviction that the ultimate constituents of social reality have been unimpeachably defined as 'individuals' and that only facts about them figure in both descriptions and explanations. How then is the individual conceptualized, which is another way of asking what is meant by facts about individual people and in what sense these can be considered as 'ultimate'? Since the Individualists are as concerned as anyone else studying society about social action rather than behaviour, then the relevant facts are not physiological but mentalistic; they are our dispositions to find things meaningful and intelligible and to act on that basis. We have already seen Watkins stating that 'According to this principle, the ultimate constituents of the social world are individual people who act more or less appropriately in the light of their dispositions and understanding of their situation'.[7] Leaving aside the queasiness which these unobservable dispositions presumably induce in the full-blooded empiricist, it must follow that if the crucial facts about people are their dispositions, then statements about things *other* than individuals are excluded as are statements which are *not* about dispositions.[8]

Yet Methodological Individualists immediately break with both these requirements of their position, since the facts about people which are allowed to figure in 'rock-bottom explanations' are neither solely individual nor solely dispositional. Instead the acceptable predicates can include 'statements about the dispositions, beliefs, resources and interrelations of individuals' as well as their 'situations ... physical resources

---

[6] L. J. Goldstein, 'Two theses of methodological individualism', in O'Neill (ed.), *Modes of Individualism and Collectivism*: 'For the most part, people are born into their kinship relationships, and it seems entirely a reversal of actual fact to say that such relations "are the product of people's *attitudes* to each other, though these are partly determined by their *beliefs* about their biological relations". It seems more reasonable to say that for the most part the proper attitudes towards one's various kin are cultivated during the enculturation process' (p. 284).
[7] J. W. N. Watkins, 'Methodological individualism and social tendencies', in Brodbeck (ed.) *Readings*, p. 270.   [8] Gellner, 'Holism versus individualism', p. 257.

and environment'.[9] Firstly, inspection of this list reveals that some of its constituents logically cannot be construed as facts about *individual* people (the environment, physical resources, situations and interrelations – since definitionally a relationship is a fact about at least two people). Very arguably none of them should be, for my belief in the theory of relativity is only individual in the sense of my believing it, but its existence does not depend upon my holding it. Secondly, some of the elements on the list are obviously not about *dispositions* (the environment, physical resources, situations) and again, arguably, none is, for beliefs are independent of the disposition to believe just as many of our interrelations are non-voluntaristic and autonomous from whatever dispositions we bring to them. Thirdly, it can then be contended that none of these aspects of social reality is about *either* individuals *or* their dispositions and thus cannot be construed as facts about individual people.

Matters become even more difficult when the shift is made from discussion of determinate individuals to that of anonymous people, a move accepted as necessary and legitimate by Individualists. When dealing, for example, with the French Huguenots, the third point made above comes home with full force, for as Goldstein comments, 'What we have are not the characteristic dispositions of people we don't know, but the social behaviour of people in given situations quite apart from their personal dispositions'.[10] In other words, where anonymous individuals are concerned, we are not dealing with dispositional individuals at all, since neither element is identifiable, all that is subject to identification are non-individualistic features of the social context and socially induced ways of acting within it.

Because social reality cannot be confined to individuals and their dispositions, then those aspects of the social context which are indispensable for both identification and explanation are themselves incorporated into individual terms. As Lukes puts it, 'the relevant features of the social context are, so to speak, built into the individual'.[11] There are two serious ontological objections to this procedure. On the one hand, in what recognizable sense are we still talking about 'the individual' when he or she has now been burdened with so many inalienable features of both social and natural reality (cultural systems, socio-cultural relations,

---

[9] Watkins, 'Methodological individualism', pp. 270–1.
[10] Goldstein, 'Two theses', p. 286. This point plays an important part in the debate, for Watkins contends that 'Mandelbaum is able to prove the existence of what he calls "societal facts" because he defines psychological facts very narrowly as "facts concerning the thoughts and actions of specific human beings". Consequently the dispositions of *anonymous* individuals which play such an important part in individualistic explanations in social science are "societal facts" by definition' ('Methodological individualism', p. 272n). [11] Lukes, 'Methodological individualism', p. 125.

physical resources and the environment)? On the other hand, can the social context (let alone the natural world) really be disaggregated in this way, such that role relations are purely interpersonal matters, belief systems are only what certain people hold and reject, and resources are just what you or I have laid our hands on? Leaving the latter consideration aside for the moment, this social ontology has only been made to work descriptively by bundling complex and diffuse social relations into the individual as predicates of people.

In fact, this type of Monadism characterized both sides of the debate. In order to work at all, the Individualist ontology had grossly to inflate 'the Individual' by incorporating into people anything social to which it may be necessary to refer. In strict parallel, the strong form of Collectivism strips the individual of everything of interest, leaving him or her as nothing but Durkheim's 'indeterminate material', by bundling personal properties (thoughts, convictions, feelings) into collectivities – as the collective conscience – and thus representing them as predicates of 'the social'. These then constitute equal and opposite ontological defects and one of their deficiencies concerns their methodological implications.

Consequently, this is where Gellner concludes that the Individualist leaves us: 'Algy met a bear, the bear was bulgy, the bulge was Algy'; the individual may consume what Durkheim and others have called social facts, but he will bulge most uncomfortably, and Algy will still be there. I suspect that actual investigators will often . . . prefer to have Algy outside the bear'.[12] This preference is due to what 'desperate incorporation' necessarily precludes, and rules out both ways round (whether the bear eats up Algy as in the Individualist version, or Algy eats the bear in the Collectivist version), namely the interaction between the two. Whether Algy stands for the Individual or the Social, what is the most interesting thing is their meeting and its outcome, neither of which can be disposed of by ontological cannibalism. In short, the methodological outcome of social Monadism is epiphenomenalism. That which might *seem* to be separate (and the Individualist does not deny the existence of groups any more than the Collectivist denies the existence of people) is now engulfed, can be fully explained by the engulfing factor, and presented as part of its digestion process – reductive breakdown (in Individualism) or energization (in Collectivism). In the end, instead of investigating the interplay between individual and society or agency and structure, social theory developed on these two bases is an endorsement of Upwards Conflation by the Individualist and Downwards Conflation by the Collectivist, because of the methodological and ontological principles they have

---

[12] Gellner, 'Holism versus individualism', pp. 267–8.

adopted. This, however, is to get too far ahead. Instead, let us pause for a moment to see what this process of bundling the social context into individual terms actually does for (and to) the Individualists' claim that their individual is the ultimate constituent of the social world.

The individual as the ultimate constituent of social reality

In what sense can facts about individuals, as now defined in this generous way, be considered as 'ultimate' constituents of social reality? This bulging entity is not just a semantic device, it is meant to do a great deal of work. Being held to be ultimate, the individual of Individualism is also considered to be immune from (further) reduction himself, whilst all things social can be methodologically reduced to her. Calling individuals ultimate is like making them the terminus: explanations of things social come back to them, but this is the end of the line, for no further reduction is possible. I want to challenge this ontological claim to 'ultimate status' and its joint methodological implications, viz. that *in principle* all things social can be reduced to the individual whilst *in principle* such individuals are immune from further reduction to things psychological. Basically, the argument is that the postulated relations between the three areas represented by Psychologism, Individualism and Collectivism are inconsistent and cannot secure any kind of ultimate status for the Individualists' individual.

Let us consider first the relationship between Psychologism and Individualism. Here for a change the Individualist stands as the anti-reductionist *vis-à-vis* the advocates of psychologism who argue that there are yet 'lower level' entities, that is, psychological properties, which should be regarded as the real, rock-bottom constituents of social life and everything above them can be reduced to them and thus be explained by them,[13] Now, the Individualist rejects the view that society can be explained as some sort of *reflection* of psychological characteristics. Although I have no trouble in accepting this conclusion as correct, the grounds upon which it is based are troubling. Here the Individualist contends that mirror-image explanations must fail because they do not take into account the intended, 'the unintended and unfortunate consequences of the behaviour of interacting individuals'.[14] But this is exactly what the Collectivist repeatedly said to the Individualist (there are results

---

[13] Thus to Homans, 'if the ultimate units of social behaviour are men and their actions, then the general propositions used to explain social behaviour must be propositions about men and their actions; that is, they must be what I have called psychological propositions' (G. C. Homans, *The Nature of Social Science*, Harcourt Brace, New York, 1967, p. 62).

[14] Watkins, 'Methodological individualism', p. 276.

of interaction and results of these results, which make for the social context whose effects are not then those of individuals). To this the Individualist responded that all such matters were amenable to reduction in terms of individual dispositions and composition rules. The claim went further: *in principle* composition rules must be able to reduce collective phenomena to their real ultimate constituents. What then is to prevent the protagonists of Psychologism from invoking the same principle? Their argument would be that of course individual psyches do combine together, so that what goes up on the big screen is not a mirror-image but is modified by the unintended consequences of psychological interaction. Nevertheless, *in principle* the composition rules can be found for reduction to take place to the ultimate *psychological* constituents. The fact that this is a bad argument because such matters of fact cannot be determined *a prioristically*, does not rescue the Individualists, for it is *their* argument and what is sauce for the goose is sauce for the gander. In short, they cannot fend off further downwards reduction to psychology by appealing to unintended consequences and thus cannot sustain their claim to have identified the 'ultimate constituents' of social life *on this basis*.

Therefore, a different kind of argument must be introduced to support the Individualists' ontological claim, and one which proofs it against any question of reduction to psychological terms. Were the Individualist to argue that such reductionism simply doesn't work, they would doubtless recall that they dismissed similar Collectivist criticisms by adversion to the principled necessity of reduction, on pain of committing reification. Advocates of psychologism could be equally stern and maintain that by not adhering strictly to their principle, the Individualists' individual, far from being the ultimate constituent of social reality, is yet another reified entity! The only way out for the Individualist is to claim that their 'individual' is different in kind, *sui generis*, that is emergent from psychology, by virtue of those internal and necessary relationships developing between people which render the 'individual' both real and irreducible. Moreover, it is a good way out, for the 'socialized individual' of Individualism can only be such given that certain enduring relationships do pre-date him or her: English speakers do require existing English speakers in order to become such themselves. But then how is this different from the Collectivist argument that to be what they are, tribespeople do indeed require tribes; pupils, schools; and soldiers need armies? Therefore, adopting this solution (which would establish socialized individuals as real rather than reified and make them a legitimate subject for social psychology) has the undesired consequence for Individualists that they have now endorsed emergence and accepted that we live in a stratified social world comprised of two strata. Yet if they have had to concede the *principle of emergence*, how can they continue to deny *social* emergence, that is the existence of a third and higher stratum made up of just those entities to which the Collectivists referred? But this is exactly what they want to do.

The Individualists are now on the horns of a dilemma and either way their ontological claims about individuals as the ultimate constituents of social reality seem bound to crumble. If reductionism is possible, and they of all thinkers are badly placed to deny it, then their ultimate constituent can (at least 'in principle') be further reduced. If emergence is possible, and in self-defence they have surely had to concede it, then it becomes an open question whether further strata also emerge which are just as 'ultimate' as the individual. Therefore, neither reductionism nor emergence allows the claim to be upheld that the Individualists' individual is the ultimate constituent of social reality.

If then the Individualists have conceded that emergence occurs, does any way remain for protecting their position against its Collectivist critics? Only one. Although emergence can no longer be denied in principle, it can still be maintained that empirically nothing of the kind is the case as far as 'society' is concerned. This is where the 'inflated' concept of the individual comes into its own, for the generous definition of what can count as a fact about individuals withholds emergent status from anything but them. If every aspect of the social context can be bundled into the individual, then this is indeed the terminus. So, the argument goes, if inter-relations are individual properties, then they cannot denote something other than people; if unintended consequences can always be altered, providing only that the individuals concerned want to and know how to do so, then they have no autonomy from people; if things like environmental constraints and contextual conditioning are only the effects of others, then they are in no way independent of people. Therefore, to what else could an emergent feature of social reality possibly refer? Answer, only some reified and superhuman entity.

Now, a rather over-hasty consensus seems to have concluded that this descriptive inflation of the individual to incorporate the social context is merely a semantic matter, one which will certainly be unhelpful in future social analysis, but still an allowable manoeuvre since it is only a matter of words. However, we are not just arguing over what to call things but about what things are denoted by concepts. Here, the Individualist states that all concepts used in relation to the social context really denote nothing other than people, and this is an empirical not a semantic claim. For its justification depends not on the correct (or even the most helpful) use of words but on empirically demonstrating that the social context really does refer to nothing except 'other people'. The denial of societal emergence is an ontological claim which requires empirical demonstration. To vindicate their notion that the 'individual' *is* the ultimate constituent of social reality (and the terminus of all explanations), Individualists have to sustain their notion that 'social structure' *is* nothing but other people (as defined). Another way of putting this is that the ultimate ontological status assigned to the individual can be vindicated only when every aspect of the social context has been shown to be *epiphenomenal*. Hence, upwards conflation is indeed intrinsic to Methodological Individualism.

The Individualists' social structure

On the face of it to produce a convincing empirical demonstration of the epiphenomenal status of the social structure is a daunting enterprise because of the unending complexity of the social context. That Individualists remain undaunted is due to their empiricism itself which reassures them that, however complex, there are only two possible ways in which it can be construed: either social organization is constituted by things which are manifestly real or by reified entities, and of the two the former must be correct. This Watkins echoes: if 'methodological individualism means that human beings are supposed to be the only moving agents in history, and if sociological holism means that some super-human agents or factors are supposed to be at work in history, then these two alternatives are exhaustive'.[15] Ontologically, then, social structure can only refer to the human or the super-human: other contenders and specifically emergent properties (which being relational in nature are neither mortal nor immortal) are ruled out in advance. With empiricist confidence, the Individualist then 'insists that the social environment by which any particular individual is confronted and frustrated and sometimes manipulated and occasionally destroyed is, if we ignore its physical ingredients, made up of other *people*, their habits, inertia, loyalties, rivalries and so on'.[16]

This is an *ontological assertion*, but as we have seen it requires *empirical demonstration* if the threat posed by societal emergence is to be repulsed. Demonstrating that the social context is epiphenomenal is a methodological task which entails showing that every reference to it in explanations of social life (and no one wishes to deny that we are influenced by our social environment) actually refers to 'other people' (under the 'inflated' description particular to Individualists). Specifically, this means showing that, in relation to people, *social structure is not*: (i) autonomous or

---

[15] Watkins, 'Methodological individualism', p. 271.
[16] Watkins, 'Methodological individualism', p. 278n.

independent, (ii) pre-existent, (iii) causally efficacious. Collectivists have argued that they fail on all three counts and their arguments are persuasive.

(i) If autonomy is to be withheld from the social context and it is to be denied any independence from people, this means the Individualist must vindicate the claim that it can be treated as nothing other than an *aggregate* of individuals, which as such has no independence from its constituents – therefore our social environment is constituted by 'interpersonal relations'. It also follows that if the 'social structure' is only an aggregate, then 'the group' becomes synonymous with 'the social' to the Individualist. Here, the Collectivist queries whether in studying society we are, can, and should be, confined to the study of 'groups'. When we examine kinship structure, for example, we are not just investigating how that 'group' *does* inter-marry, transmit property, have particular obligations towards specific others and so on, but what rules govern their inter-marriage etc. Comparison of kinship structures is to compare different rules not different groups, for the rules regulate what the members do. Certainly, the continued salience of any rule depends on people continuing to adhere to it (this is merely a statement of activity-dependence) *but* their adherence is not what makes the rule, otherwise rules just become descriptions of what people do and have no regulatory or constitutive function. The identical point can be made about all other social or cultural institutions.

The same Collectivist argument serves to show the defects entailed in viewing environmental influences as nothing but 'interpersonal relations'. It highlights the fact that in dealing with the social context we are not paradigmatically concerned with groups at all. Roles, as Collectivists have often pointed out, are more important for understanding what is going on between landlords and tenants or bank cashiers and customers than their relations as persons. Moreover, the role has to be granted some autonomy from its occupant or how else do we explain the similar actions of a succession of incumbents, or that when promoted to bank manager our original cashier now acts quite differently? Once again the fact that roles are necessarily activity-dependent is insufficient to deny them the independent capacity to structure individuals' activities. In social analysis we often are and have to be less concerned with interpersonal relations than with the endurance of *im*personal role relationships.

(ii) Yet the Individualist argues that 'no social tendency exists which could not be altered *if* the individuals concerned both wanted to alter it and possessed the appropriate information'.[17] Thus, the social context has become the effect of *contemporary* other people. For it follows that whatever makes up our environment (such as enduring roles, positions

<hr />

[17] Watkins, 'Methodological individualism', p. 271.

and distributions) are all things that the 'people concerned' now do not want to change/do not know how to change or do not think about changing. In other words, whatever the origins of the social tendencies and features we observe, their present existence is due in some way to the people present. Therefore, explanation of the social structure is always in the present tense and responsibility for everything present lies firmly on the shoulders of those here present. Now, pre-existence, the fact that we are all born into an on-going social context, constrained to speak its language, take up our places in a prior distribution of resources, be sanctioned by its laws and confront its organizations is a powerful argument to the Collectivist for the existence of constraints and enablements which stem from emergent properties of society. The internal and necessary relationships between social positions (landlord and tenant, MP and constituent, husband and wife) have developed from past interaction but form a context within which we have to live. Only if their persistence *can* be attributed to the sustaining behaviour of 'other people' may they be assigned an epiphenomenal status.

If we take the example of a demographic structure (which should be agreeable to Individualists since it is made up of N people of different ages), then the relevant population, that is, those of child-bearing age who could change it, cannot significantly modify it for several years nor eliminate all its effects for many more. Yet more significantly, they themselves are constantly influenced by it since it has determined the size of this initial 'relevant population' to which they belong. Many distributions have this same property of taking time to change, even if all people present are consensually dedicated to their transformation. Their very resistance shows that they are not epiphenomenal: their differential resistance invites us to address the nature of the structure itself rather than automatically attributing its endurance to people's lack of commitment to change or information about it. Moreover, desires for persistence or transformation (and knowledge of how to effect them) are not randomly distributed, but shaped by the advantages and disadvantages which the pre-existent property distributes differentially throughout the population – and cannot be understood independently of them. In short, whether we are dealing with unintended consequences, aggregate effects or emergent properties, we are neither dealing with 'present tense' phenomena nor with epiphenomenal.

(iii) Denial of the pre-existence of social forms was intended to deprive them of any causal efficacy, yet this claim also fails if such properties are resistant to change or take a considerable time to alter. Although many of them may *eventually* be changed by human action, nevertheless *while* such environmental factors endure, they can constrain and facilitate different activities and may have consequences which are not trivial for future social change. The Individualists, however, make the opposite assumption. In effect, they argue that because such social tendencies are ultimately reversible, nothing of importance will happen *before* they are reversed. Matters of this kind cannot be decided by theoretical *fiat*.

This was the whole burden of the Collectivist critique, namely that reference to these structural properties were often unavoidable and they therefore were necessary to adequate causal accounts. As such, this was a purely methodological critique which concluded that '*explanatory* emergence' must be endorsed contra Individualist reductionism, but one which did not move on to question the ontological foundations of the Individualist programme. Hence, Gellner's well-known summary of where the debate between Individualism and Collectivism stood. 'Perhaps in the end, there is agreement to this extent (human) history *is* about chaps – and nothing else. But perhaps this should be written: History is *about* chaps. It does not follow that its explanations are always in terms of chaps.'[18] Yet why stop there, winning the methodological point but conceding the ontological one, especially as the two are so closely intertwined? But the Individualists were fully aware of the connection and pushed it home to their ontological advantage. Basically, they conceded, given the complexity and difficulty of social reality, that it may be wise for social scientists to examine (rather than dismiss) whatever imperfect connections exist between group variables. That is, it may be sensible to work with 'half way' explanations *pro tem*, precisely because 'these, in turn, may suggest the appropriate composition rules of individual behaviour'.[19]

Such a *pro tem* and heuristic 'acceptance' of explanatory emergence did nothing to undermine the basic commitments (both methodological and ontological) of individualism; the core programme could survive this concession at what was defined as lying at its periphery. Thus in Brodbeck's words,

The most that we can ask of the social-scientist whose subject-matter requires him to use such 'open' concepts [group properties] is that he keep the principle of methodological individualism firmly in mind as a devoutly to be wished for consummation, an ideal to be approximated as closely as possible. This should at least help assure that nevermore will he dally with suspect group-minds and impersonal 'forces', economic or otherwise; *nevermore will non-observable properties be attributed to equally non-observable group entities*.[20]

Empiricism was the alpha of Individualism and here it is meant to be the omega, an ideal to which we should be devoutly committed.

However, since I have been arguing that the Individualists fail to

---

[18] Gellner, 'Holism versus individualism', p. 268.
[19] Brodbeck, 'Methodological individualisms', p. 303.
[20] Brodbeck, 'Methodological individualisms', p. 286.

establish their case that social structure is epiphenomenal, that is a mere outworking of the doings of 'other people', then it also follows that they have not succeeded in denying emergence. Their inability to withstand claims that the social context has autonomy and independence from people, pre-exists them, and is causally influential of them, means that there should at least be a pause in Empiricist devotions to entertain the case that a 'social structure' which has these properties also has a claim to existence, though not one which can be substantiated through experience as sense-data. Does Collectivism manage to sustain it?

METHODOLOGICAL COLLECTIVISM

Collectivism's social structure

The irony of Collectivism is that whilst it defends the methodological indispensability of 'structural factors', no overall conception of social structure is advanced ontologically. What accounted for this is that Collectivists were simultaneously haunted by Holism and hamstrung by Empiricism. As far as the former was concerned, the proper desire to evade any charge of reification seemed to imply that safety lay in refraining from making ontological claims as far as possible. Consequently what we are actually dealing with most of the time is Methodological Collectivism. Its overriding concern is with explanation and particularly with the deficiencies of the Individualists' programme of reductionism. In criticizing it, the Collectivists' case rests largely on the fact that references to the social context have to be included for explanatory adequacy, because accounts cast purely in terms of 'chaps' just don't work. They break down short of the goal (through failure of composition laws) and 'societal properties' are needed to supply the deficit. Although the point is also made that 'chaps', their dispositions and their doings cannot even be identified (i.e. described as 'believers' or 'voters' etc.) without further resort to the social context, this is not used to issue an ontological challenge to the Individualists' concepts of 'structure' and 'agency'. On the contrary, when Individualists defended their backs by promptly incorporating all such social features into their conception of individual people, the Collectivists noted the fact, commented that it would be unhelpful in explaining the relations between what we now call 'structure and agency', but backed away from an ontological confrontation by deeming this to be a matter of semantics. Since the Individualist was arbitrating about the ultimate constituents of social reality, it is hard to see that this could be let pass as merely an issue about the use of words – particularly when identifying explanations are often at stake.

In other words, the Collectivist was playing an inordinately defensive game. References to 'societal facts' are defended as ineradicable 'remainders', without which Individualists' descriptions remain incomplete, and also as indispensable adjuncts when Individualists' explanations come up against the 'irreducible'. The very language of 'remainders' and 'unreduced concepts' casts the Collectivist in the role of critically supplementing Individualism, rather than confronting it head on. Instead of articulating a robust counter-concept of 'social structure', the Collectivist cautiously indicates points at which some aspect of society is necessary to explain this or that and only becomes exuberant when detecting Individualists busily committing sins of commission, on their own terms, by incorporating such references anyway.

This means that the Collectivist deals with the 'social structure' in the most fragmented way, as a disparate collection of facts or factors which are only brought forward when Individualism fails. Yet when they are then adduced by Collectivists, the question cannot be evaded as to their ontological status. Here, the spectre of Holism and the fear of reification made the Collectivist response as circumspect as possible. Gellner, for instance, was far from content with 'descriptive individualism' as the necessary bulwark against Holism: whilst it warded off the reified ghoulies, he clearly considered that it also cordoned off important tracts of the field which contained things quite other in kind than 'geists' and 'group-minds'. Thus, he speculates that the patterns we are capable of isolating in our environment and reacting towards are not 'merely abstracted', not simply mental constructs. He then invites us to consider that 'For any individual, the *mores*, institutions, tacit presuppositions, etc. of his society are an independent and external fact, as much so as the physical environment and usually more important. And if this is so for each individual, it *does* follow that it is so for the totality of individuals composing a society.'[21] What then is the status of these patterns in whose terms the everyday actor thinks and in relation to which s/he acts, as does the observer who also recognizes that they cannot be eliminated from his account of social life? The way the reply is couched is revealing. 'The pattern isolated, however, is not "merely abstracted" but is *as I am somewhat sheepishly tempted to say, "really there"*.'[22]

To examine the origins of the 'sheepishness' is important for they were responsible for withholding full ontological status from 'societal properties' for decades. Tentativeness is rooted in two spectres of reification and the seeming difficulty of affirming the existence of 'societal properties'

---

[21] Gellner, 'Holism versus individualism', p. 264.
[22] Gellner, 'Holism versus individualism', p. 264.

without invoking one of them. The first was J. S. Mill's old fear,[23] namely
that to acknowledge emergence was to countenance the existence of a new
'social substance'. The second was that talk about 'societal properties'
was also talk about things produced or generated by society, independently of the activities of people and therefore superordinate to actors. In
fact, it appears that both very proper anxieties were really semantic in
origin, turning respectively on the Greek word (*ousia*) for substance
(which need never be employed in relation to emergence) and the Latin
phrase 'sui generis' (which has been misused in this connection).

The first source of unease is the doubt that any referent of a holistic
concept can have an effect upon concrete individuals, since this seems to
endow an abstraction with some kind of existence which cannot be flesh
and blood and therefore must entail a different substance (from people) if
it is real. As Gellner writes, putting himself in the shoes of the Individualist, 'Surely the insubstantial cannot constrain the substantial? I think we
can provisionally agree to this principle'.[24] In other words, the only two
alternatives seemed to be to credit 'societal properties' with some
mysterious substance or to withhold reality from them. The language of
substances proved as damaging in sociology as *ousia* has been in the
Tridentine concept of 'transubstantiation', which construes eucharistic
theology in terms of sacramental physicalism. In social science the
problem was identical, only (rightly) sociological physicalism had no
takers. The real problem was that the wrong language was being
employed, even more by the opponents of 'societal properties' than by
their sheepish advocates. In consistency, the Individualist who felt
confident when pointing to flesh and blood people, surely did not hold
that they were invoking dubious 'substances' when they (necessarily)
referred to people's personalities, attitudes or dispositions? And if so,
then why should the defenders of 'societal facts' be automatically guilty of
invoking such when referring to their 'non-observables' – for *neither*
could confine their terms of reference to sense-data, which is what
'substance' effectively stood for in this context.

The second source of concern derived from the current (and continuing) mis-assumption that to consider 'societal facts' as being *sui generis*
entailed reification because it implied that they were generated by society
itself – as a separate and superordinate entity, 'Society'. Literally, the
phrase means nothing more than 'of its own kind'. In this case, 'societal
facts' do not *pertain* to the *genus* (class of object) made up of individual
people but belong to a different *genus*, i.e. the class of objects designated

[23] J. S. Mill, *A System of Logic Ratiocinative and Inductive*, People's Editions, London,
1984, p. 573.   [24] Gellner, 'Holism versus individualism', p. 262.

by terms like society, social organization or social structure. Note, this says nothing at all about their genesis, where they come from as properties, it specifies only what kind of properties they are. The confusion arises etymologically because the same word *genus* (of which *generis* is the genitive means 'birth', deriving from the older Sanskrit verb 'jan', meaning 'to be begat'. Hence, the source of the Holistic error that (reified) Society begets or generates its own (equally reified) properties. However, when referring to things, such as 'society', it denotes merely 'sort' or 'kind'.

Collectivists were perfectly clear that they were making no such claims; neither invoking a reified Society nor denying that the origins and indeed persistence of 'societal facts' depended upon continuous human interaction. Thus Gellner underlined that where properties of groups and complexes are concerned, 'these latter can indeed exist only if their parts exist – that is indeed the predicament of all wholes – but their fates *qua* fates of complexes can nevertheless be the initial conditions or indeed the final conditions of the causal sequence'.[25] In exactly the same vein, Mandelbaum maintained that 'one need not hold that a society is an entity independent of all human beings in order to hold that societal facts are not reducible to individual behaviour'.[26] Although such statements clear their advocates of reifying Society and also distance them from their opponents' reductionist ontology, what they do not clarify is the precise ontological status of 'societal properties' themselves. Mandelbaum, after seriously damaging the Individualist conception of social reality by demonstrating the ineradicability of references to the social in description and explanation, was clear that 'one's ontology must be accommodated to the facts: the facts cannot be rejected because of a prior ontological commitment'.[27] Fair enough, for methodology should indeed regulate ontology. However, this points to a different conception of social reality, one which was not restricted to the Individual but never referred to the Social Whole, one which accepted that 'societal facts' were activity-dependent yet also maintained they were causally influential, autonomous and pre-existent *vis-à-vis* individuals. But it was not forthcoming from within Collectivism. The reason for this was the impossibility of substantiating the existence of a societal property, 'of its own kind', within the confines of an empiricist epistemology, where knowledge only comes from sense-experience. Since it was not forthcoming, then the charge of reification was repeatedly reiterated by Individualists, whilst Collectivists did not articulate a new social ontology because hemmed in between Holism and Empiricism.

[25] Gellner, 'Holism versus individualism', p. 263.
[26] Mandelbaum, 'Societal facts', p. 230.   [27] Mandelbaum, 'Societal facts', p. 232.

The empiricist barrier

We have already noted the conviction current in the 1950s to the effect that there were only two types of entities which could contend to be 'moving agents in history', the human and the super-human, and that these alternatives were held to be exhaustive. From this it was concluded that since the latter entailed reification, then the former was the only claimant. Now, both to view them as exhaustive and to conclude that, because of their observability, individuals were the only conceivable 'moving agents' (i.e. real and really causally efficacious) are twin products of Empiricism. Basically, the Collectivist sought to deny that this dichotomy was exhaustive and to show that the conclusion only followed whilst ever the dichotomy was sustained. Instead, Collectivists rejected both referents and argued for a third type of 'moving agent': 'societal facts', referring to forms of social organization, to social institutions, to persistent roles, that is to systematic and enduring *relationships*. These were neither human nor inhuman in nature but *relational*, and relations depended upon people but at the same time exerted an independent influence over their activities. However, given such a relational conception, 'one can still legitimately ask what sort of ontological status societal facts can conceivably possess if it is affirmed that they depend for their existence on the activities of human beings and yet are claimed not to be identical with these activities'.[28] The question is answerable, but it cannot be answered within the framework of empiricism. Moreover, Collectivists were aware that the answer was 'emergent properties', for Mandelbaum actually refers to 'existential emergents' and Gellner mentions the 'principle of Internal Relations' for explicating their inner constitution. Significantly, both insights are confined to footnotes, conveying the impression that to air them would invite a frosty reception, possibly withering Collectivism's more modest methodological attack upon the explanatory inadequacies of Individualism.

Most likely they were correct, for the notion of 'emergent properties' depends upon overturning empiricism itself. Instead of a one-dimensional reality coming to us through the 'hard-data' supplied by the senses, to speak of 'emergence' implies a *stratified* social world including non-observable entities, where talk of its ultimate constituents makes no sense, given that the relational properties pertaining to each stratum are all real, that it is nonsense to discuss whether something (like water) is more real than something else (like hydrogen and oxygen), and that regress as a means of determining 'ultimate constituents' is of no help in this respect and an unnecessary distraction in social or any other type of theorizing.

[28] Mandelbaum, 'Societal facts', p. 230.

We would not try to explain the power of people to think by reference to the cells that constitute them,

as if cells possessed this power too. Nor would we explain the power of water to extinguish fire by deriving it from the powers of its constituents, for oxygen and hydrogen are highly inflammable. In such cases, objects are said to have 'emergent powers', that is, powers or liabilities which cannot be reduced to those of their constituents ... Emergence can be explained in terms of the distinction between internal and external relations. Where objects are externally or contingently related they do not affect one another in their essentials and so do not modify their causal powers, although they may interfere with the effects of the exercise of these powers ... In the case of internally related objects, or structures ... emergent powers are created because this type of combination of individuals modifies their powers in fundamental ways. Even though social structures exist only where people reproduce them, they have powers irreducible to those of individuals (you can't pay rent to yourself)[29]

or swear fealty to yourself, or manumit yourself.

Therefore, to talk about 'emergent powers' is simply to refer to a property which comes into being through social combination. These are literally 'existential emergents'. They exist by virtue of inter-relations, although not all relationships give rise to them. Thus, the increased productivity of Adam Smith's pin-makers was a power emergent from their division of labour (relations of production) and not reducible to personal qualities like increased dexterity. Although he himself held that this was also a side-effect, it did not account for the hundred-fold increase in output (mass production) which was the *relational effect* of the time saved in not picking up and putting down different tools, or manipulating each pin through various angles and on different surfaces when making one from start to finish. By contrast, the Ladies' Sewing Circle was doubtless a social relationship but not one which generated the emergent power of mass production, since each member confined herself to her own work.

Just as the development of 'emergent powers' is nothing mysterious, neither is there any mystery about their constituents and certainly no invocation of dubious 'social substances':

The nature or constitution of an object and its causal powers are internally or necessarily related: a plane can fly by virtue of its aerodynamic form, engines, etc.: gunpowder can explode by virtue of its unstable chemical structure; multinational firms can sell their products dear and buy their labour power cheap by virtue of operating in several countries with different levels of development; people can change their behaviour by virtue of their ability to monitor their own monitorings; and so on.[30]

[29] Andrew Sayer, *Method in Social Science*, Routledge, London, 1992, p. 119.
[30] Sayer, *Method*, p. 105.

The existence of such causal powers has nothing to do with essentialism for as the entity changes (through natural causes such as metal fatigue or social causes such as a Third World embargo on multinational imports), so the powers change because their internal relations have altered (or been altered) in ways which nullify that which was necessary to the power in question.

Such were the ontological implications of the insights which the Collectivists already had, but failed to pursue. And their reason for this was their full awareness that such efforts would come straight up against the brick wall of empiricist epistemology. For 'societal facts' and 'emergent properties' in general are incapable of being known via sense-data, because as non-observables they cannot be 'pointed to' in the sense in which we can point to material or organic objects, or to their qualities or activities. Mandelbaum was conscious that, on this criterion, the argument would simply go round full circle:

Whenever we wish to point to any fact concerning societal organization we can only point to a sequence of interpersonal actions. Therefore any theory of knowledge which demands that all empirically meaningful concepts must ultimately be reduced to data which can be directly inspected will lead to the insistence that all societal concepts are reducible to patterns of individual behaviour.[31]

Thus the problem of how to substantiate the existence of relational properties appeared intransigent. Mandelbaum himself remained stranded in the uncomfortable position of asserting that 'societal concepts' could not be translated into individual terms without leaving an irreducible societal remainder, whilst at the time bowing to empiricist epistemology and advocating the necessity of *partial* translations in order to *verify* the concepts in question. Thus, 'It is always necessary for us to translate terms such as "ideologies" or "banks" or "a monogamous marriage system" into the language of individual thought and action, for unless we do so we have no means of verifying any statements which we may make concerning these societal facts.'[32]

Yet as we noted earlier, Gellner had seen a way round this epistemological difficulty, a method of securing the reality of relational concepts not on the perceptual criterion of empiricism, but through demonstrating their casual efficacy, that is employing a causal criterion to establish reality. What precluded its exploitation was that the empiricist conception of causation, in terms of constant conjunctions at the level of (observable) events, constituted another brick wall. The trouble with 'internally related structures' is that their powers may not always be exercised because other contingencies intervene in society, which is

---

[31] Mandelbaum, 'Societal facts', p. 232.   [32] Mandelbaum, 'Societal facts', p. 229.

necessarily an open system and can never approximate to laboratory conditions of closure. Because of this, 'emergent properties' will not necessarily or usually be demonstrable by some regular co-variance in observable events. Despite their roles, bank tellers sometimes hand over money to masked men and ideologies may be masked by tokenism. In other words, emergent properties rarely produce constant conjunctions in society and therefore almost always fail to establish a claim to reality on the empiricist criterion of causality.

Ironically, the notion of emergence was a defence against Holism which came to grief on Empiricism. It was employed purely defensively to rebut ontological objections, namely that references to societal facts or properties entailed reification, but it was never deployed in its own right for a thorough-going reconceptualization of social structure. Its drastic and premature limitation to this defensive role is starkly illustrated by Goldstein's conclusion:

No sociological theory need make explicit reference to sociological emergence; its usefulness is of another sort. When methodological individualists assail this or that theory as holistic, when in fact it simply uses concepts that are not reducible to individual dispositions, its defenders have always the possibility of pointing to methodological emergence or some variation of it. That is, since the nature of the criticism levelled against the theory is ontological rather than methodological, sociological emergence offers a way of meeting it. It affirms that social scientists may develop non-individualistic theories without being holists. And it has the further advantage of forcing methodological individualists to defend their thesis on methodological grounds. If non-individualist social science does not commit untoward ontological sins, the methodological individualists are required to find better grounds for its rejection. The doctrine that all explanation in social science is ultimately in terms of individual dispositions is not established, indeed, in no way supported, by the untenability of holism.[33]

There we have it all: the emergentist ontology relegated to the background, invoked only to repulse charges of holistic reification and thus to allow Collectivist explanations to continue to be advanced. In short, the *methodological* game can go on, but only as a battle over the proper form of sociological explanation, in a way which makes no explicit reference to emergence!

Effectively what this does is to encourage Collectivists to go on playing a game, defined in empiricist terms and according to its rules which means that they can never win. On such terms there is no way in which they can establish the *reality* of the explanatory concepts they adduce. As we have seen, either they concede the necessity of 'partial translation' into statements about individuals which re-shackles them to the empiricist

[33] Goldstein, 'Two theses', pp. 281–2.

criterion of observability (and therefore does nothing to establish the reality of their non-observable structural properties), or, if they appeal instead to the causal criterion, emergent structural properties must fail Hume's test for they do not manifest themselves in constant conjunctions (they are incapable of predicting regularities at the level of events). Consequently, at most, such properties can be inserted into explanations when reduction fails, and the most that can be hoped for by Collectivists is that this 'gives us some understanding of the unreduced concepts'.[34] It is hardly a confident expectation, because confronted with the same situation, the Individualist cherishes the opposite hope, namely that the connections established between 'group variables' may 'suggest the appropriate composition rules of individual behaviour'.[35]

Hume's heritage

In other words, Collectivists retreated to playing a methodological game which could never establish their ontological claims. They thus became closet emergentists but explanatory game players and in the process the emergent social structure, to which no 'explicit reference' was made, underwent further diminution. Once again, methodology reacts back to regulate ontology, in this case fragmenting structure into a series of discrete properties rather than allowing social structure to be considered as a distinct stratum of social reality and explored as such. It enters explanations as a set of social features adduced on an *ad hoc* basis when explanation cannot do without them, thus serving to occlude the systematic nature of social structure. But the effects go deeper still, for what now governs even its *ad hoc* admission is none other than the Humean model of causation itself! For structural features are allowed in under the rubric of (as yet) 'undefined group properties' *provided* they increase our explanatory/predictive power by helping to account for observed regularities. It is its contribution to accounting for a constant conjunction which gives a structural property its right of entry. Yet most of the time, in open social systems, regularities at the level of events are just what emergent features do not generate. Therefore, the structural elements which can pass the Humean check-point, only do so on an *ad hoc* basis but are also *atypical* 'of their own kind'! In practice, they are those which approximate to observability and are in play because of their descriptive indispensability. Thus, for example, the type of electoral system (proportional representation or first-past-the-post) will be needed to explain the kind of

---

[34] Gellner, 'Holism versus individualism', p. 255n.
[35] Brodbeck, 'Methodological individualisms', p. 303.

government to emerge from any election, in addition to statements about people's political dispositions, which in turn are only identifiable in relation to Political Parties. These two structural properties earn their ticket and the Collectivist might even manage to suggest that voters are in a (pre-structured) situation where their Party affiliation is affected by the electoral system (i.e. supporting a minority party makes more sense under proportional representation). However, what Humean gatekeeping will preclude are propositions about the prior distribution of power having affected the electoral system in operation, the Parties in existence, let alone the political dispositions of voters themselves. Yet there may well be internal and necessary relationships obtaining between all four elements.

Another way of putting this is that certain emergent effects may get through the gate, but no emergent mechanism will. Included purely insofar as they boost predictive power, some structural factors can be added to statements about individuals to improve the correlation coefficient. In this way, all that is asserted is that the two together yield better predictions. What cannot be asserted or even explored in terms of constant conjunctions is how the explanatory factors interact together to generate a given outcome. The explanatory formula is 'individual dispositions' plus some indispensable 'structural property', where the 'plus' is predictive rather than real (i.e. two independent factors which together predict better than one alone, rather than as inter-dependent variables).

Consenting to play a purely methodological game according to Humean rules gradually undermines the Collectivist programme. We have just charted the fragmentation of structure into disparate 'factors' and indicated that it is immediately followed by the exclusion of the interplay between 'structure and agency'. Yet this interaction had been just what early emergentists looked towards and saw profit in social theory exploring. Mandelbaum had argued that to hold 'that societal facts are not reducible without remainder to facts concerning the thoughts and actions of specific individuals, is not to deny that the latter class of facts also exists, *and that the two classes may interact*'.[36] Moreover he had begun to spell out how they do so, by sketching in exactly the kind of mechanism, or still better *process*, which constant conjunctions literally cannot acknowledge (for to Hume *all* we can ever say is that (a) and (b) are regularly observed to coincide). On the contrary, Mandelbaum proposed that 'if we wish to understand many of the dilemmas by which individuals are faced, we can do no better than hold to the view that there are societal facts which exercise external constraints over individuals no less than there are facts concerning individual volition which often come into conflict with these

---

[36] Mandelbaum, 'Societal facts', p. 234.

constraints'.[37] Finally, if this crucial interplay is written off the agenda, two other elements are lost with it.

The first is any notion of the 'structuring of agency', that is the processes by which our necessary involvement in society (as opposed to our equally inescapable involvements with other people), help to make us the kind of social beings we are, with the dispositions we possess and express. For the Collectivist was surely right that, for instance, an attitude of political disillusionment can be engendered by such things as a succession of coalition governments locked in immobility which were produced, in part at least, by proportional representation systems. Instead of the re-conceptualization of agency to which this points, we are left with 'the individual' plus some 'structural factor' needed for enhanced prediction and can only combine them for purposes of correlation, but cannot investigate the processes of their combination in the real world.

Secondly, since process in general is off the Humean agenda, then the strange and undesirable situation arises in which a given 'structural property' may permissibly figure in an explanation, yet the processes through which it emerged cannot be captured within the same explanatory framework. Regrettably then, the strenuous policing of which 'structural properties' might appear in explanatory statements (those which improved predictive power) also prevented any explanation of their own origins (interaction in a prior social context) and their mode of influence (through structuring the context of current interaction). By entering 'factorially' into explanations, it was allowed that these fragmented aspects of social structure co-determined outcomes (along with individuals), but never that they did so by a process of working *through* people – shaping the situations they confronted, furnishing beliefs for their interpretation, or distributing different vested interests to them in maintaining or transforming the status quo. Instead, they remained 'undefined', unexplored and unlinked (to one another or to agents): only their *deterministic* effects in accounting for regular social outcomes was upheld.

On Humean terms, such 'structural properties' as earned their keep remained both unduly mysterious and inexplicably powerful. Ironically, then, positivism served to retain them as something much more akin to Holistic factors (of unexplicated provenance and deterministic consequence) than had ever been the wish of Collectivists. Not surprisingly, many of those who found the parameters of the Humean game unduly restrictive sought stronger beer in unabashed Holism itself – structura-

---

[37] Mandelbaum, 'Societal facts', p. 234.

lism, structural functionalism and structuralist marxism. In short, the failure of Collectivism to articulate an alternative social ontology to Individualism, and the Collectivist 'retreat' to defending what they could of their methodological ground, served both directly and indirectly to foster 'downwards conflation' in practical social theory – be it through those acceding to positivism and according 'structural properties' a deterministic influence in the regular occurrence of events, or through kicking over the empiricist traces to become Holistic recidivists.

Contesting the terms of the traditional debate

Chapter 1 began by stressing the tripartite relationship between ontology, methodology and practical social theory. Since none is dispensable, then each has to be adequately conceptualized in itself and consistently related to the others. In turn, this means that we are dealing with their *mutual regulation* and matters can only go astray if what should be a flexible two-way relationship is rigidly conceived of as uni-directional. This was the purpose of going over the ground of the old debate between Individualists and Collectivists, for both programmes illustrate the deficiencies of one-way approaches.

Thus, Individualists began from an unshakeable *ontological commitment* that the ultimate constituents of social reality were 'individuals', formulated their methodological injunctions on this basis, yet were unwilling to make ontological adjustments in the light of the unworkability of their own methods and the findings of others who did not share their commitment to the necessity of reductionism. By contrast, Collectivists started from an equally strong *methodological conviction* that facts about the social context could neither be excised from the description or explanation of our subject-matter, but failed to ground this in a conception of social reality which both avoided any taint of Holism and evaded the strictures of empiricism.

The inability of either Individualism or Collectivism to establish a convincing, consistent and working relationship between social ontology and methodology can be laid firmly at the door of empiricism itself. For it fortified Individualists in the belief that since they were ontologically secure, then their methods must work 'in principle', despite all evidence to the contrary. Simultaneously, it undermined Collectivist confidence in their methodological 'success' by querying the reality of their explanatory variables, which never could be validated in empiricist terms.

The implications for practical social theorizing were equally unsatisfactory. However implicit they may be, no social theory can be advanced without making some assumptions about what kind of reality it is dealing with and how to explain it. All social theory is ontologically shaped and methodologically moulded even if these processes remain covert and scarcely acknowledged by the practitioner. This is inescapable because theories logically entail concepts and concepts themselves include certain things and exclude others (at the methodological level) and denote some aspects of reality whilst denying others (at the ontological level). Any who think they can avoid both fall into the trap of instrumentalism: those believing that the use of 'heuristic concepts' in explanation saves them from making any ontological commitment fail to recognise that terming something 'heuristic' is itself a matter of ontology.

Yet the concepts on offer from Individualism and Collectivism were fundamentally unsatisfactory. Individualism supplied an unacceptably atomistic concept of the individual, shorn of any relationship with the social context yet inexplicably bulging with social attributes; a conception of the social structure as a mere aggregate of individual activities whose every tendency was the responsibility of current actors, plus the unworkable method of reduction as the means for linking 'structure and agency'. On the other hand, Collectivists proffered a fragmented conception of structure, defined residually as that which defied reduction, an equally fragmentary concept of agency represented by individuals plus their social context, and they refrained from specifying the processes linking the two together. Insofar as working social theorists took Individualist concepts on board, this served to perpetuate the fallacy of upwards conflation in social theorizing. If they drew upon Collectivism instead, then the missing two-way link between structure and agency continued to foster the equally fallacious form of downwards conflation in social theory.

Of course much of this went on in the state of inarticulate unawareness and often consisted in practical analysts cutting their theoretical cloth to suit their coat or vice versa.[38] Thus, at one extreme interpretative sociologists undertook small-scale interactional studies and simply placed a big etc. after them, implying that the compilation of enough sensitive ethnographies would generate an understanding of society by aggregation. At the other, large-scale multivariate analyses pressed on towards some predictive goal without reference to the interactional processes generating their variables. However, it has already been stressed that the scope of the problem or size of entity is not what actually

---

[38] 'Factual trends may certainly be detected with respect to the preferred, strategic field of empirical inquiry. In particular, those who focus on small groups, or microsociological phenomena, are more often than not reductionistically orientated, and those who study the comprehensive historical processes, or macrosociological phenomena, tend toward antireductionistic interpretations'. Piotr Sztompka, *Sociological Dilemmas*. Academic Press, New York, 1979, p. 92.

differentiates between Individualism and Collectivism; to the former, the macroscopic is just the 'large group'; to the latter, a dyad like husband and wife or doctor and patient is unidentifiable without reference to the social context. Thus the above connections were ones of superficial theoretical affinity, but once forged the concepts used then transmitted their own deficiencies into practical theorizing. Alternatively, in some specialisms, theorizing would begin on the basis of concepts taken from one camp, realize the limitations of the concepts, and then swap to the other camp, only to repeat the process. Thus, for example, the 'old' sociology of Education (Collectivist) gave way to the 'new' (Individualist), eventually leaving practitioners calling for synthesis.

Yet as we have seen, synthesis or compromise is the one deal which cannot be struck, which is why I have continuously resisted the notion of a *via media* between the two programmes, consisting of conceding Descriptive Individualism to the Individualist and Explanatory Emergence to the Collectivist. Further modifications or revisions, such as 'situational individualism', undertaken with the same conciliatory aim in view, have not been discussed, because like the *via media* they fail – as they must – to reconcile contradictory premises. I have stuck to the pure lines of the debate, as articulated in the 1950s because if, as I maintain, there are intimate and indissoluble connections between ontology, methodology and practical social theory, then this is what we have been stuck with ever since – a choice between the two alternatives, replete with their deficiencies which are merely replicated at the practical level, which ever is chosen. This was the reason for saying 'don't choose', but it was almost impossible advice to follow when positivism was in full flood and empiricism itself was responsible for the intrinsic defects of the only two options available.

Only after the empiricist hegemony had been challenged and the closely associated domination of positivism had been similarly undermined did siding with neither Individualism nor Collectivism become a genuine option. For with the progressive demise of empiricism, not only were the terms of the old debate between them rejected, but the debate itself was re-cast in entirely different ones. These transcended the original antinomy between the 'study of wo/man' and the 'science of society' by re-conceptualizing 'structure' as intimately rather than truistically 'activity-dependent' and the 'individual' as intrinsically rather than extrinsically the subject of 'social constitution'.

What did not disappear, despite the vastly premature celebration of a new consensus by many commentators, was the enduring necessity of making a choice. For the new terms in which 'structure and agency' were re-conceptualized and linked together were again represented by *two standpoints*, thus opening up a new debate beginning in the seventies or early eighties. These I have termed 'Elisionism' (because transcending the dualism between individual and society consisted in replacing it by an insistence upon their mutual constitution), and 'Emergentism' (because structure and agency are both regarded as emergent strata of social reality and linkage consists in examining their interplay).

The first manifestations of Elisionism in social theory were distinctly idealist. Neo-phenomenological forms of theorizing construed the social context as 'facticity' rather than fact and insisted upon its 'externalization' and 'objectification' rather than allowing it externality and objectivity. However, in viewing entities such as social institutions as purely dramatic conventions which depended upon co-operative acts of agents in sustaining a particular definition of the situation, Symbolic Interactionists in particular elided 'structure' and 'agency' in three key ways which have increasingly come to characterize Elisionism as a distinctive theoretical orientation: (i) a denial of their separability, because, (ii) every aspect of 'structure' is held to be activity-dependent in the present tense and equally open to transformation, and (iii) the conviction that any causal efficacy of structure is dependent upon its evocation by agency.

Because of the centrality of 'inseparability', such premises are neither reductionist (*contra* Individualism), nor anti-reductionist (*contra* Collectivism). Whilst the untrammelled idealism, characteristic of interpretative sociology in the seventies, is no longer the hallmark of those viewing structure and agency as mutually constitutive, the fundamental inseparability of the two is what constitutes Elisionism as a distinctive approach. Those now endorsing the 'duality of structure' as the medium and outcome of social practices, under the rubric of Structuration theory, have reconstituted Elisionism on a more acceptable basis (which incorporates material resources and power rather than dealing with networks of meanings alone), whilst continuing to endorse *inseparability* and its associated premises. In contradistinction, the very notion of 'emergent properties' which are generated within socio-cultural systems is necessarily antithetic to the tenet of inseparability because such structural and cultural features have autonomy from, are pre-existent to, and are causally efficacious *vis-à-vis* agents – their existence, influence and analysis therefore being incompatible with the central premises of Elisionism.

Consequently choice is inescapable because 'Elision' (the term used for those grouping themselves around Structuration theory) and 'Emergence' (those exploring the interface between transcendental realism and social theory) are based upon different ontological conceptions, related to disparate methodological injunctions and thus have quite distinct implications for practical social theorizing. To celebrate the development of a new consensus is to concentrate upon their common rejection of the terms of the old debate whilst ignoring the different bases upon which the two re-set the terms. The unpopular message of this book is that the burden of choosing has not been removed – and we can only make a sensible choice by closely scrutinizing the nature of and connections between ontology – methodology – practical social theory which Elisionists and Emergentists respectively endorse. This is exactly what will be done: it is undoubtedly more burdensome than the conclusion that we can have the best of both worlds, but it is preferable to recognize in advance that again there can be no *via media* than to find it collapsing under us later on.

Let us briefly introduce the two new standpoints whose relative merits will be examined in the course of the next three chapters – and the reasons for the choice which is made between them here. On the one hand, the Elisionists' new 'ontology of praxis' seeks to *transcend* the traditional debate through replacing the two sets of terms in which it was conducted by their notion of 'the duality of structure', in which agency and structure can only be conceptualized in relation to one another. From this, it follows methodologically that neither the reductionism advocated by Individualist nor the anti-reductionism defended by Collectivists can play any part in the Elisionists' approach to explanation – which takes up the novel position of *areductionism*. This is the direct logical consequence of their re-defining structure and agency as *inseparable*. Whilst this frees both from being an epiphenomenon of the other, it does so by holding them to be mutually constitutive. In turn it will be maintained that although the implication of this is a rejection of both upwards and downwards conflation in social theorizing, its consequence is actually to introduce a new variant – central conflation – into social theory.

On the other hand, the realist ontology of the Emergentists is deployed to furnish that which Collectivism lacked, an activity-dependent concept of structure, which is both genuinely irreducible yet in no danger of hypostatization, and a non-atomistic conception of agents, to rectify the deficiencies of Individualism's individual – without, however, regarding the two elements as part of an inseparable 'duality'. Instead, because Realists endorse the existence of irreducible 'emergent properties', they advance a much more robustly *stratified* view of both society and people and hence resist central conflation which is the expression of Elisionism in social theory.

Emergentists' combined repudiation of both reductionist and conflationary theorizing means a principled avoidance of the epiphenomenalism which is embedded in Holism and Individualism, where 'agency' and 'structure' respectively become inert as wholly dependent features –

consequently, introducing downwards and upwards conflation into social theorizing. It also constitutes a principled departure from the 'duality of structure' by which 'structure' and 'agency' are inextricably compacted by Elisionists. In place of all three forms of conflationary theorizing, the Emergentist substitutes *analytical dualism*. Because the social world is made up, *inter alia*, of 'structures' and of 'agents' and because these belong to different strata, there is no question of reducing one to the other or of eliding the two and there is every reason for exploring the interplay between them.

These differences between the Elisionists and Emergentists have often been obscured by their common rejection of the terms of the traditional debate, but what the two replace them by is grounded in antithetical conceptions of social reality – precisely because Structuration theorists explicitly *disavow emergence itself*. Thus Ira Cohen underlines that 'structures' are 'properties of systems that do not "emerge"' and states:

> To affirm that enduring properties of collectivities are embedded in disappearing and reappearing practices and relations both clarifies and demystifies the ontological obscurities associated with emergence. In particular it is no longer necessary to pose the uncomfortable question of how emergence actually occurs: a question which no collectivist theorist, to my knowledge has answered in a persuasive fashion.[39]

Such a viewpoint stands in the starkest contrast with the Realist assertion that 'it is just in virtue of these emergent features of societies, that social science is possible'.[40]

Obviously there is an onus upon those of us who uphold the latter view to clear up the 'ontological obscurities' which 'sheepish' Collectivists did leave unresolved when they defended explanatory emergence (but failed to ground it in a non-empiricist conception of social reality). The contributions of transcendental realists over the last ten to fifteen years have served to clarify these residual obscurities: the development of the morphogenetic/static approach now provides an account of 'the occurrence of emergence' which complements the realist social ontology with a working methodology. Together they insist upon the activity-dependence of emergent properties, in their origins as in their influences. Equally, they claim that this does *not* mean generative activities and emergent consequences have to be treated as inseparable; on the contrary they firmly uphold the possibility and utility of distinguishing between them.

---

[39]   Ira J. Cohen, 'Structuration theory and social order: five issues in brief', in J. Clark, C. Modgil and S. Modgil (eds.), *Anthony Giddens: Consensus and Controversy*, Falmer Press, Basingstoke, 1990, p. 42.

[40]   Roy Bhaskar, *The Possibility of Naturalism*, Harvester, Hemel Hempstead, 1979, p. 25.

Thus in the new conspectus which I have called Emergentism (and can now be seen to be defined here as a realist ontology and a morphogenetic methodology), it is vital to distinguish between

such *causal inter-dependency*, which is a contingent feature of the process concerned, from *existential intransitivity*, which is a priori condition of any investigation ... For although the processes of production may be interdependent, once some object ... exists, if it exists, however it has been produced, it constitutes a possible object for scientific investigation.[41]

A realist ontology which upholds transfactual structures and intransitive cultural properties, and encourages their investigation as emergent entities, is thus at variance with the Elisionists' view which holds, (a) that such properties only possess a 'virtual existence' until, (b) they are 'instantiated' by actors, which (c) means these properties are neither fully real nor examinable except in conjunction with the agents who instantiate them, and only then through an artificial bracketing exercise since the two are inseparable in reality.

In conclusion, their consistent insistence upon the differentiation and stratification of the social world leads Emergentists to separate 'parts' and 'people' in order to examine their distinctive emergent properties. As Bhaskar noted of Peter Berger's early and idealist version of an elisionist theory, its fundamental error is that 'People and society are not ... related "dialectically". They do not constitute two moments of the same process. Rather they refer to radically different things'.[42] Precisely the same criticism can be levelled at later versions like structuration theory, which repeats this 'fallacy of the two moments', and will only entertain 'unacknowledged conditions of action', withholding the status of emergent properties from them by rendering them merely matters of 'knowledgeability' on the part of agents.

Hence, the separability/inseparability issue represents the ontological parting of the ways between Emergentists and Elisionists. For the Emergentist,

The importance of distinguishing, in the most categorical way, between human action and social structure will now be apparent. For the properties possessed by social forms may be very different from those possessed by the individuals upon whose activity they depend ... I want to distinguish sharply then between the genesis of human actions, lying in the reasons, intentions and plans of human beings, on the one hand; and the structures governing the reproduction and transformation of social activities, on the other.[43]

Why? Not simply because ontologically they *are* indeed different

---

[41] Bhaskar, *Naturalism*, p. 47.   [42] Bhaskar, *Naturalism*, p. 33
[43] Bhaskar, *Reclaiming Reality*, Verso, London, 1989, p. 79.

entities with different properties and powers, but because methodologically it is necessary to make the distinction between them in order to *examine their interplay* and thus be able to explain why things are 'so and not otherwise' in society.

This interplay between the two is crucial for effective theorizing about the social world, whether our concern is with everyday personal dilemmas or with macroscopic societal transformations. Yet the Elisionists insistence upon 'inseparability' precludes just that examination of the interface between structure and agency upon which practical social theorizing depends. From the standpoint of Elisionism it becomes impossible to talk about the stringency of structural constraints versus degrees of personal freedom, for in theories based upon central conflation, causation is always the joint and equal responsibility of structure and agency and nothing is ever more attributable to one rather than the other, at any given point in time.

The central argument of this book is just the opposite. It is only through analysing the *processes* by which structure and agency shape and re-shape one another over time that we can account for variable social outcomes at different times. This presumes a social ontology which warrants speaking about 'pre-existence', 'relative autonomy' and 'causal influence' in relation to these two strata (structures and agents) and an explanatory methodology which makes such talk practicable for the practising social theorist.

3   Taking time to link structure and agency

The 'problem of structure and agency' is now a familiar phrase used to denote central dilemmas in social theory – especially the rival claims of voluntarism versus determinism, subjectivism versus objectivism, and the micro- versus macro-scopic in sociology. These issues are central for the simple reason that it is impossible to do sociology at all without dealing with them and coming to decisions about them. These issues are problematic for any social theorist who cannot come down with conviction on one side or the other; and that means a great many of us, each of whom is then of necessity in the job of reconciliation. Imperative as this is, the urgency of the 'problem of structure and agency' is not one which imposes itself upon academics alone, but on every human being.

For it is part and parcel of daily experience to feel both free and enchained, capable of shaping our own future and yet confronted by towering, seemingly impersonal, constraints. Those whose reflection leads them to reject the grandiose delusion of being puppet-masters but also to resist the supine conclusion that they are mere marionettes then have the same task of reconciling this experiential bivalence, and must do so if their moral choice is not to become inert or their political action ineffectual. Consequently, in facing-up to the 'problem of structure and agency' social theorists are not just addressing crucial technical problems in the study of society, they are also confronting the most pressing social problem of the human condition.

What is to be developed in this book is a theoretical approach which is capable of *linking* structure and agency rather than *sinking* one into the other. The central argument is that structure and agency can only be linked by examining the *interplay between them over time*, and that without the proper incorporation of time the problem of structure and agency can never be satisfactorily resolved.

When discussing 'structure' and 'agency', I am talking about a relationship between two aspects of social life which, however intimately they are intertwined (as in our individual experiences of, say, marriage), are none the less analytically distinct. Few would disagree with this characterization of social reality as Janus-faced: indeed, too many have concluded too quickly that the task is therefore how to look at both faces of the same medallion at once. It is precisely this methodological notion of trying to peer at the two simultaneously which is resisted here, for the basic reason that they are neither co-extensive nor co-variant through time, because each possesses autonomous emergent properties which are thus capable of independent variation and therefore of being out of phase with one another in time.

Emergence means that the two are analytically separable, but also since given 'structures' and given 'agents' occupy and operate over different tracts of the time dimension they therefore are distinguishable from each other. Thus for example, a particular marital structure pre-dates *our* contemporary constitution as married social subjects – which is an entirely different point from the perfectly compatible statements that, (a) previous actors through their prior social practices themselves constituted the institution of marriage earlier in history (since this refers to agents long dead), or (b) that our present actions as married subjects are contributing to the transformation of this institution at some future time (since this refers to distant restructuring). To stress temporal separability is never to challenge the activity-dependence of structures: it is only, but very usefully, to specify whose activities they depend upon and when.

Time in non-conflationary social theory

Fundamentally it is maintained that the 'problem of structure and agency' is conceptualized entirely differently by non-conflationary theorists because of their emergentist ontology, which distinguishes them from every type of social theory which endorses conflation. This conception is 'analytical dualism' and it is based on two premises. Firstly, it depends upon an ontological view of the social world as stratified, such that the emergent properties of structures and agents are irreducible to one another, meaning that in principle they are analytically separable. Secondly, it asserts that given structures and agents are also temporally distinguishable (in other words, it is justifiable and feasible to talk of pre-existence and posteriority when dealing with specific instances of the two), and this can be used methodologically in order to examine the interplay between them and thus explain changes in both – over time. In a nutshell, 'analytical dualism' is a methodology based upon the *historicity of emergence*.

The main claim of the morphogenetic/static approach is that 'analytical dualism' provides the most powerful tool in practical social analysis, yet one which has been slow to develop and whose full potential in terms of its theoretical purchase and practical utility have still to be fully recognised. The reasons for this delayed development are basically that both elements, that is analytical separability and temporal distinction were needed in conjunction. Any attempt to make temporal distinctions without a complementary notion of the emergent nature of structural entities was ontologically ungrounded, leaving those who did so open to the charge of reification from others and themselves puzzled about what it was that they held to be prior to action or consequent upon it. Similarly, the reverse, that is to endorse analytical separability without simultaneously recognizing that emergent structures were pre-dated by some actions and post-dated by others (that any activity took place in a context of prior emergent structures and that determinate activities were antecedent to specific structural changes), missed perhaps the most profound methodological consequence of emergentism itself.

Until the analytical separability of structure and agency was explicitly acknowledged to entail temporality rather than simultaneity, realists did not radically recast the form of theorizing about the relations between structure and agency. Instead, they tended to become quite similar to central conflationary approaches.[1] The tardy development of analytical dualism was due to the fact that the necessary conjunction of ideas (i.e. temporal separability) was so long in coming, for firstly there was a period during which temporal distinctions were advanced without an ontology of emergence and then vice versa.

Mandelbaum, as we have seen, was already hinting in 1955[2] that 'societal' and agential properties were spaced differently in time but was hamstrung by still trying to ground structures in empirical realism and thus advocating their translation into individual (observable) terms rather than claiming real emergent status for them. More influential in social theory was Lockwood's seminal article (1964)[3] in which he put forward the distinction between 'social integration' and 'system integration'. By making it, he was claiming that it was both possible and profitable to separate-out the two analytically, that is to distinguish the orderly or conflictual relations maintaining between groups of actors from the orderly or conflictual relations prevailing between parts of the social structure. The point of the exercise was to be able to theorize about the *interplay* between the two, which in turn gave more explanatory purchase upon social stability and change than did theories based on one

---

[1] Note the numerous sources which consider there to be marked resemblances between Bhaskar's 'transformational model of social action' and Giddens' 'structuration theory'.

[2] Maurice Mandelbaum, 'Societal facts', in John O'Neill (ed.), *Modes of Individualism and Collectivism*, Heinemann, London, 1973, 221–34.

[3] David Lockwood, 'Social integration and system integration', in G. K. Zollschan and W. Hirsch (eds.), *Explorations in Social Change*, Houghton Mifflin, Boston, 1964, 244–57.

of them alone (such as conflict theory, exclusively concerned with agency relations and the extent of group antagonism, or normative functionalism, preoccupied with structural relations alone and the nature of systemic interdependencies).

What is of particular significance here is Lockwood's awareness that the distinction between 'social' and 'system' integration is more than an analytical artifice when temporality is taken into account. Thus he states that '[t]hough definitely linked, these two aspects of integration are *not only analytically separable, but also, because of the time element involved, factually distinguishable*'[4] (my italics). Equally, in using the distinction for explanatory purposes, Lockwood relied completely upon the independent variation of the two in time. Thus, when examining his key Marxist example he stresses that 'it is perfectly possible, according to this theory, to say that at any *particular point of time* a society has a high degree of social integration (e.g. relative absence of class conflict) and yet has a low degree of system integration (mounting excess productive capacity)'[5] (my italics). Indeed, the generic explanation of stability and change which he puts forward rests upon the historical coincidence or discrepancy between the properties of structure and those of agency. Since the two are not held to be temporally co-variant, then examination of their variable historical combinations can become a new source of explanatory power.

Yet Lockwood himself was fully aware of the ontological difficulties entailed, namely what exactly was the nature of the systemic 'entities' which he had analytically *and* temporally distinguished from actors and social interaction? Hence he understandably noted that 'the vital question is, of course: what are the 'component elements' of social systems which give rise to strain, tension or contradiction?'.[6] He was fully aware that they cannot be captured at all within the confines of methodological individualism (which remains confined to agential conflict and soon reaches its explanatory limits), but was equally and rightly dismissive of their restriction to observable 'institutional patterns', as in (holistic) functionalism. Although it is clear in his discussion of patrimonialism that he is dealing with internal and necessary relations between its 'component elements' (bureaucracy and taxation) and its contingent contradiction with a subsistence economy, he simply lacked the concepts of emergent generative mechanisms, operating in an open system, with which to answer his own question.

Thus, the later realist and even later morphogenetic approaches would define these 'component elements' as 'emergent properties', arising from relations between the structures which constitute a particular system:

---

[4] Lockwood, 'Social integration', p. 250.
[5] Lockwood, 'Social integration', p. 250.   [6] Lockwood, 'Social integration', p. 250.

social systems being seen as specific configurations of their constitutive structures where the emergent features of the former derive from the relations between the latter. Thus, unlike the 'institutional pattern', rightly dismissed, which confines components to observable entities, structures themselves contain non-observable emergent powers whose combination (relations between relations) generate the further emergent properties which Lockwood addressed – in particular those of contradiction and complementarity. These are not criticisms of his work which is pre-realist (in social theory) yet fully compatible with it, for its explanatory model is also anti-Humean, and this one article was also the single most germinal source for the development of the morphogenetic approach: it is merely to explain why it did not immediately issue in 'analytical dualism' as a general method of social analysis.[7] The author himself had begged too big and delicate an ontological problem among a generation who were at best sheepish about structural properties.

As a form of realism, specifically dealing with social reality, developed in the 1970s,[8] it was surprising to find that this strong ontological defence of emergence and of the stratified nature of the social world was not accompanied by an equally strenuous statement of the *temporal distinction* possible between two of the principal strata, structure and agency. 'Analytical dualism' is implicit, but it remained low key. In fact, I believe that it is not only implicit but necessary to the realist enterprise as a philosophy of social science. After all, its condemnation of empiricism and its critique of the Humean notion of causality for reducing explanation to the detection of 'constant conjunctions' did not hinge only on the assertion of the existence of non-observable emergent entities whose reality was ascertained through their causal effects. It relied equally on the acknowledgment that these were operative in open systems whose other properties could intervene to mask or emasculate these effects (thus necessitating a distinction between empirical outcomes or events and real generative mechanisms which often lacked any empirical manifestation). Yet ultimately what makes society quintessentially an open system (rather

---

[7] Lockwood's article was used as the springboard for developing this approach in my *Social Origins of Educational Systems*, Sage, London and Beverly Hills, 1979. This work which was begun in 1970 relied upon Methodological Collectivism when dealing with explanatory emergence at a time prior to the articulation of realism in social theory. Equally, Lockwood's distinctions furnished the basis for my *Culture and Agency*, Cambridge University Press, Cambridge, 1988.

[8] R. Harré and P. Secord, *The Explanation of Social Behaviour*, Basil Blackwell, Oxford, 1975; R. Harré and E. H. Madden, *Causal Powers*, Basil Blackwell, Oxford, 1975; R. Keat and J. Urry, *Social Theory as Science*, Routledge and Kegan Paul, London, 1975; Roy Bhaskar, *A Realist Theory of Science*, Harvester, Brighton, 1978; William Outhwaite, 'Toward a realist perspective', in Gareth Morgan (ed.), *Beyond Method*, Sage, London and Beverly Hills, 1983.

than just an exceedingly complex one)? What fundamentally precludes any simulation of laboratory conditions of closure, however ingeniously however many factors are 'held constant'? The answer is people and their own inalienable emergent properties. Closure depends upon two conditions, an intrinsic and an extrinsic one, both of which are ineluctably violated by what people are. The extrinsic condition of closure requires that no new emergent properties are developing *outside* the system, which can interfere with the exercise of its known emergent powers in unpredictable ways. Yet whatever social structures are examined, they are only operative in and through the world of people which props the door permanently open because human action is typified by innovativeness, a capacity for interpreting the same material conditions, cultural elements, circumstances and situations in different ways and hence for introducing novel patterns or courses of action in response to them. Since people by nature are reflective in thought and reflexive in action, this is the one factor which can never be controlled for and which therefore makes attempted closure rather like locking the stable door on a horse who knows how to undo it.

The second and intrinsic condition of closure is that there must be no change or qualitative variation (like the effects of impurities in chemistry experiments) in the entity possessing the causal powers if the mechanisms is to operate consistently and produce regular results. Closure thus implies that no new properties can develop *inside* the system or structure in question, which change it and alter its effects. Yet any social structure is dependent upon people and operative only through people, for positions have to have occupants and situations are things that people find themselves in and their own capacity for self change and social change thus violates the intrinsic condition of closure. Here, if you like, the horse remains in the stable but has a capacity denied to horses of redesigning it from within.

Now, since the aim of the realist is to explain what happens in society (and not as it is sometimes misconstrued, to posit some emergent property(ies) dogmatically and then to reel off *ad hoc* lists of factors masking its manifestation), it follows that the ability to theorize in an open system, rather than to be floored by its flux, makes it a matter of necessity to differentiate the properties of structures from those of people. In brief it is *necessary* to separate structure and agency (a) to identify the emergent structure(s), (b) to differentiate between their casual powers and the intervening influences of people due to their quite different causal powers as human beings, and , (c) to explain any outcome at all, which in an open system always entails an interplay between the two. In short, separability is indispensable to realism.

If the realist seeks to explain at all then his or her explanations have to distinguish between generative mechanisms and intervening factors – amongst which people always figure. It follows that a distinction between structure and agency is necessary to the realist enterprise in social theory. But so far that is only to say that 'analytical separability' is indispensable to realism: does it also follow that a 'temporal distinction' between structure and agency is equally a matter of necessity ? The answer is yes, for it is precisely *because* of people being the way they are that the practical consequence for structures (as for any emergent property of society) is that the latter are 'normally out of phase with the pattern of events which actually occur'.[9] In other words, they are not co-variant in time. (Their being out of phase is of course is exactly what Lockwood captured in his distinction between 'system' and 'social' integration.)

Again, this is precisely what Bhaskar maintains when arguing that in social theorizing 'the relations one is concerned with here must be conceptualized as holding between positions and practices ... and not between the individuals who occupy/engage in them'.[10] If we ask whether such an analytical separation *always* entails the temporal distinction between positions and practitioners, roles and their incumbents, the systemic and the social or structure and agency, the answer has to be that this has certainly not been common practice. Generations of sociologists have made present tense distinctions between offices and their holders or formal role requirements and informal doings, but these are confined to the empirical level, they are based on observable current affairs and this will not do for the realist since it omits, *inter alia*, the powers of many role structures to pre-determine *who* was eligible to be an occupant and the powers of incumbents to reflectively re-monitor their activities. The former introduces the past tense and the latter the future tense, but neither are observable in the present tense, if they are observable at all. Thus if the question about the necessity for temporal distinction is re-posed for the realist, the answer is yes. Structures (as emergent entities) are not only irreducible to people, they pre-exist them, and people are not puppets of structures because they have their own emergent properties which mean they either reproduce or transform social structure, rather than creating it. To explain which occurs the realist examines the interplay between the two (endorsing and utilizing separability) and in both cases, reproduction and transformation necessarily refer to maintaining or changing something which is temporally prior to these activities.

---

[9] Roy Bhaskar, *The Possibility of Naturalism*, 2nd edition, Harvester, London, 1989, p. 9.
[10] Bhaskar, *Naturalism* (2nd edn), p. 41.

Why, then, has the temporal strand remained so implicit and under-worked amongst Emergentists in general? (Even Lockwood who made great and important play of the temporal distinction between the 'syste-mic' and the 'social' actually confined his analysis to showing how the 'parts' and the 'people' varied independently of one another *over time* but made no play at all of they themselves being prior and posterior to one another in time.) Perhaps the reluctance to advance 'analytical dualism' forcefully is due to the enduring spectre of reification and to what has rightly been construed as the main bulwark against it, namely an insistence upon the activity-dependence of each and every social struc-ture as indispensable to a non-reified ontology of society. However, what seems to have escaped notice is an extremely simple though profoundly important question which in no way challenges or weakens this ontologi-cal commitment, namely *whose actions?*

The activity-dependence of structures is in no way compromised by the argument that a given structure was issued in by a particular generation/cohort of actors as an unintended yet emergent consequence of their activities, whilst it then necessarily pre-existed their successors. This is the human condition, to be born into a social context (of language, beliefs and organization) which was not of our making: agential power is always restricted to re-making, whether this be reproducing or transforming our social inheritance. The assertion of pre-existence far from nullifying activity-dependence, actually specifies upon *whose* activities the develop-ment of a particular structure depended, in contrast to those later agents who cannot be held responsible for its genesis, but only for its mainten-ance, change or perhaps ultimate abolition. Activities of the latter, of course, engender new forms of structural elaboration which, in turn, their own successors confront as existing realities. No one would seriously deny this in its common sense form, e.g. those whose activities generated the relations constitutive of industrialism, imperialism, political parties, a state educational system or a national health service, were quite different people from those who later had to live in a society made up of these structures amongst others. Some were now born into it and knew no other, in the same way that our current generation of British school leavers have known nothing other than Conservative government, though as non-voters this was not a polity of their making. However, in the future they may seek and succeed in transforming current party political organization, but only by confronting their structural inheritance through strategic action which is itself conditioned by the nature of the inherited structure of political parties. Since it seems unlikely that anyone would seriously deny this lay insight, why has it failed to be taken seriously in social theorizing?

A crucial element of this insight is a recognition of Auguste Comte's important aphorism that the majority of actors are the dead. Yet there is resistance to exploiting it because of a pervasive suspicion that this somehow denies the continuous nature of action over time. Basically this argument goes as follows and is a distorted version of activity-dependence: (a) society is consistently dependent upon action and there can be no moment in time when action is suspended, therefore, (b) action constitutes an *unbroken flow* in which talk of the separate activities of generations or cohorts is only a heuristic artifice since generations overlap and groups are continuous despite the death and even complete replacement of their members. Sometimes this argument is buttressed by the empirical observation that groups can outlast structures, which we all agree are at most only relatively enduring and can be of much shorter duration (like governments or theories) than a determinate group of agents. But the case which I am arguing is not an empirical one and the issue at stake is not one which can be resolved empirically (even were it possible to quantify whether more groups have shown greater endurance than is the case for structures). Instead, what I am challenging here is the basic idea of an *unbroken flow of activities* and particularly as supported by the notion of the continuity of social groups. To contest this in no way depends upon contesting the premiss that all aspects of the social world are continuously activity-dependent – for challenging (b) in the above argument does nothing to impugn (a). Instead, it usefully adds greater precision to it by specification of elements like 'whose' activities, 'when', and 'where'.

What needs to be rebutted here is the assertion that whilst it may be true for each individual that a structure pre-exists them (a teaching post must exist before someone can be a teacher) or even for whole cohorts (schools have to exist before pupils can enrol), it is not true for 'the group'. Critics maintain that 'groups' can have greater permanence than structures, through replacement of their members, and therefore it makes no sense to talk of a structure pre-dating such a group. However, my counter argument asserts that a position necessarily has to exist before someone can fill it and this remains the case even where certain individuals or groups have been able to define such things as new roles for themselves. For here too the defining precedes the occupancy and occupation then embroils the incumbent(s) in a network of relations, their unintended and emergent consequences. Action itself is undeniably continuous, but the nature of activities is not, being discontinuous with past activities because of the new relational constraints and enablements which now unavoidably help to shape it. In other words, we can talk of continuous action without implying a continuous unbroken flow of activities.

The real force of the objection thus comes to rest not upon critics maintaining that groups can show a greater durability than structures (because they can point to 'teachers' as a 'group' retaining continuity before and after the emergence of state educational systems, or the same for 'doctors' as far as the inception of the national health service was concerned). Rather, what I am criticizing is their (implicit) notion *that the 'group' remains fundamentally the same*, that is, they are pointing to the same entity. If this were the case, as seems quite persuasive at first glance, then it would indeed prevent one from ever talking about a pre-existent structure and would also effectively demolish 'analytical dualism' by removing its temporal mainstay which is what makes events tractable to explanation. Thus, we would be back to the simultaneity model of central conflation.

However, this critical viewpoint is fatally flawed by the naive nominalism with which it treats 'the group'. It supposes that just because we can use the label 'working class' over three centuries of structural changes in Britain, that we are talking about the same 'group'. We are not, any more than this is the case for 'teachers' or 'doctors' above. Here I need to introduce the notion of the double morphogenesis of structure and agency which will be developed later. To give one example, those who were teaching when education was a matter of private ownership, occupied positions in a particular structure which pre-dated them (the Anglican church in the case of England), which defined, constrained and enabled them in various ways including conditioning the part they played in the struggles for educational control which culminated in the emergence of the State system. Yet once the latter was in place, the actual position of teacher became radically different (change in employer, accountability, activity, expertise etc.). Nominally, one could still use the same word 'teachers' and practically some individuals made the transition, but none of that means that one is really talking about the 'same group', even if one is talking about some of the same people. For the group has changed profoundly, witness unionization and professionalization, new vested interests, forms of organization and values. In other words, at the end of a transformational sequence, not only is structure transformed, but so is agency as part and parcel of the same process. As it re-shapes structure, agency is ineluctably reshaping itself, in terms of organization, combination and articulation, in terms of its powers and these in relation to other agents. The double morphogenesis of structure and agency is taken up in detail in chapter 8. For the time being I only wish to show that nothing but obfuscation attaches to regarding any group as continuous, simply because it bears the same name, yet regardless of all that which makes it anything but 'the same'.

Already we have the first hint that agents and individuals cannot be used interchangeably – and are not by realists. However, the key point here is that it is fully justifiable to refer to structures (being irreducible to individuals or groups) as pre-existing them both, just as it is equally legitimate to refer to determinate agents being prior to the structures they transform, because through the same process they themselves are literally re-constituted as new groupings (whatever their nomenclature). The issue is not about the chicken and the egg since even were ultimate regress possible, it would not prove very revealing about either structures or agents after millennia of morphogenesis: what critics of 'analytical dualism' have tried to convince us is problematic is how to tell a chicken and an egg apart!

Finally then, it should be stressed that whilst I am arguing for temporal separability where structure and agency are concerned, to state that some structures are pre-existent to determinate agents and activities has no ontological priority over emphasizing that the self-same agents are themselves prior to later structural elaboration. Furthermore, it is precisely because such elaboration is co-determined by the conditional influence exerted by antecedent structures together with the autonomous causal powers of current agents, that society can develop in unpredictable ways. Unlike self-subsistent natural reality, it can be made to change shape through the reflexive actions of its thinking components (people), though not usually in anything like precise accordance with their intentions. Society depends upon reflection without embodying it (*contra* idealism), and is reliant upon agents wanting change yet rarely changes in the way anybody wants. And this is because of the unpredictable interplay of the two sets of emergent, irreducible and autonomous causal powers pertaining respectively to structure and agency.

Hence my adoption of the unlovely term 'morphogenesis',[11] to capture both the possibility of radical and unpredictable re-shaping (which renders misleading all those traditional analogies – of society being like a mechanism, organism, language or cybernetic system), and the fact that the genesis of this re-shaping lies in the interplay between structure and agency – a process which can only be examined because of their temporal separability and an outcome which can only be explained by means of analytical dualism. Our open society is like itself and nothing else, precisely because it is both structured and peopled.

---

[11] A term first coined by Walter Buckley, *Sociology and Modern Systems Theory*, Prentice Hall, New Jersey, 1967. Morphogenesis refers 'to those processes which tend to elaborate or change a system's given form, structure or state' (p. 58). It is contrasted to morphostasis which refers to those processes in a complex system that tend to preserve the above unchanged.

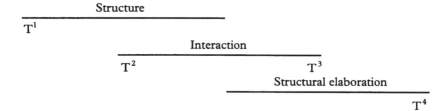

Figure 1 The morphogenetic sequence.

The previous pages have dealt with defining 'analytical dualism' and accounting for its reluctant recognition. It was maintained that its two key features, the acknowledgement that structure and agency are analytically separable and temporally sequenced, were implicit in realism. Morphogenesis/stasis can therefore be seen as an approach to social theory which is realist in its ontology and which supplements realism by making 'analytical dualism' explicit and demonstrating its methodological utility in practical social analysis. Thus in contra-distinction to every version of conflationary social theorizing, the morphogenetic/static approach stands four-square on 'analytical dualism'. By definition it hence accords full significance to the timescale through which structure and agency themselves *emerge*, *intertwine* and *redefine* one another, since this is the very format employed in the analysis of any problem.

Fundamentally the morphogenetic argument that structure and agency operate over different time periods is based on two simple propositions: that structure necessarily pre-dates the action(s) which transform it; and that structural elaboration necessarily post-dates those actions, which can be represented as shown in figure 1.

Although all three lines are in fact continuous, the analytical element consists only in breaking up the flows into intervals determined by the problem in hand: given any problem and accompanying periodization, the projection of the three lines backwards and forwards would connect up with the anterior and posterior morphogenetic cycles. This represents the bed-rock of an understanding of systemic properties, of *structuring* over time, which enables explanations of specific forms of structural elaboration to be advanced. (Since time is equally integral to morphostasis there is no question of the temporal being equated with change alone and not stability.) 'Castro's example' will be used to demonstrate how time is incorporated as intrinsic to morphogenetic theorizing since it lends itself to simple quantitative illustration.

After the revolution Castro confronted an extremely high rate of illiteracy which he sought to eliminate by the expedient of 'each one teach

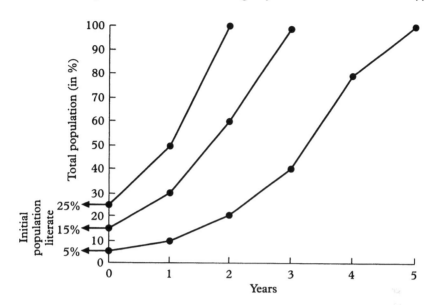

Figure 2 Time and the morphogenetic sequence: Castro's example.

one'. Now let us make a number of arbitrary and hypothetical assumptions about a situation like the Cuban one, namely that the proportion of the total population literate at the start was 5 per cent (15 per cent or 25 per cent), that to become literate took precisely a year, and that the policy was 95 per cent successful (no society ever achieves 100 per cent literacy). From these the diagram shown in figure 2 can be produced. For all its oversimplification the curves demonstrate some vital points about the relationships between time and the morphogenetic sequence.

1. *Structure*. The initial structural distribution of a property (i.e. the consequence of prior interaction) influences the time taken to eradicate it (five years versus two years for the outer and inner curves), through its effect on the population capable of transforming it. Certainly only some kinds of properties would approximate to this exponential pattern of change (skills, knowledge, capital accumulation, demographic distribution), but this does not affect the basic point that all structures manifest temporal resistance and do so generically through conditioning the context of action. Most often perhaps their conditional influence consists in dividing the population (not necessarily exhaustively) into social groups working for the maintenance versus the change of a given property, because the property itself distributes different objective vested interests to them at T^2 (rather than abilities as in the example used). This

would be the case where properties like citizenship, political centralization or wage differentials were concerned.

Furthermore, what the diagram serves to highlight is that the initial structural influence does not peter out immediately, even given a collective determination to transform it (indeed here the major burden of illiteracy is dispersed only towards the end, in the last or penultimate time interval). In other words it takes time to change *any* structural property and that period represents one of constraint for some groups at least. No matter how short, it prevents the achievement of certain goals (those which motivate attempts to change it). Structural influences thus extend beyond T^2 and it is essential to know whether this is because they (temporally and temporarily) resist collective pressures to change, remain because they represent the vested interests of the powerful, or are in fact 'psychologically supported' by the population. To regard every institutional regularity as the result of 'deep sedimentation' is to assimilate them all to the latter category. Yet without these distinctions it remains inexplicable *when* (or whether) the property will be transformed.

2. *Interaction.* On the one hand, activity initiated at T^2 takes place in a context not of its own making. In our example, those who were literate initially were not responsible for their *distribution* in the population; this group property resulted from the restrictive educational policies of others, probably long dead. Here it appears impossible to follow the methodological individualist and assert that any structural property influential after T^2 is attributable to contemporary actors (not wanting or not knowing how to change it), because knowledge about it, attitudes towards it, vested interests in retaining it and objective capacities for changing it have already been distributed and determined by T^2. Yet without analysing these we cannot account for *when the 'longue durée'* is broken, *who* is primarily responsible for changing it, or *how* it is accomplished (by collective policy, social conflict, incremental change etc.).

On the other hand, between T^2 and T^3 agency exerts two independent influences, one temporal, the other directional. It can speed-up, delay or prevent the elimination of prior structural influences. In our example, (a) popular commitment to self-instruction could reduce the time taken to eliminate illiteracy, thus improving on all three curves (though not obliterating them entirely because of the need for personnel to prepare, disseminate and guide in the use of materials); (b) lack of enthusiasm or ability to teach among literates and lack of willingness to participate and learn among illiterates can delay the process and damage the project. (Determinism is not built in to the morphogenetic perspective.) Simultaneously, agents, although partly conditioned by their acquirements (whose contents they did not themselves define) can exercise a directional influence upon the future cultural definition of 'literacy' thus affecting the nature of elaboration at T^4. (Voluntarism has an important place in morphogenesis but is ever trammelled by past structural and cultural constraints and by the current politics of the possible.)

3. *Structural elaboration.* If action is effective, then the transformation produced at T^4 is not merely the eradication of a prior structural property (illiteracy) and its replacement by a new one (literacy), it is the structural elaboration of a host of new social possibilities some of which will have gradually come into play between T^2 and T^4. Morphogenetic analysis thus explains the timing of the new facilitating factors and can account for the inception, in this instance, of say a national postal service, mail-order businesses, bureaucratization and less obvious but more significant developments like international communication with its ramifications for religion, technology, political ideology, etc. From the elisionist perspective, these remain the capricious exploits of indeterminate 'moments'.

Simultaneously, however, structural elaboration restarts a new morphogenetic cycle, for it introduces a new set of conditional influences upon interaction which are constraining as well as facilitating. T^4 is thus the new T^1, and the next cycle must be approached afresh analytically, conceptually and theoretically. Giddens is completely correct that laws in the social sciences are historical in character (i.e., mutable over time), but whereas his endorsement of this view rests principally on the reflexive knowledge and behaviour of actors, mine resides on changes in the social structure itself which require us to theorize about it in different ways since our subject matter has altered. A new explanandum calls for a new explanans. Our theories are transitive, not solely for epistemological reasons, but because our subject-matter itself undergoes change over time.

Time in conflationary social theory

The obverse of 'analytical dualism', is what I have termed the Fallacy of Conflation since the basic defect of any theory which embodies it is that structure and agency are elided.[12] Later on I will try to demonstrate that such an elision fundamentally precludes an adequate account of social stability and change. The reason for this is that such theories entail a truncation of the time-span which comes or can come under their purview. Time-referents are always too short, whether it is that too much of time past or time future (or both) are excluded. In brief, the Fallacy of

[12] An earlier version of this section first appeared in Herminio Martins (ed.), *Knowledge and Passion: Essays in Honour of John Rex*, Tauris, London and New York, 1993.

Conflation always entails a failure to incorporate temporality into social theory properly. This it seems is a logical consequence of conflation itself.

However a little more needs to be said about the different forms of conflationary theorizing in order to put some meat on the bare bones of the argument. Conflation of the two levels of analysis – of the properties of structures with the activities of social groups – always takes place in a particular *direction*. There are three possibilities and two of these are the antithesis of one another since conflation takes place in precisely the opposite direction: in the one, social structure is held to organize social interaction whilst in the other, inter-personal interaction is presented as orchestrating the structure of society. Thus in what can be called the 'downwards' version, structural properties engulf agency through the basic processes of regulation and socialization, whilst in what will be termed the 'upwards' version, social interaction forms and transforms structures whose properties are merely the resultants of domination or objectification.

In brief, both versions treat one level as an epiphenomenon of the other level: they differ about which of the levels is held to be epiphenomenal but not about the legitimacy of elision *per se*. However, epiphenomenalism is not the way in which the more general process of conflation operates. There remains the third possibility, namely that of 'central' conflation, where the two levels are held to be inseparable because they mutually constitute one another, a view which is enjoying considerable vitality in sociology at the moment.

In both the 'upwards' and 'downwards' versions, the fundamental drawback is that by making agency *dependent* upon structure, or vice versa, they automatically preclude any two-way interplay between the levels – because in each, one level is rendered inert. Consequently, the dependent element is robbed of the capacity to exploit or to influence the determining element, for it lacks the autonomy and independence to do so. This then blocks an adequate conceptualization of the processes explaining social stability and change. Instead, adherents of both approaches advance rather crude unilateral accounts, which have equal but opposite defects. In the one, structural properties are simply pushed around by some untrammelled dominant group or placed at the mercy of capricious renegotiation by unconstrained agency. In the other, social structure imposes its choreography on interaction and agents are reduced to *träger* or bearers of its properties, whether through oversocialization or mystification. If, as my initial assertion maintained, an adequate theoretical stance is one which acknowledges the *interplay* between structure and agency, then this has to be predicated upon some autonomy and independence being assigned to each.

However, the errors attaching to conflation do not depend upon epiphenomenalism, on rendering one aspect of social life itself lifeless. Epiphenomenalism is not the only way in which either structure or agency are deprived of autonomy and thus their interplay is denied, for any form of conflation has the same two consequences. In other words, conflation is the more basic fallacy and epiphenomenalism is merely a form it can take, or rather two particular cases of it. This is demonstrated by the remaining possibility, namely 'central' conflation, where elision occurs in the 'middle'. This directional approach, which enjoys a certain vogue at the moment as 'structuration theory', interprets neither structure nor agency as epiphenomena of one another. Indeed, this is a prime article of faith amongst modern proponents of 'central' conflationism.

Instead, what happens is that autonomy is withheld from *both levels* and this has exactly the same result of precluding any examination of their interplay. Here, structural properties and social interaction are conflated because they are presented as being so tightly constitutive of one another. Unlike everyday terms which involve mutual constitution, such as 'riding' (where horse and rider have separate properties, some of which are irrelevant to the practice – horse's colour or rider's colour – and some of whose interplay is vital to it – horse's size and rider's size), in central conflation the intimacy of reciprocal constitution amounts to an actual elision of the two elements (via the ontology of praxis) which cannot be untied and hence their influences upon one another cannot be teased out.

These are the effects of the denial of emergence in all versions of conflationary social theory. The principled denial of 'analytical dualism' automatically precludes the temporal separation of structure and agency. What is perhaps less obvious is that conflation simultaneously becomes antipathetic to a proper incorporation of time into social theory at all. The temporal implications of each form of conflationary theorizing are pictured in figure 3 and compared with the 'analytical dualism' of the morphogenetic approach.

(i) *Downwards conflation* where structure and agency are conflated because action is treated as fundamentally epiphenomenal has many variants, but is encountered today in any uncompromising version of technological determinism, economism, structuralism or normative functionalism. Despite their differences, nuances and apologetics, which cannot be entered into here, the bottom line is always that actors may be indispensable for energizing the social system (no people: no society) but it is not they whose actions give it direction by shaping structural properties. Agency, it is allowed, constitutes the motor-power but agents themselves are never admitted to touch the steering wheel. So the course of social change is never pictured as a wild zig-zag as social groups

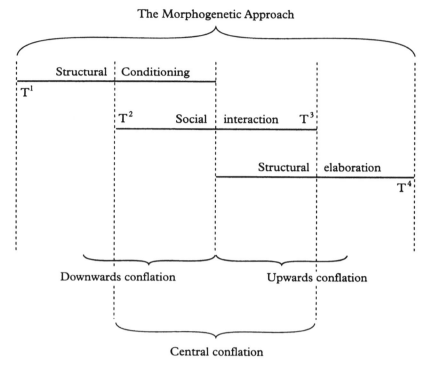

Figure 3 The limited time span of conflationary theories compared
with the morphogenetic approach.

struggle to wrest the wheel from one another, often taking them where no
one wants to go and potentially into a brick wall. (Indeed one of the
hallmarks of such theorizing is that structures stalk in straight lines.)

At most it might be allowed that social interaction is a sort of white
noise or Brownian motion in the system, but one whose very randomness
deprives it of any decisive effect upon the state of society. This apart, we
are presented with either the 'oversocialized view of man' or the 'overde-
termined view of man' depending on whether the epiphenomenal character of agency is grounded in idealism or materialism, which are the twin
fountainheads of downwards conflation.

Consequently to any downward conflationist, action leads nowhere
except where structure guides it. Hence, with reference to figure 3, there
is never anything *to* examine after T^2 *other* than the imprint of structure
upon agency. Since people are literally the agents *of* structure – its
embodiments-cum-executors – then socio-cultural change results from
some autonomous unfurling process which is operative at the structural

level, and although this may be conceptualized in all sorts of different ways, the common denominator is that human actors are never granted the autonomy to have any independent effect upon it. Since social interaction is never credited with the capacity to generate intended, unintended, aggregate or emergent properties which are of structural magnitude or consequence, then T^3 is never approached in analysis because 'the future' is the unfolding of immanent structural tendencies which are *already* present in the system. (At most they might be considered to develop in adaptation to an external environment, often a purely physical one, but even if it is made up of other structures, these of course are held to have the same relationship to their own agents.)

Looking backwards instead, if action *is* epiphenomenal then logically structure must predate it. Yet because action is not held to create it (i.e. there is never a T^3 at *any* point in history) then the sources of structure are located elsewhere since they have to come from somewhere. Social systems thus become the progeny of holistic or psychologistic factors. The explanation of how things got to be the way they are is handed over to impersonal forces or factors – the hidden hand of systemic adaptation, the iron grip or material progression, the unseen grasp of a destiny ideal or architectonic principle. The psychologistic alternative makes the grid of the human mind the ultimate though unconscious progenitor of social structure. This method of dealing with the historicity of socio-cultural systems is encapsulated in Ruth Benedict's statement that they are 'individual psychology thrown large upon the screen, given gigantic proportions and a long time span'.[13]

However, what this means about the time span over which any particular social structure emerges and develops is that it is *not* by examining group interaction during that period that we can arrive at an explanation of it. On the contrary, social structures are *never* admitted to have *social* origins. (In contradistinction, social agents are always assumed to be structural products.) What follows from this is that the proper investigation of the T^1 to T^2 period, in which social structures crystallize, is withdrawn from the explanatory ambit of social theory proper. From the viewpoint of downward conflation structure does indeed predate action, though not in the acceptable sense that this particular structural property at T^1 predates these specific actors at T^1, but in the primordial sense that no anterior action sequences are ever credited with the genesis of structures (even if care is taken to emphasize

[13] Ruth Benedict, 'Configurations of culture in North America', *American Anthropologist*, 1932, 34: 24.

that previous interaction is itself conditioned by an even earlier structural context).

Thus, insofar as advocates of downwards conflation address the future, this future is never one which actors intentionally define or unintentionally produce through the conjunction of their promotive interests. And, insofar as they address the past, they immediately cede the explanatory rights of social theory to human biology, individual psychology, economic inevitability, evolutionary adaptation or simply to speculative metaphysics. Insofar, then, as downward conflation does incorporate temporality, it ceases to be sociological. Finally it follows from all this that downwards conflationists basically restrict their treatment of structure and agency to an examination of *the impress of structure upon agency in the present*. Thus, instead of an investigation of their linkage over time, this perspective reduces every actor to the eternal humanoid and endorses the reification of structure in perpetuity.

(ii) *Upwards conflation* represents the exact opposite since structure is held to be the creature of agency. The social context of action may not look that way to the investigator upon first inspection and it may never feel that way to the actor because of lasting objectification. Nevertheless, to upward conflationists it is always a major descriptive error to treat structural properties as having the ontological status of facts rather than facticity, and it is equally erroneous to allow them to figure in explanatory statements as external conditioners of action. Thus, for instance, the neo-phenomenological school asserts the primacy of agency by reducing the structural context of action to a series of intersubjectively negotiated constructs. However, the basic charter of all versions of upward conflation, of which interpretative sociology is only one variant, is methodological individualism. Its prime injunction is to view so-called structural properties as reducible to the effects of other actors, which are in their turn always recoverable by agency.

Essentially, structure becomes epiphenomenal in classic statements of methodological individualism because the social context is defined as made up of nothing more than other people. For this strategy of 'personalization' to work in social theory, its protagonists have to show that *all* structural properties (every aspect of the social environment), which figure in explanations, refer to nothing more than the activities and attitudes of other people. Thus, the argument goes, since society is made up of people there is nothing in the environment (although it may appear to be non-people) which people in turn cannot change, leaving aside its physical components. Hence, to Watkins, the 'central assumption of the individualist position – an assumption which is admittedly counter-factual and metaphysical – is that no social tendency exists which could not be altered *if* the individual concerned both wanted to alter it and possessed the appropriate information'.[14]

Note here that the structural properties and the constraints they exert have now become the effects of *contemporary* action. For it follows that what constitutes our social context are things that the 'people concerned' do not want to change/do not know how to change/do not think about changing. Thus any temporal back reference to the T¹ and T² phase in figure 3 is ruled out. For whatever the origins of the structural tendencies and characteristics we observe, their present existence is due in some way to the people present. A big jump has thus been taken from the truistic descriptive statement 'no people: no society' to a much more contentious explanatory one, 'this society because of these people here present'. Yet the 'central assumption' upon which this is based is not metaphysical, it is a hypothesis and one which can be tested *provided* the time dimension is reintroduced. But if it is, then this assumption is undoubtedly counter-factual for there appear to be some structural properties which cannot be eliminated at will (given any amount of information, thought or desire) by contemporary actors – at least not for a considerable period of time!

This would be the case for demographic structures, for levels of literacy or of national education. Such structural influences are the unintended consequences of past actions which came into play between T¹ and T², but their conditioning and constraining effects at T² cannot be reduced to or made the responsibility of contemporary agents who quite literally inherit them. The fact that such structural properties are *ultimately* reversible by human action is not at issue, the point is that they exert constraints *until* they can be changed. There are then some aspects of our social environment which obstruct us (e.g. certain kinds of military recruitment or pension policies are impossible with a particular kind of demographic structure) but these cannot be attributed to the sustaining behaviour of contemporary actors.

This severance of present from past not only raises problems about structure, but also about agency itself. If the bed-rock of any acceptable explanation of a social phenomenon is individual dispositions, i.e. something is accounted for when related to the motives, aims, beliefs, or any other intelligible reaction of contemporary people to their social circumstances, then another difficulty appears. As Gellner has pointed out, this view of agency presupposes the possibility of always isolating more elementary dispositions 'as they are prior to their manifestations in a social context. The real oddity of the reductionist case is that it seems to

[14] J. W. N. Watkins, 'Methodological individualism and social tendencies', in May Brodbeck (ed.), *Readings in the Philosophy of the Social Sciences*, Macmillan, New York, 1971, p. 271.

preclude *a priori* the possibility of human dispositions being the dependent variable in an historical explanation – when in fact they often or always are'.[15] It is as if, in explaining any contemporary phenomenon, we were constantly starting afresh since it is assumed that we can detect dispositions which influence the explanandum without their being dependent upon it or on other earlier social phenomena. It was of course in response to this charge that the attempt was made to allow for environmental influences, *provided* these could be construed as the 'innocent' effects of (contemporary) other people, which I have argued cannot always be done.

However not only is the historical conditioning of current action discountenanced (unless it can be 'personalized'), but also too the future is cut off from the present – for agency as for structure. On the one hand, if dispositions can never be the dependent variable, then the things which today the individualist explains as the unintended results of independent elementary attitudes, must simultaneously be held by such theorists to be incapable of influencing the attitudes and actions of tomorrow's agents. On the other hand, structural complexity (properties like inflation or social differentials) can be viewed as the final result of social interaction: indeed it is precisely the reductionist aim of the methodological individualist to trace such social consequences back to their individualistic origins. Yet although the development of structural properties from human interaction is admitted beyond T^3 (as long as they are construed as the 'innocent' products of people), the analysis is then firmly end-stopped. What the individualist can never allow, as far as the complex structural consequences of interaction are concerned, is that 'their fates *qua* fates of complexes can nevertheless be the initial conditions ... of a causal sequence',[16] for this would be to countenance 'explanatory emergence'.

In other words, they cannot accept that unintended consequences from past action, may, at T^4 become consequential in their own right – as emergent properties or aggregate effects which represent new structural influences upon subsequent action. For structural factors are inefficacious without the sanction, as it were, of contemporary other people. So at some point prior to T^4, any such property has become something which agency does not want to change/does not know how to change/does not think about changing. Consequently methodological individualists endorse a perpetual 'autonomy of the present tense' and have to truncate temporality if they are to eliminate emergent structural properties and view agency as responsible not only for their origins but also for their maintenance and influence.

[15] Ernest Gellner, 'Holism versus individualism', in Brodbeck (ed.), *Readings*, p. 260.
[16] Gellner, 'Holism versus individualism', p. 263.

(iii) *Central conflation* is an approach based upon the putative mutual constitution of structure and agency and finds its most sophisticated expression in modern 'structuration theory'. Now the general principle of mutual constitution is entirely unobjectionable; what I resist is the representation of their bonding as contact adhesion such that structure and agency are effectively defined in terms of one another. For the net result of this is that mutual constitution ultimately implies temporal conjunction between the two elements. Thus, structural properties (defined reductively as rules and resources) are held to be outside time, having a 'virtual existence' only when instantiated by actors. In exact parallel, when actors produce social practices they necessarily draw upon rules and resources and thus inevitably invoke the whole matrix of structural properties at that instant. All of this is condensed in the brief statement that 'structure is both medium and outcome of the reproduction of practices'.[17] This represents the key notion of the 'duality of structure' which is advanced in direct opposition to the analytical dualism advocated here.

Ironically, Giddens maintains that 'the conception of structuration introduces temporality as integral to social theory'.[18] While agreeing whole-heartedly that the incorporation of time is a condition of theoretical adequacy, one may doubt whether 'structuration' does integrate the temporal dimension adequately. Instead I will argue that, on the contrary, the time-referent of structuration theory is in fact restricted to the T^2–T^3 span in figure 3. The reason for this is an inability to examine the interplay between structure and agency over longer temporal tracts because the two presuppose one another so closely. The intimacy of mutual constitution thus means that the only way in which structure and agency can be examined 'independently' is through an artificial exercise of 'methodological bracketing'.

I will maintain that an ineluctable consequence of this procedure is the actual suppression of time. On the one hand, institutional analysis brackets strategic action and treats structural properties as 'chronically reproduced features of social systems'. This image of recursiveness figures prominently, but many would deny that these features necessarily are 'chronic': though they *might* be long lasting they are nevertheless temporary (e.g. feudalism) or may change frequently (e.g. interest rates). Instead, through this kind of institutional analysis, they acquire a spurious methodological permanence.

On the other hand, to examine the constitution of social systems as strategic conduct, institutional analysis is bracketed and what is studied is

[17] Anthony Giddens, *Central Problems in Social Theory*, Macmillan, London, 1979, p. 69.
[18] Giddens, *Social Theory*, p. 198.

the mobilization of rules and resources by agents in their social relations. This leads immediately to the reverse image – 'Change, or its potentiality, is thus inherent in all moments of social reproduction'.[19] Here an equally spurious changeability appears as a product of this methodological device – structural malleability is not only high but is constant over time. On the contrary many would argue that it is variable and that its temporal variations are partially independent of strategic action, however intensely it is mobilized or knowledgeably it is conducted. This methodological bracketing has produced a pendular swing between contradictory images – of chronic recursiveness and total transformation.

It might be replied in defence that since both occur simultaneously in reality, then no contradiction is involved as social reality is inherently Janus-faced. Insistence upon this entails a principled refusal to unravel the interrelations between structure and agency since this would be an unacceptable lapse into dualistic theorizing. Yet, ironically, what does the bracketing device do other than traduce this very principle, since it merely transposes dualism from the theoretical to the methodological level – thus conceding its *analytical* indispensability.

Most importantly this bracketing approach has serious implications concerning time which seem inconsistent with the aim of making temporality integral to explaining social reality. What is bracketed are the two aspects of the 'duality of structure', structural properties and strategic conduct being separated out by placing a methodological *epoché* upon each in turn. But because these are the two sides of the same thing, the pocketed elements must thus be *co-terminous in time* (the co-existence of the *epochés* confines analysis to the same *époque*); and it follows from this that *temporal relations between* structure and agency *logically cannot be examined*.

The attempt to reunite the two elements under the rubric of 'structuration' consists in the introduction of three 'modalities', drawn upon by actors strategically but at the same time constituting the structural features of the system – 'interpretative scheme', 'facility' and 'norm'. Hence, the notion of 'modality thus provides the coupling elements whereby the bracketing of strategic or institutional analysis is dissolved in favour of an acknowledgement of their interrelation'.[20] But the interrelationship is not really at issue (outside of hard-line ethnomethodology or the most extreme structural determinism). The real theoretical issue is not whether or not to acknowledge it but how to analyse it, and how to explain the structural elaboration generated from it. Yet little of this can

[19] Giddens, *Social Theory*, p. 114.   [20] Giddens, *Social Theory*, p. 81.

be tackled from an approach which precludes theorizing about the *temporal relations* between structure and agency.

The basic notion of the 'duality of structure' militates against the latter because it resists untying structure and action, except by the bracketing exercise. In turn, this means that structuration theory cannot recognize that structure and agency work on different time intervals (however small the gap between them). This, paradoxically, leads to the full importance of time in social theory being seriously underplayed. What is stressed is that theorizing must have a temporal dimension: what is missed is that time is an actual variable in theory. In consequence, advocates of central conflation assert that 'social systems only exist through their continuous structuration in the course of time',[21] but are unable to provide any theoretical purchase on their *structuring over time*.

Paradoxically, for all Giddens' stress upon the importance of time, it is the past *in* the present which matters for him; the present being a succession of 'passing moments' in which, quoting William James approvingly, 'the dying rearward of time and its dawning future forever mix their lights'.[22] This continuous flow defies periodization. Consequently he has to stress the quintessential polyvalence of each 'moment', both replicatory and transformatory (reproduction always carries its two connotations). Yet he is nevertheless driven to recognize the existence of 'critical phases' in the long term and to accord (excessive) theoretical significance to them (as times of institutional spot-welding). What is lacking in Giddens' work is the length of time between the 'moment' and the 'critical phase' – in which the slow work of structural elaboration is accomplished and needs theorizing about.

Envoi

Morphogenetic analysis, in contrast to the three foregoing approaches, accords time a central place in social theory. By working in terms of its three-part cycles composed of (a) structural conditioning, (b) social interaction and (c) structural elaboration, time is incorporated as sequential tracts and phases rather than simply as a medium through which events take place. For the very occurrence of events, like the progressive structuring of an educational system, necessitates our theorizing about the temporal interplay between structure and agency. What is crucial then is that the morphogenetic perspective maintains that structure and action operate over different time periods – an assertion which is based on

---

[21] Giddens, *Social Theory*, p. 217   [22] Giddens, *Social Theory*, p. 3.

its two simple propositions: that structure necessarily predates the actions which transform it; and that structural elaboration necessarily post-dates those actions.

In *structural conditioning*, systemic properties are viewed as the emergent or aggregate consequences of past actions. Once they have been elaborated over time they are held to exert a causal influence upon subsequent interaction. Fundamentally, they do so by shaping the situations in which later 'generations' of actors find themselves and by endowing various agents with different vested interests according to the positions they occupy in the structures they 'inherit' (in the class structure, in the social distribution of resources, or in the educational system for example). From this follows a conviction that 'the properties of social structures and systems . . . must be taken as given when analyzing the processes of action and interaction'[23] because of the conditional influence exerted by the former on the latter. In short, when we talk about structural properties and their effects from the morphogenetic perspective, we are also endorsing the realist notion of emergence and its causal powers. Thus we accept that the results of past actions have effects in their own rights later on, as constraining or facilitating influences upon actors, which are not attributable or reducible to the practices of other agents.

However *social interaction* is seen as being structurally conditioned but never as structurally determined (since agents possess their own irreducible emergent powers). On the one hand, the mediatory mechanism which transmits structural influences to human actors consists in the former moulding frustrating or rewarding contexts for different groups of agents, depending upon the social positions they occupy. In turn, it is argued that these experiences of frustrations or benefits condition different situational interpretations and dissimilar action patterns: groups experiencing exigencies seek to eradicate them (thus pursuing structural change) and those experiencing rewards try to retain them (thus defending structural stability). Regularities of this kind, detectable in subsequent patterns of interaction, are reflections of these objective opportunity costs. None the less their effect is only conditional: they force no one, but simply set a price on acting against one's self-declared interests and a premium on following them (consequently detectable regularities do not even approximate to constant conjunctures). To acknowledge this involves nothing more sinister than the Weberian assumption that most of the time for most people there is a rough congruence between their interests, interpretations and actions. On the other hand, since conditioning is not determinism, the middle element of the cycle also recognizes the promotive

---

[23] Percy. S. Cohen, *Modern Social Theory*, Heinemann, London, 1968, p. 205.

creativity of interest groups and incorporates their capacity for innovative responses in the face of contextual constraints. Equally, it accommodates the possibility of reflective self-sacrifice of inherited vested interests on the part of individuals or groups.

The *structural elaboration* which then ensues is interpreted as being a largely unintended consequence. The modification of previous structural properties and the introduction of new ones is the combined product of the different outcomes pursued simultaneously by various social groups. The unintended element largely results from group conflict and concession which together mean that the consequential elaboration is often what no-one sought or wanted. (This is what separates the morphogenetic approach from simple cybernetic models based on goal steering: here the positive and negative feedback loops, resulting in structural elaboration and reproduction respectively, run free of any control centre. It is also what unites it with the realist assertion about the non-predictability of change in open systems.) The end-point and the whole point of examining any particular cycle is that we will then have provided an analytical *history* of emergence of the problematic properties under investigation. At this point, which is also the start of another cycle, the elaborated structure constitutes a new conditional influence upon subsequent interaction, and the concepts and theories we employ to deal with this next cycle may well have to change in order to explain this change our subject matter has undergone.

Thus every morphogenetic cycle distinguishes three broad analytical phases consisting of (a) a given structure (a complex set of relations between parts), which conditions but does *not* determine (b), social interaction. Here, (b) also arises in part from action orientations unconditioned by social organization but emanating from current agents, and in turn leads to (c), structural elaboration or modification – that is, to a change in the relations between parts where morphogenesis rather than morphostasis ensued. The cycle is then repeated. Transition from state (a) to (c) is not direct, precisely because structural conditioning is not the sole determinant of interaction patterns. Only Holists conceptualize a movement straight from (a) to (c), without mediation; the realism endorsed here cannot countenance such a move.

What Methodological Individualists claim is that action alone, (b), constitutes the necessary and sufficient conditions for the explanation of (c). To them (a) can be eradicated. Advocates of the morphogenetic perspective do not deny that social interaction is the ultimate source of complex phenomena (which include both unintended aggregate and emergent consequences): they simply maintain that because this causal chain unravels over time and each anterior action sequence was itself structurally conditioned, we must acknowledge that we cannot deduce (c) from (b) alone and thus have to consider agents' activities to be necessary but not sufficient conditions of structural change. Therefore to account for the occurrence of structural elaboration (c), interactional analysis (b), is essential, but inadequate unless undertaken in conjunction with (a), the study of structural conditioning.

Hence the distinctive feature of the morphogenetic approach is its recognition of the temporal dimension, through which and in which structure and agency shape one another. Time is incorporated quite explicitly in the delineation of successive cycles and their component phases, which of course constitute the explanatory framework itself. However, it is not merely the *importance* attached to time in morphogenetic theorizing which sets it apart from other approaches which conflate structure and agency. The actual time-span which any morphogenetic explanation addresses is in fact *longer* than in every version of conflationary theory. Back-reference to figure 3 serves to illustrate how the elision of structure and agency in conflationist approaches means that each of them works with a narrower time referent.

Obviously all theories have to make some reference to time since events occur in space/time, but however long the chronological span may be, as dictated by the substantive problem in hand (it is longer if the problem is the development of monarchy than if it is the development of state socialism), in morphogenetic analysis it must always be longer still than these substantive considerations alone dictate. In contradistinction, it has been argued that conflationary analysis effectively confines itself to a sociology of the 'present tense'. Referring back to my preliminary argument, this then prevents any conflationist solution of the 'problem of structure and agency', since examination of the interplay between the two elements over time is ruled out – in all three versions of it.

4 Elision and central conflation

Duality: structure and agency as ontologically inseparable

To view structure and agency as fundamentally *inseparable* is certainly novel, for it asserts something much stronger than their necessary relationship. It means that we are basically talking about one thing, since even if it is an amalgam then it can only be treated as such. This is Craib's view: 'instead of separate and opposing things in the world or as mutually exclusive ways of thinking about the world, they are simply two sides of the same coin. If we look as social practices in one way, we can see actors and actions; if we look at them another way we can see structures'.[1]

If someone were to insist in the Elisionists' defence that an amalgam still has two constituents, it nevertheless remains the case that for them we are compelled to see the two only in combination and constrained to regard this combination of being of a particular kind. As Thompson puts their view of the matter, 'Rather than seeing action and structure as counter-acting elements of a dualism, we should regard them as the complementary terms of a duality, the "duality of structure".'[2] In turn, this spells a shift away from traditional procedures and indicates a new focus for social analysis. Now what 'must be grasped is not how structure determines action or how a combination of actions make up structure, but rather how action is *structured* in everyday contexts and how the structured features of action are, by the very performance of an action, thereby *reproduced*'.[3] From this it follows for Layder that to Elisionists like Giddens, 'the proper locus for the study of social reproduction is in the immediate process of the constituting of interaction'.[4] By enjoining the examination of a single process in the present tense, issues surrounding

[1] Ian Craib, *Anthony Giddens*, Routledge, London, 1992, pp. 3–4.
[2] John B. Thompson, 'The theory of structuration', in David Held and John B. Thompson (eds.), *Social Theory in Modern Societies: Anthony Giddens and his Critics*, Cambridge University Press, Cambridge, 1989, p. 58. [3] Thompson, 'Structuration', p. 56.
[4] Derek Layder, *Structure, Interaction and Social Theory*, Routledge and Kegan Paul, London, 1981, p. 75.

the relative independence, causal influence and temporal precedence of the components have been eliminated at a stroke.

These are indeed the implications of *'inseparability'*. They derive directly from the assertion of the mutual constitution of structure and agency, where the 'production and reproduction by active subjects are the constituting processes of structure. There cannot be one without the other', because 'They cannot refer to separate processes or separate structures'.[5] Since all three of the commentators just cited (whose views I fully endorse) draw out these implications as part of their critiques of elisionism, it remains to be seen *why* Giddens finds such virtue in his major premiss about inseparability as contained in the notion of the 'duality of structure'.

Basically the answer lies in what he hopes to wrest social theory away from – the reified notion (in his view) of emergent properties, as prior to and autonomous from action and the reductionist conception (in his view) of individuals, with personal properties which are independent and detachable from the social context of their formation and expression. The proposal is that all of this can be transcended by substituting a social ontology of praxis. Thus to Cohen, there is a real virtue in the idea that 'the non-emergent description of the structural properties of systems, all revert in one way or another to the central notion that institutionalized practices and relations may be regarded as more basic constituents of order than either individuals or the properties of collectivities'.[6] Actual transcendence is held to consist in the assertion that a consideration of 'social practices' suffices for the analysis of all levels of the social world. Simultaneously, it re-valorizes the agent as someone with knowledgeable mastery over their social doings whilst eradicating the idea of external hydraulic pressures upon them. Society as a skilled accomplishment restores dignity to agency whilst upholding that the practice of accomplishing life in society is itself ineluctably social.

The first question, then, is how can the concept of 'social practices' alone deal with the complexities of the social world, which many others regard as being a stratified reality where different properties, powers and problems pertain to the layered strata? To begin with, it only does so by considerably flattening out the ontological depth of the social world by denying the existence of emergent properties which pertain to a 'higher' stratum when they do not obtain at a 'lower' one. Thus the furthest that Giddens will go towards acknowledging differences between the micro-

---

[5] Layder, *Structure*, p. 75.

[6] Ira J. Cohen, 'Structuration theory and social order: five issues in brief', in J. Clark, C. Modgil and S. Modgil (eds.), *Anthony Giddens: Consensus and Controversy*, Falmer, Basingstoke, 1990, p. 42.

scopic and the macroscopic is to recognize the difference between face-to-face interaction and distanced interaction – the qualitative distinctiveness of these types of relations thus replacing the traditional 'problem of scope',[7] where new properties were held often to attend quantitative increases in the size and/or composition of groups.

Within this context, and regarded as a justification of it, face-to-face interaction depends upon individuals drawing on 'structural properties' (defined as rules and resources), and in so doing, serving to recreate them. Thus, the smallest item of our day-to-day activity is related to the entire matrix of structure as the necessary medium of action and outcome of it, such that 'when I utter a grammatical English sentence in a casual conversation, I contribute to the reproduction of the English language as a whole'.[8] For the time being I will simply leave a question mark over this linguistic analogy and its presumption that in the same way as many elements of syntax are mutually implicative (compound tenses imply simpler ones), this is also the case for social structure. Although such a parallel stresses the necessary *involvement* of the entirety of structure in even the most trivial act, Giddens is equally at pains to emphasize the simultaneous absence of social *determinism* in small scale interaction. Hence, the concept of 'role' is jettisoned as being too 'given' and replaced by the notion of 'positioning', which is produced and reproduced through 'social practices' and consequently contains the potential for transformation at every moment. Again let us place another question mark over the jettisoning of conditioning along with determinism through the abandonment of roles, their rights, obligations and associated expectations.

'Social practices' are also the bedrock of 'institutions', for the latter are held to be nothing more than regularized practices, structured by rules and resources. When 'structural properties' are drawn upon in a routinized fashion, an institution becomes 'sedimented' as a clustering of the practices constituting it. In turn this means that 'institutions' are never something concrete to which we can point but are essentially processual; ever in a fluid process of becoming and never in a (temporally or temporary) fixed state of being, because all structural properties and all actions are always potentially transformational. Practical social analysts may want to insert their own question mark over how the investigation of processes within and surrounding an institution can proceed without the capacity to identify a relatively enduring institutional context through

---

[7] Cf. Helmut Wagner, 'Displacement of scope: a problem of the relationship between small-scale and large-scale sociological theories', *American Journal of Sociology*, 1964, 62: 6.

[8] Anthony Giddens, *Central Problems in Social Theory*, Macmillan, London, 1979, pp. 77–8.

properties which are necessary and internal to it being what it is (while it lasts). Many of these would not be content to substitute a study of 'routinized practices' on the grounds that they would first need to invoke a structural context – e.g. educational or medical – to know which practices to examine.

At the largest scale of interaction, the social system (defined by him as the visible pattern generated from agents transforming the modalities of structural properties to produce this patterning), Giddens is still not dealing with anything separable from action. The only difference is that, at the systematic level, he is dealing with relations between 'groups and collectivities' rather than individual actors. Thus there is complete continuity, for here too 'the integration of social systems is something which is constantly reproduced by the actions of agents',[9] through their social practices – there are simply more of both. The first implication of this is that at the systems level, there are no new properties present, only this concatenation of practices. It is allowed that such practices may result in important unintended consequences of actions but disallowed that these might represent emergent properties or powers. Moreover the link with agency remains intact since it is stipulated that these can be recovered and brought under regulative monitoring by agents, in which case, to Giddens, 'the reflexive monitoring of action rejoins the organization of social systems, and becomes a guiding influence in it'.[10] Until this happens (if it does) some may wish to query whether such 'unintended consequences' should not be granted an influence independent of agency, even within structuration theory. Otherwise, the Elisionist argument has to be that since agents *can* (eventually) regain control, nothing of social consequence will ensue until this (supposedly) occurs. The weakness of this supposition is highlighted by analogy with the skidding car.

Yet because of the commitment to inseparability, no state of the system can vary independently from that of agency. Since the system merely refers to relations between larger numbers occurring at a distance, then 'the basic definition of social integration is the reciprocity between actors; of systems integration, reciprocities between groups and collectivities'.[11] In other words, while Lockwood[12] saw considerable explanatory advantages deriving from distinguishing between 'social' and 'system' integration, insisting that the two could vary independently and that different conjunctions between them made for stability or change, this is precluded by elisionism. On the contrary, in structuration theory, they must co-vary

[9] Craib, *Giddens*, p. 57.   [10] Giddens, *Social Theory*, p. 79.
[11] Craib, *Giddens*, p. 58.
[12] David Lockwood, 'Social integration and system integration', in G. K. Zollschan and H. W. Hirsch (eds.), *Explorations in Social Change*, Houghton Mifflin, London, 1964.

because they are inseparable. Hence, Giddens writes that 'the systemness of social integration *is fundamental to the systemness of society as a whole*'.[13] Cohen reinforces the point and in so doing, underlines the fact that this is a direct consequence of the 'ontology of praxis'. Thus he argues that whereas Lockwood maintained 'that for certain purposes system integration may refer to holistically conceived properties of systems, Giddens preserves his pivotal emphasis upon structured praxis by maintaining that systems integration involves social reciprocities between agents at a distance'.[14] Indeed he does, but some will still want to question the price, in terms of loss of explanatory power, which Lockwood's analysis supplied by enabling one to distinguish between ubiquitous social conflict which generated no change, due to 'high system integration' (*not contra* Cohen, conceptualized holistically, but in terms of emergence), and conflict which does issue in transformation through actualizing a systemic contradiction. This loss is the cost of sustaining 'duality' by focusing exclusively upon the amalgam of 'social practices' – which elides structure and agency.

Yet what others question is considered by Elisionists to be the unquestionable strength of their position, because the reconceptualization of structure and agency as inseparable is their strategy for transcending the dualism of the traditional debates. However, to sustain the mutual constitution of the two does mean that redefining the terms of this dispute also entails re-definitions of 'structure' and 'agency' themselves, as has already been noted. Since 'inseparability' is held to be a step forward it is important to note what their reconceptualization has left behind. In particular, this means that Elisionists deliberately turn their backs upon any autonomous features which could pertain independently to either 'structure' or 'agency'. Otherwise such features could be investigated separately. Their distinctive properties would potentially make a difference, because of which the nature of their combination would become problematic, and in view of that their interplay would require examination – in which case dualism would once more be the name of the game. In avoiding this turn of the wheel, 'structure and agency' become even more closely compacted together.

Because 'structure' is inseparable from 'agency' then, *there is no sense in which it can be either emergent or autonomous or pre-existent or causally influential*. Instead, 'structural properties' (i.e. defined as 'rules and resources') are 'instantiated' in social practices and have no existence outside this instantiation by agency. In this consistent ontology of praxis, structural properties exist and have any efficacy only by courtesy of

---

[13] Giddens, *Social Theory*, p. 77.   [14] Cohen, 'Structuration theory', p. 45.

agents. Without 'instantiation', they have only a 'virtual existence' as 'material' entities; materials belonging to the physical rather than the social world (land, resources, or printed paper labelled, for instance, the Highway Code). Here the physical realist, the defender of a self-subsistent natural world, will query their designation as 'virtual', to which the Elisionists would reply that they are not contesting the reality of 'a field' in nature, they are merely claiming that it has to be endowed with social significance by agents to become 'The Field', of the film. The question mark has not vanished, for many would doubt whether we can legitimately erect ontological brick walls between physical and social reality in this way and would ask whether there are not properties of the natural environment such as famine or shortages of resources which constrain the meanings which can be associated with them and the activities possible in the light of them. Certainly interpretations can vary, but whether a famine is seen as punishment from the gods or the result of international capitalism, it neither changes the ineluctable fact that people starve nor the impossibility of engaging in certain actions (from waging effective war to reducing infant mortality). Since these are real influences and effects, how can they be consigned to only a 'virtual' existence?.

Thus if 'structural properties' really only exist when instantiated in social practices, where, apart from their 'material existents' do they actually have their existence? Where do we look to find that which transforms them from being 'virtual' into actual features of social life? The answer is agency itself which carries 'structural properties' as memory traces which are transmitted from one set of agents to others. Thus to Craib, 'if structures have a locus of existence, it is in the heads of social actors'.[15] Kilminister draws the same necessary conclusion; 'In this sense "structure" in Giddens' theory is *internal* to actors'.[16] The Elisionist is quite prepared to bite this bullet, and spits its remains back at critics in the form of Outhwaite's economical challenge – 'where else?'[17]. Yet there are other places, which generically could be called 'the Library'.

The defence of 'memory traces' immediately raises questions about the Library, where we store all the information which we do not carry around in our heads, which we ourselves do not know fully, and thus are incapable of transmitting. Since we are not collectively the walking/talking books of *Fahrenheit 451* (if in doubt consider just how little sociological knowledge alone could be retained by a Department mar-

[15] Craib, *Giddens*, p. 42.
[16] Richard Kilminster, 'Structuration theory as a world-view', in Christopher G. A. Bryant and David Jary (eds.), *Giddens' Theory of Structuration*, Routledge, London, 1991, p. 96.
[17] William Outhwaite, 'Agency and structure', in Clark et al. (eds.), *Anthony Giddens*, p. 69.

ooned on a desert island), in what sense is bibliothèque knowledge ontologically dependent upon 'instantiation'? It exists and if it works, if it is true or false, this is the case independently of agents knowing it. Certainly they can activate it or leave it to gather dust, but its ontological status is not determined by which they do. Knowledge without a knowing subject would be ruled out in elisionism, but would still leave many questioning what the Rosetta Stone was before it was discovered and decoded, yet was capable of decoding. The one answer which won't do is 'a memory trace'. The discoverers had no memory and they could well have got it wrong, dismissing the carved symbols as being art or of ritual significance. Nor was decoding a meeting of minds with the original carver whose intentions will always remain unknown. It was the object itself which had carried the meaning over the centuries and under the sand, providing an instance of objective knowledge in transit, capable of being understood but independent of understanding.

A second necessary consequence of defending the 'inseparability' of structure and agency is that to the Elisionist, 'structures only exist at the point when they are produced and reproduced by actors in concrete instances of instantiation'.[18] This assumption of their *simultaneity* is the corollary of 'structural properties' having to be instantiated in order to have either social existence or effect. It disallows the pre-existence of structures (roles, positions, relations) which are thus made both *co-existent* and also *co-terminous* with agency. Structures then become the responsibility of agents in the present tense which leaves behind a final splatter of question marks. What about 'structural properties' which entire populations would consensually seek to eliminate? What explains some seeking their reproduction and others their transformation if we cannot appeal to prior structured distributions of vested interests? What accounts for struggles between groups of actors if we cannot refer to either the benefits or disadvantages which their structural positions deal them, nor to prior ideological definitions of their situations which are matters of imposition rather than 'instantiation'?

Looking at matters the other way around, the result of treating structure and agency as mutually constitutive is identical for agents; they too have to be denied autonomous properties and independent influences, above and beyond the biological, all of whose tendencies are anyway held to require 'social specification'. None is admitted to give rise to psychological differences of a socially unmediated kind, through, for example, interactions with the natural world. Now, it has often been noted that Elisionists privilege agency over structure (perfect symmetry between the

---

[18] Layder, *Structure*, p. 64.

terms cannot be sustained because it is agents who do the instantiating upon which structural properties depend for their existence). Here, Elisionists themselves often mention it as a strong point that the insights of Goffman can readily be acknowledged within this approach. Yet it would seem that the absence of personal psychology creates similar difficulties for both. Certainly the celebration of the highly knowledgeable actors leads, like Goffman, away from the over-socialized 'cultural dope' who only does things, on the Parsonian account, because required to by the roles and positions occupied. Instead, agents in their life world play out their positionings with style, skill and distance. Yet if they can perform socially with such virtuosity they must have a personal identity, yet one which is not thrust upon them or defined for them – by prior structural conditioning and cultural processes of socialization. Thus, we need to know who this 'self' is and how it came to be; a debt Goffman leaves unsettled by his question-begging definition – 'a self is a repertoire of behaviour appropriate to a different set of contingencies'.[19] Goffman owes us a theory of the self as a social subject, for his second definition makes matters even more mysterious since selfhood without psychology reduces to an organic parcel: 'by "personal identity" I mean the unique organic continuity imputed to each individual, this established through distinguishing marks such as name and appearance'.[20] Elisionists would presumably respond that all such difficulties can be overcome simply by saying that the self is formed 'through social practices'.

Yet this would seem to leave them on the horns of a dilemma since it is valid and important to ask 'which practices form which people?'. Here, the Elisionist could either concede that positions and relations pre-date people, thus conditioning the types of social selves they can become, but their commitment to inseparability makes this unacceptable to them. Alternatively, resort would have to be made to a personal psychology of the self, allowing individuals variable propensities and abilities which influence those social practices to which they are drawn and those which they can accomplish. Obviously this too is repugnant since to allow that individuals have different propensities, *not* all of which are socially mediated, enforces a discussion of the interplay between two types of properties – individual and social. Although many who are not Elisionists would not want to make a case for a 'given self', they would appeal to the development of individual psychology for, unless there is some continuity of the self (beyond an organism which bears a proper name), unless allowance is made for differential learning ability, information process-

[19] E. Goffmann, *The Presentation of Self in Everyday Life*, Doubleday, New York, 1959.
[20] E. Goffmann, *Relations in Public*, Penguin, Harmondsworth, 1971, p. 189.

ing, transfer training and creativity, proclivities and antipathies, another question mark hovers over the source of rules and manipulation of resources and the differential ingenuity and willingness with which different agents handle the 'transformative potential' held to inhere in these structural properties. Yet, to grant the existence of individual psychology would be to acknowledge personal properties which at least have relative autonomy from social practices.

The questions which have been raised in this introduction will be tackled in the last two sections of this chapter.

The deficiencies of central conflation: structure and agency as methodologically areducible

To treat 'structure' and 'agency' as inseparable is central to the notion of 'duality'. This method of transcending dualism then produces an ontology of 'social practices' which are held to be the ultimate constituents of social reality. There is a decentring of the subject here because human beings only become people, as opposed to organisms, through drawing upon structural properties to generate social practices. There is an equivalent demotion of structure, which only becomes real, as opposed to virtual when instantiated by agency. These ontological assumptions have direct implications for practical social theorizing, for they enjoin that social theory should concern itself exclusively with 'social practices'. These alone are the subject matter of the social sciences. If this is the case then its corollary is central conflation, for the implication is that neither 'structure' nor 'agency' have independent or autonomous or anterior features, but only those properties which are manifested in and reproduced or transformed through 'social practices'.

Now, the view defended throughout this book is that conflation is always an error in social theory. The deficiencies of its 'upwards' and 'downwards' versions were those of epiphenomenalism; that structure and agency respectively were deprived of relative autonomy and could thus be reduced to one or the other. Central conflation instead deprives *both* elements of their relative autonomy, not through *reducing* one to the other, but by *compacting* the two together inseparably. Yet this very compression is what advocates of structuration theory consider to be its strength – a method of conceptualizing social life where there is no divorce, rupture or disjunction between the minutiae of everyday activities and the structures which are necessarily reproduced or transformed in the practices of everyday living. We do not intend to reproduce the English language each time we generate a grammatically correct sentence in it, but this is the inexorable consequence of our so doing. Enter the knowledgeable actor and exit the cultural dope; enter structure as a medium of action and exit structural properties as constraints upon it: these are the attractions of central conflation, the bonuses accrued by abandoning traditional dualisms and transcending them through the notion of 'duality'.

For the critics of central conflation, the central question is whether 'duality' merely throws a blanket over the two constituents, 'structure' and 'agency' which only serves to prevent us from examining what is going on beneath it. Twelve years ago I referred to this approach as 'sinking rather than linking the differences between structure and agency'.[21] In similar vein, Smith and Turner criticized it as a vicious circle where 'agency presupposes structure and structure presupposes agency'.[22] More recently, Thompson comments that the problem of structure and agency has not so much been 'resolved as dissolved' in structuration theory.[23] In other words, elision is hailed as a virtue by advocates of central conflation, whereas the compression of structure and agency into 'social practices' is condemned as a vice by its critics because it entails the repression of properties which are distinct to each and distinguishable from one another.

At the end of the day, the fundamental argument between the Elisionists and their opponents (at both the ontological and methodological levels) is about the stratified nature of social reality. Whilst the Elisionist does not deny the stratification of the world, basically only three strata figure in their theorizing – the natural, the biological and the social. These three alone are credited with independent properties and therefore it is only the interplay between these (relatively) autonomous entities which can permissibly figure in Elisionist theorizing. The crucial difference is that those opposed to elisionism delineate at least two additional strata, with their own distinctive emergent and irreducible properties – personal psychology (mind as emergent from body) and socio-cultural structures (structure as emergent from social relations). For the latter, therefore, 'the social' is not one and indivisible but made up of heterogeneous constituents. Because of this, examination of their interplay is central to any adequate form of social theorizing (since the relative autonomy of each stratum means that its properties are capable of independent variation, combination and above all, influence).

The debate is thus about whether an adequate theory of social reality

[21] Margaret S. Archer, 'Morphogenesis versus structuration', British Journal of Sociology, 1982, 33: 455–83.
[22] J. W. Smith and B. S. Turner, 'Constructing social theory and constituting society', Theory, Culture and Society, 1986, 3: 125–33.
[23] Thompson, 'Structuration'.

can be cast in homogeneous terms, that is referring only to 'social practices', or whether it must deal with heterogeneous elements because of its stratified nature. Cohen is perfectly clear that the former is the position adopted by Elisionists and upholds an unstratified view of social reality: 'Giddens lays the foundations of structuration theory at the intersection between theories of action and theories of collectivities, arguing as he proceeds that the division between these theoretical domains obscures the fact that collectivities and action do not comprise heterogeneous constituents of social life'.[24]

Effectively, this debate invokes one which has a long history, namely the traditional dispute about the relations between the two disciplines of psychology and sociology, one which found the Individualists and the Holists on opposite sides. The point at issue is not about the boundaries between these disciplines, which in academia are largely artificial, but whether the two do and should possess separate and identifiable bodies of concepts *because* they refer to heterogeneous entities (individual and society: agency and structure: subjectivity and objectivity). As an issue it is quite distinct from admitting that frequently 'Psychologists, dealing in principle with individuals, have not been able to abstract from the societal environment, nor sociologists, dealing in principle with social wholes, from individual motivations, purposes, beliefs and attitudes'.[25] Certainly, this correct observation points to a legitimate area of study, 'social psychology', whose claims to existence represent a difficulty for Holistic downwards conflationists and Individualist upwards conflationists alike. Obviously the Methodological Individualist in search of 'rock bottom explanations' seeks to make individual dispositions the terminus of their explanations and thus *does* wish to abstract from the social environment. In consequence, 'social psychology' is limited in scope and by principle to the study of how 'other people' (and purely as people, never as incumbents of positions or as parties in structured relationships) serve to affect individual dispositions, attitudes, opinions etc. What is vaunted as the principled explanation of individualistic theorizing is psychology itself – hence the attempt to isolate 'primordial' dispositions, prior to their expression in any social context, as the ultimate bedrock of any acceptable account. The methodological Holist takes the opposite point of view, with the individual seen in Durkheim's famous phrase as 'indeterminate material' upon which social forces and factors imprint themselves. Again 'social psychology' is reduced in scope to the study of circumstances in which societal socialization fails and the consequences of the resulting

---

[24] Cohen, 'Structuration theory', p. 34.
[25] Piotr Sztompka, *Sociological Dilemmas*, Academic Press, New York, 1979, p. 115.

'deviance' for the social whole – with the implication that appropriate (re)socialization can always mould the individual 'material' appropriately. What is vaunted as the principled explanation of holistic theorizing is 'sociology' alone – hence the injunction to explain one social fact only by another.

The Elisionist, of course, differs from each of these stances. While they both, for entirely different reasons grounded in their divergent ontologies, sought to *minimize* the brief of 'social psychology', the central conflationist seeks to *maximize* it. Individual dispositions cannot be abstracted from their social environment, whose structural properties must be drawn upon for their expression yet such properties depend upon individual intentionality for their instantiation. (The intention need not be *to* instantiate, as in the English language example, but individuals have to intend something when deciding to speak, for this to be the result.) In short, because 'social practices' are the central concern of the Elisionist and because these are an inseparable compound of structure and agency, central conflationists are not dealing with heterogeneous constituents of social life, but with one homogeneous though Janus-faced entity which is how 'social practices' are conceptualized. It follows from this that the entirety of their theorizing could very properly be called 'social psychology', since their weakly stratified ontology of the world as a whole only acknowledges that autonomous properties pertain to 'biology' and 'nature', which would require their own concepts and propositions, but denies heterogeneity to anything 'in between' them. Homogeneous 'social practices' take up all this terrain and can thus be conceptualized in the same way which is at once 'social' and 'psychological'.

It follows that those who defend the existence of a more robustly stratified social world will agree in repudiating the psychological reductionism of the Methodological Individualist and rejecting the sociological reductionism of the Methodological Holist, but they cannot conclude from this that there is nothing but 'social psychology', as conceived of by the central conflationist. They cannot concur because their stratified view of social reality means they acknowledge emergent properties at different 'levels' within it, which must be conceptualized in their own terms – ones which are neither reducible to one another nor, because of their relative autonomy (and hence capacity for independent variation) such that they can be compacted together and treated as a homogeneous entity.

Thus, one the one hand, 'social psychology' can tell us nothing about individual characteristics such as perception, consciousness and cognition nor about the psychology of personal proclivities and antipathies. Although it may add a great deal about their exercise and even modification in social settings, these autonomous individual properties have to be granted *before* we can talk of their exercise or modification, and, as features emergent from the biological stratum, they themselves constrain (and enable) what *can be* socially expressed and modified. On the other hand the properties and powers of structures themselves, such as electoral systems, banking or capitalism, are not explained by 'social psychology' (let alone psychologism) since they form its very context. 'Social psychology' may again add a great deal to our understanding of their maintenance or modification but what is maintained and how it is transformed means that these structural properties have *first* to be granted *before* analysing their stability or change, since they themselves distribute interests in change and are differentially malleable to it. In brief, the Emergentist stands opposed to 'one-level' explanations, based on a homogeneous view of the social world, whether this be the 'psychology' of the upward conflationist, the 'sociology' of the downward conflationist, or the 'social psychology' of the central conflationist. However, it is the latter which concerns us here.

We have just seen how the Elisionists' stand-point confronts considerable opposition. To vindicate themselves against their opponents, they have to demonstrate two things in order to defend construing the social as a homogeneous entity, i.e. such that 'structure' and 'agency' do not comprise heterogeneous constituents with relatively autonomous properties:

1. How structures can be rendered in terms of 'social practices', without any remainder save their material element. In other words can structures be adequately conceptualized as *nothing but* part of the parcel that is 'social practices'?
2. How agents can be construed in terms of 'social practices', without any remainder, save their biological element. In other words can people be adequately conceptualized as *nothing but* the other part of the parcel which makes up 'social practices'?

Let us examine these two points in turn.

Structure and the ontology of praxis

The Elisionist defence requires a complete reconceptualization of 'structure', in conformity with the ontology of praxis, and therefore one which breaks with both traditional and contemporary alternatives. Thus, the definition of social structure which is generic to Methodological Individualism, namely, 'patterns of aggregate behaviour that are stable over time', is jettisoned, primarily for its explicit atomism, secondarily for its assumption that nothing but a process of aggregation is involved in structuration, thirdly for making the visible pattern reproduced synonymous with 'structure' and finally for the presumption that to be a structure *is to be* relatively enduring. Next, the definition most closely associated with Methodological Holism, namely, 'lawlike regularities that govern the behaviour of social facts', is dismissed firstly, for the explicit reification of structure by its severance from action, secondly, for the assumption that regularities are lawlike in producing ineluctable consequences, thirdly, for holding that these operate in steam-roller fashion immune from human intervention, and lastly, for assuming that structures endure and unfold over the heads of actors like mechanical and naturalistic forces.[26]

Finally, social structure which is conceived of by Methodological Realists as 'systems of human relations among social positions' is rejected primarily because structures refer to actual forms of social organization, that is, to real entities with their own powers, tendencies and potentials, secondly, because the social relations upon which they depend are held to have independent causal properties rather than being mere abstractions from our repetitive and routinized behaviour, and, most importantly, because these relations which constitute structures pre-date occupants of positions within them, thus constraining or enabling agency. In short, realists, who would also disassociate themselves from the definitions endorsed by Individualists and Holists, see social *structure as quintessentially relational* but none the less real because of its emergent properties which affect the agents who act within it and thus cannot be reduced to their activities. Because the Elisionist seeks to conceptualize structure (and culture) in terms of 'social practices', this relational conception is not acceptable since relations themselves are credited with properties distinct from practices, potentials irreducible to practices, powers influential of praxis and are pre-existent to practitioners. Instead, the Elisionist needs a concept of structure which is implicated *in* social practices and not one like the relational, where structures cannot be compressed into practices and exert their own, relatively autonomous, influence over them.

Hence, Giddens deliberately advances a non-relational conception of structure, redefined as 'rules and resources' which are implicated in social practices and have no existence independent of them. Thus he writes, 'by the term structure I do not refer . . . to the descriptive analysis of relations of interaction which "compose" organizations or collectivities, but to the system of generative rules and resources'.[27] Conceived of as 'rules and

---

[26] Douglas V. Porpora, 'Four concepts of social structure', *Journal for the Study of Social Behaviour*, 1989, 19: 198. These generic definitions of social structure are also taken from here.

[27] Anthony Giddens, *New Rules of Sociological Method*, Hutchinson, London, 1976, p. 127.

resources', several more refinements are needed before structural properties can become co-extensive with social practices, without remainder,
that is, without their possessing any existence or influence autonomous
from, or anterior to, or influential of social practices. For obviously, to
concede any of the last three points would leave structure with a surplus of
features which lie beyond practices, yet which influence them – thus
rendering the ontology of praxis both inconsistent and incomplete.

Firstly, then, the re-definition shifts the referents of 'structure' away
from identifiable forms of social organization (the division of labour,
educational systems, political parties ...) and links them instead to
underlying organizing principles, which generate what they do only
because agents draw upon them in particular ways in the course of the
social practices in which they engage. Thus, what others had taken to be
real entities constitutive of structure (e.g. an educational system), become
here, not structures themselves but only the 'visible pattern' produced by
agency manipulating 'rules and resources' in ways which perpetuate this
patterning. Secondly, when it is objected that even here things like
educational systems still figure in Elisionist theory, it is quickly countered
that this visible pattern has no independent existence or influence but is
only an abstraction from the repertoire of repetitive or routinized
practices surrounding education. Institutions themselves are thus recon-
strued as 'regularized practices', whose very regularity (i.e. endurance)
depends upon agency invoking the same structural principles in the same
way because praxis has become routinized. Finally, one of the most
obvious difficulties in these re-definitional manoeuvres is that the very
'rules and resources' which are drawn upon to generate social practices
could therefore be held to be something other than (i.e. autonomous,
external, anterior to) social practices. Here, the defence consists in
placing 'rules and resources' outside time and space and endowing them
with only a 'virtual existence' until or unless 'instantiated' by agents in the
course of social praxis. Undoubtedly this raises ontological problems of
two kinds. The first set are those which arise within the terms of the
theory and concern that which is *included and yet deemed to be 'virtual'*,
and thus agency-dependent. The second set concerns what is *excluded
because it cannot be conceived of as instantiated*, that is aspects of social
reality which cannot be accommodated within the 'social practices' of
agents. These twin difficulties of inclusion and exclusion will be examined
in turn, though the source of both is rooted in the linguistic analogy which
shadows the text, the notion of language as the exemplar of a 'virtual
property' and the disanalogies which surface when the *langue/parole*
distinction is transferred to structural properties/social practices.

The ontology of instantiation: structures as virtual

The first set of problems begins with 'structure' (defined as 'rules and resources') being assigned a virtual existence, until instantiated by agents and boils down to questioning what is 'virtual' about either a rule or a resource? Stated economically, 'if they have a real existence, then it does not help to say that their existence is virtual and if they are real we must be able to distinguish them from agency'.[28] The standard response in structuration theory is to admit that the material component of resources exists (as part of nature) but only acquires social significance in conjunction with rules (gold is more valuable than silver). However, such rules themselves only have their locus in the heads of agents as 'memory traces', hence it is invalid to distinguish them from the agents who are their bearers, or their practices which alone control their invocation and efficacy – which is what instantiation means.

The equally standard riposte is to insist that the reality of structure does not depend upon instantiation. Where rules are concerned this consists in arguing: (i) many rules have an actual existence as in Law, Constitution, Liturgy or contracts, are anchored in time and space and exist (as penalties, entitlements, rights and obligations) independent of their invocation, i.e. they have *autonomy*; (ii) also they are pre-existent, that is they are already there to be invoked (appeal can be made to them and sanctions introduced through them), i.e. they are *anterior*; (iii) and it is not necessary for them to be known in order to have an effect (ignorance of the law is no excuse), i.e. they have an independent *causal influence* .

Identical points are made about the ontological status of resources, such as land, food, weapons or factories: (i) sometimes rules and meanings are both unidentifiable and unintelligible without reference to them (political attitudes without reference to parties or voting patterns without mention of electoral systems) i.e. they have *autonomy*; (ii) their prior existence frequently constrains the meanings which can be imposed or made to stick, i.e. they are *anterior*; (iii) they impinge upon people rather than awaiting instantiation and their effects are often independent of interpretations placed on them, i.e. they exert a *causal influence*.

What is curious about these critiques is that they are confined to making these perfectly valid points about either 'rules' or 'resources' without proceeding to subject the formula, structure = 'rules and resources', to a full-frontal scrutiny. When it is, then the under-theorized nature of both components raises major internal problems about *which is which*, and

---

[28] Craib, *Giddens*, pp. 153f.

therefore about *what* is materially grounded and what not, and thus about the assignment of the terms actual and virtual.

The issue arises the moment we consider Giddens' proffered definition of 'resources' as 'the media whereby transformative capacity is employed as power in the routine course of social interaction'.[29] Since in his view all action entails the exercise of power, then an effective verbal request of the 'Pass the salt' variety, turns language itself into a *resource* as well as a body of *rules*. While there is nothing objectionable about this *per se*, nevertheless since language is the guiding image behind the notion that all structural properties share a 'virtual existence', the guide itself is fundamentally ambivalent on the issue of 'what's what'. This turns out to have some very far reaching implications for the terse formula that structures do equal 'rules and resources' and are dependent upon instantiation through the 'social practices' of agents.

One Elisionist at least has recognized these difficulties and sought to rescue the 'duality of structure' from them. William Sewell's[30] brave attempt is very instructive. He begins by conceding that resources are *not* virtual, since by definition, material things exist in time and space, and only in particular times places and quantities can material objects serve as resources. Thus they have to be deemed actual rather than virtual and this is so not just for 'allocative resources', but also for human ones, since human beings are embodied and their bodies like other material objects cannot be virtual. Yet this necessary admission creates a major problem for Giddens, who as has just been seen wishes to construe language as a resource and yet to sustain its virtual nature. It arises because although Giddens would immediately insist that *langue* was virtual whilst *parole* (entailing instantiation) was actual, none the less *langue* refers to rules and *parole* now to resources. Is the implication that only 'rules', but not resources, have a virtual existence?

This is Sewell's conclusion, but since he again accepts what the critics had to say about the reality of formal rules, his admission leads him to re-classify them as resources! Thus, 'publicly fixed codifications of rules are actual rather than virtual and should be regarded as *resources* rather than rules in Giddens' sense'.[31] In itself, this is an unacceptable move because by definition 'resources' are things which one can have more of than others and can accumulate or increase. Yet much of the law is not like this: whilst one can think of some possessing more or less civil rights, nevertheless, one cannot sensibly speak of having more of the Highway

---

[29] Giddens, *Social Theory*, p. 92.
[30] William Sewell, 'A theory of structure: duality, agency and transformation', *American Journal of Sociology*, 1992, 98: 1–29.   [31] Sewell, 'Theory of structure', p. 8.

Code than other people or of accumulating the law of Trespass. Further-more this now means that only *informal rules* (renamed as 'cultural schemas') retain 'virtual' status, what is virtual about them being that they can be generalized or transposed to new situations. 'To say that schemas are virtual is to say that they cannot be reduced to their existence in any particular location in space-time: they can be actualized in a potentially broad and unpredetermined range of situations'.[32] However, this new defining feature of the virtual, namely transposability, does not map onto the informal/formal distinction between rules because case law and legal precedent are inherently transposable and canon law is genera-lizable through conscience. Even more serious is that what now remain as 'virtual' rules, apart from etiquette and protocol (which seem mis-classified since they are in part at least publicly codified) include Lévi-Straussian binary opposites (lacking any context of justification), aes-thetic norms (which are quintessentially contestable) and partially con-scious schemas (which put a strain on agential knowledgeability). The crucial point is that this category of virtual rules now lacks *precisely* the Wittgensteinian quality of enabling the agent to 'know how to go on'. (In the above instances family resemblances are not invoked to impose limits, so transposability implies 'anything goes, anywhere it sticks'.) Equally they have now lost the strong Winchian quality of being public criteria which establish what correct rule-following is and is not (transposability becomes a lot more like 'what can you get away with').

The whole point of these manoeuvres was to rescue the basic structure = rules and resources equation, yet Sewell recognizes he has merely created a new problem. 'If I am right that all resources are actual rather than virtual, Giddens' notion of structure turns out to be self-contradic-tory. If structures are virtual, they cannot include both schemas and resources. And if they include both schemas and resources, they cannot be virtual. He, and we, can't have it both ways. But which way should we have it?'.[33]

There are two paths out of the wood. The left pathway would be to maintain that structure refers only to rules, whereas resources should be thought of as their *effect* not their co-equal in the basic equation. In this way, structures would retain their virtual quality whilst resources could be allowed an actual quality, and become media animated by the former. Yet Sewell knows this leads via cultural idealism and determinism to just where he does not want to go – to the denial of the 'duality' of structure through negating its active instantiation by agents. Were this path to be followed, then, 'stocks of material goods and people's knowledge and

---

[32] Sewell, 'Theory of structure', p. 8.   [33] Sewell, 'Theory of structure', pp. 10–11.

commitments become inert, mere media for and outcomes of the determinative operations of cultural schemas. If we insist that structures are
virtual, we risk lapsing into the de facto idealism that continually haunts
structuralism'.[34]

Therefore, Giddens' notion that structures are virtual has to be
abandoned. Instead, the right and correct pathway to follow, 'if the
duality of structure is to be saved',[35] means re-defining the terms of the
equation. 'Structure, then, should be defined as composed simultaneously of schemas, which are virtual, and of resources, which are
actual'.[36] What follows from this are two of the most contentious
propositions, namely that 'it must be true that schemas are the effects of
resources, just as resources are the effects of schemas'.[37]

The first proposition asserts that if informal rules are to be reproduced
over time, and without this sustained reproduction they could not be
counted as structural, then 'they must be validated by the accumulation of
resources that their enactment engenders'.[38] Even if one recalls that
'texts' of all kinds now constitute 'resources' in Sewell's redefinition, the
statement seems far from true and the examples offered are unconvinc-
ingly forced. His notion of the Eucharist as a 'resource', whose reception
suffuses communicants with a sense of spiritual well being, thus 'validat-
ing' the reality of the rule of apostolic succession which makes a priest a
priest, not only entails an unacceptable theology of sacramental sensatio-
nalism but challenges the sociological proposition it was supposed to
illustrate. Does it follow that a priest is not a priest when pronouncing
absolution, since the sacrament of reconciliation involves no 'resources'?

Similarly both prayer and philanthropy are sustained social practices,
yet there is no accumulation of 'resources' in the former, whilst the latter
foresees their diminution. Were the rejoinder to be that millennia of
praying have produced countless volumes of 'texts', this in no way makes
the current practice of prayer dependent upon them: were it maintained
that philanthropy is self-limiting at the point where 'resources' have been
exhausted, then what is ruled out is that a practice can be sustained by
example and that various forms of altruism involve a self-giving which
cannot be represented as 'resources', that is reduced to things like 'time
and effort' (in which case they would anyway suffer depletion not lead to
accumulation). In short, it is true neither that beliefs have necessarily to
be 'validated' by 'resources', nor that accumulation rather than diminution is entailed if resources are involved, nor that enactment engenders
resources at all. The relation between 'rules and resources' is a matter of

[34] Sewell, 'Theory of structure', p. 12.   [35] Sewell, 'Theory of structure', p. 12.
[36] Sewell, 'Theory of structure', p. 13.   [37] Sewell, 'Theory of structure', p. 13.
[38] Sewell, 'Theory of structure', p. 13.

contingency not necessity; their relationship is only necessary in order to salvage the theory rather than being a truth about social reality.

The same can be said of the second proposition, namely that 'resources are the effects of schemas', with the former depending upon the latter for 'instantiation' or 'embodiment' without which they would eventually dissipate or decay. In other words, the actual, that is 'resources' (now including every variety of text), is held to be dependent upon the virtual. This is a curious statement, given that it purports to be about ontology rather than social efficacy. As far as cultural items are concerned, it basically asserts that the existence of books depends upon readers and is thus a classical assertion that knowledge requires a knowing subject. Consequently it confuses the fact that knowledge does indeed require holders/practitioners/believers in order to have a social effect at any given time with the ontological existence of a text whose dispositional capacity to be understood remains inviolate despite millennia of neglect (Dead Sea Scrolls etc.).[39]

This difficulty is compounded when material resources are considered, for it is maintained that these 'are read *like* texts, to recover the cultural schemas they instantiate'.[40] Both the assumption that resources need to be read or interpreted in order to remain in existence *and* that they have no social effects independent of the constructions placed upon them, are equally unacceptable. As far as the object world is concerned, the first claim repeats the denial of self-subsistent reality which contradicts the actual status previously assigned to material resources. Again, this not only confuses the question of existence with that of social efficacy but also makes the latter depend upon the activities of knowing subjects. What this neglects are the real effects of the real world upon us, independent of any act of 'instantiation' or interpretation. After all, why do the effects of famine, conquest, of a demographic structure or an income distribution require reading? Their objective influence may be to leave many dead, enslaved, poor or disadvantaged, in a way which can be consequential in itself, could be independent of their having readers (nuclear holocaust), and often have an efficacy regardless of any readings which are placed on them (inflation may not be identified at all by pensioners, it may be interpreted as the effect of governmental incompetence or excessive wage settlements, but its inescapable effect for those on fixed incomes is that they can buy less).

However, despite the sweeping assertions which have just been criticized, Sewell can dodge their impact by moving the target, which is what

---

[39] For a full discussion of this matter, see Margaret S. Archer, *Culture and Agency*, Cambridge University Press, Cambridge, 1988, especially ch. 5, 'Addressing the cultural system'.   [40] William Sewell, 'Theory of structure', p. 13.

he does in his final redefinition of structures, only to jump from the frying pan into the fire. Finally, then, 'sets of schemas and resources may properly be said to constitute *structures* only when they mutually imply and sustain one another over time'.[41] In so doing, he has not rescued Giddens' equation, structures = *rules* and *resources*, but has in fact replaced it with the more limited formula, structures = rules *and* resources. In other words, by insisting upon the two mutually 'implying and sustaining' one another, he is now defining them in terms of *internal and necessary relations* between them. This means he is shifting towards a definition of structures as emergent properties and, while this is welcome in itself, it means that he is no longer dealing with properties which are reducible to 'social practices'.

This Sewell resists, still wishing to maintain the central tenet of structuration theory that 'all social action is generated by structures',[42] but now of course he is leaving outside the bounds of structure those 'rules' and 'resources' which are not mutually implicative and reciprocally sustaining. Thus his statement about 'all social action' means here that this is generated by a much more limited range of 'structural properties'. In other words, he would have to vindicate this statement in order to sustain his claim to have rescued structuration theory. Yet it is precisely because of what is now *excluded* from the redefinition of 'structure' that the claim is not sustainable. For there now remain two categories of relationships between properties (rule to rule relations and resource to resource relations) which are specifically omitted, but which may indeed be claimed to generate social action, although not through any kind of instantiation in social practices. In fact, there is a double objection here. On the one hand, rule-to-rule relations (caste and khama, theoretical deductions or the implications of ideas) are omitted as are resource-to-resource relations (e.g. private property/house ownership/rent). On the other hand, since the relationships defining structure are ones which are held to 'mutually imply and sustain one another', the concept of structure is automatically restricted to relations of complementarity and necessarily eliminates relations of material or cultural *contradictions*.

In other words, if we think of (a) possible relations between rules and resources in a two by two table, Sewell's definition confines structure to half of the possible combinations, and (b), if we assume that all relations in this table can be either complementary or contradictory ones, then this definition covers only four out of sixteen possibilities. Yet we have no reason to assume that complementarity prevails over contradiction in society (this being an empirically variable matter), nor is there any

[41] Sewell, 'Theory of structure', p. 13.   [42] Sewell, 'Theory of structure', p. 22.

justification for assuming that 'all social action' is generated by this particular kind of relationship and not by the other types of combinations. All sixteen combinations are emergent properties (if they are internally and necessarily related) and thus as the results (or the results of the results) of social relations are *not homogeneous* with 'social practices'. Yet, equally, *all sixteen* can generate social action through shaping the socio-cultural situations in which people find themselves – complementarities moulding problem-free ideational or material contexts and contradictions generating problem-ridden contexts of action. As such they *all* possess heterogeneous properties of autonomy, pre-existence and causal influence in relation to the people who have to confront them (as enablements or constraints), *but* the particular pair, 'complementary rules and resources' enjoys no *a prioristic* privilege over the other three-quarters as influences upon social action and therefore there is no justification for defining 'structure' in terms of them.

The attempt to rescue a re-defined notion in which structure = rules *and* resources thus fails for the same reasons as did Giddens' original equation, namely that there are now even larger 'remainders' of 'rules' (emergent cultural properties) and of 'resources' (emergent material properties) which the re-definition cannot accommodate. In turn, these 'remainders' represent not only theoretical deficiencies but constitute parallel methodological obstacles to the Elisionist.

The methodological implications of instantiation

The latter repay a brief inspection for they point up the practical deficiencies which arise from the Elisionist failing to take account of the stratified nature of the social world. This is the same critical path which Thompson pursued when seeking to establish that 'while rules of various kinds are important features of social life, the study of rules (and resources) is not identical to but rather distinct from and on a different level from, the analysis of social structure'.[43] To begin with there is the problem that we cannot make our entrée into practical social analysis through 'rules and resources' because (a) these rules are too vaguely defined as a formulaic ways of knowing how to go on in everyday life to direct our attention to anything in particular, and (b) since instantiation of any single rule invokes the whole matrix, we are no better off, and (c) since the potential for transformation is inherent in every instantiation of a rule, we are even worse off in terms of being given a sense of direction. It follows therefore that it is necessary to work the other way round. If we

---

[43] Thompson, 'Structuration', p. 64.

seek to investigate education then we must first address the 'visible pattern' of things educational to know *which* rules are relevant to it. Were 'visible patterns', like educational systems, nothing more than the embodiment of rules and resources in practices to do with education, a problem would still arise for the Elisionist, namely that we have indeed had to resort to precisely that descriptive analysis of organizations which Giddens reproved, in order to get the investigation going. To know what rules are important, we have first needed to investigate 'education' itself, which leads Thompson to query 'what justifies this implicit criterion of importance if not an analysis of social structure which is separate from the study of those rules which are singled out in its name?'.[44]

This is a valid methodological point, but one which would not fundamentally damage the Elisionists' case if the 'visible pattern' were indeed nothing more than a temporary embodiment or expression of 'rules and resources'. Thompson of course is already hinting that institutions and organizations are more than this, that they have features independent of such 'structural properties' and thus an existence and influence which cannot be conceptualized in terms of social practices -and his argument seems well founded.

Analysis of institutions like schools and universities universally shows that certain groups or classes of individuals have restricted opportunities for entry, yet how can these forms of discrimination be construed in terms of 'rules' since they actually traduce the rights of the agents concerned? Thus, 'what is at issue is the fact that the restrictions on opportunities operate differentially, unevenly affecting various groups of individuals whose categorization depends upon certain assumptions about social structure; and it is this differential operation or effect which cannot be grasped by the analysis of rules alone'.[45] Indeed it cannot, which is why Emergentists stress the need to acknowledge the prior structuring of groups, that is the differential distribution of life chances among them as independent structural features which affect how anyone goes on or gets on educationally. Yet Elisionists have the avowed intention of avoiding any notion of structure as pre-constituted which means that reproduced relations between classes, sexes or ethnic groups 'cannot be admitted to the definition of structure. To do so would be to contradict the idea that structures only exist in their instantiation, since to talk of reproduced relations implies structures of social relationships which endure (exist) over time'.[46]

Were the Elisionist to counter that it was the 'resources' element which

---

[44] Thompson, 'Structuration', p. 65.
[45] Thompson, 'Structuration', p. 65.   [46] Layder, *Structure*, p. 66.

was at play in accounting for differential restrictions on things like educational opportunities, two difficulties would be encountered. On the one hand resources are held only to be 'material existents' which acquire significance solely in conjunction with rules. Therefore rules would have to be adduced governing the uses of financial and cultural capital in educational situations. Yet even if there were such a rule as 'buy the best you can' there would still remain the same intractable problem that the prior distribution of these resources itself differentially constrains who can buy what, that is, in which educational practices they actually can engage. On the other hand, the Elisionists' remaining way out is to conceptualize such educational restrictions as the unintended consequences of social practices. Thus, Giddens himself gives the example of a poverty cycle where maternal deprivation – poor schooling – low paid employment – maternal deprivation operate as a homoeostatic loop coordinated and controlled exclusively through the unintended consequences of day-to-day social activity. What this does not explain is why some groups enter the loop in the first place, for it is not *their* practices which set their life chances, determine the definition of instruction, the linkages between educational and occupational opportunity etc. Nor can any of their practices extricate them from the loop without overcoming stringent constraints whose differential distribution again begs the question of why and how they *are* differentially distributed in society. Any attempt to dispose of these questions by simply invoking the unacknowledged conditions of action, which is part of the Elisionist equation of social structure with practical knowledge, finds itself in the same cul de sac. Victims of educational discrimination are not victimized by their lack of 'discursive penetration' of the situation in which they find themselves. We could endow them with all the findings of educational sociology without changing the fact that their situation places objective limitations on the resources at their disposal and the rules they are *able* to follow. To know that public schools convey educational advantages which inner city comprehensives do not is only useful to those with the means to turn their knowledge into practice.

Thus, when 'structural properties' are defined as 'rules and resources' in order to construe them as co-extensive with 'social practices' there is always a remainder which cannot be accommodated. The ontology of praxis constantly comes up against an interface with another level of social reality whose features cannot be construed as practices themselves, their unacknowledged conditions or unintended consequences. Structure asserts a stubborn relative autonomy from social practices because of its prior and independent influence which shapes the practice of different groups in different ways. Structural features which mould our practices

are clearly indispensable for explaining them, yet if they cannot themselves be assimilated to the category of practices then our explanations are
made up of these two heterogeneous elements – structures and practices.
This remainder, those aspects of structure which 'rules and resources' do
not encompass, are properties emergent from social relations which
constitute a distinct stratum of social reality.

Agency and the ontology of praxis

'It is social practices which constitute (or socialize) us as actors, and which
also embody or realize structures.'[47] This comment of Craib's seems a fair
summary of how the actor is conceptualized by Elisionists, who 'almost
talk about the actor constituted in and by practices'.[48] Once again the
main criticism is that this concept is far too under-stratified. In this
connection, it is particularly significant that the terms 'agent', 'actor' and
'person' are used interchangeably within structuration theory. Yet I will
argue in chapter 8 that this triple distinction is indispensable because all
three contain emergent properties and are thus irreducible to one another.
Instead, Elisionists proceed as if all that were involved was one homogeneous entity, with uniform powers, who is constantly related to society
and constantly active within it. These are the consequences of attempting
to construe the broad concept of agency within the narrow confines of
'social practices', without remainder.

At rock bottom, for Elisionists to insist that we are constituted through
'social *practices*' makes us relentlessly active, and to emphasise that all our
daily life is constituted by '*social* practices' makes us unremittingly social
(High Society and no Private Lives). Basically this generates an under-
stratified notion, one which captures some salient features of the 'actor'
but cannot accommodate all the distinctive properties of either the 'agent'
or the 'person'. These I will maintain are the 'remainders' which cannot
be encompassed by an ontology of praxis, yet are indispensable to
adequate social theorizing. They will be dealt with in turn, in this section,
which is structured around the triple distinction (agent, person, actor)
whose lack is held to be the main deficiency of the Elisionist conceptualization and one which derives directly from the ontology of praxis.

The over-active view of the agent

What is questioned first are the basic Elisionist equations; agency = action, action = an ability to do otherwise, and therefore, agents = those who

---

[47] Craib, *Giddens*, p. 34.   [48] Craib, *Giddens*, p. 37.

could have done otherwise. This I maintain produces the 'over active agent' and the crucial remainder which is omitted is agents' capacity 'to make a difference' *simply through their existence as members of collectivities with particular properties*, which no amount of activity on their part can make other than they are at any given time.

How this omission arises is clear if we consider the notion of 'social practices' themselves. For the Elisionist to emphasize that agents are constituted through involvement in 'social practices' is to make them unremitting 'doers', and their 'doings' the only important thing about them. Whilst this may be justified for 'actors', it is misguided in relation to 'agents' who may well be inactive in Giddens' terms (that is, incapable of doing otherwise so as to become something other), yet none the less can still generate important social consequences – in terms of their aggregate effects. Here my argument is that the actor and agent have been unhelpfully elided: agents have activity unwarrantably thrust upon them so that the definition can embrace them.

Activity then is quintessential to agency in Giddens' view and it is this which I challenge. His definition states that an agent is one who 'could have done otherwise'.[49] Thus because activity is the central defining feature (given his ontology of praxis), Giddens denies any structural constraints which may so limit options that agency is effectively dissolved (on his definition). Hence, he is at pains to insist that even the bound and gagged prisoner in solitary confinement remains an agent as his ultimate refusal, namely suicide, is supposed to indicate (on the questionable assumption that this is always possible).

Here, Thompson rightly remarks that 'Giddens manages to preserve the complementarity between structure and agency only *by defining* agency in such a way that any individual in any situation could not *not* be an agent'.[50] His critique rests on underlining that a person's actions may be severely restricted by the *range of alternative courses of action* available to them and that restrictions (such as job shortages) are constraints stemming from structural conditions which cannot be construed as rules instantiated by agents drawing upon them in social practices.

Indeed, the logical extension of Thompson's critique is to maintain that even when the stringency of constraints precludes any alternative course of action, agency is not necessarily dissolved and agential effects can continue to make an important difference. Thus I would argue that the most important aspect of 'agency' is the capacity to 'make a difference'

[49] Anthony Giddens, *A Contemporary Critique of Historical Materialism*, Macmillan, London, 1979, p. 63.   [50] Thompson, 'Structuration', p. 74.

to society, but do not see that this necessarily entails activity *especially* if this means an ability 'to have done otherwise'.

What I have in mind here are collectivities whose very *presence* has an effect on its own right. It is their 'being' rather than their 'doing' which is efficacious, since it is consequential either for society as a whole or for some social organization. Thus if there are simply too many or too few in a given place or time (to feed or to fight) their very *presence* creates exigencies for decision-makers and makes a real difference to what policies can be enacted. *Their being there* constitutes part, the human part, of the *environment* which those actors who can do otherwise have to confront and in confronting it they are constrained in what they actually can do.

After all it does make sense to talk about the effects of under- and over-population on various aspects of society, independently of the activities in which people making up these populations engage. Similarly, when we speak of the 'dumb pressure of numbers' (on the housing or job market), the phrase carries its literal meaning: that it can constitute a pressure in its own right as an aggregate effect. The more people on the dole, the harder it becomes (*ceteris paribus*) to prevent unemployment benefits from falling and the more children in reception classes then pupil/staff ratios rise. Yet the things which can be done in these circumstances are constrained by the sheer numbers involved. This influence of agency is not limited to constraining effects; the dumb pressure of numbers can be enabling too, as in Durkheim's discussion of 'dynamic density'. These are all agential effects but they have nothing to do with the activity which is inseparable from the notion of 'social practices', except in the truistic sense of their *actes de présence*.

Elisionists might counter that the above examples entail activity in that, for example, signing on the dole implies knowledgeable agents activity drawing upon social rules and resources in order to go on in their daily lives. This however is not the point. Of course, as living human beings people cannot be inactive (in the common meaning) but this does not commit agents to activity in Giddens' sense of being able to do otherwise, for the point here is that *whatever* their actions, they cannot become other than they are as a collectivity. In this way they have no option, but this does not mean they have no effect. Given a shortfall between jobs available and the jobless, unemployment exists and not because people sign up for welfare benefits, for it does not disappear (except in official statistics) if they refrain from registering. The shortfall between jobs and jobless, constitutes the unemployed, between houses and unhoused, the homeless, between teachers and pupils, the illiterate, between food supplies and numbers to feed, the starving. It is the existence of these collectivities of agents which *through* their shared characteristics, i.e. *being* unemployed, homeless, illiterate, hungry or old, makes a difference to what can be done for them, about them, in view of them or despite them. In short, we will not be able to understand why *strategic actors* make decisions *so* and not *otherwise* unless we allow for the difference made to their designs by the effects of the very existence of collectivities of agents with particular properties in common.

Thus some of their effects, qua agential collectivities, are *irrespective* of their doings, because *whatever* their activities these cannot make the collectivity otherwise than it is at a given time. Certainly there are ethnomethodological tales to be written about 'doing unemployment', but ones whose importance lies in what unemployment does to people and how they live out something they have no option but to live with. It might seem that the Elisionist could counter that through some or enough doings these agents could themselves abolish the category as such (e.g. by mass migration), but this in turn depends upon that option being open, a matter which is not determined by the collectivity's actions (at that time).

Nevertheless, Elisionists might still claim that *how unemployment* is 'done' (criminality, militancy or depression for example) affects the *kind of problem* that it represents. Yet this would be a political misrepresentation, for the original problem remains unchanged, the collectivity unaltered in this respect since it cannot *be* 'otherwise'. What has really occurred is that more problems have developed (those now needing treatment for depression do not stop being unemployed). In these circumstances politicians might be tempted to say that we have a problem of 'mental health' or 'law and order' rather than of unemployment. The social theorist should resist such masking manoeuvres which conflate the positions to which collectivities of *agents* are confined without option, with what *actors* make *of* such situations. Of course being jobless can be personified in different ways by different depressive, militant or criminal actors, but rather than removing unemployment, it merely reinforces the need to distinguish between *collective agents* and *individual actors*. The reality experienced by the collectivity is not reducible to the personal reactions of its members; nor is the subjectivity of the latter understandable without reference to the objectivity of the former.

Moreover some properties cannot be transformed, like being old, where the aged themselves can do nothing as a collectivity to transform a top-heavy demographic structure. Of course the Elisionists could sustain their theory by suggesting that it remains open to this collectivity to play their last degree of freedom in a voluntary genocide pact. Yet if they seek to eliminate (*sic*) the problem of agential effects in this way, I will be suggesting that the other neglected 'residue' in their under-stratified view of people, that is personal psychology, would work to resist this 'ultimate solution'.

The over-social view of the person

Just as in the last section I argued that the equation of agency with action wrongly compacted the two, thus omitting crucial aspects and effects of agency, so now the argument is that the equation of the actor with the person has equivalent defects and that what is omitted here is the stratum of individual psychology. In short, what is lacking is what we might as well refer to as 'personality', used as a portmanteau term for all the psychological differences which differentiate between us as individual people.

If the constitution of the self in social practices (as a process inseparable from the constitution of society) had remained implicit in earlier works, it is fully explicit in Giddens' *Modernity and Self-Identity*.[51] Effectively, this represents another 'oversocialized view of man', or more strictly an 'oversocial' view. It does differ significantly from the Parsonian emphasis on learning specific values and automatically acquiring a normative attachment to them, since it is both more generic to humankind (sociality is a predicate and not an acquisition) and less determinate in its social consequences (because all things learned are susceptible of novel transformations, there are no adaptive outcomes). This 'oversocial view' is fully consistent in Elisionist thinking; were a distinction to be made between the individual personality and the socio-cultural system, this would allow the old dichotomies between 'self' and 'society', 'agency' and 'structure' etc. to re-surface which are precisely what the 'duality' approach is attempting to transcend, through vaunting their inseparability. The end result however, is to leave us with the single concept of a 'social self' which is under-stratified because it ultimately denies personal psychology.

The success of the Elisionists' enterprise depends upon their being able to eliminate any reference to selfhood which is independent of social mediation, for otherwise a stratum of individual features (personal psychology) would have to be acknowledged and its interplay with social properties would then require examination. Giddens instead begins with a sweeping (though purely anti-Cartesian) dismissal of *any* transcendental notion of the 'self', by the blanket assertion that 'a transcendental philosophy of the ego terminates in an irremediable solipsism'.[52] In

[51] Anthony Giddens, *Modernity and Self-Identity*, Polity, Oxford, 1991.
[52] Giddens, *Modernity*, p. 51.

preference he endorses what he holds to be Wittgenstein's view that the 'I/Me' distinction is internal to language. Here I want to question two things without entering philosophical controversy over the elusive 'I', but rather to assess the adequacy of this sociological account of self-consciousness. Firstly, the blanket nature of the dismissal rests exclusively upon a rejection of Husserl's discussion of *social* relations and that understanding others is exclusively reliant upon empathetic inferences from the self. Such a critique can stand (it is an inadequate solution to the problem of Other Minds) but it does not dispose of the transcendental need to predicate our interactions with the *world* upon an 'I' who engages in them. Secondly, if language is the medium through which self-identity is developed in a socially mediated manner, then considerable difficulties arise over the Elisionists' conception of pre-linguistic children, specifically *who* is interacting with *what* and *how*. These two questions, and the difficulties encountered by Elisionists over them, are closely intertwined.

The Elisionists' strategy is basically to deny the existence of *any* socially *un*-mediated experiences at any stage of human development, concluding that prior to language learning – 'learning about external reality hence is largely a matter of mediated experiences'.[53] This statement becomes objectionable, not in insisting upon mediation but on the *social nature* of mediation. The latter by *fiat* blocks off alternative mediators, such as nature itself, biological needs or transcendent divinity. Indeed, Giddens argues that we do not have non-social interaction with the *object world*, since this only comes to 'us' via emotions which are themselves constituted by social routines. Thus he maintains that these

acquired routines, and forms of mastery associated with them, in the early life of the human being, are much more than just modes of adjusting to a pre-given world of persons and objects. They are *constitutive of an emotional acceptance of the reality of the 'external world'* without which a secure human existence is impossible. Such acceptance is at the same time *the origin of self-identity through learning what is not-me*.[54] (my italics)

These are extremely sweeping claims and to sustain them Giddens has to demonstrate (a) that the self-subsistent natural world (whose reality is acknowledged) impinges upon us through social mediation alone, and (b) that possession of the 'I' differentiated from all that which is 'not-me' is socially and only socially conferred.

Similar to this treatment of the *object world*, the cursory and Durkheimian dismissal of our spirituality as something which 'religious cosmologies may play on'[55] *once* we have acquired the linguistic grasp of 'finitude'

[53] Giddens, *Modernity*, p. 43.
[54] Giddens, *Modernity*, p. 42.   [55] Giddens, *Modernity*, p. 50.

entails an unwarranted sociological judgement on *ir*reality of the divine which merits the same criticisms as Durkheim's claims to know better than the believer the (social) reality to which beliefs really relate. Since Giddens considers his approach to be explicitly Wittgensteinian, one wonders whether Wittgenstein believed he was merely recording the play of socially constructed religious cosmologies upon him when he kept his lengthy spiritual diary.

The purpose of denying other mediators of the world (seen and unseen) to us is to insist upon all reality being socially mediated. From there, he can immediately move to the statement that 'all existential problems are answered in a social context',[56] precisely because there are now no other sources from which people derive them. Consequently Mead's 'I' as the unsocialized and pre-social part of the individual, far from being taken as given, can now give way to the counter-claim that 'intersubjectivity does not derive from subjectivity, but the other way round'.[57]

There are two related difficulties with this view. The first is that as far as babies are concerned, the experience of others is the experience of *objects*. Persons impinge from the outside world, but in a manner initially undifferentiated from other objects, both animate the inanimate, which do likewise. Therefore, Giddens' assertions that 'trust in others is at the origins of the experience of the stable external world' or that 'self-consciousness has no primacy over awareness of others'[58] entail category mistakes. They involve the illegitimate imputation of adult concepts (distinguishing people from animals and objects) to a baby who has no ability yet to make such distinctions. Trust in others cannot be the source of experiencing the stable external world, since at the start of life other people can only be experienced as part and parcel of that external world.

The second difficulty arises directly from this, for if our earliest interaction can only be with an undifferentiated object/people world, then someone (a self) is again required to do the interacting and gradually to learn to do the differentiating. After all, when Laing gave currency to the notion of 'ontological security',[59] this referred directly to a self which knew itself to be continuous over time and space and therefore could either become secure, or was enough of a self to feel itself endangered in these crucial respects. In its security or insecurity, the 'I' necessarily had to be there as prior to either. Giddens wishes to reverse the sequence, but I have maintained this is impossible in principle and 'through practice' given that the notion of 'trust', which to him secures reality, depends on distinctions which have not yet been acquired by the baby.

[56] Giddens, *Modernity*, p. 55.
[57] Giddens, *Modernity*, p. 51.   [58] Giddens, *Modernity*, p. 51.
[59] R. D. Laing, *The Divided Self*, Penguin, Harmondsworth, 1965.

The only way in which Giddens can avoid these twin difficulties is essentially by making the subject/object distinction an inherited rather than acquired ability. Hence, 'unconscious sociality' is simply *posited* in the newborn. 'The *mutuality* with early caretakers *which basic trust presumes* is *a substantially unconscious sociality which precedes an 'I' and a 'me'*, and is *a prior basis* of any differentiation between the two'[60] (my italics). Thus he supplies, by imputing it to the inborn unconscious, that which practical consciousness cannot deliver through involvement in undifferentiated object/person interactions where *social* routines are indistinguishable from routine occurrences which may be wholly mechanical (incubator-reared babies). By theoretical *fiat* 'sociality' has been *imputed* to the newborn in order to underpin the theoretical assertions that (a) the self-subsistent natural world only impinges upon us through social mediation, and (b) that the distinction between 'I/not-me' is socially conferred. Yet these points require demonstration; they cannot be dealt with by imputation – of non-demonstrable properties.

This is particularly the case when such imputations not only lack a context of justification but are actually unnecessary. It is not only unnecessary, but so is its antithesis, the 'given' self. Instead it seems plausible that the biological urges of the baby organism interacting with the environment can supply the root solution to problem (b), the differentiation between the 'I/not-me', in the form of the 'realization' that 'I' cannot satisfy my own hunger and thirst, the use of all 'my' resources only witnessing to their intensification. In turn, if it is allowed contra-Giddens that the organism confronts the natural world through biological mediation, a different solution to problem (a) emerges, the reality of the external world initially being established through bodily testing of the food and drink coming to it from 'outside' which generates an 'inner' satisfaction only available from 'outsider' sources. In this case of course we do really encounter objects first (the teat rather than the hand which holds the bottle or even the breast which enfolds it). Such routine occurrences may indeed depend upon social routines (as with incubator feeding) but we do not illicitly have to impute awareness of this to the baby – plenty does go on behind their backs! Such testing in the *object* world (including people) and the naturalistic solution to the 'I/me' distinction, far from entailing solipsism is exactly what precludes it, for let 'me' believe that my cries produce food and 'I' will be denied this presumption often enough by reality.

Finally, this also answers the other basic problem in Giddens' discussion, namely *who* experiences the emotions attributed to them, in the form

---

[60] Giddens, *Modernity*, p. 38.

here of a self forged between the experiencing of its own organismic needs and inner inability to satisfy them. Equally, this provides a rudimentary asocial account of the origins of self-consciousness and reflexivity by reference to interactions with the environment, which demarcate the self from the world in terms of which can supply what. Giddens, instead, would have matters the other way around, with the self as socially derivative, namely it is only thanks to 'the sense of ontological security, that the individual has the experience of self in relation to a world of persons and objects organized cognitively through basic trust'.[61] Trust, to me would be a secondary and subsequent development, contingently dependent upon objective routines turning out to be really and reliably routine – and thus contingent upon the outside world being so, rather than a predicate for meeting stable external reality. After all, that interactional encounter cannot be postponed for one day for the newborn.

The positing of 'unconscious sociality' is used as the bridge by which Giddens hopes to get to linguistic dry land – a home ground where concepts can proliferate and the elisionist can make play of the fact that to be a person is not just to be a reflexive actor but entails the *idea* of being a person, which is socially mediated as can be demonstrated by cross-cultural variations in how persons are conceptualized. Although this is true (unique personhood being a Christian endowment), it still has to be admitted that 'the capacity to use "I" in shifting contexts characteristic of every known culture, is the most elemental feature of reflexive concep-tions of personhood'.[62] Yet if the 'I' is an exclusively social gift, the fact of its being 'elemental' should cause surprise, for it has certainly been the aim of strong collectivist regimes to replace it. Thus its resilience would have to be explained by the universal existence of countervailing forms of socially mediated individualism, whose very success would beg for explanation in its turn, probably returning us to its anchorage in the nexus between the biological organism and nature. Indeed it is where the latter is weakest (in Siamese twins) that selfhood seems most fragile, judging by reported comments about 'my other half' or 'having lost part of myself'. Interestingly, even where it is weakened, in identical twins reared together who according to Luria[63] mutually satisfy many of their require-ments, a high proportion of autonomous vocabulary develops whereas sociality (as indicated by language acquisition and learning) is actually retarded.

By theoretically construing all our relations with the world as socially mediated, Giddens seeks to block off the influence of anything non-social

[61] Giddens, *Modernity*, p. 45.   [62] Giddens, *Modernity*, p. 33.
[63] A. R. Luria and F. Y. Yudovich, *Speech and the Development of Mental Processes in the Child*, Staples, London, 1959.

in making us what we are. Thus his following definition of self-identity is overly social in three respects: 'Self-identity is not a distinct trait, or even a collection of traits, possessed by an individual. It is the *self as reflexively understood by the person in terms of her or his biography*.'[64]

The first objection is that our biographies have already been unduly restricted by Giddens: truncated to reflections on a personal history constituted entirely of social practices (unique to each person as a constellation, but uniquely social in composition). This seems to offer a neat solution to squaring the uniqueness of persons with the notion of all people as social beings. Yet can our biographies be edited in this way? If we are denied socially *un*mediated relations with objects, with nature and with the transcendental, we are surely being deprived of much that makes each of us what we are and different from others.

Secondly, were these interactions reallowed in our lives, then the sequence, as Giddens presents it is often reversed. If, for example, early biographical encounters with nature help to make us animal lovers or hydrophobics, then it cannot be denied that this is *prior* to the type of social practices which the person will later sift in order to seek or shun. After all it seems impossible to construe being bitten by a dog as a socially mediated experience (and of no avail to say this depends upon a society which keep domestic pets for the same goes for near-drowning incidents), yet this event may be responsible for the person later selecting those social practices to which they *will* expose themselves. In other words, interactions with the natural world, physiologically mediated and reflexively understood, can *shape* our social biographies, and not vice versa as Giddens suggests is always the case. Similarly, wordless spiritual experiences are prior to the quest for a mystical language which partially captures then, rather than being the products of its adepts. Why else search for them and how else be surprised that another (long dead and in another country) had found the words in which we recognize our own wordless experiences, especially when we can have no part in the historical context of religious practices in which such texts were produced – and often questioned!

What is at issue here is not a question of the most appropriate *psychological terminology* with which to describe 'personality' (talk of fixed traits is usually limited and often inappropriate), it is that 'personality' itself is denuded if presented in purely *sociological terms*. If it is, and if all socially unmediated interactions are disallowed, then the third objection is that we are denied any form of private life. Our reflexivity is thus confined by a social medium (language) and restricted to that which can

[64] Giddens, *Modernity*, p. 53.

be socially mediated to us. Yet, at the most mundane level, my reasons for taking a walk (private enjoyment) and my belief that I should do it more often (for more such enjoyment) need to draw upon no 'rules and resources', but could constitute a practice which becomes routine, without any call upon society. This then raises the question of why some of us become regular walkers (a personality difference between people which could remain even if the health and fitness campaigners advocated only indoor pools and ergo-machines). That such differences can be socially augmented or diminished is not at issue, for even here there are *prior* proclivities to contend with – why else are there reluctant joggers, those who cheat on their own work-outs and the drop-out from aerobics?

More seriously, *all* our loving, feeling, praying, dreaming and reflecting cease being part of our private lives and become facets of our social selves. Maintain otherwise and the Elisionist promptly declares a foul for supporting 'private language', since all such activities are held to depend upon socio-linguistic mediation. Basically, I have never been convinced that this is foul play. If we reintroduce physiological interaction with nature, then there seems nothing objectionable about the notion of asocial rules being forged in this process. Instead, repeated experiences of falling through thin ice, with physically unpleasant consequences, could lead to the personal 'formulation' of a rule about prior testing. Obedience to the rule is umpired by natural reality, which, being incapable of abrogating its own laws, leads to cracked ice and re-dunking, thus physically reinforcing the advisability of rule-keeping. However, just as the defence of personal psychology did not turn upon defending the traditional terminology of traits and attributes, neither does the defence of private life ultimately rest upon the possibility of private language. It is perfectly possible to grant the universal use of public language for the *expression* of private experience, without accepting that the feelings, urges or beliefs which people express in it are social rather than personal.

The Elisionist response is to deny that we are actually talking of two things, inner projects and outer expressions. In other words, inseparability, which I am challenging, is again brought in to rescue the enterprise. Thus, Giddens wants to insist that 'action is a continuous flow, a process which cannot be broken down into reasons, motives, intentions etc., to be treated as separate entities'.[65] This is consistent with the flow being made up of nothing but social practices: to treat motivation, affectivity or intentionality separately would be to acknowledge a stratum of individual psychology whose partial independence or temporal priority *is* separable and therefore inconsistent. Yet can this be avoided by Elisionists since

---

[65] Craib, *Giddens*, p. 35.

they too must provide an account of where desires and beliefs, necessary for intentional action, come from?

Certain psychologists have advanced an account of intentionality which is explicitly consonant with structuration theory. These seek to dispense with the notion that actions require mediation by some 'inner' reference ('ideas', 'images', 'representations') which indicate desired end states in the 'outer' world. Instead 'the concept of duality of structure suggests something quite different. To be appropriate to its circumstances, an action need not be guided by an 'inner' representation of the 'outer' circumstances at all . . . an action can be informed not so much by factors present in the source from which it issues, as by the context *into* which it is directed'.[66] Intention formation thus becomes a *process* of the progressive social specification of biological tendencies. Nothing else intervenes between the two (or alongside them) for the interactional process is *interpersonal* and the 'context' is therefore exclusively *social*. Thus 'motives, intentions, sentiments are not inner things represented in outer behaviour, but are in the mediatory activity (joint action) going on between individuals . . . As such, one might say, motives etc. exists less 'in' us than in the institutions between us.'[67] Again, individual psychology is lost because the social context alone is charged with the canalization of biology. Yet the social context can only be elevated to this formative role on the premiss that there are not socially unmediated interchanges fostering inner motive formation. Since this is precisely what is at issue, another re-statement of it does not advance the Elisionists' case.

Furthermore, something extra is now being smuggled in through the notion of an action/intention being 'appropriate to its circumstances' (above), namely society as the only arbitrator of appropriateness, since there is no longer a robust enough self to sustain an inner vision which could redefine what s/he deems appropriate. The 'oversocial' view is not identical with the 'over-socialized' view of people, but the former is in permanent danger of slippage towards the latter. Within Elisionist thought, the frail barrier is the allowance made for personal permutations on rules *within a* context, where innovativeness can be (re)construed as a particular permutation which is contextually given an encore.

It is too frail because from where, other than the inner vision (be it sacrificial or sadistic) do the 'inappropriate' motives of the martyr or the mass murderer originate? The only two sources left to the Elisionist are 'inadequate socialization' or 'bad genes'. Similarly, if motives etc. exist less 'in' us than in the institutions between us, how can individual

[66] John Shotter, 'Duality of structure and intentionality in an ecological psychology', *Journal for the Study of Social Behaviour*, 1983, 13: 19–20.
[67] Shotter, 'Duality', p. 39.

decisions about appropriate action collide with institutional definitions, as they often do ? If inner visions cannot be conceived within our private lives, then how can those human intentions which repulse their social context be construed as being 'specified' within it? The fact that it can be refused (the hermit), reviled (the prophet), re-visioned (the idealist) or rejected (the recidivist) are forms of repudiation too varied to be explained by reaction formation. Presumably we would be invited to undertake a detailed socio-biographical investigation of such cases, which not only commits us in advance to social determinism but also only (potentially) answers the question of *who* becomes different. It is mute about the *content* of their differences: unable to explain why some people seek to replace societies' rules and unwilling to allow that this originates in people themselves, from their own personality characteristics, forged in the space *between* biology and society – or *between* divinity and humanity.

Yet, in Elisionist thought personality properties are nullified. Instead, 'there need be no fundamental elements at all, only principles distinguishing one activity from another, each existing in terms of its difference from the others – it is the dance not the dancers which is important'.[68] Yet, the objection remains that a 'self' is still needed as a *focus* for such principles and that an 'over-social' self remains inadequate as a *locus* of their origins. This under-stratified view of persons turns out to be a danse macabre for the 'self' who is more than his biology and irreducible to her sociality.

The under-stratified view of the actor

Despite the much vaunted role of active agents and society as their skilled accomplishment, actors themselves are the casualties of an approach which de-centres the subject by truncating their biographies and giving priority to history and not its makers. What makes actors act has now become an urgent question because, as was seen in the last section, the answer cannot ever be given in terms of people themselves, who have neither the personal resources to pursue their own aims nor the capacity to find reasons good if they are not in social currency. In terms of the long-standing debate between neo-Humeans and neo-Kantians, the 'social self' of the Elisionists has been deprived of 'internal' reasons (because, stripped of personality as other than a social gift, actors have no 'inner passions' which reason can ingeniously service); equally they have been denied a robust enough self which could heed the 'stern voice of duty' if this meant setting a flint face against routine social practice. Effectively

---

[68] Shotter, 'Duality', p. 41

this means that the Elisionists' actor can only be moved by reasons *appropriated* from society,[69] which is of course implicit when they state the necessity of actively drawing upon structural properties (rules and resources) in order to act at all.

We have already examined the impoverished view of persons which results from denying them *their* 'passions' (or, in Bernard Williams' terms,[70] from confining them to a socially constructed subjective mental set). Now we need to demonstrate how the actor becomes poorer still in motivational sources because a whole tract of 'external reasons', which can be considered as levers to action, are denied existence in the ontology of praxis, namely those structural constraints and enablements which supply reasons for different courses of action amongst different categories of actors yet are not dependent upon actors' knowledge of them.[71] These work through the situations in which people find themselves (the unacknowledged conditions of action) and the objective bonuses and penalties which they associate with different courses of action amongst those differently placed. Certainly, these compel no one, but they do set a premium on defending vested interests and a price on going against them. These may be collected or paid uncomprehendingly, though reflective actors can discern them and then morally decide whether to promote or discount them. Here motivation is shaped by/between circumstances independent of current actors (since they pre-date them) and by selves strong enough to arbitrate upon them; both elements being absent in Elisionist accounts.

What is crucial here is that central conflationists sever human motivation from a prior distribution of interests vested in social positions which antedate their holders, because the idea that interests are built into positions *by* the relationship of that position to others, would be to give structure an unacceptable independence from social practices held to be constitutive of it. Hence, Giddens 'speaks of structure as constraining and enabling, but never of it motivating'.[72] When Realists speak in these terms they are talking of conditional influences, not determinants of action, i.e. the objective costs and benefits mentioned above which constitute reasons for action, yet have to be weighed by actors. Elisionists, who instead seek to *transcend* the dualism between voluntarism and determinism are left with the question, 'what leads someone to do one thing rather than another?' If individual personality cannot be invoked within the ontology

---

[69] For an extended discussion of three categories of reasons which move agents to act, see Rosemary Watson, 'Reasons as causes', unpublished PhD thesis, University of Warwick, 1993.

[70] Bernard Williams, 'Internal and external reasons', in his *Moral Luck*, Cambridge University Press, Cambridge, 1981.   [71] See Watson, 'Reasons as causes.

[72] Porpora, 'Four concepts of social structure', p. 208.

of praxis, then the need to allow for structural influences is even more pressing.

Instead, we are offered a peculiarly one-dimensional view of 'actors' who differ from one another (or in particular situations) only by virtue of their knowledgeability, including tacit skills. That is to say, agents have different degrees of 'discursive penetration', 'practical knowledge' or 'unconscious awareness' of their situations which in turn affect their social practices. The standard objection here, which is well founded, is that 'whilst it may be true that lay actors in the routine vicissitudes of social life must be knowledgeable in some, particularly the practical sense . . . this does not require us to say that they are all equally knowledgeable (in whatever sense), nor, more importantly, does it require us to say that such knowledge enables lay actors to control or produce the conditions of their existence'.[73]

The question being posed here is 'what accounts for differential knowledgeability?', especially if the central conflationist will not accept an answer given in structural terms. It is a good question and a valid point that knowledge does not yield control over social conditions. However this argument can be pushed further to ask why, if knowledge is all that differentiates between people, is knowledge itself considered to be sufficient to account for differences in human motivation?

Usually action is considered to derive from a desire plus a belief. One has both to want something and believe one knows how to attain/obtain it in order to act to that end. Knowledge alone is no spur to action: to know the train times to Scotland and to have the price of a ticket will not find me there without some desire, motive or reason for going. Central conflationism is mute on desires: they can have no external locus, that is finding their promptings in structured positions, in vested interests or induced wants and they can have no internal locus in psychological proclivities.

An account of desire framed exclusively in terms of social practices would seem to face two intractable difficulties. Firstly, how to account for regularities in the action patterns of those similarly positioned when this cannot be explained by reference to social rules (e.g. why is there educational discrimination in terms of class, gender and ethnicity, as reflected in action patterns like early leaving with low qualifications, when this actually traduces the educational rules?). Giddens' approving citation of Willis' *Learning to Labour*,[74] showing the 'lads' appropriating their own self-defeating class practices, only begs the structural question of why the cards are pre-stacked against such practices. Secondly, why if

---

[73] Layder, *Structure*, p. 69.
[74] Paul Willis, *Learning to Labour*, Saxon House, Farnborough, Hants, 1977.

every action is potentially transformative, do some settle for routine reproduction whilst others pursue change? Talk of constraint and enablement needs something to talk about; namely desires which are frustrated and wants which are facilitated, yet we find no source of these within an ontology of praxis. In telling us that actors have to invoke rules and resources to engage in action, yet are never determined in how these are invoked since they could 'always have done otherwise', central conflation leaves us with three perennial questions: Wittgenstein's problem, 'where do rules come from', Winch's problem 'how do rules change' and, above all, Weber's pre-occupation with 'why are things so, and not otherwise?'.

Without a stratified view of agency which allows of prior structural conditioning *and* individual personality differences, we lack an account of *both* the regular patterning of wants in different parts of society *and* of the personal differences which do indeed make actions something quite different from mechanical responses to hydraulic pressures. It was the latter from which the Elisionist sought to escape through the image of endlessly variegated permutations upon rules and resources. Yet without any external (structural) spur to action or any internal (psychological) prompting, 'social practices' appear random in origin and kaleidoscopic in result. Theories based upon central conflation may be able to account for the fact that actors know how to go on, but what is it that keeps them going?

The need for analytical dualism

In the last sections I have tried to establish two crucial points: (1) That structure cannot be rendered in terms of 'social practices', without any remainder, save their material element. In other words structures cannot be adequately conceptualized as *nothing but* part of the parcel that is 'social practices', for their relatively autonomous powers, the irreducibility of their influence and their pre-existence means they cannot be accommodated within a homogeneous ontology of praxis, but need to be acknowledged as constituting a different stratum of social reality. (2) That agents cannot be construed in terms of 'social practices' without remainder, save their biological element. In other words, people cannot be adequately conceptualized as *nothing but* the other part of the parcel making up 'social practices', for again the relatively autonomous psychological properties of individuals, the impossibility of deriving their influence from practices yet their indispensability in accounting for praxis, all point to the necessity of conceding that social reality is further stratified and contains a psychological stratum which is heterogeneous to the practical doings of actors in their everyday social lives.

Taken together these fundamental criticisms of central conflation have two implications. The first is negative, namely that since the two 'remainders', i.e. 'structural characteristics' and 'psychological characteristics' defy compression into 'social practices' then the elisionary enterprise fails. Social reality cannot be encompassed by an ontology of practice which negates important strata of social reality. Theories based upon central conflation will be deficient precisely because of these two missing 'remainders', and most of the critiques to which they have been subjected refer to one or other of these lost dimensions. Ultimately they relate to the lack of ontological depth which is the central fallacy of elisionist thinking about society.

If the first implication was a rejection of the 'duality' approach, the second advances the case for putting 'analytical dualism' in its place. If social reality is indeed made up of different strata, each with heterogeneous properties, then it becomes imperative to examine the interplay between them. Far from it sufficing to lay the foundations of theory 'at the intersection' between action and organization, that is, in social practices, an adequate social theory is one which sees this intersection as leaving far too much out of account, and bases its account on an interplay between real agents and real structures without conflating them. For 'these lost dimensions point not only to the existence of external social structures but also to the existence of internal psychological structures of much more complexity and ambiguity and to more complex relationships between the two than is allowed for in structuration theory',[75] Theorizing about this complexity turns then upon examining *the relationship* between 'structure' and 'agency' which central conflation precludes by eliding them.

What it points to is an approach explicitly based upon analytical dualism, where structure and agency are interrelated but not viewed as mutually constitutive since each possesses emergent properties particular to that level. The task of social theory, being

to explore the space between the differential distribution of options, on the one hand, and the wants and needs of different kinds and different categories of individuals, on the other, is to examine the degrees of freedom and constraint which are entailed by social structure. Such an analysis would show that, while structure and agency are not antinomies, nevertheless they are not as complementary and mutually supporting as Giddens would like us to believe.[76]

Analytical dualism is a method for examining the interplay between these strata; it is analytical precisely because the two are interdependent but it is dualistic because each stratum is held to have its own emergent

[75] Craib, *Giddens*, p. 166.   [76] Thompson, 'Structuration', p. 74.

properties. Their denial by elisionists produces central conflation in social theory. The next chapter seeks to show the difference between social theorizing which is non-conflationary rather than conflationist, because based upon emergence rather than elision and therefore one which works in terms of analytical dualism rather than 'duality'. It does this by contrasting structuration theory with social realism and its methodological accompaniment the morphogenetic/static approach.

5   Realism and morphogenesis

Social theory has to be useful and usable: it is not an end in itself. The vexatious fact of society has to be tackled *in* theory and *for* practice. These two tasks cannot be separated, for were practical utility to be the sole criterion we would commit ourselves to instrumentalism – to working with theoretically ungrounded rules of thumb. Conversely, a purely theoretical taming of the vexing beast may give a warm inner glow of ontological rectitude but is cold comfort to practical social analysts. They want a user-friendly tool kit and although it cannot come pocket-sized with an easy reference manual, customer services have every right to complain when handed an unwieldy device without any instructions on the assumption that if they handle it sufficiently this will somehow sensitize them to something.

Yet, because social theorists have fought shy of 'emergence' we are very short indeed of concrete exemplars, that is of ways of approaching the vexatious fact of society which are based four-square upon the acknowledgement of its emergent properties. Instead, there is a glaring absence of bold social theories which uncompromisingly make 'emergence' their central tenet. With the exception of Lockwood's[1] seminal though incomplete attempt to beat a pathway, others have laid a few more paving stones before losing their nerve and heading back for shelter in either the Individualist or the Holist camps. The former was the case with Buckley, who having launched the notion of morphogenetic/morphostatic processes of structural development then withdrew their ontological underpinnings, by construing emergent properties as heuristic devices: 'the "structure" is an abstract construct, not something distinct from the ongoing interactive process but rather a temporary, accommodative representation of it at any one time'.[2]

Conversely, Blau,[3] after painstakingly working on the derivation of

---

[1] David Lockwood, 'Social integration and system integration', in G. K. Zollschan and H. W. Hirsch (eds.), *Explorations in Social Change*, Houghton Mifflin, Boston, 1964.
[2] Walter Buckley, *Sociology and Modern Systems Theory*, Prentice Hall, New Jersey, 1967.
[3] Peter Blau, *Exchange and Power in Social Life*, Wiley, New York, 1964.

complex social properties from simpler forms of exchange, seems to have become absorbed by the holistic impact of the former on the latter rather than remaining exercised by their interplay. Full-blooded emergentist theories are hard to find because their prototypes failed to negotiate a passage between Individualism and Holism without coming to grief on one or the other.

Forewarned that the signposts reading 'reductionism' and 'reification' are roads to hell paved with bad conceptualizations, no doubt central conflation promises ontological security to more and more theorists. Yet theirs is a very pharisaical self-satisfaction. They expect thanks for not being guilty of grasping at atomism, or unjustly privileging society or the individual, or of whoring with social facts. They congratulate themselves on their theoretical abstemiousness in dieting only on areduction and on the tithes of hard syncretic endeavour it has taken to consolidate their position. Then they compare themselves favourably with those of us who freely confess that theory is in a mess, that we can point to few worthwhile offerings – but believe the only thing to do is to admit it, confront it, and hope to do something about it.

Consequently, Bhaskar's work is of considerable interest since his ontological realism, premissed explicitly upon emergence, is used to develop the framework of a social theory which seems set fair to navigate a passage between Individualism and Holism. Although a 'realist metatheory is however clearly compatible with a wide variety of theoretical and methodological approaches'[4] and Bhaskar's philosophical realism is therefore a general platform, capable of underpining various social theories (though incompatible with any form of downwards or upwards conflationism because their epiphenomenalism nullifies the stratified nature of social reality), his Transformational Model of Social Action (TMSA) can claim to be a social theory in its own right. Of course it is incomplete (taking on the philosophical under-labouring doesn't mean finishing the job for us), but this very incompleteness leaves room for exploring whether it can be complemented and supplemented by the morphogenetic/static approach. (Henceforth this is referred to as M/M).

Although the answer will be in the affirmative, there are certain qualifications to be made, for this is what the whole business of clambering on theoretical shoulders is all about. Moreover there are some crucial clarifications and disassociations which also have to be established. In particular it is undeniable that many commentators (and, at times and with caveats, Bhaskar himself) have noted affinities between TMSA and

---

[4] William Outhwaite, 'Realism, naturalism and social behaviour', *Journal for the Theory of Social Behaviour*, 1990, 20: 4, p. 366.

central conflation in the form of Giddens' structuration theory. Thus before being able to build upon the affinities between TMSA and the morphogenetic approach, because of their common grounding in realism, it is necessary to provide a convincing demonstration that Bhaskar's model contains basic assumptions which prevent it from being swept into the central conflation camp. Specifically, these concern emergence itself; fundamental to realism but fundamentally unacceptable to central conflationists. Certainly, there was a moment when the siren call of mutual constitution proved strong, indeed there are passages of dalliance with the sirens, but the emergentist groundings of TMSA were too robust for the spell to last. Ulysses made his getaway and might not have paused at all had there been other obvious ports of sociological call at the time. Equally, had there been no elective affinity between Emergentists and Elisionists, based on their common rejection of the terms of the Holist/Individualist debate, there would not have been the inclination to think that the enemy of one's enemy must be a friend. Thus some ground clearing is needed to identify where the positive affinities lie between three social theories which are equally negative about the terms in which the old debate was conducted.

Morphogenesis, structuration and the transformational model of social action

To begin with, it seems as though the objective and approach of the TMSA and M/M approaches are very close indeed. In *The Possibility of Naturalism*, Bhaskar drafts what can be called a 6-point Charter, which becomes embodied in his TMSA.

I argue that societies are irreducible to people and ... sketch a model of their connection. (1)

I argue that social forms are a necessary condition for any intentional act, (2)

that their *pre-existence* establishes their *autonomy* as possible objects of investigation and that (3)

their *causal power* establishes their reality (4)

The pre-existence of social forms will be seen to entail a transformational model of social activity ... (5)

the causal power of social forms is mediated through human agency (6)[5] (my notations)

---

[5] Roy Bhaskar, *The Possibility of Naturalism*, Harvester Wheatsheaf, Hemel Hempstead, 1989, pp. 25–6.

Point (1), which talks of the need for a model which *connects* structure and agency resonates well with the aim of the M/M approach which is to link the two rather than to sink the differences between them. Nevertheless, it is far from decisive. After all, structuration theory does not argue that societies are reducible to people; there are structural properties even if these are held to require human instantiation and the concept of 'modalities' is advanced to account for their interconnection. Fifteen:all to analytical dualism and the duality of structure. Point 2, sees structuration edging ahead since there structural properties are the very medium of social action, whereas M/M has serious reservations about social forms being a necessary condition for *any* intentional act, seeing the break with nature as too great and arguing that natural interaction can supply the necessary and sufficient conditions for intentionality. This point has already been defended in the last chapter and the reader must adjudicate, but in any case it leaves the score at 30:15 to structuration.

Point (3), insisting upon the *pre-existence* and *autonomy* of social forms (and both are crucial) marks a real turn of the tide. Temporality is integral to the M/M approach and contained in its first axiom 'that structure necessarily predates the action(s) which transform it'. Because of this there is always a Phase 1 in any sociological enquiry where it

is assumed that some features of social structure and culture are strategically important and enduring and that they provide limits within which particular social situations can occur. On this assumption the action approach can help to explain the nature of the situations and how they affect conduct. It does not explain the social structure and culture as such, except by lending itself to a developmental enquiry which must start from some previous point at which structural and cultural elements are treated as given.[6]

Autonomy is also temporal (and temporary) in the joint senses that such structural properties were neither the creation of contemporary actors nor are ontologically reducible to 'material existents' (raw resources) and dependent upon current acts of human instantiation (rule governed) for all their current effects. These effects do produce a 'visible pattern', the well-known detectable regularities in human interaction which are never a matter of social hydraulics in the M/M approach. Yet this is very different from Giddens's assertion that 'social systems only exist through their continuous structuration in the course of time'.[7] Pre-existence and autonomy denote *discontinuities* in the structuring/restructuring process which can only be grasped by making analytical distinctions between the 'before' (Phase 1), the 'during' (Phase 2) and the 'after' (Phase 3), none of

[6] Percy S. Cohen, *Modern Social Theory*, Heinemann, London, 1968, p. 93.
[7] Anthony Giddens, *Central Problems in Social Theory*, Macmillan, London, 1979, p. 217.

which is to deny the necessary continuity of human activity for the endurance of all things social.

Here Bhaskar is equally uncompromising about the need for examining a 'before': 'society pre-exists the individual'.[8] The church-goer or language user finds their beliefs or language *ready made at birth*, so 'people do not create society. For it always pre-exists them ... Social structure ... is always *already made*'. Consequently, Bhaskar's own comment upon Giddens is that he himself is 'inclined to give structures (conceived as transfactually efficacious) a stronger ontological grounding and to place more emphasis on the pre-existence of social forms'.[9] Because the 'relations into which people enter pre-exist the individuals who enter into them, and whose activity reproduces or transforms them; so they are themselves structures'.[10] They are structures by virtue of being emergent properties which are irreducible to the doings of contemporary actors, yet derive from the historical actions which generated them, thus creating the context for current agency. This brings the score to 30:all.

Now, it follows for Bhaskar that if this is the case, then what I term central conflation 'must be corrected in a fundamental way'[11] and the other forms of conflation rejected. The three models which Bhaskar criticizes correspond respectively to what I have called upwards, downwards and central conflation. The critique of the three is identical. Thus 'on Model 1 there are actions but no conditions; on Model II conditions but no actions; on Model III no distinction between the two'.[12] The distinction is indispensable, not just because of their pre-existence and autonomy but because relational properties have causal powers (Point 4), though not ones which work in a naturalistic manner (on which more later, especially in chapter 7, for this is where M/M has much to add). If prior emergent properties really condition subsequent interaction, then their reality cannot be withdrawn by reducing them, as Giddens does to 'memory traces' which falls back onto the 'personalization' strategy of Individualism. This is a case of the 'desperate incorporation' of the vexingly social into seemingly more tractable individual terms; as Gellner[13] caricatured it, 'Algy met a bear, the bear was bulgy, the bulge was Algy ... the individual may consume what Durkheim and others have called social facts, but he will bulge most uncomfortably, and Algy will still be there ... I suspect that actual investigators will often, though

[8] Roy Bhaskar, *Reclaiming Reality*, Verso, London, 1989, p. 77.
[9] Roy Bhaskar, 'Beef, structure and place: notes from a critical naturalist perspective', *Journal for the Study of Social Behaviour*, 1983, 13, p. 85.
[10] Bhaskar, *Reclaiming Reality*, p. 4.
[11] Bhaskar, *Reclaiming Reality*, p. 76   [12] Bhaskar, *Reclaiming Reality*, p. 77.
[13] Ernest Gellner, 'Explanations in history', in John O'Neill (ed.), *Modes of Individualism and Collectivism*, Heinemann, London, 1973, p. 262.

perhaps not always, prefer to have Algy outside the bear.' Uncomfortably mutually constituted as they now are, there is no question of examining their interplay or talking about their independent causal powers. Conditions and actions have to be examinable separately in order *to* talk about conditioned action. The real literacy levels in Castro's example (chapter 3) exert their effects even were there complete Cuban amnesia about their origins or the nature of this distribution. Morphogenesis is now leading 40:30.

Thus in *making* this temporal distinction, Bhaskar employs the image of a sculptor at work fashioning a product out of existing materials using the tools available. The M/M approach would merely add that some materials are more resistant than others, that tools vary in their adequacy and that the sociological identification of such differences is indispensable. What this is indispensable to is the key question, 'when are we going to get transformation rather than reproduction, or vice versa'?

Morphogenesis and morphostasis are very close indeed to the notions of transformation and reproduction, and all four terms only make sense as processes which come 'after' something which existed 'before' them. Thus for social structure 'it is no longer true to say that human *agents* create it. Rather we must say; they *reproduce* or *transform* it . That is to say, if society is already made, then any concrete human praxis . . . can only modify it: and the totality of such acts *sustain or change it*.'[14] Again Bhaskar is driven to part company with Giddens because of the latter's restricted use of the present tense alone. Thus,

it is because the social structure is always *given*, from the perspective of intentional human agency, that I prefer to talk of reproduction and transformation rather than of structuration as Giddens does (though I believe our conceptions are very close). For me 'structuration' still retains voluntaristic connotations – social practice is always, so to speak, *restructuration*.[15]

In my own terms, morphogenesis is always a transformation of morphostasis. Thus Bhaskar's fifth point, namely, that the 'pre-existence of social forms will be seen to entail a *transformational* model of social activity', also seems to represent game point. Since the TMSA has a 'before' (pre-existing social forms), a 'during' (the process of transformation itself) and an 'after' (the transformed, since social structures are only relatively enduring), the same goes to Morphogenesis and is clinched because TMSA must also see its last phase as being the start of a new cycle. As Bhaskar notes, emergence implies 'a reconstruction of the historical processes of their formation out of 'simpler' things'.[16] Logically

---

[14] Bhaskar, *Naturalism*, pp. 33–4
[15] Bhaskar, 'Beef', p. 85.   [16] Bhaskar, *Reclaiming Reality*, p. 80.

it follows that we can also theorize about the ongoing emergence of more complex things provided we see these as spaced out over time, clearly differentiate between antecedence and consequence in this succession, and above all retain the demarcation between pre-existing conditions and current actions.

The sting is in the tail, in the very last clause. The M/M approach insists upon the need to sustain an analytical distinction between structure and agency if a transformational model is to prove workable, that is to do the work which practising social analysts need it to do. The reason why this is not game, set and a rather dreary match to morphogenesis is that Bhaskar displays some qualms about adopting the analytical dualism between the two upon which the workability of his TMSA depends. The vexatiously unique character of the social makes many of Giddens's ways of grasping it particularly appealing. This is the seductiveness of central conflation and it signals the start of another game.

The siren call of inseparability

The peculiarity of all things social is that they are activity dependent. Without human activity nothing in society could have its genesis, continuation, or undergo change. On this we can all agree: unlike nature, social reality is not self-subsistent. This is its ontological oddity and what makes it peculiarly vexatious to tackle. However the problem becomes less vexing if we concentrate steadily on the question 'specifically whose activities are responsible for what and when?' In the past debate and in the present vacillations we are examining, it seems that the root of confusion lies in an over precipitous and quite unnecessary leap from the truistic proposition 'No people: no society' to the highly questionable assertion, 'this society; because of these people here present'. The leap has its attractions when we think in the most general terms about the historical panorama of 'the societal', for how could this have kept going from age to age without the continuous sustaining activities of succeeding generations of actors and how, in any particular age, can its on-going be divorced from the myriad of meanings and praxes without whose interweaving there would be no social fabric? The attraction does depend, however, upon the powerful imagery of the 'seamless web', an endless bale of material unrolling through time, without break or cut; a tissue which at any point in time can only be grasped in its totality, for it has no distinct parts since each is woven into the rest, so at most it has a pattern – albeit a changing one which is always the product of the weaving and inseparable from the woven.

Powerful images are rarely dimmed by counter-arguments, this is the wrong medicine for the bedazzled, so we have to deal (initially) in their own currency. Let us counterpoise a variant image in the same terms; society as a garment handed down through the human family, showing the wear and tear accumulated on the way, the patching and over-patching, the letting out and taking in done for different purposes, the refurbishing performed at different times, until the current garment now contains precious little of the original material. It has been completely re-fashioned (which brings us back to Bhaskar's sculptor) until perhaps the original only figures as 'something old' in a new wedding outfit. Why does this help? Because this image points up disjunctions, the ability to inspect different parts, the purposes and times at which they were introduced, by whom, and how these were treated by the next recipient. This is precisely how I propose treating social structures and the relations between them and human activities. Giddens remains rivetted by the first image and Bhaskar too is still impressed. What is wrong with it is what it fosters in theorization.

To start with we all endorse the obvious; 'No people; no society'. Furthermore, those we are considering would also concur that 'there is an ontological hiatus between society and people',[17] the properties possessed by the former may be very different from those possessed by the latter, upon whose activities the first depend. Agreement might just stretch as far as Bhaskar's statement that 'People and society are not ... related 'dialectically. They do not constitute two moments of the same process. Rather they refer to radically different things.'[18] However, it is at this point that Giddens makes the leap to 'this society because of these people here present'. Structural properties only become real (as opposed to having a virtual material existence) when instantiated by actors, instantia-tion therefore becoming dependent upon current activities which, in turn, depend upon the knowledgeability of contemporary agents about what they are doing. Bhaskar is tempted to make the same leap and for the same underlying reason, namely that in society we are not dealing with a self-subsistent reality. Dwelling upon this he advances three propositions about its distinctive nature, which if true would indeed land him on the side of conflationism. The first two which point to the activity-depen-dence and concept-dependence of social structure are indeed very close to Giddens' stance on society's constitution in the activities of highly knowledgeable human agents, as Outhwaite has noted.[19] I want to argue that the first two propositions do not work, that Bhaskar has recognized

[17] Bhaskar, *Nuturalism*, p. 37.   [18] Bhaskar, *Reclaiming Reality*, p. 76.
[19] William Outhwaite, 'Agency and structure', in J. Clarke, C. Modgil and S. Modgil (eds.), *Anthony Giddens: Consensus and Controversy*, Falmer, Basingstoke, 1990, p. 70.

this and that his proposition three (the effects of social structures are only operative through human activity) eventually persuades him not to jump at all.

Proposition 1, is that social structures, 'unlike natural mechanisms ... only exist in virtue of the activities they govern, and cannot be identified independently of them'.[20] As Benton[21] has argued persuasively, if the operative word is 'govern', then the statement cannot be upheld. On Bhaskar's own argument, power for example, may exist unexercised thus governing nothing at all at the present time. Benton however, left a loophole for activity-dependence, through allowing for those activities necessary to sustain the *potential* for governance. Thus, in the case of a State, its full coercive power may remain unexercised but actions such as the (current) raising of taxes and armies may well be necessary for it to retain its potential power of coercion. Bhaskar accepts the criticism and grasps the loophole. Thus to him

a structure of power may be reproduced without being exercised and exercised in the absence of any observable conflict ... so long as it is sustained by human practice – the practices which reproduce or potentially transform it. In this sense the thesis of activity-dependence of social structures must be affirmed. Social structures exist materially and are carried or transported from one time-space location to another only or in virtue of human praxis.[22]

This could indeed have been written by Giddens and to be fair, it works for some aspects of social structure. The really crucial point is that it does not work for all. If we think of a demographic structure, this might appear activity-dependent – it goes on being structured the way it is if people literally go on reproducing and not reproducing in a particular pattern. Yet suppose all activities were harnessed to transforming it, the (top-heavy or whatever) structure would not disappear for several generations. Whilst it endures, whose activities are sustaining it? Those who constitute it just by being alive? Certainly, but this is simply the 'no-people: no demography' truism, for it was not *their* intention to structure it that way nor the unintended consequence of *their* actions, nor the intentionality of contemporary agents for we have presumed they all seek its transformation. *Here the activity-dependence of such structures can be affirmed in only one acceptable way: by reference to the activities of the long dead.* This demographic structure is not due to the people here present in anything other than the truistic sense. We are dealing with a relatively enduring

[20] Bhaskar, *Reclaiming Reality*, p. 78.
[21] Ted Benton, 'Realism and social science: some comments on Roy Bhaskar's *The Possibility of Naturalism*', *Radical Philosophy*, 1981, 27, p. 17.
[22] Bhaskar, *Naturalism*, p. 174.

emergent property, (proportional relations between age cohorts are internal and necessary to a top heavy demographic structure) which temporarily proves resistant to concerted activities to transform it.

How much of a maverick is this example? Not one at all, for there are at least three classes of properties which work in identical fashion. To begin with, the same argument can be used of many other levels and distributions (such as capital), though not all (such as eye colour). Secondly, and especially where emergent properties are those involving human relations with nature (from dust-bowl effects and green-house effects, through the consequences of extinction of species and exhaustion of minerals, to pollution and puncturing the ozone layer), there seems to be a growing fund of properties *upon which* the future *of* human activity depends, which may be irreversible in the present yet some of which require no continued reproduction, for past activities have made them permanent or chronic features of contemporary life. It is unnecessary to be bright Red or Green to acknowledge that our unfriendly relations with nature have consequences which are visited on the heads of subsequent generations, some of which they strive not to reproduce and others which they are incapable of transforming. Instead they suffer if they must and circumvent if they can – but both activities are constrained by properties and circumstances which are not of their making.

In case the above examples look as though they have been extracted from close to the point where Giddens freely grants them the status of 'material existents', or where others might object that the property which is not activity dependent in the present consists in physical laws which were triggered by past actions, we can point to another huge area replete with properties immune from such criticisms. If we think of culture then all knowledge was certainly activity dependent for its genesis and elaboration. Nevertheless, once recorded (chiselled into runes or gathering dust in the British Museum), it constitutes knowledge without a current knowing subject. It is knowledge because it retains the dispositional character to be understood, though it persists unrecognized, sustaining potential powers (of contradiction and complementarity with other cultural items) which remain unexercised. Ontologically it exists and if the theory it states is true, if the technique is describes works, or if the belief it articulates is justifiable, these remain the case quite independently of current actors knowing it, using it or believing it. We know that they are real by virtue of their releasable effects, because the old recipe, if workable, will still work if tried a hundred years later when someone rediscovers it and has the motive to try it. In this case they activate it which is very different from saying that they instantiate it, for the item in question does not *become* real, true or useful simply because someone tries it out. The significance of a Cultural System which exists (is existentially independent of knowledge about it) yet has crucial causal relations with Socio-Cultural level, which is indeed activity dependent, will be explored much further in chapter 7. Emergent cultural properties have been introduced at this point merely as another large category of the social which is ontologically independent from the activities of those people here present.

Thus, where emergent properties are concerned, the preceding arguments show that it is an *empirical question* whether their activity-dependence is *present tense or past tense*. Each and every instance of the latter makes the leap to 'this society because of these people here present' entirely unjustified.

Bhaskar's second thesis about the distinctive oddity of social structures is that 'they do not exist independently of the conceptions that the agents have of what they are doing in their activities'.[23] Again this is very close to Giddens' assertions about actors being very knowledgeable indeed about their social doings, that little goes on behind their backs, and that society depends upon their skilled performances. Bhaskar's own thesis is open to three interpretations. Firstly is he asserting that social structures only exist because agents have *some* conception of what they are doing? As Benton rightly points out this has no bite whatsoever: 'it seems to me hard to sustain the concept of an agent at all without the notion of conceptualization of activity, so that insofar as human agents are a necessary condition for the existence of social structure (and this is hardly disputable) then the thesis is sustained'.[24] It is, but what is sustained here is simply the truistic 'no people; no society'. Secondly then, is the thesis of concept-dependence that the existence of social structures depends upon agents having the *particular* conceptions they do of what they are doing? Whilst a few relational properties are of this kind – friendship, loyalty, and commitment, many other structural relations are sustained by law or coercion, censorship or ideological manipulation, and sanctioning processes which maintain the relational property precisely by overriding the diversity (and conflicting nature) of agents' concepts of what they are doing – or inducing mystificatory ones. This Bhaskar concedes and has to if he is genuinely declaring war upon empirical realism and the privilege it gives to the experiential. To begin with he accepts that 'the *generative* role of agents' skills and wants, and of agents' . . . beliefs and meanings must be recognised without lapsing into an interpretative fundamentalism by conferring *discursive* and/or *incorrigible* status on them'.[25] This in itself

---

[23] Bhaskar, *Reclaiming Reality*, p. 78.
[24] Benton, 'Realism', p. 17.   [25] Bhaskar, *Reclaiming Reality*, p. 98.

neither distances him from Giddens (who talks of degrees of 'discursive penetration' and of corrigible knowledge) nor does much for his conviction that agents' particular conceptions may be systematically distorted by ideology. Since agents' conceptions may be wrong, *inter alia* because of ideological distortions, then in consistency Bhaskar has to grant that 'the *conditions* for the phenomena (namely social activities as conceptualized in experience) exist *intransitively* and may therefore exist independently of their appropriate conceptualization'.[26] The introduction of 'conditions that exist intransitively' marks the break with Giddens, for important things are now indeed going on behind our backs. As Bhaskar writes, 'of such relations the agents involved may or may not be aware'.[27] Indeed his whole emancipatory programme depends on the claim that they do at T^1, but need not at T^2. Thus when 'types of explanation succeed in identifying *real*, but hitherto *unrecognised*, conditions and patterns of determination they immediately augment our knowledge',[28] and with it our freedom. All of this has severed the entente cordiale with Giddens' 'highly knowledgeable agent', without however entailing a full retraction of the concept-dependence thesis.

For a final possibility remains. Bhaskar allows that structures may exist independently of their *appropriate* conceptualization, but could still reply that they depend upon being *inappropriately* conceptualised. In other words, the thesis may specify a causal relationship between agents' misconceptions and the endurance of social structures, implying of course that changes in the former would contribute to changes in the latter. Examples are not hard to find (like the rise and decline of the fur trade or ideology and ideological demystification) but to universalize this proposition, quite apart from its conspiratorial overtones, is to swallow a story about the functional necessity of every inappropriate concept and of the fundamental *a prioristic* coherence of concepts and reality. Again there are no grounds for demonstrating this as an *a priori* truth; the matter seems to be one for empirical investigation, particularly since we can find evidence of large conceptual shifts (feminism) which existing structures have withstood largely unchanged. And what this points to in turn is the indispensability of theorizing about them and then investigating *whose* conceptual shifts are responsible for *which* structural changes, *when*, *where* and under *what* conditions.

In short, none of the arguments about the concept-dependence of social structures justifies the leap to 'this society because of these people here present and the concepts they hold'. On the contrary many social

---

[26] Bhaskar, *Naturalism*, p. 51.
[27] Bhaskar, *Naturalism*, p. 26.   [28] Bhaskar, *Reclaiming Reality*, p. 91.

structures seem resilient in the face of profound conceptual disagreements between agents about their doings and their shifting concepts of what structures are like. Again, we return to restate that the concept-dependence of such structures can be affirmed in only one acceptable way: by reference to the concepts (ideas, beliefs, intentions, the compromises and concessions plus unintended consequences) of the long dead. These continue to feature in present structures, despite strenuous efforts of current actors to change them, as with racism and sexism.

Bhaskar's third thesis about the ontological peculiarity of society is that social structures are only present in and through their effects, that is only in and through the activities of human beings. Once again the drift towards Giddens is pronounced and threatens to impale the TMSA on the 'simultaneity model' for which Layder correctly takes structuration theory to task. For how 'can objective structures be both outside and determinative of interaction, whilst at the same time being the internally generated outcome of such interactions? This is what the simultaneity model asks us to accept'.[29] Benton too is quick to pounce, for at this point, the very existence of emergent properties is at stake, the danger being that they are simply going to disappear, being incorporated into 'other people' in typical Individualist fashion. Quite rightly, he insists that the only protection against this is if structural conditions and human activities are kept separate, namely if we adhere strictly to analytical dualism rather than succumbing to the duality of structure. Thus to sustain the existence of emergent properties 'it is necessary to distinguish between those activities of agents which are exercises of their own intrinsic powers, and those activities which are really powers which reside in social structures, but operate through the activities of human agents'. The difficulty is, though, 'if any person "A" is the agent of an activity "a", then "A" must be the possessor of the power of which "a" is the exercise. If this is accepted then it follows that, at best, we can distinguish only between powers of agents possessed in virtue of their intrinsic natures, and powers of agents possessed in virtue of their relational properties.' This is of course as far as structuration theory would go, given Giddens' mistrust of emergence. To Benton, this spells the collapse of the TMSA programme. Bhaskar's 'conception of social structures does not, after all, sustain them as autonomous possessors of causal powers, or, therefore, as *sui genesis* realities. Roy Bhaskar is, it seems, committed to a variant form of individualism in social theory.'[30] Benton admits to being both sceptical of his conclusion and intrigued to see where it breaks down.

[29] Derek Layder, *Structure, Interaction and Social Theory*, Routledge and Kegan Paul, London, 1981, p. 73.   [30] Benton, 'Realism', p. 17.

It does, though a little more work has to be done than is contained in Bhaskar's riposte. It is insufficient to state that social structures are only efficacious in and through the activities of human beings (as a condition for avoiding reification) for all descriptive individualists would assent to this. Yet the effects of emergent properties are not those of 'other people' and reification is not involved in saying so. Bhaskar most certainly would not wish to slide into the 'personalization' strategy of Individualists and he is explicit that in talking about structures he has switched the focus from *people* to *relations* (including those with positions, nature and social products such as machines and firms). Still this is not quite conclusive, for as we saw Watkins was perfectly happy to bundle the 'beliefs, resources and inter-relations of individuals' into his charter for Methodological Individualism in which 'the ultimate constituents of the social world are individual people'.[31] It is only in the final phrase of this exchange that Bhaskar gets off the hook. 'What remains of "individualism"', he writes 'is a residual truth: that nothing happens in society save in or in virtue of something human beings do *or have done*'[32] (my italics).

This unaccentuated 'or have done' needs to be given its full force. If the argument did hang on 'something people do', then there would be commitment to 'this society because of those people here present', no escaping reductionism, and no evading Benton's conclusion. The addition, 'or have done' avoids all three for it lets in *past actions* and full force can be given to Auguste Comte's insight that the majority of actors are the dead. That force is the force of emergence, namely that it is now perfectly possible to talk about emergent properties and the results (or the results of the results) of past actions, which pre-date all current actions of contemporary agents and yet condition them – in the form of enablements or constraints which are not dependent upon current activities nor influential because of their contemporary conceptualization (be it correctly, incorrectly, or not at all). Reification does not threaten. It is affirmed that social structures are only efficacious through the activities of human beings, but in the only acceptable manner, by allowing that these are the effects of *past actions*, often by long dead people, which survive them (and this temporal escape is precisely what makes them *sui generis*). Thus they continue to exert their effects upon subsequent actors and their activities, as autonomous possessors of causal powers. How they carry over and how they exert their effects is just what the M/M approach attempts to theorize. Endorsement of analytical dualism in relation to structure and

---

[31] J. W. N. Watkins, 'Methodological individualism and social tendencies', in May Brodbeck (ed.), *Readings in the Philosophy of the Social Sciences*, Macmillan, New York, 1971, pp. 270–1.   [32] Bhaskar, *Naturalism*, pp. 174.

agency (distinguishing pre-conditions from present activities) is now not only permissible, it is essential to the TMSA programme.

If the siren call of central conflation had continued, Benton had pointed to the ineluctable conclusion. In the end it was resisted and there is a world of difference between Giddens' insistence that 'structure has no existence independent of the knowledge that agents have about what they do in their day-to-day activity'[33] and Bhaskar's statement that 'the mark of intransitive objects of knowledge then becomes that they exist and act independently of the knowledge of which they are the objects'[34] and his affirmation that social structures are such intransitive objects. With the assertion in *Reclaiming Reality*, one to which no central conflationists could ever put their name, that 'society may thus be conceived as an articulated ensemble of such *relatively independent and enduring structures*'[35] (my italics) we can now move on to a discussion of the *interplay* between these structures and human agents in a manner which is closed to the central conflationist who denies this possibility by rendering them mutually constitutive.

Separability: the interplay between structure and agency

This final set proves rather easy going as central conflation steady fades as a threat to TMSA which plants itself firmly on its backline of Emergentism to make strong and decisive returns. The outcome is a necessary one because if Bhaskar holds fast to the ontological role he has assigned to emergent properties then he can really have no truck with the 'duality of structure', as conceived of in structuration theory. It seems *logically* inescapable that if the 'powers', 'tendencies', 'transfactuality' and 'generative mechanisms' inhering in social structures can exist unexercised (or unrecognized), in open systems like society, then there *must* be a disjunction between them and the everyday phenomenal experiences of actors. This Bhaskar asserts forcefully in his repudiation of empirical realism and the privilege it accords to the experiential. However, it follows from the fact that the two often or usually are 'out of synch' with one another that analytical dualism then becomes a logical necessity when Bhaskar moves from his general consideration of realism to advance the TMSA as a contribution to social theory. Because the emergent properties of structures and the actual experiences of agents are not synchronized (due to the

---

[33] Anthony Giddens, *The Constitution of Society: Outline of the Theory of Structuration*, Polity, Cambridge, 1984, p. 26.
[34] Bhaskar, *Naturalism*, p. 14.   [35] Bhaskar, *Naturalism*, p. 78.

very nature of society as an open system), then there will always be the inescapable need for a two-part account. Part I seeks to disengage the properties (their 'powers' etc.) *per se* of social structure: part 2 conceptualizes the experiential, namely that which is accessible to actors at any given time *in* its incompleteness and distortion and replete with its blind spots of ignorance. Thus the two accounts will not be the same, but written from different standpoints, for one will include elements which the other lacks and vice versa.

Thus, Bhaskar writes that he 'wants to distinguish sharply, then between the genesis of human actions, lying in the reasons and plans of human beings, on the one hand; and the structures governing the reproduction and transformation of social activities, on the other; and hence between the domains of the psychological and social sciences'.[36] The need for this distinction and the two accounts which it calls for are entirely alien to Elisionism. Unfortunately the phraseology in which this is expressed has to be read carefully, for parts of the formulation are only too redolent of structuration theory.

This is the case with the following statement: 'Society is the ever-present *condition* and continually reproduced *outcome* of human agency: this is the duality of structure. And human agency is both work (generically conceived), that is (normally conscious) *production*, and (normally unconscious) *reproduction* of the conditions of production, including society: this is the duality of praxis.'[37] Although the first sentence sounds as if it comes straight from structuration theory we established in the last section that something very different from 'simultaneity' is meant by Bhaskar, and that therefore 'condition' should actually be read to mean 'pre-condition' and 'outcome' to imply that which post-dates given actions. (This of course is identical with the two basic theorems of the M/ M approach.) However, Giddens means one thing and one alone: that structural properties require 'instantiation' by present agents to *be* efficacious and that 'outcomes' are part and parcel of the self-same and simultaneous process – in what is a unitary account. On the contrary, Bhaskar underscores the need for two accounts in the above quotation, one which deals with the 'duality of structure' (though to him spread out over time, as a 'tensed' process, rather than compacted in the present) *and another*, dealing with the 'duality of praxis' (where 'production' and 'reproduction' are again spaced in time and may well involve different agents altogether). This need for *separate accounts* of 'structure' and 'praxis' firmly separates the TMSA from structuration. For in the latter the two can *only* be separated by the artificial bracketing exercise, which

---

[36] Bhaskar, *Reclaiming Reality*, pp. 79–80.   [37] Bhaskar, *Reclaiming Reality*, p. 92.

recommits structuration to simultaneity because the *epoché* confines us to the same *époque* and prevents exploration of the interplay between structure and agency over time. In contradistinction Bhaskar's 'two accounts' entail a commitment to analytical dualism and issue in the need to investigate their interplay (in a third account), an interplay whose exploration is firmly blocked in structuration theory.

In fact a little reflection shows that, realism itself is *predicated* upon analytical dualism. This is underscored when it quits the realm of abstract ontology and enters the domain of practical social theorizing. At any given T^1, *both* accounts are required, since at any point in time, what Lockwood distinguished as 'system integration' may be at variance with 'social integration' – and explaining the outcome at T^2 involves examining their interplay. The admission of two accounts, *contra* central conflation, always implies the need for a third which combines them. This is what sets analytical dualism apart from any of the triple versions of conflation whose common fallacy is always to issue in one-dimensional accounts; crude epiphenomenal reductionism in the upwards and downward versions, more sophisticated but still 'compacted' in the central version since only an artificial bracketing exercise can separate them, not in reality but purely for analytical convenience dependent upon one's interests.

Once Bhaskar has differentiated in his TMSA between the need to *retain* 'No people: no social structures' (in order to avoid reification) and the need to *reject* 'these structures, because of these people here present' (in order to avoid the slide into Individualism), then the widening of the time frame to include the emergent and aggregate consequences of past actions and past agents, actually makes analytical dualism a methodological necessity to the TMSA itself.

Human activity is seen as 'consisting in the transformation by efficient (intentional) agency of pre-given material (natural and social) causes'.[38] Although there is one sense in which social forms have to be *drawn upon* (to Bhaskar for the very framing of intentions), there is another sense, which is entirely alien to conflationary theorizing, in which these *pre-existing* properties *impinge* upon contemporary actors and cannot be subsumed under voluntaristic concepts like 'instantiation'. The prior emergence of relational properties impinge willy nilly on current actors and their situations, implying no compliance, complicity or consent from the latter. This relational conception of structures, explicitly incorporating time past as well as time present, then

allows one to focus on the *distribution* of the structural conditions of action, and in particular ... differential allocations of: (a) productive resources (of all kinds,

---

[38] Bhaskar, *Reclaiming Reality*, p. 92.

including for example cognitive ones) to persons (and groups) and (b) persons (and groups) to functions and roles (for example in the division of labour). In doing so, it allows one to situate the possibility of different (and antagonistic) interests, of conflict *within* society, and hence of interest-motivated transformation in society structure.[39]

In this we have a clear statement that the actors here present are not responsible for creating the distributions, roles and associated interests with which they live. Equally important is the crucial recognition that the *pre-structuring* of actors' contexts and interests is what shapes the pressures for transformation by some and for stable reproduction by others, in the present. Theories of change are not defied by infinite social complexity, reproduction is anchored in vested interest and not mere routinization, and transformation is not an undifferentiated potential of every moment, it is rooted in determinate conflicts between identifiable groups who find themselves in particular positions with particular interests to advance or defend.

The foundations of analytical dualism have now been laid down, yet to complete the TMSA as a social *theory*, the 'third account' of the *interplay* between social structures and human agents is now required. Bhaskar recognizes this, namely that mediating concepts are called for to explain *how* structure actually does impinge upon agency (who and where) and *how* agents in turn react back to reproduce or transform structure (giving rise to morphogenesis or morphostasis in my terms). In the following description of these 'mediators', it should be noted that what a large distance now separates them from Giddens' free-floating 'modalities' (i.e. the 'interpretative scheme', 'facility', or 'norm', that is stocks of knowledge, power and conventions, which are universally available rather than being *differentially distributed* and *concretely located*). By contrast, Bhaskar claims that 'we need a system of *mediating concepts*, encompassing both aspects of the duality of praxis, designating the "slots", as it were, in the social structure into which active agents must slip in order to reproduce it; that is a system of concepts designating the *"point of contact"* between human agency and social structure. Such a point, linking action to structure, must *both* endure and be immediately occupied by individuals'[40] (my italics). These types of *linkages* are concrete ('slots'), located ('points of contact'), and are differentially distributed (not all can 'slip' into the same 'slot'). Conceived of as relationships, they satisfy the requirement of temporal continuity and are irreducibly emergent since they include but do not reduce to the 'interactions' between the individuals who occupy or engage in them.

Their precise designation overlaps with that employed in the M/M

[39] Bhaskar, *Naturalism*, p. 41.   [40] Bhaskar, *Naturalism*, p. 40.

approach, though it might prove slightly too restrictive for the latter. Thus, Bhaskar claims that it 'is clear that the mediating system we need is that of *positions* (places, functions, rules, duties, rights) occupied (filled, assumed, enacted etc.) by individuals, and of the *practices* (activities etc.) in which, in virtue of their occupancy of these positions (and vice versa), they engage. I shall call this mediating system the position-practice system'.[41] Now 'position' is an ambiguous concept. If it means 'position as the passive aspect of role', which is a fairly common usage, then it is too narrow for my purposes. Agents certainly do have an important 'point of contact' with structure through the roles they occupy/assume, but it is *not the only one*. If, on the other hand, 'position' conveys its more everyday meaning ('the position in which they find themselves'), that is problematic (or felicitous) *situations* or *contexts* which are not tightly associated with specific normative expectations – therefore making it is otiose to call them 'roles', as for example, with the 'underprivileged', or 'believers' or those 'holding theory x'), then the overlap would be complete. The latter meaning seems acceptable to Bhaskar from the quotation above and given that his own usage often embraces it. For example, when discussing the experiential lifeworld at T^2, he comments that this is 'dependent upon the ontological and social *contexts* within which the significant experience occurs'.[42] Although this does not seem to be a bone of contention between us, it is raised here because in M/M approach a great deal hangs upon *not confining* all the problems which agents confront in the structures they inherit from the past to roles (and thus *not limiting* morphogenetic potential to those exigencies confronted in them or *confining* interests to those vested in roles). As far as interplay itself is concerned, the M/M approach will have much more to add about the *way* in which structures impinge upon agents at the 'points of contact'.

A final and major source of agreement with the TMSA deserves highlighting. From the M/M perspective, the structural conditioning of action (by constraints or enablements) is *never* a matter of 'hydraulic pressures' – which is why it is preferable to speak of 'mediators' linking them rather than 'mechanisms' connecting them, for there is nothing mechanical about the processes involved (and none of the concomitant denial of human subjectivity). The same goes for the TMSA, since to Bhaskar, intentionality is what demarcates agency from structure. Hence, 'intentional human behaviour is caused, and ... it is always caused by reasons, and ... it is only because it is caused by reasons that it is properly characterized as intentional'.[43] The M/M approach reflects the same conviction and therefore actually conceptualizes the conditional effects of

[41] Bhaskar, *Naturalism*, p. 41.
[42] Bhaskar, *Reclaiming Reality*, p. 97.   [43] Bhaskar, *Naturalism*, p. 90.

structure upon action in terms of the former supplying *reasons* for different courses of action to those who are differently positioned. Exactly how it does so, by shaping the situations in which people find themselves, will be explored in chapter 7. It is raised here merely to show the general congruence of the two approaches.

Picturing transformation and morphogenesis

We have talked about two accounts of 'structure', of 'interaction' and of a third account of the 'mediating processes' linking the two. These now need picturing in a form which sets these linkages out in a way which is quite different from the simple upwards and downwards or sideways arrows, distinctive of *any* diagrammatic representation of conflationary theorizing. The main difference, of course, is that while conflationary theorists *may* assign importance to the passage of time, they entirely fail to acknowledge the intrinsic *historicity* of the process. Time instead, is a medium through which things happen rather as air is to breathing-beings. But at any moment in time, the assumptions of epiphenomenalism or mutual constitution mean that the process can be depicted in exactly the same way. The reverse is the case for non-conflationists for whom the process itself is strung out over time (and each moment does *not* conform to the same eternal diagram but to a specific phase on a historical flow chart). Both analytically and in practical analysis, different phases are disengaged, not as mere aspects of a unitary process, but as parts of a temporal sequence. Moreover, since structures are held to be only relatively enduring and transformation/morphogenesis characterizes the final phase, then the model also indicates subsequent cycles of the on-going process.

Thus any one cycle which happens to rivet our attention, because of its substantive interest, is also recognised to be preceded by anterior cycles and followed by posterior ones – whether these are reproductive or transformatory, morphostatic or morphogenetic. Necessarily action is continuous ('no people: no society') but because of their actions over time, structures are discontinuous (only relatively enduring) and once they are changed, then subsequent activities are conditioned and shaped quite differently (this society is not exclusively the product of those here present any more than future society is solely what our heirs produce). How specific analytical cycles are carved out historically depends upon the problem in hand: what follows are generic diagrams whose contents the investigator would supply. Having argued that there is considerable congruence between the TMSA and the M/M approach, this will finally be clinched if, and only if, they picture the process in a manner quite

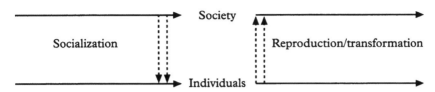

Figure 4 Bhaskar's model of the Society/Person connection.

distinct from conflationary theorists, and through generic diagrams which closely resemble one another. Both it will be argued are indeed the case, though to sustain this argument it is necessary to pin-point important developments and refinements in Bhaskar's picturing.

In the earlier *Possibility of Naturalism* (1979) he supplied what can be called his preliminary model of the society/person connection. In many ways it is too fundamentalist. As can be seen in figure 4, (i) although it contains a 'before' and an 'after' it lacks real historicity: despite the break in the middle, it could be well construed as a heuristic device which represents each and any moment, not a determinate phase in an historical process: (ii) in several ways it is 'overpersonalized'; structural influences appear to work *exclusively via socialization* and seem to exert their influence directly upon (all) *individuals*: (iii) the 'before' and 'after' are unconnected by *inter*action and unmediated by the 'relations of production'. In short, (i), (ii) and (iii), respectively point to the down-playing of historicity, emergence and mediation.

Now, although the existence of *two-way* arrows sets this model at variance to both upwards and downwards conflation, the features which are repressed in this representation (historicity, emergence and mediation) are exactly those which it has been argued, firmly separate the TMSA from central conflation. Were this the end of the story, then this model could readily be appropriated by central conflationists and it is perhaps largely responsible for the affinities which some have noted with structuration theory.

However, ten years later, Bhaskar elaborated on this fundamentalist model and did so by inserting precisely those features which were repressed in the above. In *Reclaiming Reality* (1989) crucial revisions are introduced into the following diagram; (a) the prior *emergence* and current influence of structural properties at points 1 and 2, as the unintended consequences of past actions and unacknowledged conditions of contemporary activities, are now explicitly introduced: (b) their influence is to limit actors' understanding of their social world which is compounded, at 3 and 4, by limitations in self understanding, thus rendering the *necessary*

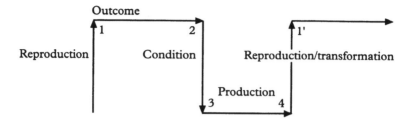

Figure 5 Bhaskar's refined transformational model of structure and praxis.

production process (which is now introduced) the *mediated* product of agents who are far from highly knowledgeable about why they find themselves in the relations they do and why they do whatever they then do in those situations: (c) the *temporal* phasing of the process is now prominent, the diagram is now a sequence through time – 1 is the explicit outcome of an antecedent cycle and 1' signals the start of a new and different posterior cycle (if transformation ensues). If reproduction is the outcome, then we are in for a structural replay in the next cycle but not necessarily an action replay.

Given these three refinements, the model now superimposes neatly onto the basic morphogenetic/morphostatic diagram. Superimposition seems fully justified by some of Bhaskar's comments which explicitly distance TMSA from central conflation and structuration theory in particular. (1) Because of emergence, he insists upon the influence of *prior* structures on *subsequent* interaction which transforms them, and now represents this *historically* rather than *sub specie aeternitartis*, as in the first diagram. (2) He remarks that he 'inclined to give structures (conceived as transfactually efficacious) a stronger ontological grounding and to place more emphasis on the pre-existence of social forms' than is Giddens, but now also stresses that 'theory need not be static, but can depict, in abstract fashion, flows, cycles and movements ... tendentially applicable to concrete historical situations'.[44] In fact, *temporality* is not an option but a necessity, for as he states 'social structures are to be *earthed* in space and *situated* in time and space/time is to be seen/scene as a *flow*'.[45] (3) Thus it is justifiable to introduce the flow explicitly as historicity *but also* to break it up into phases for he maintains that the TMSA 'generates' a clear criterion of historically significant events, namely those that 'initiate or constitute ruptures, mutations or generally transformations of social

[44] Bhaskar, 'Beef', p. 85.   [45] Bhaskar, 'Beef', p. 93.

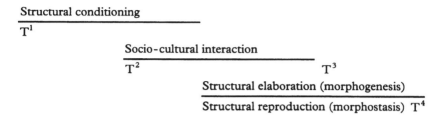

Figure 6 The basic morphogenetic/static cycle with its three phases.

forms'.[46] (4) Finally, his refined diagram now contains *mediating* processes, that is it deals with relations between positioned praxes which are not reducible to interpersonal interaction between their occupants/encumbents. Similarly in the M/M approach, interaction is held to emanate from those in positions/situations which are not of their making yet which condition much of what they can make of them.

The basic Morphogenetic/static diagram is presented in figure 6. Its basic theorems, which constitute analytical dualism are (i) that structure necessarily pre-dates the action(s) which transform it (Bhaskar as we have seen agrees but adds weight to the analytical decoupage when he emphasizes that 'the games of the life-world (Lebenswelt) are always initiated, conditioned and closed outside the life world itself'[47]), and; (ii) and that structural elaboration necessarily post-dates those actions which have transformed it (to Bhaskar structures are only relatively enduring and whether they do last or become transformed is the product of positioned praxis not voluntaristic interaction).

With minor alterations the TMSA and M/M diagrams now readily combine as in figure 7, with Bhaskar's notations entered above the lines and my own corresponding ones below them in brackets.

Since all the lines in figure 7 are in fact continuous, the dualism is *analytical* rather than philosophical, a theoretical necessity for unravelling and explaining the processes involved in the *structuring* of society and the specific forms of re-*structuring* to take place – *over time*. The projection of all horizontal lines forwards and backwards connects up with anterior and posterior cycles of the historical *structuring process*. This is equally generic to both the TMSA and the M/M approach, and accounts for the possibility of their co-picturing. However, I retain a preference for my own graphics for the simple but important reason that my T² and T³ period (where prior structures are gradually transformed and new ones

[46] Bhaskar, *Reclaiming Reality*, p. 77.   [47] Bhaskar, *Reclaiming Reality*, p. 95.

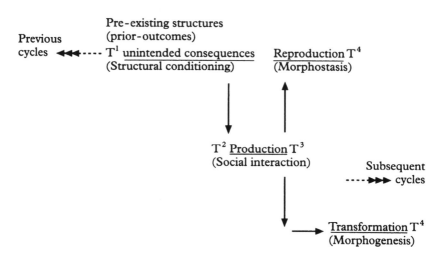

Figure 7 Superimposing the Transformational Model of Social
Action and the morphogenetic/static cycle.

slowly elaborated) shows diagrammatically that there is no period when society is *un-structured*. In a purely visual sense, Bhaskar's T^2–$T^{1'}$ (contrary to his intention) *could* convey that structural properties are suspended for this interval, whilst they undergo 'production'.

I have been arguing that *analytical* dualism is a matter of theoretical necessity if we are to obtain purchase on those processes which are accountable for determinate social changes – that is if we are to advance usable social theories for working investigators (for whom a social ontology which asserts *tout court* that the potential for reproduction or transformation inheres in each act at every moment is a white elephant). As Bhaskar maintains, the TMSA 'can sustain a genuine concept of *change*, and hence of *history*'.[48] The same claim is made for the M/M approach, and is one I hope to have demonstrated substantively in the *Social Origins of Educational Systems* (1979).[49] There is agreement that this is something which upwards, downwards and central conflationary theories cannot do. Indeed, in the latter, change remains 'something of a mystery'[50] for Bhaskar. It does indeed, and what has been examined earlier are the reasons why it must for those who uphold the 'duality of structure'. Thus structuration theory bows out at this point with Gid-

---

[48] Bhaskar, *Reclaiming Reality*, p. 77.
[49] Sage, London and Beverly Hills, 1979.   [50] Bhaskar, *Reclaiming Reality*, p. 77.

dens' anticlimatic statement that there is 'little point in looking for an overall theory of stability and change in social systems, since the conditions of social reproduction vary so widely between different types of society'.[51] Consequently his social ontology hands the practitioner a 'sensitization' device; the TMSA and M/M approaches try to provide tool kits, and whilst tools presume that practitioners have to do considerable (substantive) *work* with them, they are also designed to be worked with and to be of practical use on the job.

Given this objective, it is important to emphasize that the compatibility established between the TMSA and the M/M approaches are anchored in realism itself. Just as Individualism and Holism represented social ontologies whose commitments to what constitutes the social world then issued in programmatic injunctions about how it should be studied and explained (that is Methodological Individualism and Methodological Holism as conflationary programmes working in opposite directions), so the realist social ontology also enjoins a Methodological Realism which embodies its commitments to depth, stratification and emergence as definitional of social reality. Thus the burden of this chapter has been to demonstrate that given these fundamental tenets of realism, they can only be respected and reflected by a Methodological Realism which approaches structure and agency through 'analytical dualism' – in order to be able to explore the linkages between these separate strata with their own autonomous, irreducible, emergent properties and which consequently repudiates any form of conflation (be it upwards, downwards or central) in social theorizing.

Certainly Outhwaite[52] is correct that this means social realism is compatible with a wide range of social theories, but I believe this breadth is a matter of substantive rather than formal complementarities. In other words, whilst it is perfectly possible to have fierce realist debates about the relative *substantive importance* of different structures and generative mechanisms (of the marxist versus anti-marxist variety), nevertheless in *formal terms*, such antagonists would also be co-protagonists of Methodological Realism. This is because formally, realism itself is committed to an explanatory framework which acknowledges and incorporates (a) *pre-existent structures* as generative mechanisms, (b) their *interplay* with other objects possessing causal powers and liabilities proper to them in what is a stratified social world, and (c) non-predictable but none the less explicable *outcomes* arising from interactions between the above, which take place in the open system that is society. In substantive terms, disagree-

---

[51] Giddens, *Social Theory*, p. 215.
[52] William Outhwaite, 'Realism, naturalism and social behaviour', *Journal for the Study of Social Behaviour*, 1990, 20: 4, p. 366.

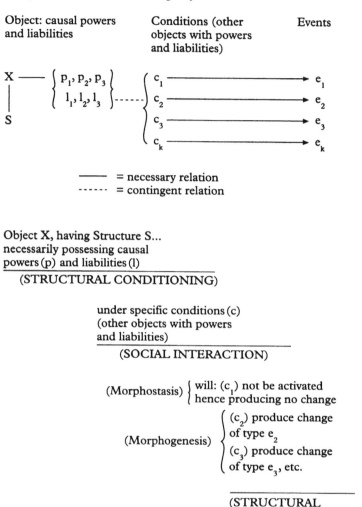

Figure 8 Co-picturing Methodological Realism and the morphogenetic/static approach.

ments can flourish about which structures, what types of interplay and what outcomes should be prioritized and how they ought to be analyzed, but without any discord over the nature and format of explanation itself. Therefore, since the M/M approach makes no substantive judgements either, it is not surprising to find that its generic diagram, founded four-square upon 'analytical dualism', also superimposes directly onto the basic explanatory framework as pictured in the only full-length book to date which is devoted to Methodological Realism. By introducing the common headings, 'Structure', 'Interplay', and 'Outcome', the similarities with Andrew Sayer's[53] figure (here figure 8), entitled the 'Structures of causal explanation' are clearly marked – as they should be if the arguments which have been advanced in this chapter, namely, that 'analytical dualism' is intrinsic to social realism, are sustained.

The TMSA is the generous under-labouring of a philosopher who has actually dug beyond disciplinary bounds: the M/M approach is produced by a working sociologist, recognizing the obligation to go deeper into precision tooling to supply a social theory which is pre-eminently usable. Thus the M/M approach seeks to go further than providing 'a clear criterion of historically significant events': it attempts not merely to identify but also to unpack. Thus there is yet more fine-grained work to be done on the conceptualization of structural conditioning, on the specification of *how* structural influences are transmitted (as reasons not hydraulics) to particular agents in determinate positions and situations (the who, the when and the where), and on the strategic combinations which result in morphogenesis *rather than* morphostasis (which outcome).

This is precisely what the next chapter sets out to do, although it will take the following three to complete the exercise by dealing with the tripartite phases making up the morphogenetic cycle. This undertaking appears to have Bhaskar's recent blessing, given that he endorses the need to think of the flow of social reality as 'differentiated into analytically discrete moments' and as being 'rhythmically processual and phasic to the core – a feature which distinguishes it from structuration, or more generally any 'central conflation' theory'.[54] This constitutes an important methodological gloss on his earlier statement that, 'it is, I suggest, in the (explanation of the) differentiation and stratification, production and reproduction, mutation and transformation, continual remoulding and incessant shifting, of the relatively enduring relations presupposed by particular social forms and structures that sociology's 'distinctive theoretical interest lies'.[55] So it does, and my main concern goes beyond producing an acceptable social ontology for it seeks to present a workable social theory. Yet the latter has to be predicated upon the former (or the slippage into instrumentalism is fatal). This is precisely the reason for the present chapter, namely to demonstrate how an Emergentist ontology necessarily entails analytical dualism, especially if it is to generate a workable methodology – for the practical analysis of vexatious society.

---

[53] Andrew Sayer, *Method in Social Science: A Realist Approach*, Routledge, London, 1992.
[54] Roy Bhaskar, *Dialectic: The Pulse of Freedom*, Verso, London, 1993, p. 160
[55] Bhaskar, *Naturalism*, p. 41.

Part II

The morphogenetic cycle

6 Analytical dualism: the basis of the morphogenetic approach

Society is that which nobody wants, in the form in which they encounter it, for it is an unintended consequence. Its constitution could be expressed as a riddle: what is it that depends on human intentionality but never conforms to their intentions? What is it that relies upon people's concepts but which they never fully know? What is it that depends upon action but never corresponds to the actions of even the most powerful? What is it that has no form without us, yet which forms us as we seek its transformation? And what is it that never satisfies the precise designs of anyone yet because of this always motivates its attempted reconstitution? To recognize the unique kind of reality with which we are dealing in this 'vexatious fact of society' is to acknowledge the difficulty of the theoretical enterprise but also the impossibility of taking analogical short-cuts.

On the one hand, in asserting that society is never exactly what anyone wants, in emphasizing this as the underlying motor of change, in stressing that the social origins of particular transformations lie in structured struggles, in underlining that resulting social forms are generated and elaborated from this parallelogram of pressures, it is also acknowledged that social *structuring*, as a process which is continuously activity-dependent is also one which is uncontrolled, non-teleological, non-homeostatic, non-adaptive and therefore unpredictable. Its form is shaped by the processes and powers whose interplay accounts for its elaboration. At any given time, structure itself is the result of the result of prior social relations conditioned by an antecedent structural context. As such it is moulded and re-moulded but conforms to no mould; it is patterned and re-patterned but is confined to no pattern; it is organized and re-organized but its organization needs comply with none of its precedents.

On the other hand, because of this quintessential ability of social structures to change shape, all traditional analogies prove misleading. Society is not a mechanism with fixed, indispensable parts and determinate relations between parts, pre-set preferred states and pre-programmed homoeostatic mechanisms. Society is not like a language with an orderly, enduring syntax whose components are mutually invoking.

Society is not a simple cybernetic system, which pre-supposes a particular structure capable of carrying out goal directed, feedback regulated, error-correction. All of these are special kinds of system and society is another, which is only like itself and is itself because it is open, and is open because it is peopled, and being peopled can always be re-shaped through human innovativeness. Hence the use of the term 'morphogenesis' to describe the process of social structuring; 'morpho' indicating shape, and 'genesis' signalling that the shaping is the product of social relations. Thus 'Morphogenesis' refers to 'those processes which tend to elaborate or change a system's given form, state or structure'.[1] Conversely, 'morphostasis' refers to those processes in complex system-environmental exchanges which tend to preserve or maintain a system's given form, organisation or state.

To argue that the form society takes at any given time is an unintended consequence is not the same as to assert that all things social are a matter of contingency. If we were sure (*per impossibile*) that everything were subject to pure contingency, then any notion of the study of society, let alone more presumptuous notions about some version of 'social science' could not even be voiced. It is not that we would have to fall back on history, for history would fall too. If all the referents of historical concepts were in shifting and contingent relationships there would be no story to tell. Not only would this preclude grand narratives of history, but neither could there be any modest and honest chronicler of the social equivalent of Brownian motion. In any domain, if all occurrences are contingently related, such that everything is flux, then verifications and falsifications alike are deprived of significance and the Popperian bold conjecture, like the historical grand narrative, is not brave but inane. Only on the metaphysical assumption that some relations are necessary and at least relatively enduring can we reasonably set out to practise science or to study society. Transcendentally, the world has to be ordered for science to have any success as a practice and its cumulative successes (not construed as undeviating linear progress) furnish increasing warrants for this metaphysical assertion.

Analogical social theorists made exactly the same assumption. However, their analogues were not just a rejection of contingency and a commitment to society being ordered, they began from a prior commitment to *how* it was ordered. The social relations of natural necessity, without which its study was precluded, were presumed in advance to be 'like x'. Now whilst the analogical imagination[2] can perform a variety of

[1] Walter Buckley, *Sociology and Modern Systems Theory*, Prentice-Hall, New Jersey, 1967, p. 58.
[2] Cf. David Tracy, *The Analogical Imagination*, S. C. M. Press, London, 1981.

useful tasks in relation to the full tripartite variety of reality itself (natural, social and transcendental), it cannot presume to furnish *a priori* judgements about the nature of order in any domain. Every such attempt has led social theorizing astray because it has led away from addressing social reality in its own right, thus denying what is ontologically vexatious about it and sometimes evading the significance of its human constitution.

The morphogenetic approach begins the other way around, that is with the essential transcendental commitment to society not being wholly contingent, but with no substantive pre-conceptions that its ordering resembles any other form of reality (mechanical or organic), nor that the whole is homologous with some part of it (language), or some state of it (simple cybernetic systems). Society is only like itself and the basic task is to conceptualize how ordered social forms have their genesis in human agency, just as social beings have their genesis in social forms.

In other words, although it is contingent *that* any particular social structure exists (for they are historically specific and only relatively enduring), nevertheless *whilst* they do persist, as the unintended consequences of previous social interaction, they exert systematic causal effects on subsequent action. Yet the systematic*ness* of these effects cannot be attributed to the entire shifting flux of unintended consequences, precisely because these combinations are ephemeral and contain inconsequential items, but rather only to a special sub-class – that is emergent properties, whose differentiating features are relative endurance, natural necessity and the possession of causal powers. Since the existence of effects cannot serve to explain origins (a prime error of functionalism) then the task of social theory cannot be restricted to the mere identification of social structures as emergent properties, it must also supply an analytical history of their emergence which accounts for why matters are so and not otherwise. Equally, once they are so, they constitute part of the social environment, and, as with any other environmental influence, we can neither assume that agents are determined by them nor are immune from them, but can only examine the interplay between the powers of the two.

In short, neither the analytical history of emergence, nor the identification of emergent properties, nor their part in the shaping of agency itself can be investigated without separating the parts from the people. Because emergence is held to be activity-dependent and operative in open systems, both social realism and morphogenesis (which is held to be its methodological complement) face identical problems. Both need a means of identifying structure(s) independently of their occupants and incumbents, yet of showing its effects upon them (establishing the reality of structures via the causal criterion), whilst coping with the intervention of other contingent relations, and accounting for the eventual outcome which either reproduces or transforms the original structure. Both follow the same basic strategy in attempting to extract explanatory order out of what otherwise appears to be an intractable flux. As was argued in the last chapter, this is predicated upon the non-conflation of structure and agency and their analytical separation on a temporal basis. It rests on endorsing the two theorems that, (i) structure necessarily pre-dates the action(s) which transform it, and, (ii) that structural elaboration necessarily postdates those actions.

Thus, the identification of structures is possible because of their irreducible character, autonomous influence and relatively enduring character, but above all because this means that they pre-date any particular cohort of occupants/encumbents. A position necessarily has to exist before someone can fill it and this remains the case even in circumstances where individuals and groups have been able to define positions for themselves. (For here, too, the defining precedes the occupancy and occupation then embroils the occupant in a network of social relations.) It is this which leads Realists[3] to insist that agency does not create structure, but only reproduces or transforms it in any 'generation'. Hence, what is involved is breaking up the sequence analytically into three stages, which for both realism and morphogenesis could be termed Emergence-Interplay-Outcome. Thus, although structure and agency are at work continuously in society, the analytical element consists in breaking up these flows into intervals determined by the problem in hand: given any problem and accompanying periodization, projection of the three phases forwards and backwards would connect up with anterior and posterior analytical cycles. This represents the bed-rock of understanding structuring over time, which then enables specific forms of structure elaboration to be explained.

The practical application of morphogenetic/static analysis to the structures which constitute the social system entails four basic propositions. As a methodological approach it is necessary for each and every one of them to command assent – *viz*:

(i)   there are internal and necessary relations within and between social structures (SS);
(ii)   causal influences are exerted by social structure(s) (SS) on social interaction (SI);
(iii) there are causal relationships between groups and individuals at the level of social interaction (SI);
(iv)   social interaction (SI) elaborates upon the composition of social structure(s)

[3] Roy Bhaskar, *The Possibility of Naturalism*, Harvester Wheatsheaf, Hemel Hempstead, 1989, p. 34.

(SS) by modifying current internal and necessary structural relationships and introducing new ones where morphogenesis is concerned. Alternatively, social interaction (SI) reproduces existing internal and necessary structural relations when morphostasis applies.

Proposition (i) represents the charter for analytical dualism for it entails the possibility of being able to make statements about the components of social structure(s) without reference to current agents, precisely because the former are held to be emergent properties whose emergence depended upon the activities of previous 'generations'. Propositions (ii), (iii), and (iv) represent the three phases of the basic morphogenetic/static cycle – which is built on the foundations of proposition (i).

The use of analytical dualism to approach the analysis of structure and agency is directly paralleled by the manner in which it is used in relation to culture and agency and entails four equivalent propositions which again pivot upon (i), that is identifying properties pertaining to Cultural Systems in such a way that they do not collapse into those characteristic of Socio-Cultural Interaction:

(i)   there are internal and necessary logical relationships between components of the Cultural System (CS);
(ii) causal influences are exerted by the Cultural System (CS) on Socio-Cultural interaction (the S-C level);
(iii) there are causal relationships between groups and individuals at the Socio-Cultural (S-C) level;
(iv) there is elaboration of the Cultural System (CS) due to Socio-Cultural Interaction (S-C) modifying current logical relationships and introducing new ones, where morphogenesis is concerned. Alternatively Socio-Cultural Interaction (S-C) reproduces existing internal and necessary cultural relations when morphostasis applies.

Taken together they sketch in a morphogenetic cycle of Cultural Conditioning–Cultural Interaction–Cultural Elaboration. Cycles are continuous: the end product of (iv) then constitutes the new (i) and begins another cycle of cultural change.

Obviously for both structure and culture, it is not difficult to identify theorists who enthusiastically subscribe to one of the last three propositions whilst rejecting the rest. Thus, although they would not use my notation because they reject the underlying conceptualization (based on proposition (i)), nevertheless downwards conflationists, whose explanatory format is SS → SI, would fully assent only to proposition (ii), which is where they see social actors being moulded by holistic entities. To them proposition (iii) would at most be theoretically redundant (just the sort of noise that people make in the process of energizing the system), whilst proposition (iv) is entirely repugnant to their approach since it postulates a two-way relationship, giving agency the power to modify structure. Exactly the opposite is true of upwards conflationists, who adopt the explanatory format SI → SS, and therefore reserve their enthusiasm for proposition (iii), since causal relations between groups are what to them constitute structure. They would see proposition (iv) as inoffensive but superfluous since the manipulation of structures in the interests of domination is what the causal relationships are all about. But they would totally repudiate proposition (ii), again because it postulates a two-way relationship – according structure the unacceptable power to mould even the most powerful groups. Central conflationists endorsing the explanatory framework SS ↔ SI, could only tentatively approve proposition (iv), which highlights the transformatory capacity of human agency, but would require its reformulation and would also strenuously deny the propriety of advancing (ii) and (iii) as separate propositions – since to them any systemic influence depends upon the instantiation of rules and resources by agents and, equally, social relations between actors are reliant upon their drawing on shared systems of signification, domination and legitimation.

Consequently, in the various versions of conflationism we have either downright rejection of some particular proposition or outright condemnation of the propriety of stating these as distinct propositions. Both have the effect of damning the morphogenetic enterprise. All of this is eminently understandable, given that conflationists as such are intransigently opposed to the analytical dualism upon which the former is based. Correspondingly, however, each version of conflationary theorizing threw up the problem of 'structure and agency' and 'culture and agency' in different guises, precisely because of epiphenomenalism or elision themselves. In order to avoid both, the morphogenetic/static approach has to reject the premiss which gave rise to them, that is any type of conflation of structure and agency. Simultaneously to get non-conflationary theorizing off the ground it has first to establish both the *possibility* of separating the 'parts' from the 'people' and then to demonstrate the *profitability* of analytical dualism – in structural as in cultural analysis.

The parts and the people: system and social integration

David Lockwood's seminal article on 'Social integration and System integration'[4] began by distinguishing the 'parts' from the 'people' and then examining their combinations in order to account for variable

---

[4] David Lockwood, 'Social integration and system integration', in G. K. Zollschan and H. W. Hirsch (eds.), *Explorations in Social Change*, Houghton Mifflin, Boston, 1964.

outcomes which otherwise eluded theorization. The profitability of analytical dualism was shown by demonstrating the increase in explanatory power which derived from concentrating upon neither element but rather from forging explanations in terms of their *variable* combinations. As an explicit rejection of methodological individualism in the form of 'conflict theory', his concern was to show that 'social (mal) integration' is a necessary but insufficient basis upon which to account for social change, unless complemented by examining its interplay with 'system integration':

> While social change is very frequently associated with conflict, the reverse does not necessarily hold. Conflict may be both endemic and intense in a social system without causing any basic structural change. Why does some conflict result in change while other conflict does not? Conflict theory would have to answer that this is decided by the variable factors affecting the power balance between groups. Here we reach the analytical limits of conflict theory. As a reaction to normative functionalism it is entirely confined to the problem of social integration. What is missing is the system integration focus of general functionalism, which, by contrast with normative functionalism, involved no prior commitment to the study of social stability.[5]

Writing in 1964, Lockwood understandably noted that 'the vital question is, of course: what are the 'component elements' of social systems which give rise to strain, tension or contradiction?'.[6] The question is actually broader still, namely, what conceivable kinds of properties can pertain to social systems which exert *any causal effects* whatsoever – in conjunction with people, but exerting an independent influence upon them? The irony for social theory at the time was that Lockwood had difficulty in answering his own question: he could and did justify the explanatory profitability of utilizing analytical dualism but could not supply an ontological account of how it was possible to differentiate systemic properties from people and attribute causal powers to them.

This left the 'component elements' employed open to the charge of reification from the uncharitable, or their construal as heuristic devices by the more charitable. Lockwood's was clearly aware of the difficulty confronted: his first inclination is indeed only to be advancing heuristic claims, maintaining that his distinction is a 'wholly artificial one'.[7] Yet five pages later artificiality gives way to the ontological and methodological claim that the two are 'not only analytically separable, but also, because of the time elements involved, factually distinguishable'.[8] Once

[5] Lockwood, 'Social integration', p. 249.   [6] Lockwood, 'Social integration', p. 250.
[7] Lockwood, 'Social integration', p. 245.   [8] Lockwood, 'Social integration', p. 250.

accepted as being real, the attribution of causal or generative powers to the 'component elements' quickly follows: 'there is nothing metaphysical about the general notion of social relationships being somehow implicit in a given set of material conditions'.[9] The problem remains and is becoming more pressing now that *specific* causal powers are being attributed to ontologically ungrounded 'component elements' whose mode of influence is also methodologically unspecified. Of one thing Lockwood remained crystal clear – that his question could not be answered at the level of observable events and entities, thus rightly dismissing the 'institutional patterns' of normative functionalism as an inadequate solution.

Later on Social Realists (and the morphogenetic/static approach) would define these 'component elements' as 'emergent properties' arising from the relations between structures which constitute a particular system: social systems being seen as specific configurations of their component structures, where the emergent features of the former derive from the relations between the latter. Thus, unlike their restriction to 'institutional patterns', which confine components to observable entities, structures themselves contain non-observable emergent causal powers whose combination (relations between relations) generate the further emergent systemic properties which Lockwood addresses. The answer to his question is given in terms of real but non-observable *relational terms*, and not, as he rightly thought, by pointing to observable social patternings at the level of events.

Structure and culture as emergent properties

Any emergent property is held to be something quite different from an overt and relatively enduring patterning in social life. That is, in the structural domain, they are something other than observable features such as 'institutional patterns', 'social organizations' or 'socio-economic classes'. Each type of observable entity like the above is heterogeneous: containing a mixture of the taxonomic and aggregative (e.g. 'Class V'), and/or an admixture of people and positions (e.g. the police force or the Health Service). Such heterogeneity is inevitable because these observable features are culled from and categorized at the level of *events* and thus unavoidably incorporate a host of contingent *regularities* arising from a variety of undifferentiated sources. What is privileged is any manifestation of regularity, what ever its source, and in some cases including spurious (that is sourceless) correlations. Basically, such unity as categories and patterns have at the level of events are those imposed by the

⁹ Lockwood, 'Social integration', p. 251.

investigators' categorisation of them as observables. What is automatically discounted are the real sources of phenomena, which may generate no manifest regularities, yet would show those detected to be conglomerations, that is contingent combinations of disparate elements from different strata which happen to co-manifest themselves at a given time.

Fundamentally, what distinguishes an 'emergent property' is its real homogeneity, namely that the relations between its components are internal and necessary ones rather than seemingly regular concatenations of heterogeneous features – of unknown provenance, undetermined internal influence and uncertain duration. In contradistinction, the primary distinguishing feature of any emergent property is the natural necessity of its internal relations, for what the entity is and its very existence depends upon them. To focus upon internal and necessary relations between components as constitutive of an emergent property is to set them apart from relations which are external and contingent. In the latter case, two entities or items can exist without one another and it is thus neither necessary nor impossible that they stand in any particular relation to one another, for the nature of either does not depend upon this.

Hence, for instance, feudal agricultural production and medieval educational provisions co-existed but the two were not even contingently related, for the doings of the one had little if any effect on those of the other. Yet on the one hand, the internal relations between feudal lord and serf, and on the other of Bishops or Priors and clerical teachers, were those on which the practices of 'agriculture' and 'education' respectively depended. These are necessary relationships because there cannot be a serf without a lord or a catechist without a source of doctrinal authority. Yet in no sense are these reducible to 'interpersonal relationships' for their existence *as* relationships depends upon further internal and necessary relations (rights to landholding and associated obligations of fealty and protection, in the one case, and hierarchical authority, and provision of material resources such as premises and texts and the authorization and support of teaching personnel, in the other case). Equally, two other practices, such as early nineteenth-century 'education' and 'industry', each entailed separate internal and necessary relations (on the one hand, between the Anglican Church, its hierarchy, financial endowments and its licensed teachers and, on the other, between industrialists, capital accumulation, factories and wage labour) yet their contingent relations to one another had the important effect of the former obstructing the latter through instilling inappropriate values in the workforce and inculcating skills irrelevant to entrepreneurial development.[10] To state that the

---

[10] Cf. Michalina Vaughan and Margaret S. Archer, *Social Conflict and Educational Change in England and France: 1789–1848*, Cambridge University Press, Cambridge, 1971, chs. 3 and 5.

relationship between two entities is contingent is not to assert that the one exerts no influence upon the other (reciprocally or asymmetrically): it is merely to maintain that the two can exist on their own for they are existentially independent.

Instead, where emergent properties are concerned to talk of natural necessity is not to imply some social *deus ex machina* which means that such relations have to exist (as the invocation of functional imperatives insists). *Whether* given relations of this kind do in fact exist is itself contingent (which is why analytical histories of emergence are needed). Natural necessity only states that X cannot be what it is without certain constituents A, B, C, N' and the relations between them. But what is it about X which leads us to attach the concept of 'emergence' to it rather than simply viewing X as the name given to the particular combination or permutation of A, B, C, N'? The crucial distinguishing property is that X itself, and itself being a relational property, has the generative capacity to modify the powers of its constituents in fundamental ways and to exercise causal influences *sui generis*. This is the litmus test which differentiates between emergence on the one hand and aggregation and combination on the other. Thus, for example, a demographic structure is often treated as a mere aggregate of so many people of such and such ages, yet this structure itself can and does modify the powers of people to change it, that is, it affects the powers of its constituents – by defining the size of the relevant group of child bearing couples whose reproductive behaviour could transform the structure and thus restricting their influence upon it, however prolific or non-prolific they may be. Furthermore other powers of people are curtailed (or enhanced) by its particular structural configuration at a given time which exerts causal powers proper to its internal relations themselves. For example, with a top-heavy demographic structure, it is extremely difficult to introduce or sustain a generous pensions policy, and the emergent effect of the structure *qua* structure can be ascertained by asking 'what does need to be the case demographically' in order to supply generous pensions? (This is unlikely to be the only requisite; some commitment to taxing the active population obviously will also be needed – entailing beliefs and the power to implement them – but the structure does affect *what* level of taxation will be required in relation to this goal). Such generative powers are the hallmarks of emergent properties and their reality is ascertained by causal effects like the above.

Yet such causal powers may be unexercised (a generous pension policy is not mooted or is defeated, perhaps in the knowledge of what it would do to taxation levels), or is exercised but obscured at the level of events (as with two countries which are both demographically top-heavy yet one has considerable scarce natural resources which the other lacks. Given similar policy intentions, the former does grant better pensions than the latter, but demography is still exerting its effect by, for example, subtracting from reinvestment capital). The difficulty of unequivocally establishing the existence of such powers *is* intransigent were we to confine ourselves to observable effects at the level of events for this would re-commit the enterprise to a neo-Humean quest for manifest regularities. Instead, the morphogenetic approach makes no leap from the real to the actual, but rather dwells on the ground between them by analysing the generative mechanisms potentially emanating from structures (and cultures) as emergent properties and their reception by people, with their own emergent powers of self and social reflection. Outcomes never simply mirror one or the other, but are the products of their interplay. This will be fully addressed when we examine the morphogenetic cycles involved.

In society there are a variety of emergent properties – structural, cultural and agential, each of which is irreducible to the others, has relative autonomy, and is also relatively enduring. Here of course is another parting of the ways *vis-à-vis* Structuration theory, whose proponents also elide these three since material resources are confined to a 'virtual existence' until instantiated by agency drawing upon interpretative schemes.

What differentiates a *structural* emergent property is its *primary dependence upon material resources*, both physical and human. In other words, the internal and necessary relations between its constituents are fundamentally material ones: these make it what it is and without them it could neither exist as such nor possess the causal powers which characterize it. With regard to distinguishing structural emergent properties from cultural ones, the force of the word 'fundamentally' is defined in terms of natural necessity itself.[11] Thus, certainly material relations may and frequently are legitimated by reference to ideas, but the two should not be elided, for a material relationship can be sustained by coercion and manipulation, thus its legitimation is not a matter of necessity. Similarly, I trust that enough was said in chapter 4 to undermine the conviction that material resources had no real existence in their own right and that insuperable difficulties attached to the structurationists' insistence that they could only become real rather than 'virtual' in conjunction with rules, that is certain kinds of ideas. The basic argument consisted in sustaining the ontological status of resources such as land, food, weapons or factories because (i) rules and meanings are often unintelligible without

[11] On the metaphysical necessity of presupposing natural necessity, see Andrew Sayer, *Method in Social Science: A Realist Approach*, Routledge, London, 1992, pp. 169–171ff.

reference to them (paying rent without reference to property ownership), i.e. they have *autonomy*; (ii) their prior existence frequently constrains the meanings which can be imposed or made to stick, i.e. they are *anterior*; and (iii) their effects are often independent of the interpretations placed on them, i.e. they exert *causal influence*. The extended argument to cover Sewell's reformulation,[12] which reassigned material resources to an actual status and cultural schemas to a virtual status, but insisted that structures were confined to cases where the two were mutually implicative and reciprocally sustaining, was that this *excluded* precisely what is under discussion now. In other words, resource-to-resource relations (of the type, food production – drought – famine; or Public Schools – fees – higher paid jobs) were just what were lost in attempting to confine structures to combinations of rules *and* resources. Symmetrically, rule-to-rule relations also went by the board, yet as will be seen in a moment these are exactly what the morphogenetic approach defines as cultural *emergent* properties.

More seriously, because not only conflationary theorists would have reservations about it, is the fact that *structural* emergent properties (and also cultural ones), are defined and identified independently of their occupants or encumbents and of the social interaction taking place between the latter. Now we have already seen that every kind of conflationary theorist will resist untying the two because all maintain some form of SS–SI connection (or some variant of CS–S–C connection for culture). Yet even some of those who do not insist upon sustaining it on theoretical grounds would maintain that the two are *methodologically* inseparable, because of either (i), the present-tense version of activity-dependence, or (ii) the contextual dependence of any SS feature on its SI environment for intelligibility and therefore for purposes of correct identification.

Now argument (i) has already been considered (above, pp. 142–9). It was countered that any given structure was one which a current population could only reproduce or transform (these processes *are* present-tense), but the structure encountered at any T^1 is activity-dependent in the past-tense since it represented the material resultants of the combined doings of previous agents and their unintended consequences. In material terms these outcomes of previous SI 'games' constituted structural emergent properties (distributions, roles, institutional structures, social systems) whose necessary and internal relations the next 'generation' of agents then confronted. The response to argument (ii) is that the relevant

[12] William H. Sewell, 'A theory of structure: duality, agency and transformation', *American Journal of Sociology*, 1992, 98:1, 1–30. See ch. 4, pp. 137–44.

context for the correct identification of structural emergent properties is *not* that of Social Interaction, which only yields the fallible partial appreciation which agents have of their structural context (we do not identify structures by interviewing people about them). Transcendental arguments ask what else needs to be the case, what else must be present for X to be such as it is, and not what people think notice, tell or believe is the case. Natural necessity makes appeal to other constituents at the SS level and not to beliefs about them, including mis-information and dis-information at the SI level. Failure to make this distinction runs together precisely the three things which we wish to explore and theorize, namely structures, their causal powers and their social reception. In falsely privileging the discursive penetration of agents it deprives us of any means of understanding their distorted perception, its sources and the interests it serves.

Therefore, *structural* emergent properties (SEPs), irreducible to people and relatively enduring, as with all incidences of emergence, are specifically defined as those internal and necessary relationships which entail material resources, whether physical or human, and which generate causal powers proper to the relation itself. As such, this serves to differentiate SEPs from the totality of unintended consequences, of which the former is indeed a sub-class. Yet every unintended outcome is not irreducible, enduring, involved in internal and necessary relations with others and *because* of this possessing determinate causal powers. Unintended consequences may indeed prove influential but in a wholly contingent manner. ('For the want of the nail the shoe was lost' to 'the loss of the Kingdom' is a pretty story of contingencies, but one whose finale is dependent upon no ready supply of blacksmiths, spare mounts or reinforcements.) Equally, emergent properties (of which SEPs are but one type) are distinguished from aggregate consequences, for however important the effects of the latter may be, they can always be disaggregated into the sum of individual actions, that is they are reducible. Sometimes the sums add up badly for those concerned, as in the cases of sub-optimality with which Elster deals.[13] For example each and everyone may be able to walk to safety through some exit, but all cannot do so simultaneously and if they try, then tragedy rather than safety will result if the building is on fire. What is involved here are actions and their combinations plus the human capacity to reflect upon them and sometimes devise approximations to optimal forms of re-combination (procedures for an orderly exit as practised in fire drills). Where this is not possible (e.g. each firm competes for profits but when all do so profits

[13] Jon Elster, *Logic and Society*, Wiley, Chichester, 1978.

shrink, wages are reduced, industrial unrest cuts into profitability, yet price-fixing is undermined by those fearful of going under etc.), we may legitimately question whether this is a pure aggregate phenomenon since the constraints denying approximation to optimal combinations (international markets, industrial organization, legal controls on pricing) all represent irreducible elements whose interrelations embroil 'producers' in the causal powers of SEPs. When structural constraints condition enduring sub-optimalities for a given category, then these outcomes cannot be construed as the summativity effects of combination alone.

In turn this raises a general difficulty in practical social analysis, namely the frequent tendency of those working exclusively at the level of events, to *treat* emergent properties as mere aggregate consequences. A SEP, of course, is entirely different from a taxonomic category constructed by investigators, for there are no internal or necessary relations whatsoever between those, for instance, making up the Registrars' Generals 'classes', those listed in the Telephone Directory or the world's anglers, although material requirements (income, subscription, equipment) determine inclusion in these categories. The generic problem is that something like 'social stratification' is treated in individualistic/aggregate terms by means of observable atomistic attributes (earnings, supervisory responsibility etc.) of people who are assigned to categories which refer not to real collectivities but to the investigator's constructs. In this manner, distributions are treated as purely additive. They elide the effects of necessity and contingency (placing a chief executive and the lottery winner in the same wealth band). In so doing, they occlude the fact that the most crucial distributions making for stratification of the population (class, status and power) are expressions of SEPs, of internal and necessary *relationships* between real collectivities and their further relations with entities like the prevailing mode of production, market arrangements, the institutionalisation of power and formal mechanisms for status conferral. Treating distributions as merely summative, and thus mixing together the expression of SEPs with various contingent consequences not only misconstrues social reality but also immediately forfeits explanatory purchase. Where stratification is concerned, though we do understand something from the fact that many *are* poor and powerless, we understand a great deal more about how this collectivity and its members will react by exploring structured poverty and powerlessness, whether the structures involved are congruent or incongruent and how they gel with the contingencies which have landed others in the same overt position of under-privilege. For within this category, different structural relationships will account for why different people find themselves there (exploitation, ethnocentricism, welfare policy), and in turn will condition those with whom they are and are not objectively predisposed to collaborate.

As with every other type of SEP (roles, institutions and systems), it is crucial to distinguish between structural conditioning and the emergent powers of different categories of people (primary and corporate agents, as well as individual actors). For it is the interplay between the powers of the 'parts' and the powers of the 'people' which is decisive for the outcome and not merely whether this can be characterized as reproduction or transformation but in order to explain the precise form of structural elaboration to take place.

Culture is approached analytically in exactly the same way as structure,[14] for it is just as appropriate to speak of cultural as of social structures. Equally it is the pre-existence, autonomy and durability of the constituents of the Cultural System which enables their identification as entities distinct from the meanings held by agents at any given time. The distinction is made by virtue of the fact that there are *logical* relations prevailing between items constituting the Cultural System, whereas it is *causal* relations which maintain between cultural agents.

The logical consistency or inconsistency which characterizes relationships within the Cultural System is a property of the world of ideas, of World Three as Popper put it, or, if preferred, of the contents of libraries. In fact, we utilize this concept everyday when we say that the ideas of X are consistent with those of Y, or that theory or belief A contradicts theory or belief B. These are quite different from the other kind of everyday statement, to the effect that the ideas of X were influenced by those of Y, in which case we are talking about causal effects which are properties of people – such as the influence of teachers on pupils, ideologists on their audiences or earlier thinkers on later ones.[15] The latter generates *causal consensus*, that is the (degree of) cultural uniformity produced by the ideational influence of one set of people on another through a whole gamut of techniques – manipulation, mystification, legitimation, persuasion and argumentation. Causal consensus tends to be intimately allied to the use of power and influence, whereas logical consistency is entirely independent of them since it exists whether or not it is socially exploited or concealed and regardless of it even being recognized. Therefore, causal relationships are contingent (they *may* pertain) whereas logical relationships *do* obtain, and when internally and necessarily related they constitute cultural emergent properties (CEPs). All items in society's propositional 'register', which have been 'lodged' there by previous thinkers, have

---

[14] For a full discussion of culture from the morphogenetic perspective, see Margaret S. Archer, *Culture and Agency*, Cambridge University Press, Cambridge, 1989. Chapter 5 is particularly relevant to this section.

[15] 'So we have actually these two different worlds, the world of *thought-processes*, and the world of the *products* of thought-processes. While the former may stand in *causal* relationships, the latter stand in *logical* relationships.' Karl R. Popper, *Objective Knowledge*, Clarendon, Oxford, 1972, pp. 298–9.

to stand in some *logical relationship* to one another (which of course can be one of independence) whilst *causal relationships* are reliant upon agential instigation. Thus, the Cultural System refers to relations between the components of culture whilst Socio-Cultural interaction concerns relationships between cultural agents. The CS/S-C distinction therefore maps on to that between culture without a knowing subject and culture with a knowing subject.

Clearly, the Cultural System and Socio-Cultural life do not exist or operate independently of each other; they overlap, intertwine and are mutually influential. This is precisely the point, for what is being defended is not philosophical dualism but the utility of analytical dualism, which allows their interplay to be explored. The generalization of this distinction depends upon using the laws of logic itself and appeals to the universality of the law of non-contradiction.[16] In other words, culture as a whole is taken to refer to all intelligibilia, that is to any item which has the dispositional capacity of being understood by someone. Within this, the CS is distinguished as that sub-set of items to which the law of non-contradiction can be applied – that is propositions, for only statements which assert truth or falsity can be deemed to be in contradiction or to be consistent with one another. In turn this makes the propositional register equivalent to the CS at any given time; a distinction which is not only workable but justifiable because of the indubitable importance of what is held to be true or false in any particular society.

Obviously we do not live by propositions alone (any more than we live logically); in addition, we generate myths, are moved by mysteries, become rich in symbolism and ruthless in manipulating hidden persuaders. But these are precisely the stuff of S-C interaction, for they are all matters of inter-personal influence whether we are talking at one extreme of hermeneutic understanding (including religious experience at the furthest extremity) or of the manipulative assault and battery of ideas used ideologically, at the other, between which lie the many other non-propositional things over which we dissent – tastes and prejudices, affinities and animosities etc. All of this takes place beyond or outside of the canons of logic, whether knowingly on the part of agents (proclaiming the mystery of faith), whether imposed on unknowing others (recipients of symbolic machinations), or whether as that state of semi-knowledgeability called 'public opinion'.

As an emergent entity the CS has an objective existence and autonomous relations amongst its components (theories, beliefs, values, or more strictly between the propositional formulations of them) in the sense

---

[16] See Archer, *Culture and Agency*, pp. 111–27.

that these are independent of anyone's claim to know, to believe, to assent or to assert them. At any moment the CS is the product of historical S-C interaction, but having emerged (emergence being a continuous ideational process) then *qua* product, it has properties of its own. Like structure, culture is a human product but it too escapes its makers to act back upon them. The CS contains constraints (like the things that can and cannot be said in a particular natural language), it embodies new possibilities (such as technical applications undreamed of in the pure theory on which they are based), and it introduces new problems through the relationships between the emergent entities themselves (the clash of theories), between these and the physical environment (mastery or ruin), and between these and human agents (makers and openers of Pandora's box).

Consequently, as CEPs, ideational contradictions exist independently of people noticing them or caring about them – indeed since there are an infinite number of situations upon which any theory may bear, it might well contain contradictions of which no one is aware. Similarly, the relationship between a problem and a solution, which is one of compatibility, is ultimately divorced from whether anyone *does* understand it, though not from the ability of someone *to do so*. Thus, as a CEP, a soufflé recipe might not have been used by anyone living, but would still work for the cook who eventually tried it.

This use of analytical dualism in relation to culture faces three sources of opposition from those who argue respectively that Cultural Systems, (i) have no independent existence to study; (ii) are socially relative and only understandable in their own terms; and (iii) cannot in practice be examined separately from the S-C context. The first objection comes from those like Winch who maintain that nothing may admissibly be dissociated from the S-C level since all things are only knowable through it. Hence, his formula that the 'logical relations between propositions . . . depend on social relations between men'.[17] (This of course is a philosophical version of upward conflation, taking the typical S-C → CS form, and depending here on the elision of 'meaning' with 'use'.) From this view, the last thing we can do is to stand outside any community or aside from its linguistic conventions and then legislate about what is real for them or what counts as a contradiction in their beliefs.[18] Thus Winch seeks to pull the ontological rug from under the CS, making it collapse back into the S-C realm, just as later more trenchant relativists sought to complete the process under (ii).

---

[17] Peter Winch, *The Idea of a Social Science*, Routledge and Kegan Paul, London, 1958, p. 126.

[18] Peter Winch, 'Understanding a primitive society', in Bryan Wilson (ed.), *Rationality*, Basil Blackwell, Oxford, 1979, p. 93f.

However, critics have regularly pointed out in response to objections (i) and (ii) that although there is undoubtedly plenty of variation in the social relations between people, no one has provided a convincing demonstration that logical relationships are capable of the same variability nor that comprehensibility could be sustained in the absence of universal obedience to the law of non-contradiction.[19] Next, not only has the use theory of meaning attracted considerable criticism but it has also suffered the final indignity of being stood on its head – namely by the counterclaim that the usage of concepts often depends upon exploiting their lack of meaning, double meaning or ambiguity.[20] In other words the intelligibilia are not always or even usually the dependent variable, as the S-C → CS formula assumes *a prioristically*. Thus, if meanings can be separated from use, this buttresses the case for the ontological status of CEPs, in principle though not necessarily in practice.

For objection (iii) remains and denies that this is methodologically practicable. Here it is argued that the identification of CEPs is context-dependent and that the relevant context is a matter of local socio-cultural practices, which therefore undermines the possibility of maintaining the CS/S-C distinction since reference to the latter constantly has to be made in order to elucidate the meaning of any given CEP. The response to this is identical in form to that made when the same objection was raised in connection with SEPs and it turns on determining the *appropriate* context for identifying emergent properties of any kind. As far as CEPs are concerned, these properties of the CS level are not dependent on any of the goings on at the S-C level, since logical relations are independent of causal ones at T^1 (though not vice versa). Analytically, at any given point in time, the items populating the CS realm have escaped their creators and have logical relationships among one another which are totally independent of what people know, feel or believe about them. At future time what agents do about them *may* be highly significant for the CS universe, but only if the things done in turn enter the CS register (as a new theory superseding an old one, a new ethic replacing a previous one and so forth) in which case they too escape their progenitors and immediately assume logical relations amongst themselves and with prior ideas. The crucial point therefore is that analytically, at any given T^1, CS relations are not context-dependent upon S-C relations, but only upon the context made up of other ideas.

Consequently in asserting the existence of a CEP, we never need and

---

[19] See Steven Lukes, 'Some problems about rationality', and Martin Hollis, 'Reason and ritual', both in Wilson (ed.), *Rationality*; also Martin Hollis and Steven Lukes (eds.), *Rationality and Relativism*, Blackwell, Oxford, 1982.

[20] Ernest Gellner, 'Concepts and society', in Wilson (ed.), *Rationality*, pp. 45–6.

never should descend from the logical to the causal level, for of all the interesting bearings that S-C interaction has upon the CS, the ability of the former to arbitrate on the logical status of the latter is not one of them. Those who attempt to treat the S-C level as the context of the CS can learn nothing more about existing logical relations from existing causal ones. Instead, they are embarking on an entirely different enterprise of trying to understand the meaning of X and Y to participants, of attempting to explain how people can hold X and Y simultaneously, or why others consider X and Y to be antipathetic. These are questions about how people live with logical contradictions or consistencies in the CEPs which figure in their culture. Yet this socio-cultural response to emergent features of the cultural system is precisely what we want to explore; to make it part of our tools of identification is to rob us of our topic – which is why it is profitable to sustain analytical dualism.

The parts and the people: stability and change

Basically, analytical dualism is possible due to temporality. Because 'structure' and 'agency' are phased over different tracts of time, this enables us to formulate practical social theories in terms of the former being prior to the latter, having autonomy from it and exerting a causal influence upon it. In other words, we can talk about 'system integration' conditioning 'social integration' which necessarily confronts the former, since 'social integration' *always applies to the here and now* (where ever that is situated historically), whilst 'system integration' is antecedent to it. This is the case for every level at which SEPs or CEPs are produced[21] and given the fact that realists defend a much more robustly stratified view of social reality, then the 'problem of scope'[22] exercises them considerably more than is the case for all versions of conflationary theorizing.[23]

---

[21] Lockwood himself suggested, in relation to his macroscopic distinction between 'social and system integration' that 'It may make sense to apply such a distinction to some particular sub-system of society or to some particular type of corporate group' – indeed it does ('Social integration', p. 253).

[22] Helmut Wagner, 'Displacement of scope: a problem of the relationship between small-scale and large-scale sociological theories', *American Journal of Sociology*, 1964, 69: 6.

[23] Central conflationists minimize the problem, partly by reducing the difference between 'social' and 'system' intergration to differences in the *size* of groups and then by viewing *their* main difference as a *qualitative one*. This, for Giddens, 'is the nearest I shall come . . . to admitting the usefulness of a differentiation between "micro" and "macro-sociological" studies'. Anthony Giddens, *Central Problems of Social Theory*, Macmillan, London, 1979, p. 77. Downwards conflationists regard the macro- and micro- as homologically related, such that the small is simply a miniaturized version of the large. Typically Upwards conflationists displace scope in the opposite direction, and by placing a big etc. after their micro-sociological expositions, imply that by aggregation we will arrive at a satisfactory portrayal of the macroscopic. See ch. 1, pp. 8–15.

However, whilst structural and cultural antecedence means that they exert conditional influences upon agency, predisposing towards different courses of action, the former in no way determines the latter. It cannot do so on two accounts, both of which hinge on the fact that agency itself is the bearer of emergent powers. Thus, on the one hand, *any form of socio-cultural conditioning only exerts its effects on people and is only efficacious through people.* Hence, no conditional influence works as a hydraulic pressure, but is subject to reflective (if often imperfect) evaluation by agents who weigh it against their other concerns, due to their own emergent properties of self-consciousness and self-monitoring. On the other hand, agential relations themselves represent emergent powers (PEPs or people's emergent properties) with their two defining features – that is they modify the capacities of component members (affecting their consciousness and commitments, affinities and animosities) and exert causal powers proper to their relations themselves *vis-à-vis* other agents or their groupings (such as association, organization, opposition and articulation of interests). At any given T^1, these agential features (PEPs) are the outcome of prior interaction in anterior socio-cultural contexts during previous morphogenetic cycles. As such, their pre-grouping is the equivalent of the pre-distribution of material resources and the pre-constitution of ideational sources at the start of any new morphogenetic/static cycle (and all three will undergo re-grouping, re-distribution and re-constitution respectively, during morphogenesis).

When we differentiate between the 'parts' (SEPs plus CEPs) and the 'people' in order to examine their interplay, this is *not* therefore a matter of investigating the impact of structural and cultural emergents upon an undifferentiated and unstratified environment whose constituents happen to be people. Instead, it is a question of the confluence between two sets of emergent powers – those of the 'parts' and those of the 'people' (PEPs). The key to Lockwood's understanding of how this contributed to accounts of stability or change lay in his grasping that the two sets of powers could be synchronized with one another or out of synch. Transformation resulted from congruence between both sets of powers, which when 'disorderly' together amplified deviations from the status quo (conditioned by structure and actualized by agency). Their incongruence was unproductive of change because it rendered structural powers inoperative (since structural conditioning was unrealized by agency). Similarly, reproduction again ensued when agential powers became ineffectual because of countervailing structural influences. Certainly, the formulation of his account dealt only with 'given' states of the two types of generative mechanisms and thus needs to be supplemented by the dynamics of their development – the morphogenesis of structure and culture (taken up in chapter 9) and the double morphogenesis, where agential powers are elaborated in the process of socio-cultural transformation (examined fully in chapter 8).

Let us now briefly examine the importance which attaches to this independent variation between the different emergent powers of the 'parts' and the 'people' at each of the various levels characterized by different types of SEPs (identical points obtain for CEPs, which range from the macroscopic doctrinal level down to that of single propositions). Unless their independent variability is first established (as is essential to analytical dualism), then the notion of linking mechanisms is otiose – they are only a necessity in non-conflationary theorizing. The same is obviously true of any notion that the confluence of the two sets of generative mechanisms can interact to reinforce or nullify one another's powers.

(i) We have already begun to discuss the *positional level* and how the structured distribution of resources pre-groups collectivities into the privileged and under-privileged. Thus, each 'generation' begins life stratified and these different collectivities have vested interests in maintaining their advantages or improving their lot. What is crucial for the outcome is whether they merely remain as Primary agents, inarticulate in their demands and unorganized for their pursuit, in which case they only exert the aggregate effects of those similarly placed who co-act in similar ways given the similarity of their circumstances. Here their potential transformation into Corporate agents, with emergent powers of promotive organization and articulation of interests (such that they become party to negotiated societal transformations) depends jointly on the conditional influences of SEPs and how these mesh with social factors influencing the cohesion possible within collectivities. For example, as has often been noted, the poor of modernity are a disparate collectivity and one which is less and less synonymous with the working class. Though still structured by the complexities of late welfare capitalism, the members of this collectivity are more reflexively concerned with their differences than their similarities. Thus generational differences divide the young unemployed from the old-aged (two of the largest categories of the poor), ethnocentricism erects a racial barrier to cohesion, whilst the handicapped, homeless and single parent families increasingly pursue their interests through special interest groups rather than by more generalized forms of collaboration. Social affinities and antagonisms thus fuel fissiparousness: they do not preclude the development of Corporate agents, but mean that these will be in the plural (addressing single-issues) rather than in the singular (confronting the plurality of vested grievances shared by the underprivileged).

Collectivities *per se* are only the tangential instigators of structural change. Precisely because they are Primary agents pre-grouped as such by the anterior distributive structure (a 'class in itself' was a fairly appropriate designation of the underprivileged in nineteenth-century England), response to their positions takes the form of disorganized and localized antagonism. Since the poor are always with us, so is Luddism in its changing historical expressions. Consequently, though they do create problems for decision makers at higher levels, they themselves are largely the *recipients* of struggles over decision-making between Corporate agents. Yet as an enormous human resource, they are not immune from these since they will be the targets of constant efforts to mobilise and manipulate them in order to determine the outcome of issues which were not of their making. Bombarded and often bamboozled and betrayed, Corporate agents drag them into the fray and, in entering it, they do not remain unchanged but undergo regrouping. Thus, those early entrepreneurial dissenters who sought to challenge the Anglican educational monopoly courted working class enrolment in their own schools, leading the Anglicans promptly to do likewise, yet the effect of this unprecedented educational mobilization of the working class generated disillusionment within three decades. It produced a new literate leadership capable of articulating both educational and socio-economic grievances and also promoted corporate re-grouping of the Chartists and their successors who developed their own schools and Institutes for politico-economic enlightenment. As pre-grouped human resources they had been mobilized to advance the struggle of others, but as self-reflective agents, the collectivity underwent regrouping in the process: in future time they were no longer a mere resource but had started to become a force – in a struggle which had now become their own.

(ii) At the level of *roles* each of which is necessarily and internally related to others (doctor/patient; landlord/tenant; teacher/pupil) and to material requirements such as hospitals, pharmaceutical supplies, equipment and trained personnel, the distinction between the 'systemic' and the 'social' is the difference between roles and their occupants – the relative autonomy of the role being secured by the fact that they endure a succession of incumbents possessing very different personal characteristics. One of the 'micro-level' problems to explain is different 'performances' of the same role and how this simultaneously leads both to role re-definition and personal development – *through the process of double morphogenesis*. Again, we need to begin by distinguishing between the properties pertaining to the role itself and the contingent properties belonging to its current holders. The latter are quite different from the types of 'social integration' which characterize collectivities at the *positio-*

nal level; for one cannot talk of a single lecturer having organization (a collective property), but only of her being well organized (a personal characteristic).

A person occupying a particular role acquires vested interests with it and is both constrained and enabled by its 'dos and dont's' in conjunction with the penalties and promotions which encourage compliance. Yet these are not determinants, because there is leeway for interpretation, especially given that they are only partial in their coverage and clarity. Even the small print of my university contract is silent on whether I can offer my students a drink or my political opinions. Thus, far from roles being fully scripted and their occupants as comprehensively programmed robots, it seems more useful to think of people *personifying* them in different ways,[24] thus making for different kinds of lecturers. To do so entails differentiating between two sets of emergent properties: the role itself (that is a prior definition of obligations, sanctions and interests) and the personal qualities an actor brings to it – and develops in interplay with it – though some are debarred through active discrimination and structurally conditioned self-selection.

Real actors bring their own ideals and objectives, skill and incompetence, dedication or distancing, inflexibility or creativeness to the roles they occupy. All such features are not formed by the job (though they may be positively or negatively reinforced in doing it and undergo transformation through learning); otherwise we would be committed to the undesirable image of robotic executors. Nor is the occupant solicitously prepared in advance by some infallible hidden hand or unerring allocative mechanism; this entails the twin defects of normative functionalism – 'the overintegrated view of society' and the 'over-socialized view of man'. Instead, the realist insists that there are emergent properties pertaining to individual people: personal psychology cannot be upwardly reduced to sociology. Only by examining the interplay between a role and its occupants is it possible to account for why some roles are personified in routinized ways whilst others can be cumulatively transformed in the hands of their incumbents.

In the self-same process of role transformation, actors' personalities will undergo some re-formation through these experiences; not in every respect, which implies social determinism, but in certain respects (such as expectations themselves). Without this we are committed to a 'self' which is entirely independent of society: yet too strong a notion of the '*social* self' deprives us of actors who actively re-make, rather than passively take,

---

[24] Cf. Martin Hollis, *The Cunning of Reason*, Cambridge University Press, Cambridge, 1987, ch. 10.

roles themselves. The modification of personality, which itself depends on the emergent human capacity to learn, reflect, weigh consequences and to self-monitor, is a process of being re-moulded in the self-same process of re-moulding roles and it is these modified personal characteristics which actors will bring to the next roles they occupy, including any role they may have contributed towards re-defining or creating.

(iii) At the *institutional* level, we can start to illustrate the importance of 'social integration' (relations amongst the relevant population) and its capacity for independent variation by imagining a very simple pastoral tribe, whose structural emergent property is the capacity to sustain more people than is the case for the neighbouring food-gathering tribe. This power derives from the necessary and internal relations which maintain between land/animals/water/people, and can only be sustained if the population is nomadic (otherwise water-holes dry up, land becomes over-grazed etc.). There are various ways in which 'social integration' can threaten or suspend the power of pastoralism to sustain a larger population than among the food-gatherers. Internal animosities could lead to the splitting-up into smaller nomadic bands, the consequent deterioration of stock through in-breeding, which thus threatens the subsistence of all. Equally, were the strongest consistently to monopolise the products for their own consumption or disposal, then although the means of subsistence are still there for all, their distribution now precludes this outcome. Rather differently, were a belief to develop that a particular water-hole would never run dry if certain rites were routinely performed by all tribal members, their new sedentary pattern, leading to the impoverishment of land and then stock, would eventually reduce the population itself because they had fundamentally disrupted the relations necessary to pastoralism. This is an instance of the negative effects which can arise for agency through the double morphogenesis. In this case, it could of course be said that the tribe had simply stopped being pastoralists, which is true, but they have not destroyed the powers of pastoralism as would be demonstrated were they to resume the nomadic life.

(iv) By definition, complex societies have a variety of institutional structures whose co-existence means that there will necessarily be further second order relations between them, some of which will be emergent properties. These are relations between relations or, if preferred, the results of the results of interaction in an anterior structural context. This state of affairs is usefully referred to as 'system integration' because such relations pertain to the highest stratum of social reality. Systems are made up of structures; they do not 'have' them as in Holistic parlance, but rather are constituted by them and the relations between them. Incompatibilities and complementarities between institutional structures may either be internal and necessary, signalling emergence at the systemic level, or external and contingent. Because of this, the generic notion of 'systemic integration' indicates variable states of the system at different points in time. High system integration thus refers to a predominance of complementarities and low integration to a system characterised by serious incompatibilities. The fundamental point here is that social systems, as unregulated configurations, themselves contain both types of relational properties, above and beyond those pertaining to each institution alone. Because 'system integration', deriving from pre-existent institutional structures is prior to those who confront it, then it can be differentiated from the relations of 'social integration' which maintain between agents, and especially Corporate agents who play the major part in institutional decision-making.

When first advancing the concept of 'system integration', it is clear from the examples given that Lockwood had systemic emergent properties in mind. Thus, his examination of how Weber treated patrimonialism shows that he is acutely aware of dealing with the incompatibilities between internal and necessary relations at the system level, that is treating it as an emergent entity, where the realization or containment of this potential for breakdown, is dependent upon the interplay with 'social integration'. Thus, 'the relationship between bureaucracy and taxation is a highly interdependent one'[25] since the efficiency of the bureaucracy depends upon the effectiveness of its taxation system; and the effectiveness of the taxation system depends upon the efficiency of the bureaucratic apparatus. Thus the strategic problem is 'one of maintaining a taxation system that can effectively meet the material needs of a bureaucracy in the context of a subsistence, or near subsistence, economy. The centralizing goal of bureaucratic institutions is constantly *liable to sabotage by the potential social relationship structure* of the subsistence economy which favours the decentralization and 'feudalization of power relationships'[26] (my italics). Here again we have the crucial notion that the fate of 'systemic' tendencies is at the mercy of their confluence with 'social' integration, resulting in containment and stability in the cases of Egypt and China and breakdown in the later Roman Empire where the defence mechanisms strategically introduced by the bureaucracy actually intensified the trend towards the subsistence economy and actualized the potential for decentralized relationships.

[25] Lockwood, 'Social integration', p. 254.
[26] Lockwood, 'Social intergation', p. 254.

SYSTEM INTEGRATION   SOCIAL INTEGRATION

Systemic	——	Interplay	——	Populations
Institutional	——	Interplay	——	Organised groups (corporate agency)
Roles	——	Interplay	——	Individual actors
Positions	——	Interplay	——	Collectivities (primary agency)

Figure 9 Analytical dualism in social theory.

The double morphogenesis

The points made in this section can be summarised in figure 9 which serves to bring home the central implication of employing analytical dualism, namely that its power in explaining (structural and cultural) transformation or reproduction depends on the recognition that we are *always* dealing with the double *morphogenesis/stasis* – of structure and of agency as part and parcel of the self-same processes.

Realists insist that the social world is *stratified* by virtue of the distinctive emergent properties and powers which develop and prove relatively enduring and this is expressed in a *stratified model of social structure* (involving SEPs, CEPs and PEPs). Since this is necessitated by the acknowledgement of emergence itself, it is unsurprising that it differs considerably from the more flattened models with which central conflationists work (which only differentiate between large and small group relations and between face-to-face and distanced interaction), precisely because Elisionists repudiate emergence itself. Hence the different levels delineated on the left hand side of figure 9 under the heading 'system integration', according to their distinctive emergent properties (different SEPs and CEPs). Equally, the underlying theme of this section has been that exactly the same holds on the right hand side of the diagram (represented by different PEPs).

In other words, a *stratified model of people* is also entailed by the recognition of emergence. There are emergent properties of collectivities and individuals which differ from the emergent properties of corporate groups, which differ yet again from those pertaining to populations. Yet these different levels of 'social integration' are not discrete from the powers of 'system integration', despite their capacity for independent variation at any given time. Although separable because phased across different sequential tracts of time, they are intertwined in the 'double morphogenesis', where agency undergoes transformation, acquiring new emergent powers in the very process of seeking to reproduce and transform structures. For in such structural and cultural struggles, consciousness is raised as collectivities are transformed from primary agents into promotive interest groups; social selves are re-constituted as actors personify roles in particular ways to further their self-defined ends; and corporate agency is re-defined as institutional interests promote re-organization and re-articulation of goals in the course of strategic action for their promotion or defence. All the above processes are reinforced or repressed by the overall state of systemic integration, whose incompatibilities foster their actualization and whose coherence serves to contain this transformative potential of agency. Consequently, chapter 8 will be devoted to the morphogenesis of agency itself, where the case will be made for a triple distinction between 'human beings', 'actors' and 'agents' since these concepts refer to different emergent properties of 'people' (PEPs).

This is in complete contrast to the understratified view of agency employed by Elisionists where it is common practice to find the terms 'human being', 'individual', 'actor' and 'agent' being used interchangeably. Central conflationists will only allow for the differential knowledgeability of 'people', which oddly and unhelpfully confuses a general characteristic with a differentiating one. For it is maintained here, in contradistinction, that differences in knowledgeability or 'discursive penetration' actually characterize all levels (it is not just collectivities and individuals, but also corporate groups and populations who can be short on knowledge, information and awareness); this is not what distinguishes between them.

Instead, through the double morphogenesis, we acknowledge the stratified emergent powers of both the 'parts' and the 'people' and by examining their interplay, acquire the theoretical wherewithal to explain how distributional pre-grouping means that some collectivities are better placed for becoming more influential agents than others, how certain roles are differentially available to different collectivities who then become actors in very different sections of the total role array, how and why Corporate agents pack more punch in defining and re-defining structural forms, and are key links in determining whether systemic fault-lines (incompatibilities) will be split open (introducing morphogenetic structural or cultural elaboration) or will be contained (reproducing structural or cultural morphostasis). All of this must remain a closed book to the Elisionists who have denied themselves the tools with which to treat 'structure' and 'agency' in anything other than an undifferentiated and unstratified manner and consequently means that central conflation represents a self-imposed, self-denying ordinance on exploring their interplay – which is the source of explanatory power.

Conclusion

Analytical dualism underpined Lockwood's vital distinction between 'system' and 'social' integration, but what was left unanswered were the crucial questions about *what* constituted the 'component elements' of social systems and *how* they could be held to exert causal effects upon people. Social Realism supplied the answer in terms of emergent properties and their generative powers. Complementary as these two contributions are, there nevertheless remains a gap between them which requires filling. Thus, whilst the strength of Lockwood's explanatory approach was its capacity to account for when transformation rather than reproduction would predominate, this was presented in terms of different conjunctions between states of 'social' and 'system' integration. Issues surrounding where the two states originated, how they were mutually influential and what processes actually produced distinctive outcomes were left in abeyance. Basically, the explanatory formula was of the 'if . . . then' type: what it lacked was a specification of the mechanisms or processes involved (though the frequent insistence that the linkage involved interaction avoided any suspicion of reification).

Correspondingly, whilst Realism could ably ground these 'component elements' in emergent properties, and the fundamental notion of a stratified social world justified the distinction between the 'parts' and the 'people', the insistence that the exercise of generative powers was at the mercy of contingent interventions within the open system of society left a gap between their robust ontology of the social world and purely tendential explanations. Basically, this explanatory formula was of the 'if . . . possibly' type, which though fundamentally correct since openness is undeniable, can be tautened to turn possibilities into likelihoods. What was usually missing here was due allowance for the confluence of *plural* generative powers and their *reciprocal influence*, rather than consideration of one emergent property alone confronting the morass of contingencies.

The gap between the two, between the explanatory power of the practical social theory and the ontological strength of the realist philosophy, is fundamentally methodological, and it is this which the morphogenetic/static approach attempts to bridge. Because of the complementarity of the two contributions under discussion, analytical dualism possesses both a firm ontological grounding and the promise of explanatory profitability. The morphogenetic cycle is advanced as the means of operationalizing analytical dualism to span the gap between the two.

It begins by accentuating that since we are indeed dealing with emergent properties in the analysis of structure, culture and agency, then in fact we are also concerned with three kinds of cycles, each of which has

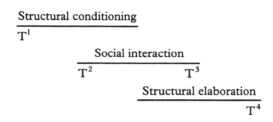

Figure 10 The morphogenesis of structure.

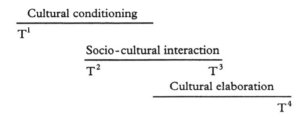

Figure 11 The morphogenesis of culture.

relative autonomy and yet interacts with the others. These have been briefly introduced in the present chapter and can be represented in the figures 10–12.

For this approach to supply the methodological complement which bridges the gap between Lockwoood's practical theorizing and the Realist social ontology depends upon the contribution it makes to their unfinished business. On the one hand, Lockwood's question marks arise within each kind of morphogenetic/static cycle and what needs to be supplied are the missing mechanisms by virtue of which structure and culture causally condition agency and also the subsequent processes through which agents introduce structural and cultural elaboration (or perpetuate reproduction). On the other hand, what is problematic in Realism can be made more tractable through according due weight to the relations between the three cycles. The three are continuously operative in society and are always interrelated because they intersect in their middle element – since all generative mechanisms are only influential through people. Yet they also have relative autonomy from one another and therefore may be out of synchrony; with one fostering morphogenesis and another morphostasis. Whether they are or not, what is involved is the confluence of *three sets of emergent properties* and by theorizing how

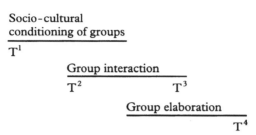

Figure 12 The morphogenesis of Agency.

(the different states of) their generative powers interlock, then we can extend firmer expectations as to outcomes than if dealing with emergence confronting nothing but contingency.

Finally, of course, it does remain contingent which properties actually do exist at any given T^1 (though this can be explained by investigating anterior morphogenetic cycles) and also precisely what is elaborated in terms of structural, cultural and agential change at T^4; because the social system is open, open because peopled, and therefore of no fixed form due to human powers of unpredictable innovation. Hence, the kind of explanation which the morphogenetic approach proffers takes the form of analytical histories of emergence for the practical issue under investigation. It does so by examining the interplay *within and between* the three cycles, for the ultimate benefit of analytical dualism is that it is not a static method of differentiation but a tool for examining the dynamics by which the 'parts' and the 'people' shape and re-shape one another through their reciprocal interaction over time.

7   Structural and cultural conditioning

The Realist is committed to maintaining that the 'causal power of social forms is mediated through social agency'.[1] This commitment protects against reification and endorses the view that agents are the only efficient causes in social life. Nevertheless, agents are not exhaustive of social reality, since both material and ideational emergent properties (SEPs and CEPs) exist and are the bearers of causal powers. There seems to be a difficulty with the preceding sentences. They assert the existence of two kinds of entities and of two kinds of causal powers – those of the 'parts' and those of the 'people' – yet allow that only the latter can be responsible for efficient causality. This raises a duo of important questions, namely, 'why this difference between them?', and, if there is such a difference, then 'how can structure and culture be influential at all' – since it is not reducible to people who are the only efficient causes? Structural and cultural conditioning it will be maintained are quintessentially matters of mediation, *and the first phase of the morphogenetic cycle is therefore concerned with mediatory processes.*

Mediation through human agency

In open systems, emergent properties (SEPs and CEPs) can exist unexercised due to a variety of intervening contingencies. The one factor which guarantees that social systems remain open (and even precludes thought experiments about closure), is that they are necessarily peopled.

People, in turn, are capable of resisting, repudiating, suspending or circumventing structural and cultural tendencies, in ways which are unpredictable because of their creative powers as human beings. In other words, the exercise of socio-cultural powers is dependent *inter alia* upon their reception and realization by people: their effect is not direct but mediated, for there are no other ways in which it could be exercised

---

[1] Roy Bhaskar, *The Possibility of Naturalism*, Harvester Wheatsheaf, Hemel Hempstead, 1989, pp. 25–6.

without invoking impersonal social forces. What adds to the complexity is that it is equally the case that the exercise of agential powers (whether of individuals or of groups) can be suspended, modified, re-directed etc. by the social forms in which they are developed and deployed. There is no need to deny these influences or to minimize their effects, for however profound these are they still work through people who remain the efficient cause of their actualization. The difference then between the two kinds of entities and their respective powers is not one of relative influence but of mode of operation, where the effects of the 'parts' are necessarily mediated, whilst the agents stand as mediators.

This introduces the second question, for if structural and cultural influences have to be mediated, how can this be conceptualised in a manner which avoids the extremes of determinism (downward conflation) or of voluntarism (upward conflation), both of which effectively deny independent powers to either the 'parts' or the 'people' by introducing epiphenomenalism into social theorizing? Central conflation, on the other hand, deprives us of the capacity of knowing when there is more voluntarism or more determinism at work since although it treats social forms as necessary *media* of action, these only become efficacious through an *act* of 'instantiation' which serves to summon up the entire matrix of structural properties and hence precludes differentiation between them in terms of their relative influence.

Invariably, from the morphogenetic perspective, *all* structural influences (i.e. the generative powers of SEPs and CEPs) *are mediated to people by shaping the situations in which they find themselves.* The circumstances confronted by each new generation were not of their making, but they do affect what these contemporary agents can make of them (structural and cultural elaboration) and how they reconstitute themselves in the process (agential elaboration). At any given time, structures are the results of human interaction, including the results of the results of that interaction – any of which may be unintended, unwanted and unacknowledged. As such they are activity-dependent (past tense) but irreducible to current practices (present tense). This 'ontological hiatus' not only permits their differentiation, but also is what enables us to construe these pre-existents as constituting the environment of contemporary action (wherever that happens to be situated historically). We can now be more precise about how mediation takes place and will characterize this as an *objective influence which conditions action patterns and supplies agents with strategic directional guidance.*

To begin with, emergent structures represent objective limitations upon the situations and settings which agents can encounter. Thus what is 'logged' within the register of the cultural system defines the doctrines, theories, beliefs etc. in existence and thus circumscribes that which can impinge upon agents as their ideational environment. Objectively, it delimits that which *can* be reproduced, re-formulated, rejected or transformed. There may be the most sophisticated conversations in so-called primitive societies, but they will not be about atomic physics. Similarly material structures have to exist before agents can engage in practices which sustain or change them: industrial action is dependent upon factory production and wage labour. As such, there is nothing contentious here for even the assertion that we are dealing with objective limitations is unobjectionable to a symbolic interactionist such as Blumer, who accepts that social organization enters into action 'to the extent to which it shapes situations in which people act and to the extent to which it supplies fixed sets of symbols which people use in interpreting their situation'.[2] From his position he is unwilling to engage in an analysis of structural and cultural conditioning sufficient to reveal its systematic rather than episodic character. Nevertheless even such an atemporal and ahistorical recognition of such influences protects again the difficulties encountered by those who consider the definition of the situation to be independent of its objective properties.

Such difficulties are not confined to the extremes of ethnomethodology, they also dog any who adopt the anti-realist position that the unacknowledged conditions of action lack determinate influence because agents are not cognizant of them. Yet what we can do in such conditions is influenced by how they actually are. The constraints and enablements of the situations we confront are not the same as our powers of description or conceptualization. What made the social environment the way it is can remain a mystery (the streetwise don't have to know about town planning): but the way social reality has come to be is not synonymous with how we take it to be. We can misconstrue situations or be led to misconstrue them, but if we do get them wrong then our actions can go wrong. In other words, the situations which have been structured by past actions 'exist and act independently of the knowledge of which they are the objects'.[3]

For some, alarm bells will have been triggered by the words 'act independently'. There are many who willingly concede that the multifarious situations we necessarily encounter do indeed exist as the objective resultants of past actions, and who even accept that they mark out an environment containing certain limitations and potentialities, but who would resist the notion that they *condition us involuntaristically*. Yet this is

---

[2] H. Blumer, 'Society as symbolic interaction', in A. M. Rose (ed.), *Human Behaviour and Social Processes*, Routledge and Kegan Paul, London, 1962.
[3] Bhaskar, *Naturalism*, p. 14.

precisely what I am committed to defending and need to do so without endorsing reification or treating conditional influences as social hydraulics. These are the twin embargoes placed by non-conflationary theorizing upon the conceptualization of mediation (because quite apart from their other defects, both reification and hydraulics would entail denials that we are dealing with *two* sets of powers).

Firstly, it is only by respecting the powers of people (i.e. not treating them as 'indeterminate material') that the powers of the 'parts' can exert a conditioning influence in a non-reified manner. One of the most important differentiating powers proper to people is their intentionality – their capacity to entertain projects and design strategies to accomplish them (which may or may not be successful). Here, the term 'project' stands for any goal countenanced by a social agent, from the satisfaction of biologically grounded needs to the utopian reconstruction of society. Now it is by virtue of the relationship of compatibility or incompatibility between the 'projects' of people and the generative powers of the 'parts', which make up their environment, that the latter exerts a conditional influence upon the former. In other words, structural properties (SEPs and CEPs), as features of the situations in which people find themselves can only foster or frustrate 'projects'. These situational powers are transfactual but work transitively, that is they require something to work upon and remain unexercised without it. Moreover, it is only their specific relationship to the particular projects of particular agents in particular positions which allows us to call their conditional influence a 'constraint' or an 'enablement'. It makes no sense to think of any emergent social property being constraining or enabling by nature or in abstraction. These themselves are also relational terms: they designate the congruence or incongruence between two sets of powers – those powers of the 'parts' in relation to the 'projects' of the people. Only in this way, of course, can the *same* environmental property (e.g. a given distribution or an official language) give rise to situations which some agents find enabling and others constraining.

Certainly it is possible to formulate matters so that they appear otherwise. Take the following two propositions (whose substantive claims are not at issue): 'Without a given level of primitive capital accumulation, capitalism cannot develop', or, 'without a certain form of knowledge, this problem would be insoluble'. Even if both are true, this would not mean that everywhere they were found lacking, they constituted a cultural or structural constraint upon the development in question. Only when some Leonardo conceived of the project of flying are he and his successors constrained by the cultural absence of appropriate knowledge about propulsion. Similarly, only if the accumulators of capital actually projected the building of factories rather than palaces are they materially frustrated. The generative powers of the 'parts' and the 'people' are both necessary conditions for the development in question, but only together do they supply the sufficient conditions for the accomplishment of the project. To omit reference to material and ideational conditions is to endorse agents who can will any outcome regardless of their circumstances. To make no mention of agential projects pretends to explain outcomes in the absence of efficient causation. A non-reified account of structural and cultural conditioning thus *requires* an active agent in order to mediate the process.

Secondly, it therefore follows that in non-conflationary theorizing, which seeks to capture the interplay between structure and agency, the influence of the former on the latter cannot be conceptualized in the deterministic terms of social hydraulics. A conditional influence never operates as an irresistible push or pull on un-reflective matter to which things merely happen, in the absence of a self-monitoring ability which can make a difference to the outcome.

Again, it is possible to present certain instances where it seems as if structural properties indeed worked in hydraulic fashion, such that any reference to their active mediation through the projects of people was uncalled for – since under the circumstances, how could they have done otherwise? Yet in such cases, what is going on is not that agents lack any kind of project and are thus like putty, but rather that their projects are so universally human that they are taken for granted. Stringently constraining circumstances, like exile or famine, only look like hydraulic pressures *because* it is assumed that no one would harbour the project of starvation or becoming a displaced person. Doubtless this would hold for the great majority of us, but all it indicates is that human agents do *tend* to share some basic life projects. Furthermore, to omit reference to them and to the self-reflexivity which is nevertheless involved in living them out (frequently in only semi-awareness) is to render two forms of action incomprehensible. They are robbed of intelligibility which is rooted in the reflective mediation of circumstances. On the one hand, there are reasons which can move people to entertain and sustain a project of starvation (hunger strikers), and on the other, the effect of experiencing a stringent constraint entails a considered response and not an autonomic reaction (there are many different ways of projecting the exilic experience). In other words we cannot dispense with reference to human projects. Where social hydraulics appear to work, it is only courtesy of certain covert assumptions – namely that no-one would do other than evade stringently constraining situations whilst everyone would welcome felicitously enabling circumstances (like a universal pay rise). What I have been seeking to show is that where this is true it is because projects are covertly, through correctly assigned to agents, rather than that agential aims are of no mediatory relevance. Furthermore, since they are always relevant, then we had better have them out in the open and ascertain whether they do hold for all agents, without exception, all of the time.

So far what has been emphasized is that structures (SEPs and CEPs) fundamentally exert their effects in relation to and actually through the projects entertained by agents. Here it has indeed been allowed that the powers of people mean the projects they are capable of conceiving can imaginatively outstrip the social possibilities of their times. It is a necessary admission if political reform, policy formation, science fiction and research activity are to remain recognizable. All the same, it should not foster a picture of untrammelled and unassisted creativity in which projects are designed in isolation from the socio-cultural context of their conception. Although it is the case that structural conditioning always works through the 'projects' of people this is not simply a matter of the independent confluence of the two sets of powers which just happen to be congruent or incongruent. On the contrary, one of the most important conditional influences of structures (SEPs and CEPs) is their effect *upon* the projects to be conceived, entertained and sustained within a given social environment.

Because of the pre-existence of those structures which shape the situations in which we find ourselves, they impinge upon us without our compliance, consent or complicity. The structures into which we are born and the cultures which we inherit mean that we are involuntaristically situated beings. We have become English speakers before we can decide what language we would like to speak, and this cannot then become our mother-tongue. We have become the beneficiaries of parental cultural capital or the victims of the poverty trap, prior to the development of our powers to reflect upon our situation and our even later powers to monitor it. Especially due to our human nature as 'late developers', compared with other species, the circumstances in which we remain involuntaristically embedded throughout childhood condition what we project as possible, attainable and even desirable.

Just as the earlier rejection of structural determinism would have been unacceptable to the downwards conflationist, so the present unwillingness to grant that we have the freedom (either individually or collectively) to make what we will of ourselves and our social environment will in turn be repudiated by the upwards conflationist. Similarly, to accentuate the significance of involuntaristic impingement will prove unpalatable to central conflationists whose pivotal notion of 'instantiation' carries much more voluntaristic connotations. Although, according to structuration theory, people are bound to draw upon structural media in order to act, because the possibility of transformation inheres in every medium at every moment, this does not condition them to act in one-way rather than another. Therefore, the morphogenetic task is to supply an account of how the powers of the 'parts' condition the projects of 'people' – involuntaristically but also non-deterministically, yet none the less with directionality.

To repeat, *all* structural influences (i.e. the generative powers of SEPs and CEPs) work through shaping the situations in which people find themselves. It is the situations to which people respond which are mediatory because they condition (without determining) different courses of action for those differently placed, by supplying different reasons to them. This is the basic manner in which I conceive of the mediation of the tendential powers inherent in material and ideational structures to agents, who, in their turn, represent necessary mediators if structural powers are to be realized. However, there are various aspects of this mediation process which need to be clearly delineated.

Involuntaristic placement

Given their pre-existence, structural and cultural emergents shape the social environment to be inhabited. These results of past actions are deposited in the form of current situations. They account for what there is (materially and culturally) to be distributed and also for the shape of such distributions; for the nature of the extant role array, the proportions of positions available at any time and the advantages/disadvantages associated with them; for the institutional configuration present and for those second order emergent properties of compatibility or incompatibility, that is whether the respective operations of institutions are matters of obstruction or assistance to one another. In these ways, situations are objectively defined for their subsequent occupants or incumbents. Such shaping processes extend from micro to macro contexts (thus leaving no privileged life-world as a structurally neutral asylum); they persist throughout the life-course since their effect is continuous rather than once and for all; and they are pervasive because if agents extricate themselves from one structurally moulded situation, it is only to enter another. In other words, that emergent properties do impinge on people is really not at issue, because all social action is necessarily contextualized and all contexts embody social forms.

The significance of involuntarism consists not in an inability to change our situations, but rather in the fact that to evade one is merely to embroil oneself in another. Thus we are quite literally born into life chances which are defined by prior distributions of material resources; this *is* our situation at T^1 and though it is alterable by T^3, alterations entail altering our situations and this is not a matter of untrammelled choice but of confrontation and extrication which carry costs. For agents to assume particular roles within institutions may appear more voluntaristic, even if it is admitted that such choices are constrained by life chances established in advance. However, the crucial point is that even such exercises of voluntarism do not free agents from involuntaristic involvement in structures and their situational conditioning. Thus most of us have the choice of whether to marry or not, but agential awareness of the structural powers which this would entail (legal responsibility, financial communality, canonical obligations and juridical restrictions on exit) may serve hermeneutically to prompt avoidance. Yet the alternative choice of 'partnership' may dodge those particular situational constraints attaching to the marriage project, but it is not a method of gaining immunity from all structural influences; these agents have merely 'exchanged' one potential situation for another form of situational conditioning (the law still arbitrates on custody of children, relative entitlements to common goods, eligibility for certain benefits etc.). Similarly, opting for single or celibate status is not to opt out of situational constraints, but to be embroiled in a different set.

Furthermore, once within given positions and roles, the situations confronted also change involuntaristically as other structural influences impinge upon them, representing situational modifications which present agents with new problems (or advantages), neither of which were of their making. A mismatch of values, inflation, over-production, shortages of skills or anticipatory socialization are all forms of the above. Their genesis derives from those second-order emergent properties, that is relations between institutions or organizations, whose powers are exercised through re-shaping the situations which different sections of the population have to face (by virtue of their association with the respective institutional operations or identification with organizational projects) and with which they then have to deal strategically. This is the case whether they confront situational bonuses which they wish to retain (since *ceteris paribus* these make their tasks easier to accomplish and their goals easier to attain) or problems whose reverse effects provide no incentive to live with them.

The involuntaristic impingement of structures (SEPs and CEPs) upon situations is wholly objective. However, it does not necessarily follow from this that these sources are known, let alone correctly diagnosed. Indeed there may be powerful interests at stake whose advantage lies in promoting just such misrecognition. However, it is precisely due to the delineation of divergent vested interests that the real effects of structured situations cannot simply be dissolved into such subjective constructions.

Vested interests

Thus the major effect of involuntaristic placement is to endow different sections of society with different vested interests as part and parcel of the situations in which they find themselves, not episodically, but rather as features which are both systematic and enduring. Yet unless these influences which are experienced as rewards or frustrations are to be left at the mercy of subjective interpretation (i.e. fully reducible to the ideational constructions of agency), then our mediatory mechanism requires that they have something objective upon which to work. These are the *vested* interests which are embedded in *all* socially structured positions.

Indeed, one of the main antecedent effects of structures (SEPs and CEPs) consists in dividing the population, not necessarily and usually not exhaustively, into those with vested interests in maintenance and change respectively, according to the positions in which they find themselves involuntaristically. As such they are wholly objective; they are not to be confounded with agents' mental states (for a vested interest in being sufficiently competitive not to go out of business is quite different from a subjective feeling of competitiveness), nor do they stand in any particular relationship to anyone's real interests. (Despite the difficulties entailed in defining the latter, we can still conclude that it *might* not be in the real interests of the idle rich to perpetuate their idleness, while it is certainly in accordance with their vested interests.) In other words, agents' vested interests are objective features of their situations which, it will be maintained, then predispose them to different courses of action and even towards different life courses.

All of us as members of society have vested interests: the significance of involuntarism is precisely that we cannot avoid trafficking with them. Of course, this is not the only way we come by positions for some will have involved strenuous voluntaristic exertions. However, those which are acquired involuntaristically profoundly affect both what is sought and what can be achieved through even the most heroic acts of voluntarism. Vested interests are the means by which structural (and cultural) properties exert a conditional influence on subsequent action. The two elements of the term are important. To characterize an interest as a 'vested' one is to associate it with a particular position; the implication being that if positions change, then so do interests. Yet to see interests (whether real or otherwise is a matter of contingency) as being embedded in social positions, points to the fact that they bear upon things that satisfy wants yet are not equally accessible to all. The home of vested interests is amidst social scarcity. The term has no meaning in the context of natural abundance. It does of course begin to acquire it the moment scarcity is introduced into abundance through social processes of unequal distribution. This is the moral of Rousseau's myth of property inequalities, which began with the first man to fence off land and call it 'mine'. Over time, that is the longest possible *durée*, natural distributions (whether scarce, abundant or variable) become converted into social distributions; the technological effects of society upon nature 'manufacture' further distributions; and the consequence of one part of society upon another 'produces' still further distributions of non-natural goods (information, expertise, esteem). Despite the general social capacity to improve upon nature's abundance (e.g. by irrigation or medicine), vested interests are concerned with relative advantages rather than absolute well-being.

Thus involuntaristically, each new generation assumes a position in a variety of such distributions. Many authors have presented these metaphorically as the accumulated winnings of past 'games'. The connotations are misleading: we are not dealing with fun, fair play and much less with Queensberry rules. Those who find the cards stacked against them do not simply have the bad luck to come from a long line of bad card players. With any such position come vested interests and with these come motives for the reproduction of advantages or the transformation of disadvantages. In both cases we are dealing with relational properties. As Porpora puts it,

among the causal powers that are deposited in social positions are interests. Interests are built into a social position by the relationship of that position to other positions in the system . . . [Thus], capitalists have an interest in maximising profit because they are in a competitive, zero-sum relationship with all others occupying the position of capitalist . . . In other words, actors are motivated to act in their interests, which are a function of their social position. Again, this doesn't mean that actors always with necessity act in their interests, but if they don't they are likely to suffer. A capitalist who shows no concern to maximise profits is liable to cease being a capitalist.[4]

Here, the fundamental point about motivation depends neither upon zero-sum relations (it works equally for the retention of relativities), nor upon maximizing strategies (satisficing at different levels supplies equivalent motive power). What is crucial is the relational nature of those motives which are constituted by vested interests.

---

[4] Douglas V. Porpora, 'Four concepts of social structure', *Journal for the Theory of Social Behaviour*, 1989, 19: 2, p. 208.

Nevertheless, for a person to be moved by any interest they have to find it good, and for them to be moved by a vested interest they would have to find it better than other reasons for other commitments. Yet why should they do either, rather than considering the lilies, taking the golden road to Samarkand, or pursuing any other goal which can be subjectively entertained? Since a vested interest is not a 'social force' nor do people's responses have anything in common with billiard balls' unreflective movements, then their influence depends for its efficacy upon them being found good by large numbers of those who share them (though not necessarily upon them being found best by all in the same position). This is only the case because there are inducements in the form of opportunity costs which are associated with the advancement or defence of vested interests.

Opportunity Costs

The conditional influence of these structural relationships works through those experiencing exigencies seeking to eradicate them, whilst those experiencing benefits seek to retain them. The former knowingly or unknowingly contributes to morphogenesis, the latter knowingly or unknowingly reinforces morphostasis. Yet it might well be objected that this ready designation of transformatory versus reproductory pressures assumes that rewards are recognized with gratitude and protected, while frustrations are detected and combated. This objection is completely valid: for agents, interpretations of their situations are not determined, nor infallible, nor exclusively influenced by structural considerations, nor freely formed in the absence of manipulation. Yet does not assenting that this is the case prevent our mediatory mechanism from exerting even the weakest conditional influence if, however strongly situations are structurally moulded, agents can interpret them however they please (or at the pleasure of powerful others)?

This would indeed be the case if it were all there was to the mediatory process. Without in any way depriving agents of their fundamental interpretative freedom, nevertheless real structural influences mean that objective opportunity costs are associated with different responses to frustrating or rewarding situations, which condition (without determining) the interpretations placed upon them. These costs represent the next link between the structured shaping of agents' situations and their reactions to them. Objective opportunity costs exert their influence upon the vested interests of agents which are equally objective.

Certainly, nothing *determines* that agents act to promote their vested interests, but costs are involved in not doing so. Since positions on social distributions concern scarcity, then there is a bonus to be lost with ceding a high position and penalties to be shed by not acceding to a low one (compare the effects on life-chances of downward or upward mobility through marriage). Those who fail to recognize this, or are induced to mis-recognize it, pay the price uncomprehendingly, but quite objectively in terms of a worsening of their situation or a perpetuation of underprivilege. Yet as purely *conditional* influences, nothing *prevents* an altruistic renunciation of vested interests, but equally virtue carries a price-tag (which is certainly not to say that no one will ever be willing to pay it). In order to argue that costs and benefits constitute reasons for the pursuit of vested interests which will be found good by many, it does not seem to me either necessary or desirable to present people in society as bargain hunters and to construe those who appear to act otherwise and turn their backs on material incentives as merely motivated by another (non-material) form of self-interest. This 'abolition' of altruism effectively denies self-sacrifice and its costs, thus blocking exploration of what other reasons can indeed outweigh this price to the self.

There are two major ways in which opportunity costs exert their influence; firstly on the attainment of the same given project and secondly upon which projects can be entertained. The former works through allocating different costs for the *same course of action* to those who are differently situated. The costs derive from the relationship between different distributions which specific projects span, and are thus a product of the overall structured situations in which people find themselves. A given position impedes or facilitates projected access to other forms of social scarcity. Were there no such interconnection, then obviously no given position would exert any constraining or enabling influence upon any other. What this points to is that constraints and enablements are in no manner separate from structures but are their situational expressions. To constrain and to enable are not matters reducible to interpersonal relations, nor are they something additional which some people do, or are able to do to others. Structured situations are not just frustrating and rewarding in themselves, they are constraining and facilitating because they operate as bridges or obstructions to other positions which also carry premiums and penalties.

Consider middle- and working-class pupils as they approach the earliest legal school leaving age. This is a simple instance where the same action (staying on in education) entails different costs for those differently placed. Both financial and cultural capital enable the middle classes to encourage better and longer forms of education for their children, whilst the less wealthy and knowledgeable can stay on only at a price which is both relatively higher and more risky for them.

'Society' forces nothing, but the differential opportunity costs for the same course of action constitute reasons for it being adopted differentially – for middle-class children tending to take the main road to university, whilst additional education for the working class tends to involve a lower absolute price, be known and closer to home, shorter and surer in its vocational returns. Now this initial choice is corrigible, but further costs are attached, some necessary and some contingent, for life goes on as corrections are contemplated. Let's take bright working-class Sharon who left school early, took her City and Guilds, and became a hair stylist. For a time she is buoyed up by her pay packet and progress up the salon hierarchy, but she becomes increasingly frustrated with the job. The trouble is that while on day release she met and later married Darren who is unenthusiastic about the sundry costs which would fall on him if Sharon pursues the University Access course which a client has just mentioned to her. His concerns are allayed by the birth of Warren, but Sharon's costs of extricating herself have now redoubled. She has now acquired new vested interests in her family and home, which constitute new obstacles to enrolment on the Access course whose completion would be even more of an uphill struggle. It can still be done, but presented with these situational constraints, not too many will be undeterred and decide that they have good reason to do so at that time and under those circumstances. Consequently, those who do not abandon the project entirely tend to postpone it (until the children are at school), thus finally entering University as mature students, and in certain job markets thus picking up another penalty in terms of being older. Moreover, not only does Sharon now have to juggle child care and study requirements, but in realizing her abilities she is also acquiring a new set of friends, concerns and outlook, many of which bode ill for her marital stability. Divorce is another common price to accrue, often leaving Sharon as a single-parent family, with a course to complete and an uncertain occupational future.

The moral of this story is not meant to deter mature students, for in an open social system such outcomes are not predictable: it is about the structural conditioning of decision-making. Its point is to stress that transformation is not a universal potential nor a possibility which is equally distributed to all at every moment and in every situation. For opportunity costs mean that different groups have different degrees of freedom and face differentially stringent constraints when they contemplate the same project from their different positions. Neither, on the other hand, is reproduction (which in this case replicates the well-known socio-economic differences in educational attainment) merely a matter of routinization. The above scenario of those situated like Sharon, far from being an account of routine or habitual action, often entails reluctant resignation, strenuous exertions against the odds and a bitter failure to meet the costs of overcoming situational constraints. Routinization might appear to be a more appropriate characterization of the perpetuation of structural privilege, but even this is deceptive since it requires an active cooperation with enablements. Habitual action may be highly inappropriate for cashing them in. Enablements are advantageous for allowing people to stay ahead, not to stay where they are, and the former means being ready and able to innovate (taking up new subjects, courses and openings).

Secondly, differential opportunity costs not only affect the ease or difficulty of undertaking the same course of action for groups which are differently situated, they also condition which projects are entertained by them and thus serve to explain why it is that these can be systematically and diametrically opposed. The connections between the antecedent setting of life-chances, the vested interests associated with them, and the opportunity costs predisposing towards different projects can account for divergent social trends amongst those variously situated. Thus the redistribution of life chances and resources attending the industrial division of labour introduced different vested interests in different family forms amongst social groups which were differently placed. Basically, the situation of the entrepreneur was one which enabled him to entertain the project of a nuclear family – not that he would have thought of it in such terms. All the same, his surplus revenue could buy services to substitute for those traditionally supplied by the third generation, while the gain in geographical mobility would improve his position. For the working class, vested interests were reversed and included the additional objective constraint that the lack of public provisions for care of the elderly exerted on projects involving their abandonment. In other words, situations were shaped in such a way as to allocate reverse opportunity costs for different family forms to different social groups. Reification is not entailed by considering such incentives and costs as conditional, though not deterministic influences, since though objective, their efficacy is dependent upon how agents weigh them and decide to act in view of their own weightings.

Degrees of interpretative freedom

Throughout it has been maintained that agents are the efficient causes of action and far from backtracking upon this, our account of structural conditioning has to present the process of mediation as one which is actually subject to reflective evaluation by agents. So far the reflexive powers of agency have been respected by never conceiving of conditioning as a 'force' but only ever as a reason. Reasons not only have to be weighed and found good but if and when they are, discretionary judgements have to be made about what to do in view of them. Action, then, has been consistently seen as resulting from the confluence of the powers of the 'parts' and those of the 'people'.

However, in giving further precision to the process of mediation, it is necessary to talk about how structures condition action, without compromising these autonomous powers of agential reflexivity and self-monitoring. The way forward consists not only in viewing structural conditioning as a supply of reasons for actions but additionally in showing why agents tend to regard them as better than other courses of action which also may be considered good. In other words, it is argued, agential powers are not such that they can make anything they will out of whatever circumstances they confront – that is without contracting substantial losses. The factors which curtail this potential interpretative volatility are the prices and premiums associated with assigning different evaluations to the situations in question.

To recap, the objective distribution of costs and benefits conditions both interpretation and action. Agents opposing the source of rewarding experiences risk harming their vested interests: agents supporting the source of frustrating experiences invite further impediments. By setting prices and premiums on situational interpretations, the conditional influence forces no one: it operates not as a hydraulic pressure but as a material reason which favours one response over another. Yet as with any reason, agents have to find it good and material considerations are not the only motives to action. Nevertheless, as they weigh them in the balance, costs and penalties tip the scales in one direction, meaning that countervailing concerns would have to be strong enough to outweigh them. It is agents alone who do the weighing, who assign values to the weights of incommensurables, and determine the sacrifices and trade-offs they can bear. However, if they miscalculate the objective costs they believe they can pay, then circumstances can foreclose their options – educational careers are abandoned in mid-course and strikes are called-off if funds cannot see them through. Not only does morphostasis ensue in these cases, but it is reinforced by these visible casualties who failed to heed situational reasons for a less radical promotion of their vested interests.

Furthermore, the promoting of vested interests (whether to protect advantages or remove disadvantages) entails strategic action which depends upon discretionary judgements. There are always degrees of interpretative freedom about the preferential course of action, but equally there is a variable stringency of constraints which discourages certain courses because their outcomes would be antithetic to promoting or defending the interests in question. Thus, a landlord has degrees of freedom about how fairly he will treat his tenants (and fair dealing may be in his longer-term interests), yet he is constrained to extract enough rent on which both to maintain the property and generate some surplus, or he will enter a downward spiral in which he ceases to be a landlord. Similarly tenants have a vested interest in at least maintaining, though usually improving, their housing situation but are strategically constrained when pressing for tenants' rights by their need not to enter the other downward spiral which ends in homelessness. Equally, those trapped in a situation of negative equity in the present British housing market have even fewer degrees of interpretative freedom. Servicing the current mortgage may be punishing, but the objective alternative is to sell-up and contract debts which both severely constrain what rentable properties can be afforded and preclude being granted another mortgage.

However, even the most stringent constraints never fundamentally determine the agent. During the Vietnam war, United States' draft dodgers paid the price. Similarly altruism entails high costs, but relief workers make material sacrifices and contemplate further ones, those in the caring professions would usually have been better off as accountants, men and women profess vows of poverty, chastity and obedience, and passers-by go to the aid of drowning strangers. Does this undoubted variation in subjective evaluations of situations and the inalienable human capacity to resist the most stringent material constraints mean that in granting it (and not cynically defining altruism away), that degrees of interpretative freedom are in no way limited, and therefore that situational responses are quintessentially individualistic and indeterminate? Were this the case then the posited mediatory mechanism would vaporize, for the powers of people would be exercised with immunity and independence from the structural context – defying not only determinism but also voiding conditioning.

This would only follow if such interpretations were entirely individualistic and idiosyncratic, and therefore indistinguishable from personal whim – when in fact they are neither. Yet in the literature there is a persistent tendency for a crude polarity to be advanced, according to which instrumental rationality governs the pursuit of material interests, whereas an irrational leap of some kind of faith prompts the promotion of values.[5] The presumption is made that material and ideal interests are taken up in entirely different ways; the former by a process of shrewd and undiluted calculation of payoffs, and the latter by an emotive leap in the dark. If, instead, it is accepted that people have reasons for their

---

[5] Cf. Roger Trigg, *Reason and Commitment*, Cambridge University Press, Cambridge, 1973, ch. 5.

commitments (such that being committed is predicated upon having good reason for it), then we already quit the realm of inexplicable whim – which is the only domain of untrammelled interpretative freedom. (In leaving it, agents are being deprived of nothing: rather they are being relieved of something incongruent with the notion of self-reflexivity, namely making irresponsible normative judgements with unconcern as to their personal implications. After all, only in the most trivial circumstances would we ever expect to find people settling their material interests by flicking coins). If material and ideal interests are not endorsed in different ways, then the conditioning of the two kinds of choices may not be unrelated to one another, or to parallel contextual considerations.

In the first place, if we ask again, as we did of material reasons, why people should find particular ideas good (when balanced against others with much to recommend them) the answer may well lie in the *relationship between the material and the ideal*, which of course means that such matters can never be purely individualistic if they are at least partly relational. Perhaps one of the reasons why altruism is rare (and constitutes an exception to the rule which many are reluctant to grant) is indeed that much of the time most people do not tolerate too great a discrepancy between their material and their ideal interests. This elective affinity, which Weber stressed in his famous 'switchmen' image, really hinges on values not undercutting material interests (which would cost heavily), yet not being epiphenomenal either (thus supplying discretionary judgements about how they should be promoted – a process including the articulation of an 'economic ethos' which could be light years away from the maximization of instrumental rationality).

But what then of genuine acts of altruism, entailing the repudiation of material interests? To begin with, this merely shows that the latter are not deterministic for agency, as has consistently been maintained. Beyond that, it points to the very important fact that agents are not risk-discounting bargain-hunters, but do take other costs into consideration, such as potential loss of repute, authority, safety or life itself *and* sometimes find good reason to pay them. However, this does not mean that we are back in the realm of personal whims or irrational leaps in the dark. Once again these are not usually purely individualistic actions. Most sacrificial activities are embedded in cultural belief systems which may be vastly more important to the individual than any other aspect of their social context, but are still not of a person's own making (the Christian martyr did not make Christianity). This cultural context supplies both doctrinal justification for the other-worldly orientation and also a supportive ecclesia (religious, scientific, political) of others who endorse the same normative primacy.

Furthermore, the altruistic project far from being a series of emotive whims does entail a reckoning of self-sacrifice, which though it would be a misnomer to term it 'calculative', nevertheless involves weighing whether the price can be mustered (consider the rich young man in the New Testament who was attracted, then deliberated, and finally decided in the negative). It follows that just as those who seek to promote their material interests can miscalculate the objective cost which they believe they will be able to pay in order to promote their vested interests, and may have to climb down, exactly the same is true of the pursuit of ideal interests. Altruism costs (and not only in material terms) and prolonged, projected altruism, as opposed to a single, immediate decision in an emergency, can atrophy or be abandoned as the bill runs up higher over time. This point, far from being judgemental, is to underscore that a struggle is involved: the conditional influence of the costs of self-sacrifice show themselves precisely in the very force with which they have to be resisted, in the pursuit of a goal which reflectively has been deemed a greater good.

Thirdly, there would of course be an implicit endorsement of materialism if costs and benefits were confined exclusively to material terms. Once certain values have been embraced (and initial degrees of freedom in adopting them can tend towards zero in cases like ethnicity and nationality), then their abandonment would entail a loss of cultural benefits which are also objective. Although nothing ultimately prevents someone from changing their values since we are not determined, any more than nothing fundamentally prevents a landlord from deciding to stop being a rentier, there is a renunciation of benefits in both cases. Cultural benefits are not exclusively subjective and a change of values can entail losses of position (MPs who change parties or clergy who go over to other denominations), of kinship rights and expectations (for some who marry out), and of status, friendship or support (for certain religious converts, political dissidents or professional innovators).

In other words, just as material reasons derive from the structural context and objectively both encourage and discourage certain judgements about courses of action, so too, normative reasons emanate from the cultural context and have the same effects upon situational evaluations. Since structure and culture are relatively autonomous, it should not be surprising that the powers of SEPs and CEPs are often out of synchrony with one another and that instead of one universally leading the other, either structure or culture can be undergoing morphogenesis whilst the other remains morphostatic. Such discontinuities between the two will be found to have important implications for one another. However, that is to get too far ahead. The point which this section has underlined is that emergent structural and cultural properties share the same conditional mechanism which mediates how they are transmitted to and intertwine with the reflexive powers of people, through conditioning their situational interpretations.

Directional guidance

If the mediatory process of structural conditioning consisted of nothing more than the above, it would remain indefinite in several important respects. So far, what is situationally conditioned is the promotion or defence of vested interests, as previously established in a prior socio-cultural context. However, that says nothing at all about what courses of action will serve in a promotive or defensive capacity. In other words, while the goals sought are indeed conditioned, it looks as if the strategic means for attaining them rest entirely at the discretion and with the ingenuity of the agents concerned. Secondly, whilstever courses of action do appear to be completely open ended, that is guided by nothing other than the variable outcomes of agential deliberations, then it is impossible to say anything further about potential outcomes or chances of success or failure. Finally, although SEPs and CEPs have always been referred to in the plural, nevertheless discussion of structural conditioning has concentrated upon examples of how one emergent property shapes the situation in which relevant agents find themselves, but obviously conditional influences are multiple and it is their confluence and combination which performs the overall process of moulding situations for people. Again, if the matter were left here, it would appear to be exclusively a question of agential priorities as to which aspects of their social context they respond.

Now the objective cannot either be to render the course of action determinate nor its outcome predictable, for such would require a closed system to which society can never approximate. All the same, there can be incremental increases in the understanding of how structure conditions agency if instead of confining discussion to first-order emergent properties (the results of past interaction), the role of second-order SEPs and CEPs (relations between the results of the results of past actions) is introduced, because at the (macro) institutional level these affect large segments of the population if not the whole of it. Thus, if they do indeed play a part in strategic directional guidance, this will condition the actions of large numbers. However, it will not necessarily guide all in the same direction since the effect may be to polarize relevant parts of the population by impinging upon their divergent vested interests in different ways. At this point caution must be exercised and any covert assumption be resisted that these second-order influences necessarily over-ride first-order forms of conditioning. What is being discussed is an influence which is potentially of systemic magnitude, but whether that potential is realized depends significantly upon its congruence with conditioning at lower levels (which spells actualization) or its incongruence (which is when systemic powers can remain unexercised).

In general, situations are shaped very differently for agents according to whether such emergent properties are characterized by tensions between their component elements or by coherence between them. Thus, whether strains or compatibilities characterize the relations between different institutional SEPs will make a major difference to the systemic context of a major portion of the population. As unintended consequences, that is, as the results of the results of prior interaction, there is (*contra* functionalism) no *a priori* reason why emergence and equilibration should coincide, rather than incompatibilities maintaining among these resultants. Thus as Blau recognized, when distancing himself from the functionalist tradition, 'In complex social structures with many interdependent, and often interpenetrating substructures, particularly, every movement towards equilibrium precipitates disturbances and disequilibria and thus new dynamic processes'.[6] Equally, the powerful but fallacious myth of structural integration is paralleled by the equally pervasive and misguided myth of cultural integration. I have criticized this elsewhere[7] for the presumption that contradictions are absent, even in those instances where it is possible to point to a hegemonic Cultural System. Similarly, relations between structural and cultural emergent properties at the highest level (of SEPs and CEPs), may, as has already been seen, be in phase with one another or out of synchrony. In the former case, they will serve powerfully to reinforce a congruent systemic context in which the majority of agents find themselves. In the latter case, their divergence spells divergent structural versus cultural conditioning and guidance (thus simultaneously buttressing reproduction and contributing to transformation in different ways). Such possible variations, which are readily detectable historically and comparatively, serve to illustrate the futility of a general debate over idealism versus materialism.

Thus strains and compatibilities are themselves *relational properties*: they have nothing whatsoever to do with optimal or sub-optimal conditions for attaining some super-ordinate goal, but simply refer to congruence or incongruence as the state of affairs resulting from the historical elaboration of socio-cultural structures whose various ope-

[6] Peter Blau, *Exchange and Power in Social Life*, Wiley, New York, 1964, p. 314.
[7] See Margaret S. Archer, *Culture and Agency*, Cambridge University Press, Cambridge, 1989, ch. 1. 'The myth of cultural integration'. Also in *British Journal of Sociology*, 1985, 36: 333–53.

rations then have to co-exist. Incongruence (chosen as a generic term to cover what neo-functionalists term 'tensions' and neo-marxists prefer to call 'contradictions'), represents a systemic fault line running throughout the social structure. Whether it is split open remains unpredictable, but its existence will condition strategies for its containment versus its actualization among different sectors of the population. Conversely, a condition of systemic congruence (which Lockwood termed 'high system' integration) confronts agents with a smooth contextual surface and metaphorically supplies no directional guidance, in the form of clefts which pressure can prise asunder. On the contrary, such a sheer face will be found to supply a ready source of reasons to discourage any attempted assault on it.

Therefore, the relationship between second-order emergents are of particular relevance to morphogenesis and morphostasis, since the incidence of complementarities serves to identify the potential loci of systemic reproduction and the occurrence of incompatibilities the potential loci of systemic transformation. In rudimentary terms, part one of the mediatory mechanism is identical with the operative effects of first-order emergents and consists in structural or cultural relations of compatibility or incongruence distributing frustrating or rewarding experiences to the situations which agents have to confront because of the institutions in which they are involved and the roles they occupy within them.

Where incompatibility maintains at the second-order level, then strains are experienced as practical exigencies by agents whose interests are vested in the impeded institutions and their associated roles. In other words, their situations are moulded in critical respects by operational obstructions which translate into practical problems, frustrating those upon whose day-to-day situations they impinge, and confronting them with a series of exigencies which hinder the achievement or satisfaction of their vested institutional interests. On the contrary, where complementarities prevail, these are transmitted to the relevant action contexts as a series of rewarding experiences. The goals which agents pursue and the tasks they undertake by virtue of their roles can be accomplished in a problem-free manner. In other words, conditioning again begins with shaping their practical situations, and this is the bridge between real but unobservable systemic properties (complementarities or incompatibilities), and their impact upon daily experience at the level of events.

However, a closer examination of the different ways in which these systemic properties are related to one another can give greater precision to the manner in which situations are shaped for the agents involved. The mechanism by which the 'parts' causally influence the 'people' can become a good deal sharper than the rudimentary notion of their shaping frustrating or rewarding situations in relation to agents' vested interests. Instead, it is possible to show how quite distinctive *situational logics,* which predispose agents towards *specific courses of action* for the promotion of their interests, are created by the relations within and between the various SEPs and CEPs. Because of this, structural conditioning does a great deal more than differentiating between those who incur different objective opportunity costs for defending or opposing the status quo. If that were all, then the mediating mechanism between structure and agency would simply shape situations and enable us to identify loci of potential supportive or oppositional pressures. However, useful as that is in answer the 'where' question, it leaves the whole issue of *what* to do (in support or opposition) to the deliberations of agents over the most appropriate forms of strategic action. Although not seeking to eliminate such discretionary judgements, or the possibility of repudiating structural influences altogether, since we are dealing with conditioning and not determinism, nevertheless *the shaping of situations also includes strategic guidance.* This works by supplying good reasons for particular courses of action, in the form of the premiums and penalties associated with following them or ignoring them, which are again cashed in through their positive or negative impact upon vested interests.

What we are concerned with then at the second order level is how the differing relationships between the array of emergent SEPs and CEPs actually motivates different courses of strategic action amongst large sections of the population. The basic thesis, which will be spelled out and illustrated in the next section, is made up of two parts. On the one hand the second order relationships which exist at any given T^1, as the resultants of prior social interaction which took place in an anterior systemic context, can be of four different kinds. (Later it will be seen as in S^1 at T^1 not all such emergent relations have to be of the *same kind*). Firstly, these second-order relationships may themselves be necessarily and internally related to one another, like the polity and a command economy, whilst others are only contingently related, like governments and free markets if they approximate to the ideal type. Secondly, and independently of the above, their relationships may be ones of complementarity or incompatibility, that is they can help or hinder one another's operations whether they are necessarily or only contingently related. In other words, this two-by-two table yields four second-order possibilities concerning institutional relationships. These are necessary complementarities; necessary incompatibilities; contingent complementarities; and contingent incompatibilities. Although they sound off-puttingly unfamiliar, they are like M. Jourdain's prose, for we have been talking about them all our lives and they are still some of the first things we talk about with first-year students, when introducing the founding fathers. They are simply generic ways of analysing the institutional make up of different social formations or configurations.

On the other hand, the next step in the argument is that these four types of relationship not only place large sections of the population in a very different situation according to the institutions with which they are associated, but also that this embroils them in very different kinds of situational 'logics' respectively. This means, (a) that tendencies towards reproduction or transformation are distributed quite differently amongst the four types of situations because of large variations in the numbers who would sustain losses or gains depending upon which took place. Only one out of the four configurations (necessary complementarities) shapes situations in which all sections of the population confronting them have reasons to reproduce them, since transformation threatens the loss of vested interests all round. In turn, (b) all situational logics motivate different forms of strategic action by predisposing different sections of the population to see their interests served by *defensive, concessionary, competitive, or opportunist* modes of interaction with other groups. Therefore, (c) insofar as a form of situational logic is strategically carried through, it represents the generative mechanism of either morphogenesis or morphostasis. This then constitutes the final conditioning linkage which completes the mediation of structure to agency. However, (d) it is not quite the end of the chain of effects conditionally set in train. This is because strategic success or failure (which ultimately determines whether it is morphostasis or morphogenesis which ensues) is itself conditioned by the relative power of the interacting social groups. Power itself is profoundly influenced by the relations between first and second order emergents: that is between the shape of distributions (first order) which determine the *bargaining power* of those groups involved in compatibilities or complementarities (second order) and their *negotiating strength vis-à-vis* each other. This is a matter of the utmost importance to which it will be necessary to return. Before that, however, points (a) to (c) undoubtedly need much more explication and concrete illustration. The next section is devoted to that task and figure 13 merely summarizes the four forms of directional guidance to strategic action which will be discussed.

Structural and cultural formations can be described in the same terms (because the four types of second-order emergent properties obtain between CEPs as amongst SEPs) and generate parallel forms of situational logics. However, there are two reasons for presenting them separately. Firstly, there are obvious *substantive* differences between these two (the material and ideational), and thus their formal similarities have to be illustrated and demonstrated rather than merely asserted or presumed.

Second order emergent properties	Situational logic
Necessary complementarities	Protection
Necessary incompatibilities	Compromise
Contingent incompatibilities	Elimination
Contingent compatibilities	Opportunism

Figure 13 Structural conditioning of strategic action: processes of directional guidance.

Secondly, although they provide parallel forms of directional guidance for strategic action, the relative autonomy of structure and culture means that they are not necessarily in synchrony with one another. Whether they are or not can be considered as a *third-order emergent property*: that is, the relationships of congruity or incongruity between SEPs and CEPs themselves are the results of the results of the results of social interaction. As such, *their* relationship constitutes the final conditional influence upon social interaction and is ultimately responsible for conditioning whether the subsequent trajectory is morphogenetic or morphostatic (be this societally or sectionally). Therefore, figure 13 will first be discussed in relation to structure and then to culture during the rest of this chapter. The crucial relationship between them, crucial that is for whether morphogenesis and morphostasis ensues, will be held over until the final chapter. Then having introduced the powers of the people (chapter 8), the first-, second- and third-order emergent properties of structure, culture and agency can be treated together which is mandatory given that they are quintessentially relational in nature and effects.

Four institutional configurations and their situational logics

It is itself contingent, upon the past history of emergence, *which* of these four configurations is approximated to in a given society at T^1 and *whether* all, most, or what are deemed to be the 'core' institutions[8] stand in one of the four relationships. If we are disbelievers in historical hidden hands or reified mechanisms supposedly guaranteeing adaptation or equilibration,

---

[8] See Percy Cohen, *Modern Social Theory*, Heinemann, London, 1968. He advances extremely cogent arguments concerning the difficulty of designating 'core' institutions with conviction, at any given time or over time (pp. 176ff.).

then we should be courageous in our disbelief and assert that there are no *a priori* grounds for expecting to find one configuration rather than another in any given society, nor for finding that all institutional structures are related in the same way in any particular systemic formation.

The illustrations which follow deliberately highlight different social systems whose institutional configurations have conformed to one of the four possibilities outlined above (precisely to insist that both functional integration and 'core contradictions' are both only one possible state in which systems may be found). However, for ease of initial presentation, examples have been chosen where the plurality of *different* relationships is at a minimum. That social formations may well not be homogeneous must not be forgotten, for how various institutions do intertwine adds considerably to the complexities of structural elaboration. Moreover, such cases usually preponderate empirically, for although the instances to be considered are real configurations, rather than ideal types, what is distinctive about them is the institutional range and systemic scope with which they consistently manifested only one of the four possibilities.

These four concepts were the stock in trade of all the founding fathers and as such serve to show, for instance, that Marx by no means confined his practical analyses to instances of 'contradictions' nor was Durkheim fixated by approximations to the organic analogy, whilst Weber devoted a work to each configuration in profitable disregard of his own methodological charter.

Necessary complementarities

When there are necessary and internal linkages of a complementary nature between systemic structures, then institutions are mutually reinforcing, mutually invoke one another and work in terms of each other. Thus, for example, the entire matrix of ancient Indian institutions was internally related, and interconnecting lines could be drawn between caste/religion/kinship/economy/polity/law and education, representing what Parsons held was the case for all functionally integrated systems and what Gouldner pointed out was one rather rare polar state in which the components of social systems could be found.[9]

A harmonious relationship of high system integration is not born out of harmony and what Weber shows for Ancient India is that the struggles which issued in this configuration were almost as long as the following two millennia of sustained morphostasis. Weber leaves us in no doubt that

[9] Alvin Gouldner, 'Reciprocity and autonomy in functionalist theory', in N. J. Demerath and R. A. Peterson (eds.), *System, Change and Conflict*, New York, 1967.

the vested interests of a relatively privileged group (the Brahmin caste) promoted a form of institutional integration which reinforced their hegemony. Yet equally, the emergent powers of this complementary configuration were *sui generis*, fostering negative feedback loops which discouraged alterations in a coherent cluster of SEPs which were irreducible to power play on the part of these dominant beneficiaries.

On the contrary, structural resilience derived from the fact that necessary complementarities create situations in which everyone has something to lose from disruption (though in absolute terms some have vastly more to lose than others), whereas the changes which would constitute gains are less than obvious and would anyway confront the combined pressures of those threatened by ensuing losses. This is the key which generates and generalizes this *situational logic of protection*: one so conducive to morphostasis that Marx concurred that there were no internal dynamics inducing breakdown but, on the contrary, only relations which accounted for 'the *unchangeableness* of Asiatic *societies*'.[10]

It might seem obvious that those at the apex of the caste hierarchy derive benefits from interdependence – as with priesthood and kingship when it was said that 'a king without a purohita [family priest] was not a king in the full sense of the word, just as a Brahmin without a king was not a Brahmin of the highest rank'.[11] It is then understandable that this mutuality of benefits would serve to protect and intensify this institutional compatibility (as post-Vedic writings increasingly accentuated patriarchal veneration, which princes in turn acknowledged by actions like confirming land grants and appointments to the Brahminate in perpetuity). It is less than obvious why those lower down in this minutely graded hierarchy, entailing several hundred sub-castes and with ever decreasing material benefits, should find their positions conducive to the situational logic of protection. Indeed, it might even be tempting to attribute their ritual conformity to caste rules to a 'false consciousness' inculcated by a religion which legitimated and stabilized distributional injustice by reference to deficient adherence to caste duties in a past life, and then held out the promise of a higher reincarnation to those most scrupulous in their current ritual observations, thus representing that the lowest castes had the most to gain from conformity.

Cultural factors are far from insignificant, yet each caste gradation also supplied material benefits *vis-à-vis* others which could only be forfeited by failure to reinforce ritualized boundary maintenance, which operated as an inclusive and exclusive mechanism. Sub-castes, which were often

[10] Karl Marx, *Capital*, vol. 1, 1867, p. 376.
[11] Max Weber, in R. Bendix, *Max Weber: An Intellectual Portrait*, University of California Press, Berkeley, 1960, p. 180.

occupational, secured a local monopoly of practice in an area, and thus provided means of subsistence for members and their kin. As such these benefits were protected: for the more artisans ritualized their traditional skills the stronger the barriers they thus erected against any free movement of labour. Collective interests in defending such acquired rights generated protective practices, the most important being the ostracism of persons violating caste rituals – when caste and kin would terminate relations with them. The crucial point is that the collectivity has something to lose by tolerance of violations, since a generalized relaxation of ritualized observances would lead to further sub-caste differentiation in a downwards direction. On the other hand, violators were guaranteed losers since exclusion and ostracism entailed a loss of benefits and accumulation of penalties by being constrained to join the residue of untouchables, generically defined as breakers of caste obligations. Hence, the situational logic of protection operated at all levels and itself encouraged an intensification of role prescriptions and a minutely and ritualistically regulated social contact between those in different positions. As such, the generalized situational logic of protection was fostered by this matrix of compatible and interdependent institutions, for their internal and necessary relations defined a network of interlocking operations, roles and positions whose complementarity then associated premiums with reproduction and allocated penalties to disruption. In turn, these structural influences represented generative powers in their own right (working for morphostasis), which were irreducible to the power play of the privileged castes. Thus Weber himself accentuated how ritual prohibitions on *fraternization* between merchants, traders and artisans precluded the development of citizenship and urban political organization. Similarly, their effect was to repress *economic innovation*, for 'a ritual law in which every change of occupation, every change of work technique, could result in ritual degradation is certainly not capable of giving birth to economic and technological revolutions from within itself, or even facilitating the first germination of capitalism in its midst'.[12] This negative feedback loop which discouraged alterations in the complementary institutional configuration was thus the effect of the protective situational logic which repressed innovation or diversification but instead reinforced the density of traditionalism. The mediatory mechanism itself stemmed from the way in which these internal, necessary and complementary relations systematically shaped agential situations such that traditional action protected against a loss of vested interests whilst innovative action imperilled them, both individually and collectively.

---

[12] Max Weber, in H. H. Gerth and C. Wright Mills (eds.), *From Max Weber*, Routledge and Kegan Paul, London, 1967, p. 413.

Necessary incompatibilities

When the constitution of the social system is marked by incompatibilities between institutions which are none the less internally and necessarily related, this has rightly been seen as containing a potential for change which is entirely lacking in the complementary configurations just examined. Generally, when two or more institutions are necessarily and internally related to one another yet the effects of their operations are to threaten the endurance of the relationship itself, this has been referred to as a state of 'contradiction'. Thus Marx's historical analyses of the successive transformation of social formations always hinged upon the internal dynamics of the mode of production, theorized as a contradiction between the forces and relations of production. Such restrictions on which institutional incompatibilities were universally accorded priority in the dynamics of systemic change have not withstood comparative scrutiny. Nevertheless, the generic idea of a contradiction between the material conditions of production and the productive institutions of the economic system is a useful way of broadening its substantive applications, which commended itself to Weber in his studies of patrimonial bureaucracy.

The use of the concept here entails a further widening, namely that 'necessary incompatibilities' are considered to be second-order emergent properties of a general type (i.e. with the same kind of generative powers) which can characterize *any* constellation of institutions that have come to stand in this relationship. It then becomes a matter of historical contingency, empirically variable and open to empirical investigation, *which* institutions do stand in this relation. (Hence, the Marxian and Weberian exemplars would be particular instances of a more general phenomenon). Of course, it may be the case that none do so at all: thus Marx and Weber concurred that none did in Ancient India and saw their *absence* as contributing to systemic changelessness.

Our present concern is how when 'necessary incompatibilities' do exist as structural emergent properties, they shape the situations in which the relevant sections of the population find themselves and predispose them towards certain courses of strategic action. In his analysis of patrimonial bureaucracy, Weber argues that its upholders are presented with an entirely different situational logic, one of compromise. For if their vested interests are advanced, this takes place in a context such that their promotion also intensifies contrary ones, whose counteractualization threatens the relation itself. Thus, Weber notes that any 'bureaucracy as a permanent structure is knit to the one presupposition of a constant income for maintaining it'. In other words, he is defining the relationship between bureaucracy and taxation as an internal and necessary one ('a stable system of taxation is the precondition for the permanent existence of bureaucratic administration'). As far as patrimonial bureaucracy was concerned, the incompatibility consisted in how to sustain an effective taxation system, upon which the endurance of the central bureaucracy depended, in the context of a near-subsistence economy where 'the centralizing goal of bureaucracy institutions is constantly liable to sabotage by the potential social relationship structure of the subsistence economy which favours the decentralization and "feudalization" of power relationships'.[13] The necessary incompatibility concerned taxation capacity in relation to bureaucratic needs.

Because of it, the situations in which *all parties* found themselves meant that forthright promotion their vested interests, as lodged in institutional operations, role sets or distributional positions, was fraught with difficulties. These could only be overcome at a steep, if not prohibitive, price. Although central bureaucratic interests would be served by extracting the maximum in taxes, they were constrained not to impose a tax burden which would promote opposition from the large landowners. Theirs was a situational logic of containment and compromise.

On the one hand, princes were reliant upon their staff of prebendaries for tax collection and had 'to enlist its members' self interest in opposition to the subjects as far as possible'.[14] This meant conferring the right of office upon them together with a variety of benefits intended to buttress this primary external support of patrimonial authority. This compromise effectively created vested interests amongst the staff of officials, the most obvious of which being that they passed on to the lord only part of the taxes gathered from the subjects, retaining the rest. In turn, the staff, whether originating as slaves, literati, clerics or jurists increasingly consolidated further economic advantages and appropriated powers of governance:

The development, however, has seldom stopped at this stage. We always meet with a *struggle* between the political or historical lord and the owners or usurpers of perogatives, which they have appropriated as status groups. The ruler attempts to expropriate the estates, and the estates attempt to expropriate the ruler.[15]

Compromise for the ruler, who cannot dispense with a staff, consists in a see-sawing between propitiation and expropriation: generous benefices to buy their loyalty and link their interests to his own, followed by

---

[13] David Lockwood, 'Social integration and system integration', in G. K. Zollschan and H. W. Hirsch (eds.), *Explorations in Social Change*, Houghton Mifflin, Boston, 1964, p. 254.
[14] Max Weber, in Bendix, *Max Weber*, p. 347.
[15] Max Weber, in Gerth and Mills, *From Max Weber*, p. 298.

attempts to curb their autonomous powers which were themselves often compromised because of central reliance upon the military services of armed prebendaries. Given this impasse, the main central strategy was to turn a blind eye to the bribery and corruption of officialdom and to allow the tax burden to be passed down onto the peasantry and to be met from the labour of a growing corpus of slaves. Ironically, the weaker the prebendary's hold on his office (if, for instance, it were leased rather than held in perpetuity) the greater the incentive to oppression and the more unregulated and variable became administrative costs. 'If offices are leased, the incumbent is put in a position where it is to his immediate interest to get back the capital he has invested by any available means of extortion, however irrational.'[16] Thus what might seem the safest compromise for the hierocratic lord *vis-à-vis* his staff, could well be quite the reverse if it back-fired amongst his subjects, driven to revolt by such oppression.

Even the peasantry were trapped in the same logic of compromise, for given that the tax burden ultimately rested upon them, they had only two strategic courses of action: to ally themselves with the landed estates against the centre, to lighten their overall burden by eliminating central financial impositions (thus fostering feudal decentralization), or to revolt against local impositions in the hope of enlisting the centre to curb the rapaciousness of officialdom. Compromise here consisted in choosing an alliance with the less oppressive of two oppressors.

The situational logic of compromise thus arises because necessary incompatibilities means that the promotion of vested interests has to be a cautious balancing act, a weighting of gains against losses, where to accrue bonuses is also to invite or incur penalties. This is inherent to the necessary incompatibility; what was distinctive about patrimonial bureaucracy were the high stakes involved in not striking the right balance – for inadequate compromises resulted in loss of Empire, lands, offices, and heads. The configuration is inherently unstable. While ever a roughly symmetrical mutual dependency characterizes the major institutional operations then the respective corporate agents will co-exist on uneasy compromises which serve to contain the incompatibility itself. Yet if symmetry slips for any reason (such as new foreign sources of revenue, or augmented coercive powers for the centre, or increased bureaucratic demands to meet military requirements) then the counter-balancing of gains and losses which constrained all parties to compromise gives way because gain now attaches to counter-actualisation. 'Sultanism' or 'feu-

---

[16] Max Weber, in Bendix, *Max Weber*, p. 356.

dalization' are the ultimate expressions of centralization and decentralization once symmetrical dependence ceases to underpin the situational logic of compromise and coercive powers cannot contain either tendency. As Weber recognized, this was an inherently unstable balance whose tensions were only temporarily held in check by compromise. Because of the delicacy of this balancing act, then 'according to all historical experience, without a money economy the bureaucratic structure can hardly avoid undergoing substantial changes, or indeed, turning into another type of structure'.[17]

Now these two examples of complementarities and incompatibilities deriving from the internal and necessary relations between SEPs were unusual in operating consistently through society, such that all agents were involved, since at every level their situations were shaped by one (second-order) emergent property so that the same situational logic prevailed from top to bottom. Because of this, both were internally morphostatic, although the continued containment of incompatibility in the latter case clearly depended on no radical changes in the resource distribution which would have dispensed with the need to compromise in order to defend vested interests. On the contrary, change in available resources would have resulted in the pursuit of vested interests cracking through the system fault line represented by the incompatibility and realizing a different structural state of affairs.

Contingent incompatibilities

These configurations arise precisely because society is an open system and no formation is hermetically sealed against external influences. Internally, morphostasis is highly resilient (Ancient India or China) or extremely fragile (patrimonial bureaucracy) and thus they are differentially susceptible to disruption by external influences, without either formation being immune to them. Thus, for example, the *contingencies of war* impinge irresistibly on even the most highly integrated formations, disrupting the exclusive preoccupation with internal protection of the status quo and re-directing it towards an entirely different *situational logic of elimination*. For war or invasion are only extreme cases where the defence of interests consists in inflicting the maximum damage on an opposing party by seeking to eliminate it. Yet in the process of mobilization, many of the old protective strategies have to be suspended (prohibitions on inter-personal contact lifted, territorial confinement abandoned,

---

[17] See David Lockwood, 'Social integration and system integration', p. 254 for discussion of this text.

traditional occupational restrictions over-ridden etc.). If the process is protracted, and particularly if wars are lost, these changes are usually irreversible.

Weber's account of ancient Palestine, intended to be read as a counter-point to the two highly stable civilizations he examined, shows war, exile and perpetual reconquest as intensifying territorial uprooting, institutional fragmentation, political instability, social fluidity, and finally culminating in diaspora. Without the recurrence of invasion, whose outcomes were so negative because successive fragmentations were reinforcing, morphogenesis would have been less dramatic in its consequences for re-grouping. Nevertheless, this is the generic effect when contingent incompatibilities arise (whether from within or without the system in question) because both sides become party to the situational logic of elimination, where the greatest gains coincide with inflicting maximum injuries on the other side. Then the strategic mobilization of material and human resources generates new forms of social cleavage which are antithetic to (a) the stable reproduction of social relations fostered by, and constitutive of, the necessary complementarity and, (b) the containment of divergent interests promoted by and sustaining the balance of resources and forces which serve to 'preserve' necessary institutional incompatibilities (despite their internal tensions).

Contingent compatibilities

Equally, as an open system there are no effective barriers which can be erected against the incursion of contingent relationships which prove highly compatible with the interests of particular groups. In both the morphostatic configurations examined, stability itself depended upon finite resources whose distributions promoted protection of what had been secured, but could be lost, especially if it was only enforced by an uneasy compromise. The latter instances are particularly vulnerable to any increase in resources and significantly agents are constantly on the look out for these in order to break out of stalemate and counter-actualize their interests. Yet in the former too, the situational logic of protection against losses is effectively an internal calculus whose binding power weakens if some, and usually the marginal, can make new gains through external relationships.

Contingent compatibilities entail a *situational logic of pure opportunism*, for only gains can accrue from their exploitation. Yet if this effects a major influx of resources its consequences are morphogenetic since it undermines the stable distribution or delicate balance upon which both types of morphostatic formations depended. Hence the importance which Marx attached to mercantalism. Thus, the influx of gold and silver from the New World produced a sharp increase in prices to the detriment of the landowners; trade with the colonies generated large profits and an impulse to commerce which was hostile to the closed guilds; and the accumulation of capital in conjunction with mobile wage-labour finally re-combined in manufacturing. Together all of this served to displace feudal relations. What emerges then are new interests themselves and new material means for their realization, in other words an institutional re-patterning which is antithetic both to the protective reproduction of the status quo and also to the repressive containment of incompatibilities where the unavailability of alternative resources was what previously bound the parties to mutual compromise.

Implications for structural morphostasis and morphogenesis

As has already been stressed, it is only in a minority of cases that an entire social system will have all its components (institutions, roles and distributions) aligned in terms of one emergent core complementarity or incompatibility which thus enmeshes all agents in the same situational logic and means that all material resources are mobilized in that single direction. These are inevitably minoritarian because societies, as open systems, can never be proofed against the incursion of external contingencies. Such effects are not simply to shape new relations between a system and its environment and thus to introduce new situational logics as the result of 'international relations', but actually penetrate the system itself by the structural changes they induce internally. Significantly, both the examples of war and trade were institutionally destructive and re-constructive at the same time. Thus they displaced old uniform alignments with new varied patternings of relations between institutions. Given societal openness, such variety is the norm and those rare cases of uniformity were only presented earlier in order to show the different kinds of situational logics operating in pure form on a society-wide basis, without countervailing influences.

Since there is nothing to prevent institutions standing in a variety of relationships towards one another (due to openness) then there is no *a priori* reason to expect to detect any particular form of patterning in every social formation encountered. Contrary to functionalist assumptions, which hold necessary institutional compatibilities to be definitional to any enduring social system, and to vulgar marxist expectations that each social formation will be articulated around a central institutional 'contradiction', it is a matter of contingency how any particular systemic configuration is patterned. Consequently it is an empirical matter *which* second-order properties characterize institutional relationships making up the system: what is not an empirical matter is what occurs when different second-order properties characterize different institutional clusters simultaneously. When certain institutions are in relations of necessary complementarity, others in ones of necessary incompatibility, and their contingent impact upon the operation of further institutions which are unrelated to them can be ones of complementarity or incompatibility, then all constitute obstructions to one another. Crucially, this means that the situations in which those who are associated with different institutions (roles and positions) find themselves are shaped variously and entail different kinds of situational logic for the defence and promotion of the respective interests vested in them.

Correspondingly, (a) clusters of internally and necessarily related institutions foster the situational logic of protective integration, which relies upon stable reproduction of practices in the population. Yet their contingent impact on independent institutions, if obstructive, places the two in a competitive relation, where attempts at mutual elimination foster social cleavage which is inimical to orderly reproduction. If contingent relations are beneficial, the original cluster has acquired new allies, but ones with sectional interests in their own institutional operations which they may seek to extend by attempting to negotiate even more advantageous outputs from the former, which then modify pure protectionism by the changes thus transacted. (b) Clusters of necessarily related institutions, which harbour incompatibilities and contain them by compromises which repress the actualization of unbridled vested interests, may find either side making common cause with independent sources of cleavage originating from contingent competitive relations, or with sectional groupings if contingent opportunities offer better gains. In either case, the delicate balance of containment is threatened and whilst more generous compromises may sustain it (and indeed become a condition of survival), nevertheless counter-actualization is now a real possibility.

Above all, two features are of outstanding significance in the vast majority of social formations where the emergent relations between different clusters of institutions are of different kinds. On the one hand, *all agents are not involved in all of them, whilst some are involved in several.* This in turn has crucial implications for social interaction, for it conditions whether allegiances are superimposed or cross-cutting and thus influences different possibilities of alliance in pursuit of institutional reproduction or transformation. Simultaneously, alliances are not simply matters of numbers but are strategic groupings. Therefore the presence of a plurality of vested interests in institutional relations which entail different types of situational logic, will have a direct effect upon the strategy which can be endorsed conjointly. It delineates those who *can* ally in promotive action for the defence or change of a particular institutional operation.

On the other hand, the alliances which do develop will have variable degrees of access to material resources (especially wealth and power) which will affect the impact of their strategic action in relation to that of their opponents. Neither factor is deterministic of the outcome, for further agents can be mobilized in the course of any strategic struggle and resource distributions are themselves modified in the process of such struggles. Nevertheless, at the outset these two factors strongly condition who will be involved, how they will proceed strategically and what resources they have at their disposal – all of which are decisive for institutional morphostasis and morphogenesis.

Four cultural configurations and their situational logics

Culture can be conceptualized as supplying directional guidance for agency in exactly the same terms as have just been employed for structure. In other words, at the second-order level, CEPs and SEPs work in an identical manner as mediatory mechanisms, despite their substantive differences.

This section focuses on the effects of *holding* theories or beliefs which stand in particular logical relationships to other theories or beliefs – that is, relations of contradiction or complementarity. The express concern is with the influence of these cultural system (CS) properties on those who uphold ideas possessing them. It explicitly does *not* purport to explain *why* people endorsed such ideas in the first place, since this is predominantly a socio-cultural (C-S) question – the answer to which would require historical recourse to anterior morphogenetic cycles.

The crucial effects to be discussed are causal ones. It will be argued that the maintenance of ideas which stand in manifest logical contradiction or complementarity to others, places their holders in different ideational positions – as is also the case depending upon whether ideas are necessarily and internally related or whether their relationship is purely contingent. The logical properties of their theories or beliefs create entirely different situational logics for them. These effects mould the context of cultural action and in turn condition different patterns of ideational development. Subsequent Socio-Cultural interaction is marked in completely different ways by these differences in situational logic. They provide directional guidance which predisposes towards totally different (formal) courses of action.

The relations between any two given doctrines (A and B) will first be examined for logical contradiction, dependence or independence. Consequently, none of the sets of relationships listed above is presumed in advance to be more of one kind than another. This of course is the difference in theoretical starting-point from the Myth of Cultural Integration – any version of which took harmony to be *a prioristic* for all the above sets.

Constraining contradictions (necessary incompatibilities)

Here the necessary contradiction is a property of the CS (doctrinally A and B are logically inconsistent): it exerts a constraint upon the S-C level if any agent(s) wish to maintain A (whether a theory or a belief). The only S-C assumption that will be made is that someone or some group does seek to sustain A (for reasons unknown but residing at the S-C level). The whole effect of the constraining contradiction is entirely conditional upon this assumption, for the existence of the incompatibility between A and B is of no social consequence if no one asserts or advocates A, even if it is well known.

In the cultural realm, as in the structural domain, contradictions only exert a conditional influence upon the course of action and once again this is by shaping the action contexts in which people find themselves. Structural contradictions represent obstructions to certain institutional operations and these translate themselves into problem-ridden situations for the agents associated with them. Very much the same is true here. A constraining contradiction is the site of cultural tension. That part of the system in which A and B are located is characterized by a form of 'strain' which arises from their incompatibility in the context of an internal and necessary relationship. There is nothing metaphysical about this, no idealist overtones of superordinate battles between ideas: pure ideas purely sleep on in books until awoken by actors. It is dependence which generates the 'strain', which enforces the fraught relationship between A and B yet simultaneously prevents their divorce or separation.

What the constraining contradiction does in practice is to confront those committed to A who also have no option but to live with B as well, with a particular *situational logic*. According to this logic, given their initial commitment to A, they are driven to engage with something both antithetical but also indispensable to it.

There is no effective method of containing the problematic relationship between A and B and there is no way of evading the problem by the simple repudiation of B. This is precisely the force of the constraint characterizing this type of contradiction. It relentlessly fosters the ultimate clash between the two contradictory components and does so through the situational logic it creates for the actors involved. Certainly human agency often tries to get off this hook by the use of Socio-Cultural containment strategies, that is, causal manipulation of other people to prevent either the realization or the voicing of the logical difficulty. These are purely 'social solutions' which may be quite efficacious for a time at the Socio-Cultural level but do not ultimately dispose of the constraining influences exerted by the Cultural System on the Socio-Cultural level. The situational logic emanating from them bears down inexorably: agents have no choice about this, their only choice is whether or not they will try to cope with it. The constraining contradiction is never a determinant, for at any point in time, agents can make their exit, turning away from a belief or theory in scepticism or turning towards an alternative which appears less problematic or more profitable. However, for those who remain steadfast in their adherence to A, then the situational logic firmly directs the way in which they deal with the contradiction.

If A and B are logically inconsistent then no genuine resolution is possible between them (unless it can be shown that this is an apparent contradiction), but if B remains unaltered it threatens the credibility or tenability of A. Consequently, the situational logic directs that continued adherence to A makes a *correction* of its relationship with B mandatory (which is why the name 'corrective contradiction' would be equally appropriate for these Systemic properties). Corrective action involves addressing the contradiction and seeking to *repair* it by reinterpretation of the components involved. Obviously since I have cast the presentation in terms of partisanship of A, then the reinterpretative efforts will be directed at adjusting B, though, as will be seen later, they do not necessarily stop there.

One of the Durkheim's best and most neglected studies *The Evolution of Educational Thought*[18] provides a superb gist of the contradiction in which Christianity was embroiled because of its inescapable interpenetration with classicism. Paradoxically, given Durkheim's reputation as a consensus theorist, this book is a towering contribution which goes at least as far as Weber's *Ancient Judaism* in elaborating the notion of cultural contradictions.

The root of this constraining contradiction was that Christianity's 'origins were Graeco-Latin and it could not but remain more or less faithful to its origins. It had acquired its form and organization in the Roman world, the Latin language was its language, it was thoroughly

---

[18] Routledge and Kegan Paul, London, 1977. All subsequent citations are taken from this edition.

impregnated with Roman civilization'.[19] In turn, this confronted the Church with 'a contradiction against which it has fought for centuries without ever achieving a resolution. For the fact was that in the literary and artistic monuments of Antiquity there lived and breathed the very same pagan spirit which the Church had set itself the task of destroying.'[20] The contradiction between this particular A and B was profound and extensive: 'we have here two quite different and even mutually contradictory moral systems',[21] 'the one thoroughly impregnated with the eudaemonistic ethic, the other steeped in the contrary principle; the one regarding happiness as another aspect of virtue, the other sanctifying and glorifying suffering'.[22] But the incompatibility exceeds the ethical domain and spills over to affect conduct in the temporal world and conceptions both of man and of mundane reality; 'the Christian way of life . . . depends on the idea of man rising above his nature and freeing himself from it by taming and subjugating it to the spiritual laws whose object is, in a word, sanctity. By contrast, the ideal of antiquity is harmony with nature; nature is regarded as the source of information about the laws of human life.'[23]

Simultaneously this initial logical contradiction was accompanied by the lasting *dependence* of Christianity on classicism: 'The single fact that Christian doctrine is complexly involved in books, that it expresses itself daily in prayers which are said by each of the faithful and which are required to be known not only in the letter but also in the spirit, rendered it necessary not only for the priest but also even for the layman to acquire a certain amount of culture'.[24] Thus for the divines, such as St Augustine, the understanding of Holy Scripture was primary but it could only be achieved by steeping themselves deeper and deeper in profane literature. Here, comprehending the Christian God entailed acquaintance with the pagan deities; grasping the symbols of the New Testament spelled immersion in classical languages; clarifying Christian theology meant journeying so far into hostile territory that its denizens may have remained enemies but ceased to be aliens.

Moreover, if the elaboration of the faith could be left to the divines, its propagation involved teaching the people. Hence the religious origins of education in Europe, which more than anything else displayed the inextricable dependency of A on B and the incompatibilities which this invoked, institutionalized and reproduced. From the start,

this embryo of education *contained within itself a sort of contradiction. It was composed of two elements, which no doubt, in some sense, complemented and completed one another but which were at the same time mutually exclusive.* There was on the one

---

[19] Durkheim, *Evolution*, p. 21.   [20] Durkheim, *Evolution*, p. 22.
[21] Durkheim, *Evolution*, p. 210.   [22] Durkheim, *Evolution*, p. 255.
[23] Durkheim, *Evolution*, p. 209.   [24] Durkheim, *Evolution*, p. 23.

hand the religious element, the Christian doctrine; on the other, there was classical civilization and *all the borrowings which the Church was obliged to make from it*, that is to say the profane element . . . But the ideas which emerged from it *patently conflicted* with those which were at the basis of Christianity. Between the one and the other there stretched the whole of the abyss which separates the sacred from the profane, the secular from the religious.[25] (my emphasis)

Corrective repairs are equally mandatory in the realm of belief and the processes involved have formal similarities with the 'appeal procedure' in science.[26] It is the interpretation of B which is at stake, the objective is to tame it through reinterpretation and the stakes are identical – correct B or go under; make the ideational environment more hospitable or perish in it. The 'faithful' must in some way domesticate the cultural monsters confronting them. Pagan ideas were much more of a threat to Christianity than the Roman lions, for with the latter passive resignation could be seen as a sign of grace whilst with the former it could only be viewed as a sign of inadequacy. Instead the inconsistency has to be tackled, repaired and the correction made to stick. This is the task that the situational logic enforces on all those who neither make their exit nor change sides in the context of a constraining contradiction.

The basic proposition advanced is that the situational logic generated by the constraining contradiction, which is concerned with the *correction* of inconsistency, generically results in ideational *syncretism* (that is, the attempt to sink differences and effect union between the contradictory elements concerned). Since the relation between A and B is that of a genuine logical contradiction, which is therefore incapable of direct resolution, then the corrective exercise which aims to repair the inconsistency necessarily involves some redefinition of one or both elements.

(1) $A \leftarrow B$, i.e. correcting B so it becomes consistent with A.

(2) $A \leftrightarrow B$, i.e. correcting both A and B so they become mutually consistent.

(3) $A \rightarrow B$, i.e. correcting A so it becomes consistent with B.

All three paths lead to syncretism, but they differ considerably in terms of which element changes and how much it alters in the course of the repair work.

Obviously for adherents to A, the preferred solution is (1) since here it is B which undergoes the revision, then leaving A both intact and in congruence with its immediate environment. The middle solution represents the only form of symmetrical syncretism, as both A and B jointly

[25] Durkheim, *Evolution*, p. 25.

[26] See Imre Lakatos, 'Falsification and the methodology of scientific research programmes', in I. Lakatos and A. Musgrave (eds.), *Criticism and the Growth of Knowledge*, Cambridge University Press, Cambridge, 1970.

undergo reinterpretation. As such it is less desirable to adherents of A than (1), but clearly protagonists of A will find (2) preferable to (3) if repair cannot be effected by method (1). For those faithful to A, the final path is a last resort because it is their theories and beliefs which have to do all the adjusting in order to survive. The situational logic of correction fosters use of this last redoubt, since the alternative is the unbridled counter-actualization of B. Durkheim provides a compelling analysis of the gradual accommodation of Christian thought to the challenge of classical rationalism over two millennia. His presentation of the sequential syncretic shifts from (1) to (3) is summarized in *Culture and Agency*.[27]

In conclusion, whichever method is used to correct a constraining contradiction the generic result is some form of syncretism. The main thrust emanating from its situational logic is the sinking of differences and the effecting of union between its components. In other words, the existence of constraining contradictions within the Cultural System conditions *ideational unification*. However, neither this Systemic impetus towards unification nor its end-products, that is unified theories or beliefs, should be viewed as forces or results which guarantee proportional consensus in the relevant part of Socio-Cultural life. The unificatory thrust can be deflected in various ways by its Socio-Cultural reception. Everything depends on whether it happens to coincide with a prolonged lack of antagonism in society or whether it meshes with structured cleavages between social groups. Nevertheless, both the morphogenetic syncretism at the CS level and the pressure towards ideational unification at the S-C level which result from the constraining contradiction stand in complete contrast to the equivalent resultants of the other key concept – the concomitant complementarity.

Concomitant complementarities (necessary complementarities)

At the Systemic (CS) level, the direct counterpart of the constraining contradiction is what I have termed the 'concomitant compatibility', for this bears the same formal features in reverse. In other words invoking A also ineluctably evokes B, but since the B upon which this A depends is consistent with it, then B buttresses adherence to A. Consequently A occupies a congenial environment of ideas, the exploration of which, far from being fraught with danger, yields a treasure trove of reinforcement, clarification, confirmation and vindication – because of the logical consistency of the items involved. This, for example, was the generic feature which Weber analyzed as linking together the religious beliefs, the

---

[27] Archer, *Culture and Agency*, pp. 162–5.

rationale for status distribution and the economic ethos in Ancient India and China.

However, concomitant compatibilities are by no means the prerogative of traditional culture (nor were all traditional cultures seamless webs of consistency), a similar relationship obtained, for instance, between classical economics and utilitarian philosophy. Indeed, modern examples are so abundant in natural science that Kuhn was tempted into portraying the entire enterprise as a succession of paradigms, each of which constituted a cluster of concomitant compatibilities in our terminology.[28]

Nevertheless, just because A and B manifestly go together, the one being the logical accompaniment of the other, this should not conceal the fact that the concomitant compatibility, like the constraining contradiction, is a logical relationship which also conditions action (causally) at the Socio-Cultural level. To the actors involved this may seem nothing more than a felicitous facilitating influence, but facilitation is a directional influence too. It guides thought and action along a smooth path, away from stony ground, but over time this wears a deeper and deeper groove in which thoughts and deeds become enrutted.

The distinctive situational logic generated by the concomitant compatibility is problem-free to the actors involved. The consistency of its components makes exploring B rewarding for protagonists of A – the source of ideational bonuses like psychological reassurance, technical back-up, corroboration of theories and confirmation of beliefs. Thus, instead of the restricted access to B associated with the constraining contradiction, the situational logic of the concomitant compatibility fosters no limitation whatsoever on that part of B which is accessible to partisans of A. Not only are Socio-Cultural containment strategies unnecessary, they would represent self-inflicted injuries – a deliberate spurning of the rewards mentioned above. A prime indicator of this difference engendered by the two very different forms of situational logic, is the much longer and more open 'education' associated with the concomitant compatibility where nothing is risked the deeper and further adherents plunge into the ideational environment constituted by the A/B complex.

Nevertheless, this situational logic is exerting a causal influence on the Socio-Cultural level and not one which is the unmixed blessing it might appear. Its initial operative effect is the direct product of its felicitous consequences for the actors involved. It reinforces their adherence to A,

[28] Thomas S. Kuhn, *The Structure of Scientific Revolutions*, Chicago University Press, Chicago, 1962.

for the absence of exigencies leads to less turning away. Certainly, exit remains possible but desertion is not a product of the logic, this pushes no one to the door for it makes staying inside seem cosily inviting. However, cosiness is the close ally of closure. Over time the situational logic fosters a negative feed-back loop which discourages alterations in the felicitous cluster of items making for concomitant consistency. Hence the *exemplary* nature of cultural leadership whose effect is to repress internal innovation – Mandarin, Guru, Maestro or Mentor – identified by Weber and over-generalized by Kuhn.

Consequently, the adherents of A are enmeshed in the cluster forming the concomitant compatibility and insulated against those outside it. Yet because their 'truths' are not challenged but only reinforced from the proximate environment, then agents confront no ideational problems, are propelled to no daring feats of intellectual elaboration, but work according to a situational logic which stimulates nothing beyond cultural embroidery. The net effect of this is to reduce Systemic diversity to variations on a theme (which do however increase its density) and to intensify Socio-Cultural uniformity (through the absence of alternatives). In brief, the situational logic of concomitant compatibility conduces towards *protection* (the maintenance of purity), not *correction*.

The basic proposition advanced is that the situational logic generated by the concomitant compatibility, which is concerned with the *protection* of consistency, generically results in ideational *systematization* (that is, the 'strengthening of pre-existing relations among the parts, the developments of relations among parts previously unrelated, the gradual addition of parts and relations to a system, or some combination of these changes').[29]

It has already been argued that the cluster of interdependent but compatible propositions represents a kind of adventure playground, a congenial environment which can be explored with profit (for it reinforces the original idea) and without danger (since it presents no threat to it). Examples of such clusters include the Weberian studies of other-worldly religions, especially Confucianism and Hinduism. If we can establish common results stemming from the situational logic they share we might finally have succeeded in putting the Myth of Cultural Integration in its place, by showing that the concomitant complementarity is its real empirical home but also that it is not nearly so homely as the Myth depicts.

The results of concomitant compatibilities may form an integrated

---

[29] A. D. Hall and R. E. Hagen, 'Definition of system', in Joseph A. Litterer (ed.), *Organizations, Systems, Control and Adaptation*, vol. II, Wiley, New York, 1969, p. 36.

whole, but they do not get born in one piece. Formally they arise from the exploration of a pair of interdependent and mutually compatible notions, the extrapolations, implications and ramifications of which are then dovetailed together. In the process, the ties linking the initial compatible items strengthen considerably and a corpus of cognate notions are progressively incorporated. The latter represent a kind of in-filling of the environment staked out by the original compatibility, which encourages great wholeness over time. But both time and intellectual endeavour are essential.

Weber was acutely aware of the active mental nature of the enterprise. For him, in 'religious matters 'consistency' has been the exception and not the rule':[30] its achievement is an intellectual product rather than any kind of given. It entails a rational process of 'systematic arrangements',[31] which contrary to the views of the over-charitable anthropologists is both hard-won and correspondingly rare. Thus in contrast to the other-world religions reviewed, he considers the Hindu doctrine of Karma to represent the most consistent theodicy ever produced in history[32] – articulated around the interdependent notions of caste and reincarnation but consistently incorporating allied concepts of commensality, connubiality, education, politics and economic activity. What then follows is a phase of internal preoccupation with working out the inclusive linkages and tying them into the original core to form a comprehensive conspectus. With his usual perspicacity Weber appreciated these two strands of extensive exploration and inclusive formalization, which the world religions welded together.

The fact that they are conducted from and contribute to a consistent conspectus produces a distinctive end-product. There is a substantial increase in 'cultural density', by which this sector of the Cultural System becomes particularly rich in fine and subtle distinctions, possesses an elaborate and often technical vocabulary to describe them and a complex body of concepts to manipulate or capture them. The development of 1,000 words for cattle, the intricacies of caste rights and prohibitions, the bulging libraries of exegetical literature are all products of the same situational logic.

In turn, growing cultural density through which systematization is accomplished, has as its corollary the formation of a natural boundary. Quite literally, there are more internal interconnections within the field of the conspectus than external relations with components outside it. This is

---

[30] Max Weber, in Gerth and Mills, *From Max Weber*, p. 291.
[31] Max Weber, in Gerth and Mills, *From Max Weber*, p. 283.
[32] Max Weber, *Economy and Society*, New York, Bedminister Press, 1968 (orig. 1922), pp. 524–5.

an objective feature of the Cultural System which is independent of, though not unrelated to, the formation of Socio-Cultural communities the cognitive field of which remains within these bounds. Logically, the more complex the internal structure becomes, the more difficult it is to assimilate new items without major disruption of the delicately articulated interconnections. 'The more oppositions an organism is capable of distinguishing meaningfully, the "richer" becomes its assimilated environment, the more involved the corresponding structure of internal organization; but the less tolerant is the organism of even subtle vacillations of environmental state.'[33] Tight and sophisticated linkages eventually repel innovation because of its disruptive capacity.

This has implications *within* the conspectus, which progressively accommodates fewer and fewer radical innovations and can reach the stage where in Kuhn's words it 'suppresses fundamental novelties because they are necessarily subversive of its basic commitments'.[34] Precisely the same point is made by Weber about the effects of complex ritualization in Hinduism: 'A ritual law in which every change of occupation, every change in work technique, could result in ritual degradation is certainly not capable of giving birth to economic and technical revolutions from within itself, or even of facilitating the first germination of capitalism in its midst'.[35] Equally there are repercussions for the relationship between the conspectus and its *external* environment. Innovations from across the boundary do not knit in easily either. Increasingly, the systematized conspectus can only tolerate a stable, nonintrusive environment and since the world of ideas is generically lacking in these features, the solution is artificial stabilization by closure against the outside. The situational logic of protection means brooking no rivals from outside and repressing rivalry inside.

Insofar as protective insulation is successful, then closure represents a negative feed-back loop in which any morphogenetic amplification of deviations is eliminated. Instead, protective closure induces morphostasis and reduces cultural development to the embellishment of the conspectus. This steady impetus towards the stable reproduction of a cultural status quo represents a major contrast with the attempts to correct people's ideas which emanate from constraining contradictions.

Thus the generic result at the Cultural System level of the concomitant complementarity is systematization, the formation of a dense, tightly articulated set of ideas. Its main thrust at the Socio-Cultural level is reproduction, that is the distribution of *similarities* throughout the

[33] Zygmunt Bauman, *Culture as Praxis*, Routledge and Kegan Paul, London, 1973, p. 140.
[34] Kuhn, *Scientific Revolutions*, p. 5.
[35] Max Weber, in Gerth and Mills, *From Max Weber*, p. 413.

population. Insofar as reproduction is successful, it engenders shared ideas and common practices thus forming 'islands of order'[36] which are also integrated communities. These are the results of the concomitant complementarity; most especially this general scenario of systematization–density–protection–reproduction.

Competitive contradictions (contingent incompatibilities)

Formally what these different kinds of contradiction share is the logical property of inconsistency: again there is a basic incompatibility between the premises, contents or implications of two doctrines, A and B, which means that both cannot be upheld simultaneously. The two differ, however, in that where constraining contradictions are concerned the upholders of A cannot get away from B because these components are inescapably conjoined and therefore the full brunt of their incompatibility imposes itself as a problem on the partisans of A: in contradistinction, the competitive contradiction is not a matter of Systemic *constraint* for the new item is not dependent on the old because the two are only contingently related. Here, to advocate this A in no sense invokes some B. For example, secular rationalism does not entail constant reference to religious beliefs. The rationalist may set his face against these once and for all by a declaration of his atheism, or, more coherently, by opting for agnosticism and asserting that a matter which cannot be proved or disproved and for which he cannot find good reason, need not detain him. Instead, this kind of contradiction is only activated if someone else insists on counterpoising B and goes on doing so – thus enforcing debate between the two groups. In short, competitive contradictions, though systemic in substance, require Socio-Cultural activation. However, active opposition is a matter of Socio-Cultural contingency and not of Systemic inescapability.

In contrast to the constraining contradiction, where the alternative to a given set of ideas is also inextricably linked to them and thus constantly threatens them with its own counter-actualization, here the *accentuation* of an 'independent' contradiction is a supremely social matter. Accentuation depends on groups, actuated by interests, *making* a contradiction competitive, by taking sides over it and by trying to make other people take their side. In brief, these oppositional interest groups *cause* the contradiction to impinge on broader sections of the (relevant) population: it does not ineluctably confront them as in the case with constraining contradictions, the moment anyone asserts A.

---

[36] Bauman, *Culture as Praxis*, p. 122.

Competitive contradictions generate an entirely different situational logic for those confronting or brought to confront them. Basically, it is one which does not rub their noses in logical difficulties and keep them there. For to maintain A, whilst being fully knowledgeable about B, does not embroil actors in inescapable cognitive exigencies which inexorably drive them to personal or collective strategies of containment and correction – the only ways of avoiding relentless mental tension or the ultimate resignation of A. Dependency is responsible for this situation for it means that B can never be shrugged off, but this property does not feature in the competitive contradiction whose constituents are only contingently related to each other.

Because of this, their operative effect is entirely different from the workings of the constraining contradiction. By contrast the situational logic created by the competitive contradiction is one which confronts people with *choice*. To be more precise, it is a logic which forces them to make choices, by accentuating differences, by insisting on their salience, by undermining indifference and by making the *question* of alignment inescapable.

This is not to argue that the situational logic enforces alignment with one side or the other but what it does inexorably extend is the awareness of choice in society. As many have pointed out, traditionalists cease to be such from the moment that they realize this is what they are. What the logic does is to pull the rug from underneath unthinking traditionalism, habitualism and conventionalism by exposing their practitioners to the existence of alternatives. It presents the collectivity with the *possibility* of ideational diversity. The level of discursive awareness will vary enormously from the ideological protagonists and academic advocates immersed in the intricacies of the contest, through groups which having been bombarded by the crossfire have made their choice but do not penetrate the issue any further, to those who merely have the uneasy feeling that in sticking to the old ways they are somehow being old-fashioned. Even the latter are aware, however dimly, that alternatives exist, and indeed they do – this is the force of the situational logic and its objective grounding.

But as far as the active opponents are concerned, those already aligned in ideational antagonism, the logical source of their opposition further conditions their course of action. In contradistinction to the constraining contradiction, here the situational logic dictates elimination not correction. In the former case, actors were driven to cope with ideas which contradicted their own (compromising, conciliating and usually conceding much *en route*) whereas those involved (and drawn into involvement) over a competitive contradiction have every incentive to *eliminate* the opposition.

Because partisans of A and B are unconstrained by any internal and necessary relations between these doctrines, there is nothing which restrains their combativeness for they have everything to gain from inflicting maximum damage on one another's ideas in the course of competition. Victory consists in so damaging and discrediting oppositional views that they lose all social salience, leaving their antithesis in unchallenged supremacy. As in structural analysis there is, then, a different distribution of opportunity costs associated with different objective situations. For protagonists of A, who find themselves confronting a constraining contradiction, penalties accrue if B is not somehow corrected; for partisans of another A who are faced with a competitive contradiction, bonuses are associated with unbridled injurious conflict. In the first case, the actors involved are conditioned to make the best of the situation, in the latter case to make the worst of it.

Since elimination of what is inconsistent with a given belief or theory is the goal directed by the situational logic, and because two groups are involved in the activation of every competitive contradiction, what results is a battle-ground of ideas. The military simile is not far-fetched, for in ideational conflict we are dealing with charge and counter-charge (counterfactuals and counter-arguments), with offensives and counter-offensives, with defensive re-groupings, loss of ground, retreat and, of course, the problem of deserters.

Since Marx, a lack of interest in ideologies as examples of competitive contradictions has characterized approaches to this type of collective belief. Being both upwards conflationists and vulgar Marxists, then for dominant ideology theorists there is no competition (because domination spells the incorporation of all into one view) and no contradiction (because domination equals the elimination of other views). Universal socialization and internalization play just the same role in relation to the central value system within functionalist downward conflation.[37]

Certainly, many have realized the significant 'peculiarity of ideology as a belief system lies in its *connection with group interests in a given social order*. This *sectional* nature of ideology *qua* belief system may be deemed the central tenet of ideology theory proper ... the *interest nexus* is what provides ideologies with their *differentia specifica* among the various kinds of collective beliefs.'[38] However, from our point of view, this is often no more than an acknowledgement of plural interests and associated ideologies. It concedes the existence of oppositional groups at the Socio-

---

[37] Talcott Parsons, for example, assimilated ideology to the 'cognitive legitimation of patterns of value orientation', in *The Social System*, Routledge and Kegan Paul, London, 1951, p. 351.
[38] J. G. Merquior, *The Veil and the Mask*, Routledge and Kegan Paul, London, 1979, pp. 3–4.

Cultural level (indeed necessary for the competitive contradiction) but it allows of no competition or contradiction between the ideologies *themselves* at the CS level, since the latter are mere epiphenomena or reflections of the former.

This is inadequate in two respects, both of which hinge on the fact that ideologies are used against one another – they are quintessentially competitive. First, if they were no more than passive duplications of interests then it is impossible that they could advance, foster or defend those interests. Yet if they are performing such tasks then they are necessarily doing so in *competition* with others which perform the same job in relation to oppositional interests. Secondly, the epiphenomenal view is fundamentally unable to deal with 'false consciousness' or to answer the 'riddle of ideological assent': '[i]f ideology is just a "rationalization" of . . . interests, then how is it also believed by those who do not share in the advantages it rationalizes'.[39] Since we are bound to acknowledge the existence of this phenomenon and if we also accept that plural interests are at work then we have to concede that there is a competition for assent amongst the ideologies at play.

Finally, if we ask the theoretically interesting question about competition – namely, how do ideologies work against one another in fostering particular interests or commanding assent from non-beneficiaries? – then their most striking common denominator is a claim to universal acceptability and a concealment of their intrinsic sectional character. Each ideology seeks to legitimate itself by reference to

the imputed interests of the *totality* and the good of the whole. It is on this claim that the moral authority and suasion of ideology grounds itself. Ideological discourse is aimed continually at denying the legitimacy of partisan interests; sometimes it even denies the *reality* of partisanship. In the latter case, ideology may seek to demonstrate that partisan interests are only *seemingly* such.[40]

The assertive group(s) which challenges it requires the dual functions of ideology from the start: not only must an ideology be developed to legitimate its claims and activities amongst its own members (and, ideally, a wider audience), but also the same principles must be extended to constitute a negation of the legitimatory basis of the dominant group. Because the claim to legitimate domination must be undermined before challenge is possible, assertive groups, in their earliest stages, concentrate almost exclusively on negation, on condemning and unmasking the interests concealed behind the proto-ideology of the dominant party.

[39] Merquior, *Veil and Mask*, p. 9.
[40] Alvin W. Gouldner, *The Dialectic of Ideology and Technology*, Macmillan, London, 1976, p. 278.

However, a group whose domination has been unopposed for a long period may only begin to elaborate this negative function in proportion to the attacks launched against it. Hence the typical response of a well-established dominant group is the immediate reformulation of its ideology[41] – extending it to negate the claims of its new rival, and thus finally crystallizing the competitive contradiction.

However, these first rival interpretations of the problem situation do not remain frozen as static social alternatives. The further clarification of the original ideology, B, which actually crystallized the contradiction, simultaneously clarified the logical points at issue with A. Those asserting A then encroach further into enemy (CS) territory by concentrating their counter-arguments on the new (or newly clarified) claims of B. But however powerful these are, the defenders of B are never rendered speechless and, at best, can make a come-back by advancing a more sophisticated version of their ideology which both protects their initial position and answers the charges brought against it. As Lakatos argued, 'the idea of proliferation of theories can be generalized to any sort of rational discussion and thus serve as tools for a general theory of criticism'.[42] This naturally involves dismissing any view which holds the *differentia specifica* of ideology to be distortion but then no one, I believe, has ever made out an acceptable case for the existence of a separate sub-type of 'ideological ideas'. What is ideological is the uses to which they are put – in the context *of* interests but *in* argument. Both features are equally important in the competitive contradiction: it is undoubtedly the S-C interests which fuel the contest and keep it going but, also, as a (CS) argument, it can be examined like any other for features like 'progressive' or 'degenerating' problem-shifts.

Contingent complementarities

The operative effects of *contingent complementarities* can best be elucidated by comparing them with the three concepts already discussed and the different kinds of situational logic associated with them – thus at the same time summarizing the main distinctions made in this connection. Although the situational logic generated by the contingent complementarity is indeed the loosest of the four (like the job description stressing initiative rather than itemizing duties), this does not prevent it from conditioning the Socio-Cultural level in a crucial fashion. For the existence of these (socially known) compatibilities represents a source of

[41] Michalina Vaughan and Margaret S. Archer, *Social Conflict and Educational Change in England and France: 1789–1848*, Cambridge University Press, Cambridge, 1971, pp. 31–2.   [42] Lakatos, 'Falsification', p. 158.

novelty which the Cultural System extends to human agency with few strings attached. These condition action precisely because they *objectively increase the opportunity for cultural free play* – for novel combinations and applications involving conceptual integration, theoretical reduction or doctrinal extension, all of which have ideational synthesis as their common denominator.

This, indeed, is the first contrast with the other three kinds of situational logic. When confronted by a constraining contradiction, the protagonists of A have no choice but to cope with B (or abandon ship); when faced with the concomitant complementarity their choice is between adopting B wholesale or flying in the face of its manifest benefits; when embroiled in a competitive contradiction, alternatives are indeed present but actors are presented with a forced choice between A and B. Only the contingent complementarity simultaneously holds out choices to the adherents of A but leaves them free to make what they will (if anything) of B. It is not merely that the objective availability of different courses of action is greater, so is the freedom to determine what to do with these opportunities.

Thus the second point of contrast is that unlike the other types of situational logic already discussed, there are no containment strategies or exposure policies associated with the contingent compatibility. While the constraining contradiction makes social containment tempting and logical correction mandatory (resulting either in restricted access to material or restrictions on intellectual enterprise), the concomitant compatibility operates in exactly the opposite direction, encouraging maximum exposure to congruent ideas but inducing maximum closure against innovation. With competitive contradictions, alternatives are objectively available but every pressure is brought to bear to decrease their subjective attractions, to discourage synthesis, and to foster stable alignment – again reducing the potential for ideational diversity. Only the contingent compatibility is free from Socio-Cultural manipulation, designed to induce *avoidance* or *adoption* or *aversion*. Certainly, distracting Socio-Cultural practices – habitual preoccupations, established routines, traditional preserves or conventional divisions of subjects – may well reduce subjective willingness to explore new and congruent possibilities. Nevertheless, the agents concerned have substantial freedom to survey or to ignore the broader horizon which has come into view and such is indeed the distinctive feature of this situational logic.

In sum, since the contingent complementarity presents a loose situational logic of opportunity, then this requires Socio-Cultural opportunists to take advantage of it. Their capacity to take advantage of contact with B and then freely to define what can advantageously be made of it, constitutes the final contrast with our other concepts.

The need to reintroduce the people

The first part of this section on second-order CEPs was concerned with the effects upon people of contradictions and complementarities in the Cultural System. In it, social agents entered the picture only as those who held ideas and who were conditioned in various ways if they went on holding them, for without people doing so there would be no picture at all. Emphatically this is not to reduce human agents to *träger*: it is a methodological procedure deriving from analytical dualism, which directs us to look at how the cultural context is shaped for agents before examining what they do in it or what they can do about it.

The types of ideas they held could vary enormously,[43] for the conditional influences of interest examined here stemmed from relations between ideas and did not reside in their substantive character. These substantive differences were irrelevant to the main argument – namely that it was formal (logical) relations of contradiction or complementarity with other ideas which (causally) placed actors in entirely different positions, whatever the nature of their theories or beliefs.

On the one hand, if these logical relationships were *internal and necessary* ones, then they created different situational logics for their holders by moulding the context of cultural action in two distinctive ways. The relational properties of a constraining contradiction enmeshed those upholding its constituent ideas in a problem-ridden situation. The causal influence of the situational logic was one encouraging correction since opportunity costs attached to failure in repairing inconsistencies. The reverse was the case for the concomitant complementarity which placed its advocates in a problem-free situation and presented them with ideational bonuses for continued advocacy. Here, the causal influence of the situational logic fostered protection of benefits received from the cultural status quo. Consequently, these two situational logics conditioned different patterns of ideational development – syncretism (a sinking of differences) in the case of correction, and systematization (a consolidation of gains) in the case of protection.

On the other hand, there is a major operative difference between these two kinds of contradictions and complementarities and the other pair

---

[43] Throughout *Culture and Agency* I maintained that there was the same formal relationship between ideas as different as religious beliefs and scientific theories.

which are only matters of contingency. For the effects of the necessary contradiction and the concomitant complementarity are ones which impinge from the CS level *inescapably* on the S-C level. In other words, these Systemic relationships (logical) impress themselves (causally) on S-C action. This is the element of truth in downwards conflation, but it is not the whole story. There are also the effects of the competitive contradictions and contingent complementarities and these are *activated* (causally) at the S-C level by the *selective accentuation* of certain CS level relationships (logical). In other words, social action determines which logical relations shall have cultural salience in society. And this is the element of truth in upwards conflation, which makes up the other part of the story. The truth is something of both, but it does not lie in the middle as central conflationists would have it.

Thus to understand what happens next it is necessary to bring the people back in, not merely as static upholders of this or that idea, but as active makers and re-makers of their culture (and structure) in pursuit of their interests, by use of their power and through social alliances or group antagonism. In short, we need to move on to the second phase of the morphogenetic cycle – Socio-Cultural Interaction – to see how relations between people are capable of changing or maintaining the relations between ideas as between material structures. More generally this is also the next step in linking structure, culture and agency, or even more basically, the 'parts' and the 'people'.

8   The morphogenesis of agency

To talk about Social Agency at all means returning to the central problem presented by the 'vexatious fact of society' and its human constitution. That neither the structuring of society nor the social interaction responsible for it can be discussed in isolation from one another is the central tenet of the morphogenetic perspective. However in modern social theory there is nothing distinctive about endorsing this proposition which now commands near universal assent: what distinguishes between different approaches is how they conceptualize the interplay between what are generally known as 'structure and agency'. The distinguishing feature of the morphogenetic perspective is its four-square endorsement of 'analytical dualism', namely, the idea that the two elements have to be teased out over time precisely in order to examine their interplay.

In the preceding two chapters, discussion of the morphogenesis of structure and culture relied upon social agents and their interaction as the mechanism which explained structural and cultural stability or change. Thus, the focus was on the results of interaction, which are passed up to the Structural and Cultural systems and passed on to subsequent generations of people as new conditioning influences upon them. All of this meant taking systemic outcomes as the focal point. Although it is perfectly legitimate to focus upon the remodelling of structure and culture in this way, it is equally important to recognize that the self-same sequence by which agency brings about social and cultural transformation is simultaneously responsible for the systematic transforming of social agency itself.

In other words, a 'double morphogenesis' is involved:[1] agency leads to structural and cultural elaboration, but is itself elaborated in the process. Thus the focus shifts to the latter in this chapter, which presents an account of the Morphogenesis of Agency, utilizing exactly the same scheme and based on the same theoretical premisses. To do this means

---

[1] Piotr Sztompka, 'Social movements: structures *in statu nascendi*', presented at XIth World Congress of Sociology, New Delhi, 1986.

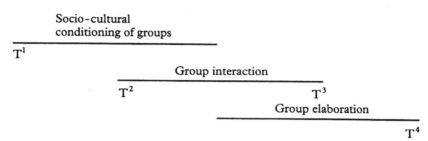

Figure 14 The elaboration of Agency.

filling in the basic morphogenetic diagram from the point of view of *outcomes for agency* rather than systemic outcomes. Figure 14 is the most fundamental representation of one such cycle and for the time being it fails to explain precisely what is meant by 'agency' or to explicate what kinds of social groups are involved. This is the task of the rest of the chapter which will progressively expand upon figure 14, whilst remaining anchored in it, just as complex discussion of structural and cultural changes never ceases to be moored in the basic morphogenetic diagram. For the time being, 'Agency' is used as a generic term which stands for the 'people' rather than the 'parts' of society. It will need to undergo refinement very soon and be broken-down further, for if a single concept sufficed, then we could simply use 'people' without more ado. However, an undifferentiated notion of Agency will be retained just long enough to make comparisons with its usage in other approaches.

Before beginning to flesh-out figure 14 it is probably helpful to indicate three other ways of conceptualizing 'social agency' from which the morphogenetic perspective explicitly dissociates itself. While the term 'agency' is employed in each of these other approaches, quite different things are meant by it. From the morphogenetic perspective the connotations and denotations are different again and 'social agency' is not just a pretentious way of referring to people or humankind.

The contrast with one-dimensional views

Indeed, perhaps the easiest way of unpacking what *is* meant by 'agency' in different schools of thought, is by asking where it stands in relationship to notions of the 'human being'. What we find here are four starkly contrasting positions. The first view in fact contains no human beings as such but only social agents, formed from Durkheim's famous 'indeterminate material', who energize the system after appropriate socialization.

The second view is the reverse. Here we have a 'model of man', an idealized human being standing for the social agent, who along with others like him generates the entirety of the social structure from his in-built dispositions to be a rational (or whatever) actor. Thirdly, there are those so intent on stressing that to be human is to be social and that society enters into each and every action, that the human being and the social agent become synonymous with one another. Finally, the morphogenetic perspective is distinctive in recognizing both human beings and social agents, but refusing to treat them interchangeably. In fact, this latter approach is more different still since it distinguishes between the 'human being', 'social agent' and 'social actor', regarding all three as indispensable in social theorizing but as irreducible to one another. This triple distinction requires considerable justification and is discussed in later sections by considering each in turn and defending all three as emergent and therefore irreducible. Right now the three other approaches mentioned require further inspection to see what it is about their conceptions of 'agency' from which this stratified morphogenetic model distances itself.

(a) Holism basically dissolves personal identity into social relationships. Selfhood becomes defined in terms of social roles in the well-known view of *homo sociologicus*. From this approach, my purposes cannot really be mine because I have been deprived of any self which allows me to find them good or appropriate ones. Where *homo sociologicus* is concerned, all purposes become entirely social, since all reasons for action are matters of role requirements.

Ultimately *homo sociologicus* is moved by social hydraulics. Any such 'downwards conflationary' view which regards people from the top down, that is as 'indeterminate material' which energizes society but is unidirectionally shaped by it, advances a passive agent and endorses social determinism rather than social conditioning. The morphogenetic perspective requires agency to be reflective, purposive, promotive and innovative, if social interaction is indeed to operate as the mechanism responsible for stability and change. Puppets will not do instead of agents for socio-cultural conditioning is not a matter of social hydraulics. It was maintained in chapter 7 that structural and cultural factors influence agents only through shaping the situations in which they find themselves and distributing vested interests in maintenance and transformation to different groups. These compel no one and are better construed in terms of structure and culture supplying good reasons for various courses of action to those in given positions, than as hydraulic pressures. However, for this to be the case, a good reason requires a reflective agent to evaluate it as such, to adopt it, and to decide then what to do about it, all of which is beyond the wits of 'passive man'. However, chapter 7 issued a promissory note on who did the reflecting and evaluating and this must be honoured, though the reader is asked to live on promises for a few more pages.

Nevertheless, whilst agents need their wits about them to decide how to perpetuate rewarding situations and to eradicate frustrating ones, they should not be endowed with the comparative insight and historical hindsight of the good sociologist. For many situations can occur only within certain structural and cultural limits[2] and these unacknowledged conditions of situated action lie beyond the ken of time-and-space-bound agents.

(b) Such unacknowledged conditions of action are one of the main problems with the opposite view which regards society from the bottom-up, seeing structure and culture as resulting from contemporary individuals, their dispositions and combinations. This, as it were, burdens contemporary agency with responsibility for all current features of society. It constitutes an under-constrained picture of 'wo/man' (or an under-enabled one for that matter). This is because it makes no allowance for inherited structures, their resistance to change, the influence they exert on attitudes to change and, crucially here, the delineation of agents capable of seeking change.

The other problem is the complementary effort to derive complex structures directly from some 'model of man', i.e. from some property pertaining to the (idealized) human being. Thus the first contender was 'rational man' of classical economics, whose calculus, consistency and selfishness organized his desires, resulting in choices which summed to produce social reality.[3] The fact that the model of 'rational man' could not cope with phenomena like voluntary collective behaviour or the voluntary creation of public goods, led some (who conceded defeat over the Prisoner's Dilemma or the Free-Rider) to complement him with an inner running mate. Enter 'normative man', who shifts to a different logic of action under circumstances in which he realizes he is dependent upon others for his own welfare.[4] Yet again, inexplicable macro-level effects remained, and 'emotional man' joined the team to mop up structural and cultural properties based on expressive solidarity or willingness to share.[5]

The trouble with this multiplication of complements, all inhabiting the

[2] Percy S. Cohen, *Modern Social Theory*, Heinemann, London, 1968, p. 205.
[3] Amartya Sen, 'Rationality and uncertainty', *Theory and Decision*, 1985, 18.
[4] See Amitai Etzioni, *The Moral Dimension: Towards a New Economics*, Free Press, New York, 1988.
[5] See Helena Flam, 'Emotional "Man"': I. The emotional man and the problem of collective action', *International Sociology*, 1990, 5: 39–56. 'Emotional "Man"': II. Corporate actors as emotion-motivated emotion managers', *International Sociology*, 1990, 5: 225–34.

same being, is that it eventually comes full circle ending up with the 'multiple self'[6] and the suggestion that we treat 'man' like an organization. Yet this is a completely vicious circle: some sort of 'man' was wanted to explain that which was problematic, namely social organization, but now we are enjoined to use the explanandum in order to conceptualize the explanans, the nature of man! What is going wrong here is the desperate incorporation of all emergent and aggregate social properties into the individual.

From the morphogenetic perspective these are irreducible group variables, unintended products of interaction, which defy reduction to individual dispositions plus any number of composition rules. Sociocultural complexity is an unintended consequence of interaction, which escapes its progenitors to constitute the unacknowledged conditions of action for future agents. It is not therefore by adducing an ever more complicated 'model of man' that social complexity can be derived from *individual* human beings. The morphogenetic perspective thus distances itself from both the conception of agency in the singular (seeing more profit in applying the terms to collectivities) and also from overburdening contemporary individuals with the agential responsibility for creating or maintaining all current features of society. (Of course, conceptions of agency in the singular need not present us with pre-social atomic individuals. However, position (b) does do so, thus conflating human beings and agents, whilst it seems that other types of singular conceptions elide agents and actors instead, as will be argued later (see pp. 275–80)

(c) Finally there is the increasing popular view, represented by structuration theory, which recognizes the tight interdependence of structure and agency, and makes a virtue out of their entanglement by the suggestion that they are indeed mutually constitutive. Here, structure and culture have to be drawn upon in the routine production of action, which in turn instantiates structural properties, thus recursively reproducing structure itself. The core notion of structure as the medium and outcome of practices, clamps structure and agency together in a conceptual vice. It does so because it precludes the examination of properties pertaining separately to the two and in consequence it prevents exploration of their interplay. This mutually constitutive conglomerate presents us with such thoroughly 'knowledgeable' agents (that very little goes on behind their backs which is not discoverable, recoverable and corrigible) and an omnipresent structure (necessarily drawn upon in each practical act, with every such enactment invoking the structural corpus in its entirety). I have given a general critique of this approach in chapter 4.

---

[6] Jon Elster, *The Multiple Self*, Cambridge University Press, Cambridge, 1986.

All that needs accentuating here is the notion of 'knowledgeability' and why, as presented in structuration theory, it is unacceptable in itself and above all by itself. To begin with, people do not have and cannot attain 'discursive penetration' of many unacknowledged conditions of action (though these are no more sinister than the results of past interaction); agents have differential knowledgeability according to social position; and some agents have defective, deficient and distorted knowledge owing to the cultural manipulation of others.

Secondly, the morphogenetic approach would also dissociate itself from this under-stratified view of agency which only differentiates between people by virtue of their knowledgeability, including tacit skills. In other words, it is only allowed that different people have differential degrees of 'discursive penetration', 'practical knowledge' or 'unconscious awareness' of their situations, which in turn affect their social practices. But why should knowledge itself be considered sufficient to account for differences in human motivation ? Yet structuration theory is mute on desires. They can have no external locus, finding their promptings in structured positions, in vested interests or induced wants, and they can have no independent internal locus in individual psychological proclivities. Without a more stratified view of people which allows for prior structural conditioning and individual differences between persons, we lack an account of both the regular patternings of wants in different parts of society and of the personal differences which make resulting actions something quite different from mechanical responses to hydraulic pressures. It was the latter from which the central conflationist sought to escape through the image of endlessly variegated permutations on 'rules and resources'. The ineluctability with which people have to draw upon these *in order to act at all* was criticized in chapter 4 as entailing an oversocial view of people. Every action needed to employ social media and no action, however personal, was conceivable without invoking all three media (i.e. interpretative scheme, facility, norm). Hence my earlier conclusion that the individual person and the social agent were being compacted together. One of the direct consequences of this is that Structuration theory does not offer a concept of collective action and has very little indeed to say about social movements, collective conflict or corporative control.

So far I have been concerned to distance the morphogenetic approach from any one-dimensional view of people, whether this took the form of 'downwards', 'upwards' or 'central' conflation. It is time to introduce the alternative, whose distinguishing feature is the endorsement of analytical dualism. This emphasizes that the two elements 'structure and agency' or, more broadly, 'society and people' have to be separated (rather than conflated) precisely in order to examine the role they play in one another's transformation over time. What is involved is the *double morphogenesis*, for the self-same process by which people bring about social transformation is simultaneously responsible for systematically transforming agency. In other words, people collectively generate the elaboration of structure and culture, but they themselves undergo elaboration *as* people at the same time. The following sketch of this process is the last occasion on which Agency is still employed as a generic term (i.e. being used interchangeably with our everyday understanding of 'people').

As usual the three phases of the basic morphogenetic cycle contain separate propositions about, (i) the conditions under which agency operates, many of which are not of its own making (this would be thoroughly congenial only to proponents of approach (a) above). We are all born into a structural and cultural context which, far from being of our making, is the unintended resultant of past interaction among the long dead. Simultaneously we acquire vested interests in maintenance or change according to the privileged or under-privileged positions we occupy and whether the situations we confront are sources of rewarding or penalizing experiences.

Next, (ii), these are conditional effects: to be socially efficacious they have to be taken up, articulated and acted upon (proponents of approach (c) above would give tepid support to this proposition alone and only when reformulated). Conditioning is mediated through agents' situations which supply reasons for pursuing maintenance or change (retaining benefits or overcoming obstacles) which work on vested interests distributed under (i). These force nobody, but they constitute objective premiums for adopting reasons which advance vested interests and equally objective penalties for endorsing ones which damage them. Conditioning thus operates through associating bonuses and penalties with different courses of action. Though these are objective, we skirt any truck with *homo economicus* by insisting that they have to be weighed subjectively and that weighers cannot be pre-programmed by nature or nurture, otherwise weights and measures would be standard across society and constant for the individual – when manifestly they are not. Far from vested interests being compelling, this view of agency in no way precludes their sacrifice for altruistic reasons. Nevertheless, their recognition by promotive interest groups is what produces regularities in the action patterns of collectivities (which otherwise would remain puzzlingly coincidental), whilst the conscientious repudiation of vested interests generates deviations (inexplicable on any positivistic account, cast in terms of hydraulics). Simultaneously, full allowance has to be made for group interaction which both manipulates knowledge and may lead to mis-representation of interests. An unrecognized vested interest prompts no protective/promotive action: penalties accrue but the price is paid uncomprehendingly.

Lastly, (iii), the resulting morphostasis or morphogenesis is the product of social agency (advocates of approach (b) above reserve their enthusiasm for this proposition alone). However the outcome is rarely exactly what any particular agent wants. Not only does it include overt compromises and concessions thrashed out during the middle phase, but also the unintended consequences of interaction. Such aggregate and emergent properties constitute features of structure and culture which condition the next cycle of interaction. *At the same time, however, agency will have transformed itself as part and parcel of the process of working for social stability or change. The elaboration of agency contains its own quota of unintended consequences which are equally potent in conditioning subsequent interaction by delineating groups standing in different relations to one another and with differential chances of prevailing over others and influencing systemic outcomes.* It is to these intricacies surrounding the morphogenesis of agency that the rest of the chapter is devoted.

However, it is now becoming urgent to know exactly *who* is being referred to in this sketch. Some readers will have been shifting uneasily at the way in which 'persons', 'groups', 'actors', 'collectivities' and 'agents' have been used interchangeably, and rightly so. The time has come to honour those overdue promissory notes issued in chapter 7 by specifying the referents of 'people' in the morphogenetic approach. The answer, as already hinted, is that we will be introducing three 'characters' rather than one, thus distancing morphogenesis still further from the one-dimensionality of the various forms of conflationary theorizing discussed.

A stratified model of 'people'

The key difference in dealing with the 'people', as with the 'parts' of society, is that from the morphogenetic perspective we again need a much more robustly stratified concept than was provided by any of those reviewed above. This is needed for describing who people are, since we identify them by different criteria for different purposes (such as taking a census, conducting a survey or promoting them at work). Of course it is one question to ask how many such strata there are, which the incidence of emergent properties and powers determines, but it is another to decide how many of these are needed in social theorizing. Since morphogenesis is intended to be a contribution to practical social theory, then it deals only with *Persons, Agents and Actors* . (Undoubtedly there are further strata, such as the linking level of individual psychology or personality, itself emergent from 'consciousness', which in turn emerges from 'mind', which is emergent from 'matter' etc.[7]) This more stratified view is also required because we may only need to draw upon the properties pertaining to the human Person, the Agent or the Actor, depending upon what we are seeking to explain. Thus, census takers only need to know who is to count as a human Person, whereas those conducting surveys have to know about the relations of Persons to various social distributions (of resources, life chances, demographic features etc.) in order to say what a sample is representative of or in relation to which properties it is stratified (these will soon be defined as characteristics of Agents). Finally, promotion boards have to consider candidates' suitability for occupying particular posts which entails reference to the social Actors they now are and judgements about the ones they might become. At any moment in time such distinctions are important not only to investigators but also to people themselves, for the things they can do *qua* human beings, *qua* agents and *qua* actors will be different things in different settings, involving different powers, different interests and different reasons. Diachronically, matters are more complex.

A notion of the 'social self' is needed here which pays due respect to both parts of the term, but this can only be seen as an emergent entity (we could just as well write 'identity') which, moreover, does not emerge in a single movement. (This is therefore quite unlike any form of conflationary theorizing which basically pictures one move – simple aggregation in upwards conflation – socialization in downwards conflation – or progressive specification in central conflation, of a sociality which is antenatally pre-inscribed and neo-natally given precise definition). The view to be advanced here is distinctivly different in presenting the human Person as fathering the Agent who , in turn, fathers the Actor, both phylogenetically and ontogenetically.

What will be given firstly then, is an account of the emergence of *Agency*, as the end-product of the '*double morphogenesis*' in which collectivities of human beings are grouped and re-grouped as they contribute to the process of reproducing or changing the structure or culture of society. In this way, they also maintain or change their collective identities as part and parcel of maintaining or transforming the socio-cultural structures which they inherited at birth.

Secondly, and literally on top of that, will be an account of the emergence of *Actors*, who develop from the '*triple morphogenesis*'. In this process, the particular social identities of individual social actors are

---

[7] The proper identification of these more primitive strata is left to those with the appropriate expertise: the above list is merely suggestive of how much social theorists have to take as given in order to be able to theorize about people at all.

forged frc n agential collectivities in relation to the array of organizational roles which are available in society at that specific point in time. Both Agents and Actors, however, remain anchored in Persons, for neither of the former are constructs or heuristic devices; they concern real people even though they only deal with certain ways of being in society and therefore not with all ways of being human in the world. Because of this anchorage in common humanity, it will be necessary to complete our account by returning to consider what social identity is thus anchored in, and what difference it makes that it has this anchorage.

Here it might be objected that to anchor the Actor in the Person may supply the needed reflexive quality and generalized ability for innovation but the snag is that the human being *per se* has no particular interests to bring to any role and to be innovative about, whilst the Actor has only those interests which come with the role. This must be readily admitted. However, admitting it is precisely the reason why reference has also to be made to the Agent: for Agents, as Collectivities sharing the same life chances, do have interests (in protecting or improving the latter) which are external to roles, yet can be pursued through them. If Persons furnish activity-potential for Actors, then Agency is a necessary mediator between them in order to supply activity with a purpose. Furthermore, Agency is also the mediating mechanism which accounts for who, out of the total population, acquires which role(s) within the total role array. For different agential life chances give differential access to different parts of the array of roles available in society at any given time. In both respects then, Agency stands as the middle element linking Persons to Actors and is needed to account for who occupies which roles – and why they do what they do when the role does not require them to do it! Hence the genealogy, Human Being–Agent–Actor.

It is as Actors that we acquire , or may acquire, a strict social identity by investing ourselves in a role and personifying it in a particularistic way. (Agents, being defined as Collectivities, and thus in the plural, cannot have strict identity.[8]) Everyone has a personal identity, but each does not, I submit, have a social identity, that is any role in which they can invest enough of themselves to feel at home with what they have become. This is one reason why personal and social identity are not the same thing. Absence of social identity occurs when the roles occupied (e.g. the

---

[8] Strict or numerical criteria for personal identity are ones which not only are, but also cannot be satisfied by more than one candidate. Currently many would dispense with attempting to supply such criteria and settle, in the tradition of William James, for 'qualitative identity'. From such a view, I am the same person that I was yesterday in that there is a present Thought which correctly judges that this Me is the same Me. However, the identity of both I and Me are not strict but 'on the whole'. This is not the path which will be followed in the present chapter.

unemployed) do not express what we would choose to be, or those which do so are lost (e.g. through redundancy), and alternatives are unavailable (e.g. because of job shortages). The other reason why we need to have and to make reference to a continuous personal identity is in order *for there to be someone* who experiences this absence or loss – a knowing subject who is aware of how society could have satisfied them but has failed to fulfil them. Again, 'indeterminate material' will not do, for it lacks potentialities which social organization can frustrate as well as a sense of self which knows them to have been frustrated. After all, talk of 'dehumanization' only makes sense if it does mean something to be human, and to experience it only makes for grief if there is a self who can sense its loss.

Agency: the double morphogenesis

Agents, from the morphogenetic perspective, are agents *of* something. Baldly, they are agents of the socio-cultural system into which they are born (groups or collectivities in the same position or situations) and equally they are agents of the systemic features they transform (since groups and collectivities are modified in the process). Fundamentally this is a shorthand account of the morphogenesis of agency: the drama of interaction may be centuries long, but the storyline is a simple one of pre-grouping and re-grouping. In many respects it is much the same story as the one which is usually called 'social stratification' and deals with the distribution of different 'life chances' to different collectivities.

Agents indeed are defined as *collectivities* sharing the same *life chances*. Internal and necessary relations maintain between these two elements, for this concept is irreducible to 'people plus some statistical probability about their future income, influence etc.' On the contrary, the major distributions of resources upon which 'life chances' pivot are themselves dependent upon relations between the propertied and the propertyless, the powerful and the powerless, the discriminators and the subjects of discrimination: and these, of course, are relationships between collectivities. (Further interdependencies are entailed with other SEPs, e.g. property forms or political organization and CEPs, e.g. forms of instruction or ethnic categories). Equally, it is their activity-dependence upon collectivities which secures the notion of 'life chances' against reification. They are neither statistical artefacts nor hypostatized entities. However, to recognize them as emergents is to acknowledge their internal and necessary relationship with structured social groups, over time.

In the morphogenetic approach, when we talk about 'social agents' we are of course referring to people, but *not* to everything about people *since it is always and only employed in the plural*. Usage in the singular (i.e.

reference to a social Agent) therefore denotes a group or collectivity, which is why nothing but groups appeared in figure 14. By contrast it is 'social actors' and 'human beings' who properly exist in the singular. Everyone is inescapably an Agent in some of their doings, but many of the doings of human beings have nothing to do with being an Agent. Membership of a collectivity, and thus sharing its 'life chances', hardly exhausts what we mean by our humanity. Yet, agents are real, agency involves real actions by real people, which is why we can legitimately talk about agents acting. For agency is not a construct, not another heuristic *homo sociologicus* which tells us about Herr Schmidt's positions but nothing about the Herr Schmidts. Here, in telling about those like Herr Schmidt as agents, we tell something real about them and their doings, but we have not told all about them as real human beings, some of which should properly remain beyond the sociological telling.

In explaining the statement that everyone is ineluctably an agent, we have to make a crucial distinction between what I have termed 'corporate' and 'primary' agents. At first glance, which probably involves selective perception induced by several decades of literature on political pluralism, it may seem that the only important agents are articulate and organized interest groups. This view is encapsulated in A. F. Bentley's well-known political dictum that 'when the groups are adequately stated, everything is stated'.[9] There is an element of truth in this, but it needs salvaging from a morass of error. Organized interest groups are indeed special and they pack a very special punch as far as systemic stability and change are concerned. For only those who are aware of what they want, can articulate it to themselves and others, and have organized in order to get it, can engage in concerted action to re-shape or retain the structural or cultural feature in question. These are termed 'corporate agents': they include self-conscious vested interest groups, promotive interest groups, social movements and defensive associations. Their common denominators are articulation and organization. Who they are, where they come from, and how the full array develops will be discussed when we come to the morphostasis or morphogenesis of agency.

Thus in *practice* I am willing to go along with Dahl[10] that macroscopic issues can hardly be said to exist unless they command serious attention in decision-making arenas – with the caveat that this is the prerogative of Corporate Agency. Where he has been rightly and repeatedly criticized is in assuming that this capacity to command attention is universal, that

[9] A. F. Bentley, *The Process of Government*, Harvard University Press, Cambridge, Mass., 1967.
[10] Robert A. Dahl, *Who Governs? Democracy and Power in an American City*, Yale University Press, New Haven and London, 1961.

nearly every group can make itself heard in decision-making. On the contrary, following Lukes,[11] many collectivities of those similarly positioned are deprived of having a say: denied an effective say since the use of non-decision-making keeps their concerns off the agenda, and denied any say at all when social organisation serves to repress potential issues and thus the possibility of stating related demands. Such agents will not and cannot be *strategically* involved in the modelling or re-modelling of structure or culture, *but they are still social agents*.

Everyone is born into an ongoing socio-cultural system and all have agential effects on stability or change, if only by merely being within it – physically and numerically. Moreover, the world, structured as they find it and are placed in it, is the one in which they live and move to have their social being: yet there is no being without doing and no doing without consequences. In short, the prior social context delineates collectivities in the same position (those with the same life chances *vis-à-vis* the major institutions) and within this context they have to carry on – 'carrying on' being conceived of more broadly than Wittgenstein's rule-governed 'going on', since some of the most crucial tracts of social life for the agent are those where the pursuit of interests is *interest-governed but not rule-governed* (i.e. rules simply do not extend to where some of their primary interests lie). In such areas it is precisely how they carry on innovatively which serves to extend rule specification to these tracts of society.

Those in this category are termed 'Primary Agents'. They are distinguished from Corporate Agents at any given time by lacking a say in structural or cultural modelling. At that time they neither express interests nor organize for their strategic pursuit, either in society or a given institutional sector. (A Primary Agent in one domain may be a Corporate Agent in another at any specific T^1 for these categories are *not fixed but mobile* over time). Nevertheless, to lack a say in systemic organization and reorganization is not the same as to have no effect on it, but the effects are unarticulated in both senses of the word – uncoordinated in action and unstated in aim. Collectivities without a say, but similarly situated, still react and respond to their context as part and parcel of living within it. Yet similarities of response from those similarly placed can generate powerful, though unintended aggregate effects which is what makes everyone an agent.

As an emergent stratum, Agency has powers proper to itself. This is the other reason why this notion of Agents cannot be rendered by any formula of the sort 'individuals plus resources'. Its typical powers are capacities for articulating shared interests, organizing for collective action, generat-

---

[11] Steven Lukes, *Power: A Radical View*, Macmillan, London, 1974.

ing social movements and exercising corporate influence in decision-making. Corporate Agents act together and interact with other Agents and they do so strategically, that is in a manner which cannot be construed as the summation of individuals' self-interest. To talk of strategic action implies that Corporate Agents are 'active' rather than 'passive',[12] that is they are social subjects with reasons for attempting to bring about certain outcomes, rather than objects to whom things happen. This is the case for the Corporate Agent but it might be queried whether Primary Agents (lacking collective organization and objectives) are not indeed of 'passive' status. Certainly they behave in that way – as people to whom things happen and who respond to happenings which are not of their making – and *whilst ever they do so* it is valid to analyse their agential effects as aggregate responses. Equally, however, it is important that they are not deemed intrinsically passive (i.e. of a kind incapable of activity), for their passivity itself represents a suspension, often a deliberate suspension, of their agential powers on the part of those Corporate Agents whose interests it serves.[13] In short, this passiveness can usually only be understood in terms of the relations between Collectivities. Moreover, unless it is understood in this way, it then becomes incomprehensible how Primary Agents frequently do form themselves into new social movements and eventually become new Corporate Agents. Yet this they do regularly and especially when Corporate groups change or step up their strategic pressures.

Corporate Agency thus shapes the *context* for all actors (usually not in the way any particular agent wants but as the emergent consequence of Corporate interaction). Primary Agency inhabits this context, but in responding to it also reconstitutes the *environment* which Corporate Agency seeks to control. The former unleashes a stream of aggregate environmental pressures and problems which affect the attainment of the latter's promotive interests. Corporate Agency thus has two tasks, the pursuit of its self-declared goals, as defined in a prior social context, and their continued pursuit in an environment modified by the responses of Primary Agency to the context which *they* confront.

At the systemic level this may result in either morphostasis or morphogenesis depending exclusively upon the outcome of interaction, but since social interaction is the sole mechanism governing stability or change, what goes on during it also determines the morphostasis or morphogenesis of Agency itself. This is the double morphogenesis during which Agency, in its attempt to sustain or transform the social system, is

---

[12] See Martin Hollis, *Models of Man: Philosophical Thoughts on Social Action*, Cambridge University Press, Cambridge, 1977.
[13] This is an instance of the third dimension of power delineated by Lukes, *Power*.

inexorably drawn into sustaining or transforming the categories of Corporate and Primary Agents themselves.

The basic question therefore which arises in relation to Social Agency is 'What are the conditions for the morphostasis or the morphogenesis of Social Agency?' Morphostasis demands an account of the divide between Corporate and Primary Agents and how some given pre-grouping is maintained during interaction, and morphogenesis calls for a discussion of how Corporate and Primary Agents are re-grouped in the course of interaction.

In a thoroughly morphostatic scenario, the two types of Agents, Corporate and Primary are starkly delineated from one another, the distinction between them is maintained through interaction and proves long-lasting. For the sake of clarity I will discuss this on a society-wide basis, taking those 'old and cold' systems which had at most two Corporate Agents who successfully confined the rest of the population to Primary status for centuries. Morphostatic scenarios do occur in modern societies – totalitarianism being a prime example – as well as in institutional sectors, but are both more complex, vulnerable and short-lived since morphogenetic influences impinge from elsewhere.

This extreme case arises where there is a conjunction between structural morphostasis and cultural morphostasis, as was discussed in the last chapter. Substantively this means that in the cultural domain there is one set of hegemonic ideas and a culturally dominant group of proficients, who have not (yet) encountered ideational opposition and are able to reproduce ideas amongst the collectivity of Primary Agents, thus maintaining a high level of cultural unification in society. On the other hand, structural morphostasis indicates a monolithic form of social organization with the superimposition of elites and a heavy concentration of resources which together prevent crystallization of opposition – this subordination of Primary Agents thus allowing the structure to be perpetuated. The reciprocal influence between the structural and cultural domains reinforces the status quo and in the process perpetuates the preliminary divide between Corporate and Primary Agents by precluding re-grouping.

Since the articulation of ideas (expressing interests) and the acquisition of organization (for their pursuit) are quintessential properties of Corporate Agents, it is clear why this morphostatic conjunction represses their proliferation through its influences upon interaction itself. First, the fund of cultural ideas which are *available* to Primary Agents engaged in structural interaction is extremely homogeneous. There are no visible ideational alternatives with any social salience for those with inaudible social grievances to adopt and thus *articulate* the sources of their smouldering discontent. Instead, by reproducing a stable corpus of ideas over time, the cultural elite (the sole Corporate Agent in this domain) works to produce a unified population. These Primary Agents may indeed be the victims of preceptual power rather than voluntary adherents to consensual precepts, but in any case they are incapable of articulating dissident views and of passing these over the intersection to stimulate structural disruption.

In direct parallel, the social structure contains no developed marginal groups or powerful malcontents with sufficient *organization* to attract the culturally disenchanted. Subordination means that there is no differentiated interest group *available* to challenge the cultural conspectus, by exploiting its contradictions or developing diversified interpretations. Thus from neither side of the intersection between the structural and cultural domains is the raw material forthcoming (i.e. organized interest groups and articulated ideational alternatives) for transforming Primary Agents into new forms of Corporate Agency. Primary Actors can neither articulate projects nor mobilize for their attainment. They cannot interact promotively but only re-act atomistically. Antipathetic reactions are restricted to the quiet cherishing of grievances or doubts, the lone rebelry of sacrilege or insubordination, or personal withdrawal – geography and ecology permitting. The major systemic effect of Primary Agency is purely demographic. There are too many or too few (to feed or to fight), in the right or the wrong places, which can create problems for the (morphostatic) goals of Corporate Agents. In the long run, even this dumb numerical pressure of Primary Agents can be a big enough environmental problem to prompt Corporate policies intended to preserve stability, but ultimately inducing change. Slavery and conquest, as copybook solutions to demographic problems, also introduce group differentiation and cultural diversification.

But this is not a necessary outcome and in any case the short run can last for centuries. So the other question which arises is why do the Corporate Agents, the structural and cultural elites whose composition was determined in a prior social context, tend to remain solidary, consensual and reinforcing, often to the point of merger? Of equal importance in this configuration is the fact that elites too are constrained by the absence of ideational or organizational alternatives, but each is simultaneously enabled by what the other is doing. Thus, the structural elite is trapped in the only kind of cultural discourse which is currently in social parlance; similarly the cultural elite is enmeshed by the monolithic power structure which is the only form of social organisation present. Given this conjunction the two elites have no *immediate* alternative but to live together, but what is much more important is that they have every interest in *continuing* to do so. Here, cultural morphostasis (through the stable reproduction of ideas amongst a unified population of Primary agents) generates an ideational environment which is highly conductive to structural mainten- ance. Structural morphostasis (through the control of marginality and the subordination of the mass of Primary agents) in turn contributes greatly to cultural maintenance.

In whatever way the elites view one another (as out-and-out barbarians or jumped-up witch doctors), the opportunity costs of turning on one another to promote a different organization or to stimulate new ideas is too high for this to become common practice. Quite the reverse. Because of mutual recognition of benefits received, the two domains often become progressively intertwined, with interlocking roles and interchangeable personnel – thus approximating to the superimposition of structure and culture which Weber described for Ancient India and China. Thus where there is unopposed cultural traditionalism and unchallenged structural domination, Corporate Agency tends to congeal into one, rather than developing fissiparous tendencies, and as a single group is even more empowered to mould and manipulate Primary Agents by controlling their opportunities for and attitudes towards greater social participation.

By contrast the morphogenetic scenario displays precisely the opposite features, namely the progressive expansion of the number of Corporate Agents, of those who are numbered among them, and a divergence of the interests represented by them, thus resulting in substantial conflict between them. Accompanying this process is a complementary shrinkage of Primary Agents, due in part to their mobilization to join burgeoning promotive interest groups and in part to the formation of new social movements and defensive associations as some of them combine to form novel types of Corporate Agency. This can be represented by the variant on the basic morphogenetic diagram shown in figure 15.

This scenario begins in exactly the same way as the morphostatic sequence already discussed, namely with self-conscious Vested Interest Groups defined in a prior socio-cultural context. What we were examin- ing there were the conditions supremely propitious to them getting away with it, that is protecting the benefits received from their pre-defined positions by being able to protract the status quo in the structural-cultural system which generated this advantageous state of affairs for them. Elsewhere I have discussed at length how in the very long run the defensive strategies of Vested Interest Groups in fact stimulate the formation of Promotive Interest Groups (both material and ideal) at variance with them.[14] They do this by spawning social differentiation and ideational diversification as part and parcel of the *pursuit* of vested

---

[14] Margaret S. Archer, *Culture and Agency*, Cambridge University Press, Cambridge, 1989, pp. 211ff.

Socio-cultural
conditioning of groups
_____
T^1 (Corporate agency and
Primary agency)

        Group interaction
        _____
        T^2 (Between corporate agents T^3
        and primary agents)

                Group elaboration
                _____
                (Increase of corporate agents) T^4

Figure 15 Corporate and Primary agency in the morphogenetic
sequence.

interests which is better pictured as an exercise in accumulation than the
protection of fixed assets. This process which expands the number of
Corporate Agents and alters the nature of their relationship is greatly
accelerated by disjunctions between morphostasis and morphogenesis in
the structural and cultural domains. Let one enter a morphogenetic
sequence and the newly differentiated groups or strata to emerge or the
new ideas made salient serve to speed up the process of re-grouping, as
ideas gain organized sponsors and nascent organizations gain powers of
self-expression.

In turn, the co-existence of a plurality of Corporate Agents seeking to
push and pull systemic or institutional structure in different directions
has profound effects on reshaping the context for Primary Agents and re-
moulding the situations in which they find themselves. Collective reactions to the new context create new environmental problems for some
Corporate Agents and constitute enabling factors for others, since
Corporate Agency is no longer consensual. Collective counter-reactions
also take the form of new Corporate Agents, thus further complicating
interaction. The complexity of the whole process can be distiled into the
ten basic propositions which follow. The first three refer to phase one of
the morphogenetic cycle, propositions 4–7 apply to the second phase, and
the last three to the final phase. These abstract statements about Agents'
different degrees of freedom and their combinatory potential are then
illustrated with a concrete example.

1. All agents are not equal: the initial distributions of structural and
   cultural properties delineate Corporate Agents and distinguish them
   from Primary Agents at the start of each cycle;

2. Corporate Agents maintain/re-model the socio-cultural system and its institutional parts: Primary Agents work within it and them;

3. All agents are not equally knowledgeable because of the effects of prior interaction upon them;

4. All change is mediated through alterations in agents' situations: Corporate Agents alter the context in which Primary Agents live and Primary Agents alter the environment in which Corporate Agents operate;

5. The categories of Corporate and Primary Agents are redefined over time through interaction in pursuit of social stability or change;

6. Actions by Corporate and Primary Agents constrain and enable one another;

7. Action by Primary Agents constitutes atomistic reaction, uncoordinated co-action or associational interaction, depending upon the extent of their participation in a given institutional context;

8. Interaction of Corporate Agents generates emergent properties: actions of Primary Agents produce aggregate effects;

9. The elaboration of Social Agency (societally or sectionally) consists in the shrinkage of the category of Primary Agents, who become incorporated or transformed into Corporate Agents, thus swelling this category;

10. Social change is the resultant of aggregate effects produced by Primary Agents in conjunction with emergent properties generated by Corporate Agents and thus does not approximate to what anyone wants.

To begin fleshing out these points, the example of educational development will be used.[15] At its most basic this involves two things – increased provisions and increased attendance. The nature of provision results from Corporate Action, but, since expansion depends equally on the enrolment of Primary Actors, the two sides of the equation exemplify the interplay between the two types of Agency. The interactional sequence which leads to State Systems with a mass intake, breaks down into three phases: the key point is that throughout them, the restructuring of education and the redefinition of educational agents go hand in hand.

The example of educational development

The story opens on a rather bare morphostatic stage. The domination of the Churches over education in mediaeval Europe was lengthy, unop-

---

[15] Margaret S. Archer, 'Theorizing about the expansion of educational systems' in Archer (ed.) *The Sociology of Educational Expansion*, Sage, London and Beverly Hills, 1982, pp. 1–64.

posed and had produced insignificant growth. Precisely because the educational investment was made by one institutional elite alone in order to service its own requirements, provision was small. Thus action begins with a single Vested Interest Group dominating education. Its private ownership of all provisions of instruction left the rest of society as Primary Agents in educational terms, whatever their standing in other parts of society (point 1).

Phase 1: Corporate competition and atomistic Primary Action

Corporate Agency Change in the educational status quo was due to groups beginning to challenge the domination of the Churches in Europe, who had monopoly control and wanted to keep it. The morphogenesis of Agency starts with the consolidation of new Corporate Actors committed to assertion and is, of course, temporarily prior to their effects on the environment of Primary Agents.

The Churches' pursuit of their vested interests in education had a negative impact on important social groups by seriously impeding their aims and operations, which were defined elsewhere in society. These obstructions were experienced as daily frustrations in practical situations related to the promotive activities of such groups (e.g. in nineteenth-century England, entrepreneurs were unable to obtain the skills or socialization sought from their workforce or for themselves; Dissenters were disadvantaged in the propagation of Denominationalism; popular mobilization was hindered by both illiteracy and a definition of instruction stressing station in life rather than the rights of man). Yet not every group (objectively obstructed and subjectively disgruntled about it) could become a Corporate Agent who engaged in educational assertion. Interest Groups do not emerge as Corporate Agents simply because they are discontented with what a Vested Interest Group is doing. A pool of diffuse grievances surrounds most such Vested Interest Groups as they busily defend their privileges. Only if resources can be brought to bear to undermine the basis of domination, only if organization can mobilize sufficient numbers to this end, and only if a counter-ideology challenging legitimacy and legitimating assertion is developed does a new Corporate Agent confront the entrenched Vested Interest Group. Thus the initial distribution of resources strongly conditions the emergence of new Corporate Agents (point 1). This is also affected by social affinities and antagonisms which determine who can work together in concerted opposition. Indeed, any new Corporate Agent usually results from alliance formation, goal dilution and ideological accommodation from the Interest Groups who constitute it, precisely in order to become an effective force.

Hostilities between those seeking to maintain the institutional status quo and those searching to re-model it are protracted for the simple reason that the original Vested Interest Group fights back and the new Corporate assertive groups have to fight harder. Elsewhere[16] I have shown how the Corporate Agents locked in a struggle over educational control, with assertive groups founding new networks of schools with the aim of dislodging or devaluing existing provisions. However, long before any decisive outcome (i.e. the eventual emergence of a State educational system), Corporate conflict generates considerable expansion as new networks of provisions are built-up and the old one tries to extend to meet the challenge. This competitive conflict between Corporate Agents was the motor for take-off in school attendance, for it altered the environment of Primary Agents, their options, their information and their dispositions (point 2).

Primary Agency In the period leading to the emergence of State Systems, Corporate Agency shaped its own environment. Primary Agents were simply confronted with a range of provisions provided by the Corporate Groups and reflecting their promotive interests. The networks of schools and their respective definitions of instruction were 'given' for the whole population and only an infinitesimal fraction had any say over their contents and practices. Primary Agents had to respond to the options available on a take it or leave it basis.

Historically, education had always been a minority affair. Consequently, the population was neither alerted to, much less aligned upon, the issue of education. The information of Primary Agents was largely purveyed by the Corporate Agents themselves, manipulating, shaping and often distorting the very perception of what education could be (point 3). The European Churches had always been in a particularly favourable position to mediate educational information, as the organization which penetrated deepest into the nation. As Corporate assertive groups developed, they assiduously sought to undermine clerical legitimacy in education, but as they attacked ecclesiastical bias with one hand, they offered their own with the other (classical economics, dissenting belief, secular rationalism, imperial nationalism, popular *kulturkampf* etc.). Thus one effect of competition between Corporate Agents was to widen the area of educational debate and put education on the popular agenda, because conflict began to reach down to the smallest communities – best exemplified by the cat and dog fights between local *instituteur* and *curé* in the market squares of rural France.

---

[16] Margaret S. Archer, *Social Origins of Educational Systems*, Sage, London and Beverly Hills, 1982.

Simultaneously, as the Corporate Agents locked in conflict they had to solicit attendance and to do so on more attractive terms. Competition forced the educational menu to vary, thus shaping new favourable dispositions towards it. This represented a two-way interplay in which the success of Corporate groups had become contingent upon concessions to the dispositional trends of Primary Agents (point 4). The educational mobilization which resulted (vastly increasing enrolment before elementary attendance became compulsory), destroyed the status of education as a minority enclave and with it the unthinking legitimacy of any one definition of instruction. Corporate Agents had thus, through their own interaction, altered the educational context of Primary Agents whose dispositions and learning gradually transformed the environment in which the former operated.

The most significant indicator of this was that new sections of the population began to reject all available alternatives and successively to transform themselves into Corporate Agents pressing for a radically different definition of instruction (like the Chartists in England and the Folk High School movement in Denmark). These then joined the mainstream of Corporate conflict, reshaping the overall context by adding novel institutions and remoulding the environment by the vision now presented to Primary Agency that education could be something other than that defined by the existing dominant and assertive groups. The two categories of agents, Corporate and Primary, had thus undergone a radical redefinition during Phase 1 which preceded the elaboration of State Educational Systems (point 5).

Phase 2: Corporate negotiation and Primary Co-action

With the emergence of State Educational Systems from the previous interaction chain, three types of negotiations between Corporate Agents universally came into play and superseded competitive conflict as the major process responsible for structural change. The shift from competition to negotiation occurs when private ownership of schools gives way to public control of education. What then induces negotiation is the fact that political accountability entails a spread of educational influence (many Corporate Agents are now officially involved in decision-making) and that public funding results in a diversification of educational services received by wider institutional sectors of society (more Corporate Agents have a stake in it). What effectively eliminates competition is the virtual impossibility of competing with the State in terms of the power and resources now needed for educational control.

The atomistic nature of Primary action (unsystematic and individualistic) simultaneously gives way to co-action, that is to groups in roughly the same position acting in approximately the same way. Co-action is the direct result of the emergence of the State System for this legally defines a school population (literally placing whole age-cohorts in the same position) and confronts the population at large with a single nationwide educational structure. Any similarity of reaction from those placed in similar positions generates powerful aggregate effects with which Corporate Agency has to deal. Basically this Phase serves to illustrate points 6–8, but especially how Corporate Agents shape the emergent System within which Primary Agents then generate significant aggregate effects.

Corporate Agency With the advent of State Systems, all three processes by which educational change is negotiated then promote expansion through the activities of the Corporate Agents using each of them. Thus, in brief, External Transactions (through which promotive interest groups, external to the system, now negotiate directly with it for novel/additional services in exchange for financial resources) lead to more diversified provisions, particularly at terminal points prior to school leavers 'joining' other social institutions. Thus wherever public instruction had got to, External Transactions took it on further with specialized vocational courses. Internal Initiation represents endogenous change, introduced by teachers. Their quest for professional upgrading, in particular, led to longer schooling by lengthening the training of the most numerous category, the elementary teachers. Finally, Political Manipulation involves the negotiation of change via the central or local political authorities (by which Corporate groups influence educational policy) and had the greatest numerical impact by widening access. While External Transactions and Internal Initiation are privileged channels of negotiation, limited to relatively wealthy Corporate groups or to the Profession alone, Political Manipulation is the sole resort of all others. Generalizing broadly this means that those who bombarded it with their demands were Corporate Agents (unions, political parties, pressure groups) representing lower socio-economic groups. In the twentieth century these demands have been variations on a single theme – equality of educational opportunity.

What accounts for Corporate action generating an extremely high growth rate is that the three processes of negotiation take place simultaneously and their effects reinforce one another. Thus more provisions plus longer schooling/more provisions plus wider access/wider access plus longer schooling are not just additive, but represent multiplier phenomena. In turn, they enabled more and more Primary Agents to be scholarized (point 6).

Primary Agents The shift from atomistic action to co-action is a direct consequence of universal scholarization (at elementary level), a new experience which constitutes a situational change for the younger cohorts. As a social category, the young are literally being made different from the rest of the ageing population and their collective action patterns do not remain the same. In turn co-action from those similarly placed produces aggregate effects (point 7). These are aggregative because the Primary Agents are not deliberately trying to change the System. Their reactions are uncoordinated but the summativity of their responses to this new national institution both constrain and enable Corporate Agents in ways unknown in the past. The constant interplay between the institutional context defined by Corporate Agency and the environment represented by Primary action now constitutes a positive feedback loop which is here to stay.

Taken together, the Corporate influences are themselves expansionist; so too are the Primary influences which basically consist in staying on longer at school. Staying on versus early leaving now carries different opportunity costs compared with Phase 1, thus transforming the objective options of Primary Agents. To remain longer confers increasing benefits in relation to income differentials: they enter the middle part of a growth curve where the social benefit deriving from length of schooling is a curvilinear function of the proportion of each age-cohort remaining at school.[17] In part the Primary Agents know this, for as more stay on and profit from it, this becomes the practical experience of increasing sections of the population.

Corporate groups work to change the structure of the System but Primary Agents work within it. The commonest orientation amongst Primary Agents was to remain longer wherever they were placed and then to proceed to whatever was available, amplifying it in the process. Thus the aggregate effects of co-action followed class lines. On the one hand, working-class Primary Agents want more schooling, but before the introduction of an educational ladder, they are positioned in the elementary sector and constrained to act within it. The result is to push the latter upwards (it grows higher 'tops' like the French *cours complémentaires* or the English higher grade schools). This creates problems at the Corporate level: structurally decision-makers try to prune, integrate and contain simultaneously. Primary action within the System meant the working class had 'grabbed' secondary education (through elongating their studies) before it was given to them: Corporate Agents responded by

[17] T. F. Green, D. P. Ericson and R. M. Seidman, *Predicting the Behaviour of the Educational System*, Syracuse University Press, Syracuse, 1980.

attempting to confine it to inferior structural channels (the English secondary modern school, the Danish non-examination middle school or the French *Collège d'Enseignement Général*). On the other hand, middle-class Primary Agents wanted the 'best': the main bourgeois impact fell on tertiary education, elongating it into postgraduate training.

Hence, Corporate and Primary influences on the growth of the System lost their past asymmetry, whereby the former dominated and manipulated the latter: instead, they become reciprocal influences promoting growth which massively reinforce one another. However, Primary co-action brings about increases in participation which precede the desires of Corporate Agents and constrain their subsequent designs. The positive feedback loop, through which those who have had some education now want more, confronts Corporate decision-makers with a dumb environmental pressure of numbers (point 8).

Phase 3: Corporate transaction and Primary interaction

In general the reciprocal influence of Corporate and Primary action intensifies and helps to foster unguided growth of the System. This serves to indicate the inapplicability of simple cybernetic models to institutions like education, which lack the necessary control centre(s) for delineating goals, monitoring processes and introducing corrective measures. If qualitatively the development of education is characterized as unregulated growth, its quantitative equivalent is inflation. Both are unintended consequences of the conjunction between Corporate and Primary action.

Corporate Agency The main Corporate Agents were affected in different ways as the educational enterprise became very large indeed. The 'big three', the Profession, External Interest Groups and the Polity now pulled in divergent directions in terms of re-structuring. For the Profession, as the size of the Systems increased, so did the scope for Internal Initiation and with it an aggressive quest for internal self-direction. The System had become a bigger and bigger employer of its own products, and, with the ladder now in place, it also became a larger and larger recipient of its own products, passed up from level to level. Conditions for the Profession to define instruction had never been more enabling. With academic expansion, new knowledge was spawned at the top of the System (inducing the internal proliferation of new courses, disciplines and specialisms): new ideas could percolate rapidly downwards to the schools as new subjects and methods, given the emergence of *de facto* academic control over teacher training.

The more sophisticated External Interest Groups themselves became part of the knowledge industry, their Research and Development departments intertwining with university projects. But for others, this collaboration which further extended the tertiary level, now landed them with too many advanced recruits who cost too much and expected too much. Yet their secular 'desertion' of the lower levels (because the new developments they introduced were clustered around terminal points) meant that less qualified recruits were products of the professional definition of instruction. And the outputs of progressive schooling revealed a mismatch of skills and values which these Interest Groups plaintively wanted correcting. Many of their grievances were transmitted to and shared by the Polity – expansion had gone too far, had cost too much and yielded the wrong thing. As *central* authorities they would have liked retrenchment, rationalization and regulation of growth: as *political* authorities they dared not repudiate all demands for equality of opportunity, of outcome, or compensatory instruction which were constantly pressed through Political Manipulation and with considerable professional support. This in-built ambivalence accounts for most governments not becoming effective regulative agencies, centrally guiding the growth of the System. Even the determined ones which attempted to impose greater accountability and financial austerity were basically hampered by the growth of interaction between Primary Agents and the steady transformation of further sections into new Corporate Agents (point 9).

Primary Agency The expanding context has two effects for Primary Agents, initially inducing them to stay on still longer to avoid penalization and secondly to engage in loose collective action to increase benefits *vis-à-vis* other social groups. Both constitute inflationary mechanisms. Firstly, the increased size of the System means that opportunity costs change yet again and liabilities come into play: instead of longer schooling carrying benefits, early leaving now confers a penalty. Schematically, as enrolment rises at the nth level, the economic benefits of those reaching it rise also. Then as the majority stay on for it, the income differentials between them and early leavers shrink. However, as universal enrolment is approached at n, then wage differentials again rise sharply, since *not* staying on for n has now become a liability. Attendance beyond the compulsory leaving age thus becomes obligatory to avoid disaster. But as more pupils move up to the n + 1 level, universal enrolment is re-approached there and the target keeps moving upwards under such inflationary dynamics.

This aggregate effect is reversible: the motor of inflation would cut out if enough dropped out by a particular level, thus making continuation genuinely optional. What militates against this is that Primary Agents increasingly engage in collective interaction (rather than personal co-action) and that further sections convert themselves into Corporate Agents (point 9). Together these supplied the fuel to keep the motor going.

Collective interaction derives from the differential learning of the two major social classes who now informally monitor the action and pay-offs of one another which condition their strategic decisions. On the one hand the middle classes have learned that benefits go to those who keep ahead of an upwardly moving norm. Since the fifties, they had accepted the necessity of going to university, then of post-graduate studies and finally of further professional training. But, in acting strategically on their knowledge, by being first in and collecting the benefits, they collectively pushed the target upwards.

Working-class learning lagged behind. It was distorted by their experience during Phase 2, when the conspicuous minority of class members with a small amount of extra schooling did indeed reap substantial advantages. However, when large numbers acted on that premiss their aggregate effect was to nullify it. Comparison with other classes gradually taught that longer attendance was now essential. Thus many of the lower classes slowly pushed themselves up – thus creating and repeating a self-defeating sequence, because *they* were always the last to enter the new level and to find that the only practical worth of this additional schooling was to give access to yet more education. When the knowledgeability of Primary Agents is stressed, it is always important to know how good that knowledge is, versus how far it has been structurally and culturally skewed.

Simultaneously, new Corporate Agents disengaged themselves to defend the educational interests of particular sections of the population, for another thing learnt is that having a say is predicated upon becoming organized, and that without organization, the aggregate effects of the 'law of last entry' fall hardest upon the doubly socially disadvantaged. These are largely defensive associations of ethnic, gender, linguistic and handi-capped groups. The concerns of these new Corporate Agents (a fair start, equal opportunity, positive discrimination, a second chance) obviously entail further expansion in proportion to their success.

In conclusion, the actual nature of educational expansion was the result of the conjunction between Corporate and Primary Agents, and, as such it was not something which *anybody* wanted (point 10). The vast increase in the scope of contemporary mass Educational Systems has no relationship to the labour market in East or West alike, being carried light years away from manpower planning, but equally from the desires of its Primary participants and regulation by Corporate Agency. This constitutes the most important contrast with the earlier periods: in Phase 1, the Corpor-ate Agents controlling their own networks all gained something of what *they* wanted (and Primary Agents only enrolled if they perceived it as advantageous). In Phase 2, the positive reinforcement of supply and demand was positively beneficial to the majority of Corporate and Primary Agents alike. The contemporary stage is distinctive in having few solid beneficiaries and little unmitigated support. This is the stuff which guarantees continuing morphogenesis, for Corporate Agents have every interest in remodelling the System and Primary Agents have a struggle to live within it. Change will continue as the combined effect of the emergent and aggregate properties they elaborate, but in the process Corporate Agency and Primary Agency will continuously redefine these very categories through their interplay over time.

Methodologically, this approach could be applied to a wider social canvas or to more localized settings since it is meant to be generic to the elaboration of Social Agency – and agents themselves come in all shapes and sizes. The appropriate morphogenetic cycle is thus delineated according to the scope of the problem in hand. Nevertheless, each such cycle will contain the basic features of pre-grouping and re-grouping, depicted below. Of course the components may need re-naming (it sounds odd to talk about 'social movements' in a sports club or 'defensive associations' in the parish church, though their micro-equivalents can be found). Furthermore, as a cycle, such features are only visible and explicable if a time-span is introduced, and this is the case regardless of the scope of problem investigated. Figure 16 therefore draws out the typical constituents of the double morphogenesis of Social Agency.

From the morphogenetic perspective, Social Agency is embedded in interaction and hence is ultimately a relational property of people. This involves relations to the prior structural–cultural context (which effect pre-grouping) and subsequent interactions with others (which effect re-grouping). Simultaneously, the context itself changes since we are dealing with a double morphogenesis, in which the elaboration of both structure and agency are conjoint products of interaction. Structure is the conditioning medium and elaborated outcome of interaction: agency is shaped by and reshapes structure whilst reshaping itself in the process. But the complexity of this process remains hopelessly indefinite unless the interplay between them is unravelled over time to specify the where, when, who and how – otherwise we are left with the vagaries of mutual constitution.

Actors: the triple morphogenesis

To view Social Agency in terms of interrelations (interactions between groups and collectivities which redefine both through re-grouping)

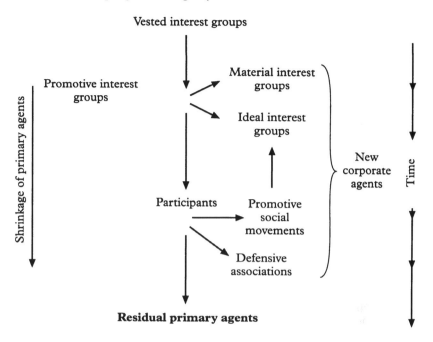

Figure 16 The double morphogenesis of Agency.

obviously means that this concept of the Social Agent (always in the plural) is not synonymous with the notion of the Social Actor (in the singular). There is a good deal more to be said about the Social Actor, most especially how s/he becomes a particular person and acquires an identity as a social self. The next emergent stratum thus concerns the Social Actor who emerges through the 'triple morphogenesis' in which Agency conditions (not determines) who comes to occupy different social roles. Social role sets entail necessary and internal relations (a pupil requires a teacher, a slave a master, and a tenant a landlord etc.), each instance of which implies further necessary and internal relationships with resources and rules (such as teaching materials, premises or buildings, expert knowledge, attendance and curricula). These are minimalistic entailments, some of which can themselves be seen to depend upon further relations (the contemporary pupil role also entails legal requirements about compulsory attendance and public resources for educational funding). Moreover, roles operate in sets rather than in isolation (e.g. teacher, head, governor, inspector, chief education officer, minister) which involve further necessary and internal relations amongst them (some of which will be ones of asymmetrical dependency, such as a schools inspector implying teachers, but not vice versa). None of this has any affinity with functionalist views of integration. On the contrary, roles and role sets may clash precisely because their associated normative expectations collide or the sum of their resource requirements exceeds total disposable assets.

Actors, then, are defined as role encumbents and roles themselves have emergent properties which cannot be reduced to characteristics of their occupants. These can be demonstrated by the pre-existence of roles, their greater durability over time, a capacity to endure despite considerable changes in the personal features of their successive holders, and the relatively autonomous powers of constraint and enablement which are lodged in the role, not the occupant, and can be lost (or shed) with loss of occupancy.

This is too big an issue to treat fully here, except in one respect. I want now to re-emphasize that the concept of Social Agency is necessarily incomplete for dealing with Actors since it is only concerned with action in or as part of a collectivity. Equally, however, any attempt to conceptualize the Social Actor needs to be completed by reference to their properties as Agents, if we are to arrive at an adequate conception of social identity.

Those who start out as 'strong actionists' with the laudable aim of defending Autonomous Man, a model of the Social Actor who is neither the passive puppet of social forces, nor a pre-social self whose adroitness at playing social games begs the question of how the individual became so endowed, hits two major snags. Both I believe could be avoided if, in the attempt to present Adam as his own 'sovereign artificer',[18] the part of Adam as Agent was fully recognized. By neglecting it, the best of such accounts ends up by having to endorse the social contract and to overplay social convention.

Such an account opens with Adam in the singular confronting the social stage, and seeks to conceptualize a *social self* for him which, whilst dependent on society, also meets the strict criteria of identity as a particular person. It proceeds by eschewing two notions, that of an actor undertaking a pre-scripted part (too much of society: too little self), or one who merely dons and doffs masks behind which his private business can be conducted (too much self: too little of the social). The proper balance is struck by a concept of the Social Actor who becomes such by choosing to identify himself with a particular role and actively to personify it in a particularistic way. The Actor's real interests come with the role s/he has chosen to personify; the snag of course is that the Actor '*qua* atomic pre-

---

[18] Martin Hollis, *The Cunning of Reason*, Cambridge University Press, Cambridge, 1988.

social individual' has no reason *to adopt* one identity rather than another[19] and he cannot have a reason on this account because he has no prior interests upon which reasons can work. Consequently, the initial choice of a position is contractarian, a contract which it is non-rational to enter in prospect but which can be rational in retrospect or rationally corrected. The trouble here is that the choice either remains inexplicable or gets handed over to depth psychology.

This can be avoided if Adam as Agent is allowed on the scene. For we become Agents *before* we become Actors. After the Fall, the rest of humanity enters society through the maternity ward doors and we immediately acquire the properties of Agents through belonging to particular collectivities and sharing their privileges or lack of them – as males/females; blacks/whites; foreigners/indigenous; middle class/working class. In short, we are always born into a system of social stratification and it is crucial to my argument that 'privileges' and 'underprivilege' are regarded as properties that people acquire involuntaristically and *not* as roles that they occupy through choice. It is defensible, I submit, to view these as positions rather than roles because of the impossibility of specifying any but the fuzziest and most highly contested normative expectations associated with them. Whilst systems of social stratification, especially rigid and unidimensional ones, may generate roles associated with particular strata (such as Brahmin, Nobles or Literati), this is contingent to stratification rather than being a necessary and internal feature of it. The quintessential features of all stratification systems, namely 'propertylessness', 'powerlessness' and the lack of prestige (together with their opposites), are thus distributions of positions with determinate life chances rather than an array of roles with clearly defined normative expectations.

Now infant Agents have a long way to go before they become mature Actors. But the kind of Agents that they start out being without any choice, due to parentage and social context, profoundly influences what type of Actor they can choose to become. Certain opportunities and information are open to the privileged and closed to the non-privileged. Options are not determined but the opportunity costs of attaining them are stacked very differently for the two. Such differential costings constitute good reasons for initially opting for different sections of the total role array. Initial choice of position is corrigible but big corrections entail increased costs which are further reasons why not very many will undertake drastic remedial measures (why, for example, so few black, female, Asian home-workers ever find their way to university).

---

[19] Hollis, *Models of Man*, pp. 104ff.

These initial interests with which Agents are endowed, through their life chances, provide the leverage upon which reasons (otherwise known as constraints and enablements) for different courses of action operate. They do not determine the particular Social Actor an individual chooses to become, but they strongly condition what type of Social Actor the vast majority can and do become. The notion of Adam as Agent literally fostering Adam as Actor can be worked to eliminate the contractual leap in the dark, since the former supplies the latter with a rational interest in accepting a social position. Here, I have only made choice of part of the role array explicable, but further argument about the differential availability of information, role models and work experience to different Agents could bring the residual contractual element into the area of sensible choice – explaining why Johnnie becomes a fireman and Tommy a policeman.

All of this is predicated upon not bundling all interests in to roles (the *locus classicus* of the Social Actor) but allowing that some interests pertain to Social Agents (privileges being the broadest way of construing these). I now want to make further use of this assumption to mount a morphogenetic assault on the role-rule set which 'strong actionism' both takes as given, but does not explain and treats as all-encompassing, which condemns Actors to a normative conventionalism, thus severely limiting their innovativeness as 'artificers'. So far I have only introduced the pre-grouping aspect of Social Agency, now this needs linking to its promotive re-grouping aspect in order to tackle this problem. For it is the latter which gives considerable purchase on how new positions/roles are constructed out of something other than role-clash and how the action involved is not restricted by rule-governed normative conventions. These are the lot of the Social Actor *qua* Actor, however much discretionary and strategic judgement s/he is allowed when pictured as an 'intelligent steward' rather than a mindless reader of the small print. Social Agents are not limited in this way.

Two things need to be stressed now. Firstly, that as Social Agents, groups and collectivities of people confront problems which are interest-related but not role-related. Secondly that as Social Agents they engage in promotive activities, when tackling these problems, which are too innovative to be construed as 'games' – since they follow no regulative rules and embody no constitutive rules. Having refused to bundle all interests into roles it is now possible to see how broader categories of Social Agents confront problem-ridden situations in relation to these wider interests (which are rooted in their life chances). Returning to the example in the previous section, when educational control was exclusively in Church hands, this created exigencies for a number of groups and where such problems represented a clash of beliefs, an obstacle to a nascent social movement, or the exclusion of a particular category, these could only be interpreted as impinging upon roles by over-stretching that concept to turn 'believer', 'radical', or 'nouveau riche' into roles.

Secondly, what such groups then did in the face of these obstructions to their self-declared interests was to seek to eradicate the hindrance by transforming the nature of educational control. Yet there was no 'game' called 'how to go about winning control of education', no regulative rules governing educational conflict, and the constitutive rules concerning governance of an educational system could only be *ex post* since the elaboration of State Systems was an unintended consequence of interaction between Corporate Agents. Out of this undoubtedly came a new role array – teachers, inspectors, administrators and Ministers. Therefore the elaboration of roles and rules is part and parcel of the morphogenesis set in train by Social Agency as it collaboratively transformed the structural context, for the very good reason that it presented them with too many environmental problems to live with. What emerged thus depended upon the conflictual *action* of Agents, without in any way corresponding to the aims which had prompted their active involvement. This is another illustration of morphogenesis rarely being what anyone wants, yet conjointly the participants retain reponsibility for the outcome which is the product of their interaction.

The argument can be broadened by considering that the 'under-privileged' confront plenty of daily exigencies, given their poor life chances, and thus have the best of reasons for struggling towards collective organization (unionization, franchise and civil rights movements, feminism), just as privileged Corporate Agents find good reason in protection of their vested interests to try to contain or repress the former. In the struggle between them (and the privileged and non-privileged are not playing some 'Us and Them' game), the extant role array undergoes considerable transformation. New positions get defined under the prompting of promotive interest groups, though they will bear the marks of compromise and concession in the course of interaction against opposition. Equally, the defence of vested interests may prompt role changes precisely in order to defend interests themselves (Kings will accept any form of constitutionalism in order to remain King – but a constitutional monarch is a very different role embedded in a much modified role-set).

In short, the re-grouping of Social Agents provides the motor which generates new role-rule sets as some of its unintended consequences, thus providing an account of their development in terms of non-rule governed action, which is not open to Social Actors as incumbents of roles hedged by normative conventions. Morphogenetically, Social Agency invents new rules for new games which contain more roles in which Social Actors can be themselves. Another way of putting it is that Agency makes more room for the Actor, who is not condemned to a static array of available positions.

Thus separating Social Agents from Social Actors ends up by destroying some of Adam's illusions but adding greatly to his powers as an artificer. What he loses on this account (because of the pre-grouping of Agents) is the spurious illusion of contractual freedom to become any social self he chooses to personify. What he gains (thanks to the re-grouping of Agents) is the collective capacity to refashion social positions, thus ultimately making society as well as himself.

Let us be clear, the Social Agent and the Social Actor are not different people – the distinction is only temporal and analytical. When we look at the Agent as father of the Actor, we are examining Adam himself at different ages. Upon maturity, Adam becomes both Agent and Actor, but it remains analytically invaluable to distinguish between what he does in the problematic or beneficial situations he confronts *qua* Agent from what he does *qua* Actor in his particular roles with their rule requirements.

Therefore, Actors themselves, as role incumbents, cannot be understood without reference to Agency. Exactly the same will be argued in relation to Personhood, although Actors are reducible to neither of these other two terms. If Actors are allowed to diminish to the point where they are nothing but the objects of roles (instead of being subjects who are active role-makers rather than passive role-takers) we not only endorse the pre-programmed executor but also exclude Actors as a source of role change themselves. This is inevitably the case because 'indeterminate material' lacks the where-with-all for innovative reinterpretation, for testing the elasticity of role requirements or exercising 'intelligent stewardship' over resources. In other words, Actors are not reducible to Persons but none the less have to be anchored in them in order to bring to any role they occupy the human qualities of reflexivity and creativity. Without these qualities, the Actor is not a subject who can reflect upon the stringency of role-governed constraints and decide whether nothing else can be done other than routine acts of reproduction, nor one who can bring his or her personal ingenuity to bear in order to exploit the degrees of freedom and thus attempt role transformation.

Persons: genesis and morphogenesis

In all of this it may seem as if the human being has disappeared, perhaps put out of business between the Agent and the Actor. Nothing could be less true, for both of these social beings need an anchorage in common humanity. Without it there can be something very dangerous about Rousseau's suggestion that we cannot conceive of individuals prior to the institutions which they live by and shape, since in every form of society individuals have reasons for their will, and these reasons vary with the form of institutions. Certainly their reasons do, yet unless Agent and Actor themselves retain their link to Adam, how can we deny that they are forged from 'indeterminate material' and, if we cannot, what prevents them from becoming inconceivable and unintelligible as future 'social products'? We need the 'Principle of Humanity' for understanding those of other times and places who live by other institutions. Without the condition that the 'pattern of relations among beliefs, desires and the world be as similar to our own as possible',[20] the thread of intelligibility breaks. Unless we hang on to the precept that 'if the natives reason logically at all, then they reason as we do',[21] then different 'social products' do become incomprehensible to us, in the past as well as in the future. Therefore, humanity is needed as an *a prioristic* anchorage for the understandability of both Agents and Actors over time, since they do change their contexts and their social selves in the process – of morphogenesis. The human being thus remains the alpha and omega of Agents and Actors alike (whose genesis can never lead to exodus from humankind).

From birth, part of being in the world is to be a Social Agent and part of living in society is to learn how to become one kind of Actor rather than another (and to decide which of these, if any, a person can and will adopt as their own social identity). Important as all of this is, it still does not exhaust our humanity. On the contrary, the arguments presented here about what kinds of social beings people become are all anchored in the fact that it is human beings who do the becoming. We need then to expand upon the statement made earlier that social identity is irreducible to, though reliant on personal identity – and to justify it. Thus it is maintained that there are properties of persons which are indispensable for being able to recognize that a (collective) interest is one's own and that it affects one's present and future. Without such a recognition, social life could simply not get going at all. Therefore, until allowance has been made for this, there is little point in discussing what keeps it going in reproduced or transformed state; for processes like self and social monitoring, goal formation and articulation, or strategic reflection on means-ends relations (all of which do indeed contribute to the transformation of both structure and agency), are themselves dependent upon more primitive properties of persons.

Justification of the above thus consists in specifying what properties

---

[20] R. Grandy, 'Reference, meaning and belief', *Journal of Philosophy*, 1973, 70, p. 443.
[21] Martin Hollis, 'Reason and Ritual', in Bryan R. Wilson (ed.), *Rationality*, Basil Blackwell, Oxford, 1979, p. 232.

define a human person and demonstrating that these same properties are necessary conditions of social life itself. Such a defining feature has appeared to many to be the continuity of consciousness. The idea that a person is something which is aware of its persistence and progress through time is thus to advance the continuity of consciousness as part of what we mean by personal identity. This continuous 'sense of self' is what will be defended here as the indispensable contribution which our humanity[22] makes to our social life. For unless there are persons who know themselves to be continuous over time, who work as persisting self-recorders, then nothing would prompt the attempt to survive in society and likewise nothing would secure the survival of society. Survival itself would not be on the agenda. Though it is otiose, perhaps it makes matters more graphic to stress that social activities which take place over time, like acting or reflecting themselves, as well as prudence, deferred gratification, strategic intervention, planning or hoping all depend upon a continuous sense of self. This being the case, then those collective and individual actions discussed for Agents and Actors who do things like acknowledging their vested interests, weighing these interests against one another and weighing them against their values, would not enter the picture. The same goes for becoming members of social movements and for personifying roles in particularistic ways. In all these cases, unless there is self-awareness that it is the *same* self who has interests upon which constraints and enablements impinge *and* that how they react today will affect what interests they will have tomorrow, then questions about the meaning and explanation of social action never arise.

This view of the person, central in the work of Locke and Kant, does not command consensus amongst philosophers[23] let alone sociologists, and more would have to be done to buttress the position merely sketched in here. Nevertheless, it is very important to be clear on what most philosophers are *not* disagreeing about. Whatever their particular objections to a continuity of consciousness sufficing to define a person, they are not defending that kind of sociological imperialism in which it is sometimes contended that a person is merely a matter of social definition.

---

[22] Here I will take the referent of humankind to be genetically typical members of the species in order not to be prematurely deflected by the occurance of amnesics etc., although it will be necessary to address such cases later.

[23] Locke put forward a definition which has considerable intuitive appeal, such that a person was 'a thinking intelligent being, that has reason and reflection, and can consider itself as itself, the same thinking thing in different times and places' (*Essay* II, xxvii, 2). From Bishop Butler onwards, critics have construed such continuity of consciousness exclusively in terms of memory and then shown that memory alone fails to secure strict personal identity. See, for example, Bernard Williams, *Problems of the Self*, Cambridge University Press, Cambridge, 1973. A defence of a modified neo-Lockean definition is provided by David Wiggins, 'Locke, Butler and the stream of consciousness: and men as a natural kind', *Philosophy*, 51, 1976, which preserves the original insight.

As certain sociologists have also stressed, there is always a crucial distinction to be sustained between the evolving *concept* of self (which is indeed social) and the universal *sense* of self (which is not). Thus Mauss[24] could trace the slow historical development of more individualized concepts of persons from the Pueblos' assumption of ancestral roles, through classical legal conceptions, to the fully individuated soul which became central in Christianity. Yet, at the same time as allowing for such progressive (and unfinished) conceptual individuation as a supremely social process, Mauss juxtaposed this with the universal sense of self – 'the "self" (Moi) is everywhere present'. This constant element consists in the fact that 'there has never existed a human being who has not been aware, not only of his body but also of his individuality, both spiritual and physical'.[25] There is a persistent danger (or temptation to those who see sociology as a colonial enterprise – of the civilizing mission variety) to try to absorb the *sense* into the *concept* and thus to credit what is universal to the cultural balance sheet.

The best way of showing *that* the distinction should be maintained is a demonstration of its necessity – i.e. a sense of self must be distinct from social variations in concepts of persons, individuals etc. because they could not work without it. Thus for anyone to appropriate social expectations, it is necessary for them to have a sense of self upon which these impinge such that they recognize what is expected of them (otherwise obligations cannot be internalized). Hence, for example, the individual Zuni has to sense that his two given names, one for Summer and one for Winter, apply to the *same* self, which is also the rightful successor of the ancestor who is held to live again in the body of each who bears his names. Correct appropriation (by the proper man for all seasons) is dependent upon a continuity of consciousness which is an integral part of what we mean by a person. No generalized social belief in ancestral reincarnation will suffice; for unless there is a self which (pro)claims *I* am *that* ancestor, then the belief which is held to be general turns out to be one which has no actual takers! Nor is this situation improved by vague talk of 'social pressures' to enact roles or assume genealogical responsibilities. On the contrary, this is incoherent for it boils down to meaning that everyone knows what roles should be filled, but no one has enough of a sense of self to feel that these expectations apply to them. The implication for society is that nothing gets done, for without selves which sense that responsibilities are their own and which also own expectations, then the latter have all the force of the complaint that 'someone ought to do something about it'. Thus the strongest versions of socialization theory

---

[24] Marcel Mauss, 'A category of the human mind: the notion of person; the notion of self', in M. Carrithers, S. Collins and S. Lukes (eds.), *The Category of the Person*, Cambridge University Press, Cambridge, 1989, pp. 1–25.   [25] Mauss, 'Human mind', p. 3.

(and in particular those 'oversocialized views of men' proffered by downwards conflationists), ultimately cannot work with completely 'indeterminate material': it has to be determinate in this one way at least, that of acknowledging itself to be the same being over time.

Moreover, it is worth pointing out that the staple material of social change for this school of thought, namely role clash, also falls to the above argument. Unless a person has a sufficiently continuous sense of self to recognize that both roles are theirs and that performing the two will mean confronting their incompatibility sooner or later, then there is neither a personal dilemma nor any social impetus to avoid the impasse (by resigning, re-interpreting etc.). If Antigone did not know that she herself were both Kreon's niece and subject and also Polynices' sister then she could have no dilemma about whether to comply with the family duty to bury her brother or to obey the royal prohibition on burial of traitors. Given no continuity of consciousness, she might still lose her life through a fleeting act of compassion, but without dying a thousand deaths in anticipation. With no continuous sense of self, she could act in a way which saved her life, but would be incapable of knowing it, just as 'she' would not keep it *as* either a loyal subject or a disloyal sister because both roles imply a continuous awareness of their on-going obligations. In other words, Greek tragedy relies upon a sense of self, even though ancient Greek concepts of persons are unlike modern ones.

These considerations have been used to introduce the argument that a continuous sense of self is a necessary anchorage for both the social Agent and Actor, necessary that is in order to unite a variety of life experiences and normative expectations in one person. Fundamentally, an enduring personal identity is essential precisely because both Agents and Actors can undergo considerable changes, amounting to changes of social identity, during their life-span. So far what has been emphasized is the indispensable contribution which our humanity makes to our social lives through furnishing this continuous sense of self. However, I am not merely arguing that personal and social identities are not synonymous, but making an additional claim which will not be acceptable to all of those who can endorse the first statement. To be precise, the addition consists in maintaining that our humanity is prior and primitive to our sociality and that social identity is emergent from personal identity.[26]

---

[26] Interestingly, Wittgenstein cannot be recruited too readily to the dissenters, at least judging from one comment he made when writing to Bertrand Russell: 'how can I be a logician before I'm a human being!' Norman Malcolm (ed.), *Wittgenstein: A Religious Point of View?*. This is likely to be congenial to Cyril Barrett, *Wittgenstein on Ethics and Religious Belief*, Basil Blackwell, Oxford, 1991, but is an interpretation which would be anathematized by David Bloor, *Wittgenstein, A Social Theory of Knowledge*, Macmillan, London, 1983.

I will use three arguments to rebut the contrary view that our humanity itself is a social gift, in order to maintain that the sense of self, which has been shown to be essential to social life, cannot be derived from life in society. Unsurprisingly, since we are (in my view) dealing with emergent strata, the arguments consist in demonstrating the relative autonomy, pre-existence and causal efficacy of human persons in relation to social selves. These properties will be treated in that order. (What follows cannot be a full philosophical treatment of these issues, but is intended to indicate the path which it would follow.)

1. The first step is to defend Kant's relatively autonomous self from Durkheimian attempts to render it socially dependent. Kant termed the locus where experiences are unified and the element which owns itself to be the focus of expectations the 'Transcendental Unity of Apperception'. To him it stood as an *a priori* condition for the ordering of experience itself, and whilst not accorded categorical status *per se*, it actually functions as the underwriter of all categories. Its existence is established transcendentally (i.e. by asking what needs to be the case to secure a world of persisting things from amongst the flux of experienced phenomena). However, the most uncontentious transcendental argument only establishes necessity; it does not answer the empirical question as to *how* the need is met or precisely by what. It is this which enabled Durkheim to attempt a typical downward conflationary move, namely to sociologize Kant by reclaiming the sense of self as a social bequest. For the sense of self 'can easily be seen in Durkheimian fashion as a "social fact", if we accept the need to pre-suppose a social milieu with public and objective rules if human consciousness – cognitive and moral – is to be possible at all. This "social origin" of the human *sense* of self can ... be seen as categorical in a Kantian way: its origin is the (empirical) fact of society, but it is given *a priori* for any given individual, and its essential authority over human thought derives from it being essential to the possibility of human thought at all.'[27] Yet this attempt to reassert the primacy of the social presents numerous difficulties.

To begin with, this argument has often been charged with circularity, for when Durkheim and Mauss contend[28] that 'the classification of things reproduces the classification of men', one of these 'things', of course, is the 'self'. Yet the obvious difficulty is that this statement does presuppose 'someone' who possesses the very ability to classify. Thus circularity arises through confusing the capacities of the (human) mind with its

---

[27] Steven Collins, 'Categories concepts or predicaments? Remarks on Mauss's use of philosophical terminology', in Carrithers, Collins and Lukes (eds.). *The Category of the Person*, Cambridge University Press, Cambridge, pp. 68–9.
[28] Emile Durkheim and Marcel Mauss, *Primitive Classification*, 1963, London.

(social) contents. Durkheim's response raises *more* problems than it resolves. He went on to admit that all animals (*homo sapiens* included) have the capacity to make 'rudimentary distinctions in the flux of experience', otherwise they could not navigate their environment, but that these are different from public, linguistically coded, conceptual distinctions. When he then proceeds to stress that 'the feeling of resemblances is one thing, and the idea of class another',[29] this does nothing to dispose of the original criticism that the former is necessary and necessarily prior to the latter. In other words, before we can receive particular concepts of self from our society, we have to be the kind of (human) being who can master social concepts.

Furthermore, one may query whether the whole 'idea of class' is really a sociological Kantianism, or whether the 'classifications' and 'categories' in question are not in fact just social variations in the conception of persons. The existence of such can readily be agreed, but their authority, it must then be granted is politically or ideologically contingent (and thus they are quite different from Kantian categories). And still, nothing has obviated the need to predicate the assimilation of these social notions of personhood upon a being who thinks in a human manner.

Finally there remains the basic problem that to accord authority to 'the social' over human thought ultimately depends upon establishing that society is essential to the possibility of human thought at all. Yet, as was argued in chapter 4, society can enjoy no such primacy, for human beings are born into an undifferentiated world such that the primary task has to be the differentiation of objects, meaning that the distinguishing of *social* objects cannot be a predicate but only a derivative of a general human capacity to make distinctions – including it was maintained, the crucial one between 'myself' and the rest of the world.

2. The second set of reasons which preclude our humanity from being construed as a gift of society all turn upon the importance of our living bodies for our identification as persons. Reference to the body is to the bodies of members of the human species and the genetic characteristics of this 'species being' are necessarily pre-social *at any given point in time* (that is, whatever role theorists assign to social factors in the course of evolution). Thus Kant's 'Transcendental Unity of Apperception' does require bodily continuity over space and time in order to connect experiences together as part of one consciousness. The embodied notion of persons, or the assertion that a person is material in the sense of necessarily being enmattered, are ideas which need treating with care.

---

[29] Emile Durkheim, *Les Formes Elementaires de la Vie Religieuse*, Presses universitaires de France, Paris, 1968, pp. 147, 443.

Before seeing what they do imply, it is worth underlining that they neither justify the reduction of the personal to the physical, nor necessarily entail physicalism at all. Let us start by disposing of the spectre of reduction. It strikes most people as obvious that mere bodily or material continuity are insufficient in themselves to define a person – otherwise personhood could be prolonged by the skill of the embalmer or would be cut short by the prevalence of cremation. The lay reaction that there is more to life than the passage of a physical parcel is quite correct as is the common feeling that it is absurd to talk of our bodies playing chess or truant or even sitting down. Instead, we are dealing with 'the body plus', and, rather than wrapping up the issue, the introduction of the physical criterion merely poses the next question, namely 'plus what ?'. Something more is required for completion and the debate often re-opens as to whether this ingredient of identity is pre-social, asocial, or exclusively social. Here this question has already been answered as 'plus the continuity of consciousness' and the impossibility of construing this in purely social terms is what I am attempting to sustain.

However, it is important to keep emphasizing that reference to the body implies no concession to reductionism, least of all to physical reduction. For there is another sense in which persons may be said to transcend their bodies. To refer to them as essentially enmattered does not mean that they are definable or can properly be described by the sciences of matter, that is in terms of physical, chemical or biological concepts, for a person is not necessarily a material concept.[30] As Wiggins puts the matter economically, 'If we understand what a living person or animal is then we may define the body of one as that which constitutes or realizes it while it is alive and will be left over when it dies'.[31] Theologians will then have their own divisions over conceptions of embodied but not enmattered persons versus concepts of disembodied spirits, but our concern here is with human not heavenly bodies. More precisely, my concern at the moment is whether this necessary reference to our bodies, in order to identify living persons, necessarily entails references to properties of persons which are non-social in nature. I am going to argue that this is indeed the case, and to endorse the stronger view that *homo sapiens* constitute a natural kind, which as such is fundamentally irreducible to the imprint of society.

To recapitulate: living persons must possess bodies, which bodies

---

[30] It is possible for a person to fail of materiality in the above sense, yet in a manner compatible with the strictest physicalism. This is because it is possible for the concept of 'person' to be (a) primitive relative to the concepts which do their job in the physical sciences, (ii) primitive relative to the concept of the human body. See David Wiggins, *Identity and Spatio-Temporal Continuity*, Blackwell, Oxford, 1967, p. 45.

[31] Wiggins, 'Locke', p. 144.

being human are those animal bodies whose properties constitute the real essence of *homo sapiens*. Although this body does not constitute the person, it defines *who* can be persons and also constrains *what* such people can do. In both respects, to view humans as a natural kind is to oppose a purely conventionalist notion of the identity of people. The response to the 'who' question is given by reference to the genetic capacity of humankind for interbreeding, and thus excludes fictional 'look-alikes' and functional 'do-alikes'. Concerning the former, we need no longer be detained to consider the inclusion of those products of bodily fission or fusion which certain philosophers wished upon us in order to undercut the claim that memory *alone* could secure personal identity. A continuity of consciousness which is explicitly embodied does not, of course, rely exclusively upon the memory criterion. Yet, since embodiment is in a natural kind, then considerations about changes of identity must conform to what is possible in the actual world, for only this can define the class of persons. Thus, brain and body splits or splinters belong to science fiction: whereas those artifacts of scientific fact, the functional 'do-alikes', such as robots or automata, could not be registered as people because they fail to qualify as animals.

Our embodied nature as a 'species being' has direct implications for the 'what' question too. Thus when talking of what the human person can do, we are also talking about the human animal since the characteristic capacities of *homo sapiens* (as a natural kind) cannot be attributed to society, even if they can only be exercised within it. On the contrary, human beings must have a particular physical constitution for them to be consistently socially influenced (as in learning speech, arithmetic or tool making). Even in those cases where the biological may be socially mediated in almost every instance or respect, such as child-care, this does not mean that the mediated is not biological nor that the physical becomes epiphenomenal.[32] Socio-biology can make valid points without over-reaching itself, if the realist principles of stratification and emergence are respected.

Furthermore, since it is our membership of the human species which endows us with various potentials, whose development is indeed socially contingent, it is therefore their very pre-existence which allows us to judge whether social conditions are dehumanizing or not. Without this reference point in basic human needs (i.e. that which because of their nature, they must have in order to flourish, as distinct from induced wants, compliance and other appetetive states), then justification could be

---

[32] Andrew Sayer, *Method in Social Science: A Realist Approach*, Routledge, London, 1992, p. 121.

found for any and all political arrangements, including ones which place some groups beyond the pale of 'humanity'. Instead, what is distinctively human about our potentialities imposes certain constraints on what we can become in society, that is, without detriment to our personhood.

One of our fundamental human potentials is also the source of the typically human predicament: *homo sapiens* has an imagination which can succeed in over-reaching their animal status. Through tools they can acquire the faculties of other species, master the natural environment, modify themselves and aspire to attributes of the gods. One crucial implication of this creativity is that human beings have the unique potential to conceive of new social forms. Because of this, society can never be held to shape them entirely since the very shaping of society itself is due to them being the kind of beings who can envisage their own social forms.

Logically, however important this point is, it does not automatically imply that persons are natural first and social afterwards (even though the pre-existence of our genetic 'species being' must surely be conceded because most aspects of our bodies are pre-social).[33] Nevertheless, if logic precludes an argument from the capacity of humanity to conceive of different forms of sociality to the primacy of the human over the social, neither does it license arguments the other way around, that is ones which collapse the two into one another or straightforwardly privilege the social in the establishment of personal identity (which are popular in central conflationism). Instead, the final set of considerations concern the need to resist both of these moves, not in order to allow more leeway for the pre-social (since giving due allowance to the body gives this its due), but rather to make room for the extra-social in making us who and what we are. My final concern is thus to establish the causal efficacy of those human relations which cannot be construed as social relations, yet which influence the people we become in society.

3. To define personal identity in a neo-Lockean or Kantian manner, as the body plus sufficient continuity of consciousness (i.e. a definition neither restricted to memory, nor in so far as the latter is invoked, dependent upon perfect recall) not only raises the issue of *who* has this sense of self, of continuous being in the world, which has just been discussed. It also poses a question about *what* in the world they are conscious of – because that which we can record helps to make us what we are. Already, in having argued that a sense of self is *a priori* to recognizably social action and to the personal recognition of social responsibilities, a

---

[33] The qualifier 'most' makes allowance for the administration of drugs, nutritional effects and other influences which social practices may have during the gestation period.

gap has been introduced between self and society. Now I want to widen the gap further by arguing that the things which the self senses (and which are therefore constitutive of personal identity) are not exclusively social (nor are they mediated to us only through society).[34]

The completion of our personal identity takes place in the world into which we are born; yet the tripartite nature of reality itself allows us neither to over-privilege nor to under-privilege the social. Society is indeed the natural milieu of humankind, but this is no less true of natural or transcendental reality. Those who do wish to privilege the social have to convince us that in one way or another (usually by reference to social relations and language) society is the gatekeeper of the whole world. Since I seek to deny it such a hegemony (without querying the advantages it confers on our practical lives or general understanding of the world), then it is necessary to show that we can have *non-social relations with non-social reality*, which as part of our consciousness is also part of what we are as persons.

This it seems to me can be readily demonstrated since it is a necessity which arises out of our embodiedness. We are born into a world which comes to us as one made up of undifferentiated objects, including people, out of which we gradually have to *learn* to discriminate the social from the non-social. In other words, the object/people distinction is an acquired one and we acquire it in that order. Not only, to repeat an earlier point, is this predicated upon our human capacity for learning such distinctions, but crucially upon our surviving long enough to do so! As animals, our bodily needs for food, drink and warmth require an immediate relation with things which are really nutritious, thirst quenching and warming. Survival depends upon these being regularly experienced and therefore these experiences cannot wait upon their social definition (instead, the basis of signification is physiological) nor upon the recognition that they are socially mediated (which is a very complex and indirect process for the incubator-reared!). In the beginning, the provenance of these necessities is irrelevant, i.e. *whether* or not they do in fact depend upon social provision, or upon divine providence for that matter. Direct interaction with the otherness of nature is necessarily prior to being able to distinguish social others: for survival, the sequence cannot be the other way round.

I suppose it does remain open to the social imperialist to deny any *continuous consciousness* of these experiences among the newborn, until they have in some manner (gesture or language) been socially encoded, but this would place us below the animals who appear to 'know' where

---

[34] An example of the type of social or sociological imperialism which is being resisted here is provided by Ian Burkitt, *Social Selves*, Sage, London and Beverly Hils, 1991.

their next meal is coming from. Moreover, there is something very worrying about a social approach to personhood which serves to withhold the title until later and later in life by making it dependent upon the acquisition of social skills. This fundamentally throws into question our moral obligations towards those who never achieve speech (or lose it) or who can never relate socially, because, having failed to qualify as persons, what precludes the presumption that they lack consciousness of how they are treated (thus justifying the nullification of our obligations towards them)? I argued above (pp. 121–9) that a plausible account of self-consciousness could be given in terms of necessary exchanges with the natural environment, which served to demarcate the self from the world through the interplay between them defining which could supply what. One advantage of such an account is that no qualification in sociality would be required from the aphasic and autistic or amnesic (or any of the rest of us) *prior* to our consideration as persons.

The general point at issue here was whether we have non-social experiences of non-social reality, and my answer has been that not only we can, but that we must – from our first day of life. Yet if we do from our beginnings, then why should we not continue to do so during the rest of our lives? Hunger, thirst and discomfort may be our first prompts to extra-social exchanges with nature, but there is also Marx's important insight that we are committed to *continuous practical activity in a material world*, where subsistence is dependent upon the working relationship between us and things, which cannot be reduced to the relations 'between the ideas of men'.[35] In this case, cumulative experiences of our environment will foster propensities, capacities and aversions which sift the social practices we later seek or shun, and thus the social identity which we then assume because of something that we already are as persons. After all, claustrophobics do not apply to become lift attendants.

Thus far, the defence of extra-social sources of the self has worked upon our feet of clay, but what about humankind as just a little lower than the angels? To the assertion that we are capable of experiencing transcendence, social imperialists press on like Durkheim 'to discover the causes leading to the rise of the religious sentiment in humanity'. Since the only causes entertained are social, the conclusion is pre-judged. Now, whilst no spiritual experience (of itself) is auto-veridical, neither is it automatically a candidate for being explained away sociologically. After all,

---

[35] To Marx, those early practices which constitute labour (the production of the means of subsistence) represent a *direct* connection between reality and consciousness, one which is indeed conditioned by human bodily constitution and whose consequences – the making of history and species' own modification in the process – could readily be represented as morphogenetic sequences.

sociology can never be robust enough to substantiate and sustain the faith of the atheist. But what is at issue here is not verification or falsification, both of which are public activities, but rather the possibility of authentic inner experience. If contemplation, or certain kinds of meditation, are essentially wordless experiences,[36] how can their authenticity be undermined (attributed to psycho-social causes) by a third party who knows nothing of this inwardness? Since it is possible to devote oneself to a life of contemplation (though not to live entirely contemplatively) this again will filter the social practices which are sought or shunned. The one thing that the sceptic cannot deny about those who take being on the side of the angels seriously, is that it makes a difference to their chosen way of being in the social world.

'In our end is our beginning'

At the end of the day, there are not too many theorists who are ready to treat personal and social identity as completely interchangeable. Even those of post-modernist temper who are readiest to obliterate the face of humankind and proclaim their anti-humanism, do retain a residual respect for the distinction between the enricher and the enriched – the social source and the synthesizing self.[37] This, I have been arguing, is not only proper but necessary. Yet if there is a gap between personal and social identity, this means that private consciousness and public character are not identical which then opens up a space in which the former can reflect upon the latter – upon which social commitments to endorse for the very reason that they publicly express the person one wants to be, versus those which cannot be embraced because they would threaten one's personal integrity. However, it is only if due allowance is given to what happens in this extra-social space, in the privacy and inwardness of individual relations with natural and transcendental reality that there can be a self who is sufficiently strong to resist collapsing into the social, but one instead who actively contributes to the social identity which s/he adopts.

Nevertheless, social reality is a partner in this development and it cannot be underprivileged for the price of doing so is the stunted development of feral children. On the other hand, since no particular social identity is itself necessary, this left the problem of how particular identities were acquired, as it was unsatisfactory to cede this to social

---

[36] The inadequacy with which language can capture ecstasy is a constant theme in Western and orthodox mystical traditions.

[37] For an exploration of this contradiction, see Richard Shusterman, 'Postmodernist aestheticism: a new moral philosophy?', *Theory, Culture and Society*, 1988, 5: 337–55.

determinism or to leave it as a matter of individual leaps in the dark. Here the bridge between personal and social identity was furnished by the concept of 'agency'. The *conditional* influence of society works through the objective life chances which are dealt to us at birth. For the collectivities into which we are involuntaristically grouped affect the 'social actors' whom we are constrained or enabled to become voluntaristically. Yet someone has to do the becoming (which is neither fully random nor fully regular) and thus it was essential not to conflate 'human beings' and their capacities with social beings. Equally, it has to be allowed that it is the latter who, in combination, transform what it is socially possible for humans to become over time by their constantly elaborating on society's role array.

'Who will become what' thus entails a genetic account that involves choices made under conditions which are not of our making: 'what there is to become' thus requires a morphogenetic account of how the active transformation of society simultaneously transforms the social identities which people can embrace or seek to evade. In the mythic setting of an as yet 'shapeless society', the author of Genesis supplies all the elements needed for the first account – the revealed presence of the transcendental, the abundance of nature, the sociality of man and woman, and, above all, the responsibility of choice. In this essentially tripartite world, our choices as to whether to acknowledge or repudiate Otherness, to use or to abuse the natural environment, to live in mutual concern or competitive conflict with one another are the processes shaping society – not once and for all at the Fall – but continuously throughout all time, by that combination of circumstances, choices and consequences which has been called morphogenesis.

9　Social elaboration

Given that the aim of the book has been to make a useful contribution to practical social theorizing, this has two implications for the way in which it concludes. On the one hand, in now turning to the final phase of the morphogenetic cycle, the objective is to set out as clearly as possible the conditions under which morphogenesis versus morphostasis ensues from particular chains of socio-cultural interaction, as conditioned in a prior social context. Obviously, given the nature of society as an open system, these will only be tendential conditions which will have to be complemented by an analysis of concrete contingencies in every research undertaking. Nevertheless, this seems to be of considerably more use to the practical social analyst than either those deterministic prophecies which fail (the currency of upward and downward conflationism which only remains in circulation given *ad lib* support by *ad hoc* hypotheses), or the indeterminate assertion that the potential for both transformation and reproduction inheres in every instance (the uphelping hand that central conflationists extend to practical researchers, which fails to supply any directional guidance at all).

However, the second aim is even more precise, namely to account for the form (though not the substantive content) of social elaboration to take place. In other words, just as the concern in discussing Phase I (contextual conditioning) was precision in pin-pointing the processes guiding action in a particular direction, so in this final Phase III, the concern is to go beyond the conditions for transformation versus reproduction in general, and to account instead for the actual configuration of social elaboration. Since what eventually transpires at the level of events is a combination of the tendential and contingent, the aim cannot be to furnish predictive formulae but rather an explanatory methodology for the researcher to employ, namely the analytical history of emergence. This transitive, corrigible narrative is the methodological hallmark of morphogenetic realism – in contradistinction to the intransitive 'scientism' of upward and downward conflationism and the intractable oscillation between recursiveness and transformation embedded in central conflation, which merely sensitizes researchers to possibilities. These two related issues will be tackled sequentially in the remainder of this chapter.

The conditions of morphogenesis and morphostasis

Once again, it is analytical dualism which supplies the key to answering this question. The generic solution was provided by Lockwood in terms of whether social and system integration gelled together: the highly integrated nature of both at any given time spelt morphostasis whilst the mal-integration of the two at the same moment tended to issue in morphogenesis. When this fundamental insight was combined with the more detailed delineation of different socio-cultural formations in chapter 7, then this yielded figure 17 which the rest of this section will be devoted to unpacking.

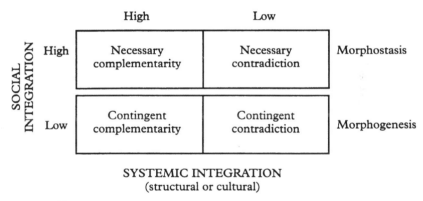

Figure 17 When morphostasis versus when morphogenesis.

Basically, then, it has been maintained that orderly or conflictual relations at the level of agential interaction (SI and S-C in the structural and cultural domains respectively) can show a significant degree of *independent variation* from those characterizing the emergent structural or cultural systems (SS or CS respectively) – as well, of course, as vice versa. In short, agential integration does not necessarily or even usually mirror systemic integration. Yet as was noted when discussing conditioning, unless supplementary *mechanisms* are introduced which link the two, our theorizing would remain shackled to a Humean model of constant conjunctures. Thus, just as conditional mechanisms through which structural and cultural properties impinged upon agents had to be adduced because conditioning only works through agency (as the sole efficient cause in social life), so the same is true of elaboration in society. The sources of transformation or reproduction arise in the middle element, that is the second Phase of the morphogenetic cycle – the locus of socio-cultural interaction – although as elaborated phenomena, their properties and powers are not reducible to it.

Hence, the conditioning linkages connecting Phase I and Phase II were seen to consist in the distribution of *vested interests* and to work by confronting agents with different *situational logics* for their attainment (chapter 7). In direct parallel, the connective mechanism between Phase II and Phase III works through *exchange and power*. However, as linkages, these are *not* generalized social media (as in functionalism), but are themselves relational properties: their status is also that of emergent properties. This is in contradistinction too to those approaches (like structuration theory) which view 'transformative capacity' as always entailing power – of agents to 'get others to comply with their wants'.[1] By highlighting power alone this serves to undercut three sources of elaboration, arising from different types of interaction – the confluence of desires, power-induced compliance, and reciprocal exchange. The origins of transformation are confined to the middle element and consequently the internal relations between the three are not explored, nor are their necessary relations with the prior structural and cultural context examined.

Here, instead, the basic notion is that exchange transactions and power relations are both responsible for social elaboration. Moreover, they are inextricably linked with one another and jointly account for the emergence of either reciprocity or control in the interaction between different groups: if a party is not sufficiently endowed with the appropriate resources to reciprocate for those it needs to receive from another, then the other can make such supplies dependent upon the compliance of the former in the issue which is at stake between them. The resources which are exchanged are varied (i.e. wealth, sanctions and expertise), but these resources do not have an exact price in terms of a single medium of exchange. This is not a methodological problem, it is a matter which is undefined for the actors involved. They have no conversion table in front of them from which to read-off constant prices to be paid for example, by industry for obtaining a particular form of technical training from public education. On the contrary, rates of exchange are socially determined through interaction and thus vary over time.

At a formal level, institutional interaction consists in using resources to transact exchanges with others in order to attain goals, whose target may be either social stasis or change. However, although the importance of the initial bargaining positions of the groups is indisputable (i.e. the amount

---

[1] Anthony Giddens, *Central Problems of Social Theory*, Macmillan, London, 1979, p. 93.

of resources at their disposal), this gives no indication of even the most general conditions under which they are likely to be successful, or of the type of interaction which would be involved. These two questions will be the concern of the present section and they are inextricably linked to one another. To specify the conditions under which changes are transacted is to indicate what, in addition to their initial bargaining position, gives a group negotiating strength. Such negotiating strength is a relational term, this means that the answer is necessarily phrased in terms of the relationships between groups. Automatically this implies examining the interaction between vested interest groups.

Exchange, power and the stratified nature of social reality

In general, social or socio-cultural interaction is explained by the changing interrelationship between the structures of resource distributions and the structure of material and ideal vested interest groups. This is how interaction mediates the social context, ultimately effecting societal elaboration (or recursiveness). Thus all transactions, as processes of exchange and power, involve the use of resources, namely political sanctions, liquid assets and expertise.

Therefore, in the first instance, it is necessary to discuss the relations between these different resource distributions and the pre-groupings of agents whom they delineate in terms of their differential life chances. These first-order relations determine the *potential bargaining power* of collectivities of primary agents. However, since the struggles which are capable of introducing societal morphogenesis/stasis are not reducible to individual jostling to advance or defend personal life chances, it will then be necessary to move to the second-order level where (a) vested interest groups are then confronted with situational benefits or penalties, stemming from complementarities and contradictions respectively; where (b) strategic action, as directionally guided by the different situational logics, depends upon how well a corporate agent can organize the mobilization of the resources potentially available, and; where (c) it is then necessary to theorize relationally about the actual *negotiating strength* which pertains *between* resource mobilizers, and, is thus a long distance removed from raw *bargaining power*.

Bargaining power (first order)

Since all methods for promoting change or protecting stability, depend upon the use of resources, then their distribution is of the greatest importance since it/they govern who has access to them and can thus participate in these processes. The differential availability of different resources to various agents is thus the bedrock of bargaining power. Resources are considered as inaccessible according to the degree to which socially significant parties do not possess them and cannot make use of them, and the extent to which other social groups can employ them to exclude these agents, their interests, and issues from processes of transaction.

The overall availability of each resource (as opposed to its availability to any particular group) varies with the shape of its distribution, i.e. distributions differ in degree of concentration from time to time and from place to place. As a general statement this appears to be uncontentious and it is endorsed from most sociological perspectives. For example, whilst Marxists stress the universality of a ruling class, commanding and cumulating scarce resources, they do not assume that its size is in constant proportion to the mass of the population (either within similar social formations or between different ones). Indeed, the changing distribution of resources is vital to various aspects of the Marxist theory of change itself – the concepts of 'capital accumulation', 'increasing immiseration' and 'class polarization' are only a few instances of this. Equally, functionalist propositions about the way in which the resource distribution parallels the contributions made to social requirements, entail no assumptions about the extensiveness of the latter and hence the concentration of the former. Finally, elite theory in general, because it distinguishes different numbers and kinds of elites who enjoy different degrees and types of privileges in different epochs and areas, obviously incorporates the notion of variability in resource distributions.

The significance of this assumption here is that the greater the concentration of resources, the fewer the number of parties who will be able strategically to transact societal change. In other words, the degree of concentration affects two basic aspects of interaction. Firstly, it influences the steepness of the gradient between elites and masses and hence their respective opportunities to participate effectively in strategic interaction. Secondly, it follows that the degree of concentration also helps to determine the volume and kinds of demands which can be transacted from different parts of society.

Both in theory and practice, the first concern is with the original institutionalized distributions of wealth, sanctions, and expertise at T^1, the start of any new analytical cycle. For this places important limitations on some of the basic aspects of transactions. (Here it is crucial not to forget that united inaction, in repulsing the ambitions of the resourceless masses, is probably the most important form of concerted 'interaction' but it is also resource-dependent.) In particular the contemporary distribution of resources restricts:

(i)   The nature and number of people admitted to transactions: these are limited to corporate agents;

(ii) their initial bargaining positions;

(iii) the volume and kinds of demands which can be strategically promoted at first.

The *original* distribution of resources does not exert such influences for all time, partly because interaction itself will bring certain agents into a better position *vis-à-vis* resources and partly because their distributions are constantly changing in response to various independent factors, thus increasing and decreasing the resources available to particular interest groups. Hence, as far as the analysis of interaction is concerned, our task is to follow through the constraining influences exerted by the changing resource distributions on transactions between vested interest groups. However, when we come to the point of elaboration itself, we will see that the original distribution of resources facilitated a series of changes in the earliest days of the new cycle which then constituted the context for further interaction and strings of subsequent changes. Later change may reverse earlier developments, but this does not mean that the former escapes from having been conditioned by the latter, and it does not remove the imprint of the original distribution of resources upon societal development.

At all times every vested interest group will have a place on the hierarchical distribution of each of the three resources considered. The general position of a group is made up of its placings on the hierarchies of wealth, sanctions and expertise. Methodologically it is impossible, at least at the present time, to express these general positions in precise mathematical terms. I have discussed the reasons for this in more detail elsewhere,[2] but the basic obstacles consist in;

Doubts about the universal character of any hierarchy, such as 'expertise', which is at least partially dependent upon the subjective attribution of prestige;

difficulties in specifying and ranking all positions, such as those carrying formal and informal sanctions, on a hierarchy;

problems of incommensurability between the three hierarchies, given the absence of a common denominator to which all resources can be reduced.

[2] Margaret S. Archer and S. Giner (eds.), *Contemporary Europe: Class, Status and power*, Weidenfeld and Nicolson, London, 1971, pp. 17–19. See also G. Runciman, 'Class, status and power?', in J. A. Jackson (ed.), *Social Stratification*, Cambridge University Press, Cambridge, 1968.

In view of this, we are forced to work in rather gross terms, merely designating groups as having high or low access to particular resources. However, working within these limitations, it is possible to advance three propositions which link agents and resources to interaction.

1. Agents with low access to all resources will be in the weakest bargaining position;
2. agents with differential access to the various resources will be in a stronger bargaining position;
3. agents with high access to all resources will be in the best bargaining position.

Therefore, it is groups in the latter position who will tend to be responsible for the majority of changes, whereas those in the first position will probably not be able to introduce significant modifications. It must be remembered, however, that the crucial overall relationship is between the position of the vested interest groups and the availability of the resources themselves. In other words, the less concentrated the distribution of resources, the fewer the number of agents who will find themselves in position (1), and the greater the proportion of groups who will be able to participate profitably in transactions. The opposite is equally true; a very high concentration of resources places a very restricted sections of society in position (3). Along the same lines a differential concentration of the three resources maximizes the number of interest groups finding themselves in position (2).

Negotiating strength (second order)

Clearly the social distribution of resources and the relations between agential groupings can change independently of one another. This is axiomatic in analytical dualism, since the former concerns the 'parts' of society and the latter pertains to the 'people'. As far as relationships amongst resource holders are concerned, these cannot be conflated with nor derived from the fact of the concentration of resources alone, but they are of great importance for the nature of interaction and change. Resource holders may be superimposed, homogeneous and united, or they may be dissimilar, mutually antagonistic, and in pursuit of independent goals.

The question is still more complex for it involves discussion of the relations *between* different kinds of resource holders as well as *amongst* each of them. Obviously as far as the former is concerned, the extent to which the distributions of the different resources are superimposed is the crucial variable – for this determines whether one is referring to the same group or section of society when talking about those who command most financial resources or political sanctions or expertise. Even if there is a high degree of superimposition, the second question remains – namely how far do corporate agents get on with one another and pull together to attain joint or mutually compatible goals?

Elsewhere I have argued (see note 2) that there are no logical reasons for assuming that the 'class, status and party' dimensions of social stratification are superimposed on top of one another, rather than significant discrepancies being found between the positions of given groups on the three hierarchies. Instead it is maintained that superimposition is a matter of contingency and degree, which have to be established in each particular case and place. The same approach characterizes the treatment of resource holders: they are neither presumed to be a single corporate group whose privileges extend over all that is scarce and socially valued, nor to consist of a plurality of corporate agents which are distinct from one another in terms of the resources upon which their privileged positions are based. Thus the analytical framework employed here is not committed in advance to either a undimensional ruling class model or a pluralist picture of multiple elites. It is neutral in the sense that if one of these models holds universally, or works well for the case(s) examined, this will show up in any substantive analysis conducted. Thus the degree of superimposition amongst resource holders must be established empirically, and it is this which then determines how far interaction approximates to a uni- or multi-dimensional affair.

However, these propositions deal only with one side of the equation, because when an interest group commands a resource(s) this represents a necessary, but not a sufficient, condition for successful transaction to take place. The very meaning of the term involves two parties, so it is inadequate to concentrate upon what one of them alone brings to the relationship. The propositions advanced under (1) above concern the relative *bargaining positions* of different interest groups, but this is a unilateral concept. For such a group to have real *negotiating strength* it must stand in a *particular relationship* to the other corporate agent involved. This concept is a bilateral or relational term, it is not a generalized capacity, possessed by some groups but not by others, but pertains to interaction itself. Negotiating strength arises in exchange situations, i.e. where group X commands resources which are highly valued but lacking (or lacking in sufficient quantities) by group Y, when Y in turn possesses resources of a different kind which are sought by X. It is a matter of degree, which ranges from (a) the ability of X to make Y utterly dependent on the resources it supplies, through (b) a balanced situation of reciprocal exchange between X and Y, to the opposite pole of imbalance (c), where X is totally dependent on the resources supplied by Y. Cases (a) and (c) are instances when power, itself an emergent relational property, characterizes interaction. This is so providing that the dependent agent cannot reciprocate, cannot get the needed resources from elsewhere, cannot coerce the other party to supply them, and, finally cannot reconcile itself to dispensing with the resources or services supplied.[3] This last caveat implies that there is always a cultural (ideological) component, inherent in negotiating strength, which is thus not a purely structural concept.

Thus the effect of (first order) bargaining power is to define who can bring what amounts and kinds of resources to bear in the struggle to promote vested interests when confronted by (second order) constraints or enablements arising from SEPs and CEPs. Yet as has been discussed in chapter 8, in the very process of seeking to affect this state of affairs, pre-grouped agents themselves undergo re-grouping. The double morphogenesis gives rise to new Corporate Agents and relations between them, that is to PEPs. Each group which is now distinguished from Primary agents is so by virtue of its internal organization and the public articulation of its objectives. But in turn, this specification of aims establishes congruence and incongruities with the purposes of other Corporate Agents and consequently conditions the possibility of alliances between them. We are no longer talking about naked group antagonism, but where PEPs are concerned, with the conditioning of strategic interaction. Negotiating Strength is itself the result of the result of prior interaction, or if preferred, it is a relational resultant. It refers to the emergent 'resources and relations' of Corporate Agents *vis-à-vis* one another and is the equivalent for agency of those forms of institutional and ideational elaboration taking place, whose pursuit generated these agential effects in the process.

Transformational and reproductive power (third order)

Matters do not stop here. The 'results of the results' discussed above are threefold: there is structural differentiation intrinsic to the emergence of

---

[3] From these conditions, Peter Blau derives the strategies required to attain or sustain control on the part of X in relation to Y. X must try to establish rates of exchange which are highly favourable to itself; bar Y's access to alternative sources of supply through monopolizing the resource or legally controlling the processes of exchange; discourage any attempt at coercion on Y's part; prevent Y from being indifferent to the benefits it offers. Equally Y's defensive strategies, aimed at keeping up its own negotiating strength, can be deduced by corollary. It must do everything it can to avoid being reduced to complete dependence on X. This involves a constant effort to prevent the exchange rate from becoming too unfavourable, by increasing the desirability and exclusivity of its own resources or services to X. It must work at keeping alternative supply lines open and accumulating supplies, thus increasing independence from X; developing strong organization in order to compel X to behave differently; and propagating counter-ideologies which undermine X's right to use resources in the way it does. See *Exchange and Power in Social Life*, New York, Wiley, 1964, ch. 5, 'Differentiation of Power'.

	Contradictions		Complementarities	
	Necessary	Contingent	Necessary	Contingent
(Situational logic)	(Correction)	(Elimination)	(Protection)	(Opportunism)
CEP's C.S. level S-C. level	Syncretism Unification	Pluralism Cleavage	Systematization Reproduction	Specialization Sectionalism
SEP's S.S. level S-I. level	Compromise Containment	Competition Polarisation	Integration Solidarity	Differentiation Diversification

Figure 18 Cultural and structural morphogenesis/morphostasis at the systemic and social levels.

SEPs; ideational diversification intrinsic to the emergence of CEPs; and social re-grouping intrinsic to the emergence of PEPs. In turn there are further results (third order) of the relations between these three developments. The generic issue now is that these structural and the cultural developments may or may not gel, yet both are exerting further conditional influences upon agency. Therefore, what transpires depends upon their reception by PEPs and the negotiating strength of Corporate groups *vis-à-vis* others. Discussion will be simplified by reference to figure 18.

For both culture and structure, the systemic level (presented on the top line for each) shows the full range of developments which can be generated if the respective situational logics are all successfully followed (and each of the relevant contingencies materializes). As we have seen, those Corporate Agents whose interests are vested in any one of these four states of affairs, in either the cultural or social system, have a corresponding ideal at the level of social or socio-cultural interaction which is most conducive to securing the systemic status quo desired by them. To this end various forms of structural and cultural power will be deployed by them as containment strategies[4] intended to preclude deviant social developments; such preferred social states are presented on the bottom

---

[4] See my *Culture and Agency*, Cambridge University Press, Cambridge, 1989, pp. 189–97 for a fuller discussion of containment strategies.

line for both culture and structure. However, as always, these are conditional effects (of the C.S. on the S-C and of the SS on SI) and their success is no foregone conclusion. Everything in fact depends upon their *social reception*. And that is determined by the relational negotiating strength between the Corporate Agent promoting the *systemic* state in question and the array of PEPs which have now disengaged in *society*, whose goals may be at variance with those of the former.

Thus, insofar as the full range of systemic states are manifest in different parts of society and their protagonists are effective in wielding structural power, then the consequence for the social level is a break up of stable groupings. Re-grouping is tantamount to re-stratification. Vertical strata reinforced by *containment* and *solidarity* are complicated by new divisions prompted by *polarization* and horizontal *diversification*; any prior form of monolithic hegemony is fragmented into a variety of powerful corporate agents; and the anterior category of primary agents shrinks quantitatively, and qualitatively loses unity as underprivilege now results from losing out in a *multiplicity* of power plays. Exactly the same is the case for culture, where the equivalent of re-stratification is cultural proliferation. Here the simultaneous growth in the *density* and *variety* of ideals induces fissiparousness at the socio-cultural level. However, all of the above is so full of 'if's, 'whens' and 'may bes' that it does little to pin-point the locus and conditions of transformational versus reproductive power – which is the object of the exercise.

The final step towards completing the task consists in recalling the *relative autonomy* of SEPs, CEPs, and PEPs. Because of this their *own* elaboration, and therefore their new generative powers, can be out of synchrony with one another. This is Lockwood's original point, that the relative orderliness or disorderliness of the systemic and the social is open to independent variation. (In the notations used here, this would be true of the CS in relation to the S-C or of the SS in relation to SI). The decisive factor is thus the extent to which the morphogenesis/stasis characterizing the structural and cultural domains, at any given time, actually gel together (i.e. are the elaborations of SEPs and CEPs in step or at variance with one another?). Another way of putting this is to ask whether structural and cultural power is pulling in the same direction or not? Since agents are always the efficient cause of change and stability, then in still other words, how does the gel between structural and cultural morphostasis/genesis affect PEPs? In answering these questions we can theorize about where, when, and with whom transformational versus reproductive power lies.

Because structure, culture and agency have been unified within the same conceptual framework, this paves the way for uniting them analytically, and theorizing about their relationship. For this conceptual unification enables a specification of the morphostatic/genetic *intersection* of the three domains, such that we can trace through the effects of one realm on the others and advance concrete propositions about the conditions of transformational versus reproductive power.

When both structure and culture are conceptualized from the morphogenetic perspective then the two *intersect in the middle element of the basic cycle.* The interactional phase, whether we are dealing with S-C interaction or with SI taking place between structured interest groups, always entails a great deal of interpenetration between the two. (This entailment is a matter of sociological necessity because ineluctably groups of agents have both vested interests and also ideas and meanings). None of this is meant to have as its corollary that the conflict of ideas is reducible to the ideational expression of the struggles between material interest groups or vice versa. On the contrary, nothing stated above rules out a conflict of ideas which gets underway independently of material interests. Even more importantly, none of the foregoing serves to deny that ideational interaction can spawn its *own* vested interest groups – collectivities, who first acquire different ideal interests through which they later develop different material interests by receiving differential material rewards from their cultural capital. Most of the time it is thus empirically the case that we have to recognize that there is structural penetration of the cultural realm, and cultural penetration of the structural domain. Hence the need to theorize about the intersection of the structural and cultural fields, for the simple sociological reason that actors themselves do have positions in both domains simultaneously.

Naked antagonism aside, it is necessary to introduce cultural factors, that is the battle between legitimatory and oppositional ideas which form part of most social struggles and transactions. It needs to be allowed that the discursive success of one set of ideas helps to account for the victory of the group advancing it, when structural factors alone (such as bargaining power, numbers, or organization) cannot explain this outcome. Similarly, cultural factors often have to be deemed accountable for the failure of conflict to manifest itself although the structural conditions appear ripe. Here, then, discrepancies between the relative orderliness prevailing between groups compared with the disorderliness prevailing between parts of the social structure has to be attributed to cultural influences. Thus, empirically and theoretically the cultural penetration of the structural field has to be recognized, for the same sociological reason as before – that social groups not only have interests, resources and sanctions but they also have ideas (and if certain groups would like not to have some of these around, then their opponents certainly would).

How does the fact that structure penetrates Socio-Cultural interaction affect cultural dynamics? Equally, how does the intersection of culture with interaction between interest groups affect structural dynamics? The answers to these 'how' questions home in on the mechanisms through which (1) culture influences structure and, (2) structure exerts its influence upon culture – but always (3) through the medium of social interaction.

(1) The basic mechanism by which cultural factors find their way into the structural field through the intersection is extremely simple. Let any material interest group (call some groups 'dominant' by all means if their societal or sectional dominance can be demonstrated empirically) endorse any doctrine (theory, belief or ideology) for the advancement of those interests (that is their articulation, assertion, or legitimation), and that group is immediately plunged into its situational logic. Structural benefits may indeed ensue from ideational back-up but they have their cultural price and not one which is paid in a single instalment.

By adopting a set of ideas the structural interest group enmeshes itself in a particular form of cultural doctrine and its associated problems. Necessarily, then, material interest groups become subject to some form of situational logic in the cultural domain. They may not make the most ingenious contributions to correction or protection, they may not provide the most inventive competitive arguments or the most innovative departures *but* they will have to keep abreast with them and attain sufficient mastery over syncretic formulae, the systematized conspectus or their ideational opposites, to engage in public discourse proficiently.

For the whole point of a material interest group adopting ideas is quintessentially public – to inform and unify supporters or to undercut opponents argumentatively, are all noisy exercises. And it is precisely because of this audible exposure of ideas that the full price of employing them is finally reckoned. The interest group had, as it were, surveyed the cultural field, selected congruent ideas from it and publicized them. In so doing, it alerts the entire relevant population (supporters, opponents, or quasi-oppositional groups) to a particular part of the Cultural System. If opposition or differentiation are already rife there, then structural opponents find ready-made cultural weapons in the CS which they have every interest in taking up and wielding against any opposing material interest group(s), by attempting to generalize and naturalize those ideas it has adopted for its own advancement. Indeed, a quasi-oppositional group may be transformed into a 'group for itself' by taking sides in a more 'advanced' cultural struggle.

(2) Structural factors find their way into the cultural field by following

the same path through the intersection, only here we have to look at what happens at the other end of it. Thus, let the advocacy of any doctrine (theory, belief or ideology) become associated with a particular material interest group and its fate becomes embroiled in the fortunes of that group *vis-à-vis* others. For all such attachments immediately enmesh cultural discourse in power play.

On the other hand, the effectiveness of cultural morphostatic strategies can be greatly extended over time given the support of powerful social groups working for the authoritarian concealment of contradictions or blocking the accessibility of alternatives. On the other hand, since morphogenesis depends not only on the elaboration of new ideas, through counter-actualization or synthesis, but also upon their achieving social salience, then their sponsorship by powerful social groups can be crucial for them attaining and maintaining high visibility in society.

Again, however, there are costs attaching to involvement in power play. The first is a form of guilt-by-association which socially restricts the appeal of ideas. Thus, for example, a set of ideas whose form is universalistic (like many religious ones) will find its Socio-Cultural reception far from universal, the more particularistic are the interests of its powerful sponsors. When the Anglican Church can become satirized as the Tory Party at prayer, this is the end of a long action sequence in which the original connection between Church, king and country eventually fostered just that particularism which it was intended to conceal. The quest by ideational groups for sponsors is a search to sign up the powerful, but the price of their support is that a second list of subscribers is simultaneously constituted – namely those willing to subscribe to practically any other ideas, providing these reinforce the pursuit of their structural hostilities. Of course, this is only an immediate reaction and soon afterwards these oppositional interest groups will be found busily engaged in ideational moulding and meddling to extract real cultural congruence out of a socially induced marriage of convenience.

These general propositions about the mechanism by which structure and culture inter-penetrate one another are crucial but they are also ones from which few but the complete idealist or materialist would dissent. For basically they state that ideas are forces in social conflict and that the socially forceful are also culturally influential. Nevertheless, it does need to be taken for granted that all ideas are generated in a material setting and equally that all material interest groups emerge within a Cultural System – in order to get to the point of establishing when one is more influential than the other.

So far we have only added a little precision to the 'how' issue. This by itself provides no escape from those banal statements that structure influences culture and that culture also influences structure, for although it tells what mechanisms are relevant, it does not specify which ones will be more important, when, where and under what conditions. Without such a specification we remain no better off than those arguing that structure and culture are 'dialectically related' or 'mutually constitutive' – which are different ways of saying that the two domains are connected, but the nature of their mutual influence still eludes us. The present aim is to improve on this by answering the two underlying questions: 'when does structure exert more influence over culture than vice versa?' and 'when is culture more consequential for structure than vice versa?' By linking the above discussion of the 'how' mechanisms to a specification of the 'when' conditions it is hoped to produce a theory of mutual influence rather than a theoretical evasion.

When is there morphostasis and when morphogenesis?

The proposition will be advanced that it is when there are discontinuities between the morphostatic/morphogenetic sequences in the structural and cultural domains that one of these is found to be *more consequential* for the other, temporally and temporarily. Correspondingly, conjunction between the two cycles coincides with *reciprocal influences* between structure and culture. Finally, the argument will conclude by attempting to demonstrate that theorizing about the interplay of structure and culture in this way also gives some explanatory purchase on what actually results under various conditions of conjunction and discontinuity, due to what agency does in these different circumstances.

Logically, there are four basic combinations between morphostatic and morphogenetic cycles in the structural and the cultural domains. As exemplifications of each readily spring to mind, they are clearly more than theoretical extrapolations and are perhaps best considered as extreme types. In contrast to Ideal Types, they are found in reality, so their discussion entails no one-sided theoretical accentuation; nevertheless, in relation to the bulk of empirical incidences they are extreme instances of perfect conjunction or total discontinuity. Probably this makes them rarities in reality, for the majority of cases are more likely to occupy slots between these two poles. The discussion will be conducted in relation to these four 'pure' combinations and theoretical statements will be disengaged in this context. It then remains an open and empirical matter whether these provide some explanatory grip on cases (societal or sectional) which are 'more like' one of the combinations discussed than any other.

The conjunction between structural morphostasis and cultural morphostasis

Let us begin from the Myth of Cultural Integration[5] and its notion of a community of shared meanings as the archetypical picture of the place of culture in society. From figure 19 it can be seen that the reality in which this image was grounded is, in fact, that particular configuration which results when structural and cultural morphostasis coincide. Far from being universal, the supposed archetype, propagated by so many early anthropologists, is dependent upon this conjunction. In turn, the manifestation of this conjunction depends on specific states of affairs occurring simultaneously in the two domains.

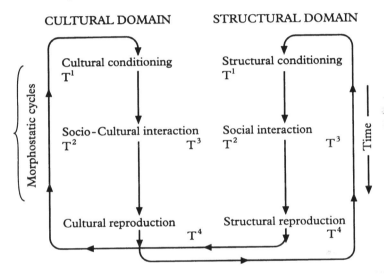

Figure 19 The structural and cultural configurations reproducing morphostatic cycles in society.

On the one hand, cultural morphostasis signifies the hegemony of systematization or syncretism at the CS level (which are not (yet) subject to ideational opposition) accompanied by the S-C reproduction of ideas amongst a unified population, which is what makes this cycle morphostatic. On the other hand, structural morphostasis usually indicates a monolithic form of social organization with a superimposition of elites and heavy concentration of resources which together prevent crystallization of opposition – this subordination of the population thus allowing the

5 Archer, *Culture and Agency*, ch. 1.

social (or sectional) structure to be perpetuated. When spelt out in this way it is obvious that this configuration is not universal; when examined more closely it is equally obvious that where it develops this conjunction will prove long-lasting. Perhaps such very durability was responsible for it acquiring the reputation of typicality among those seminal early anthropologists who confined themselves to the period of its duration.[6]

Turning immediately to the mutual influences of the two domains upon one another, these display complete reciprocity. The force of hegemonic ideas imposes itself on stable social groups and the fortune of the dominant groups reinforces the stability of ideas, the two thus working together for maintenance of the status quo. The mechanisms responsible for these reciprocal influences at the intersection of the two domains are very similar.

First, the fund of cultural ideas which are *available* for adoption by social groups in structural interaction is extremely homogeneous. There are no visible alternatives (CS) with any social salience for those with inaudible grievances to latch onto and thus articulate the sources of their smouldering discontent. Instead, by reproducing a stable corpus of ideas over time, cultural forces work to produce a unified population. Its members may indeed be the victims of preceptual power rather than voluntary adherents to consensual precepts, but in any case they are incapable of articulating dissident views and of passing these over the intersection to stimulate structural disruption. On the contrary, the cultural forces generating S-C unification and reproduction work to depress incipient forms of structural opposition.

Secondly, and in direct parallel, the social structure contains no developed marginal groups or powerful malcontents with the motive or means to increase Socio-Cultural disorderliness. Subordination implies that there is no material interest group available to challenge CS conditioning. Since the emergence of both Pluralism and Specialization are utterly dependent on social groups pushing ideational diversification forwards, these are as yet lacking in the structural domain. Hence, none traverses the intersection to stir up S-C interaction by exploiting a

---

[6] This central notion of culture as an integrated whole, grounded in German historicism (*Historismus*), echoes down the decades. Malinowski's conceptualization of 'an individual culture as a coherent whole' (*A Scientific Theory of Culture*, University of North Carolina Press, Chapel Hill, 1944, p. 38) reverberates through Ruth Benedict's 'cultural patterns' (*Patterns of Culture*, Routledge and Kegan Paul, London, 1961), Meyer Shapiro's 'cultural style' ('Style', in Sol Tax (ed.), *Anthropology Today*, University of Chicago Press, Chicago, 1962, p. 278) and Kroeber's 'ethos of total cultural patterns' (*Anthropology; Culture, Patterns and Processes*, Harcourt Brace, New York, 1963, section 122), to resurface in Mary Douglas's notion of 'one single, symbolically consistent universe' (*Purity and Danger*, Routledge and Kegan Paul, London, 1966, p. 69). All the above make the crucial prejudgement that coherence is there to be found in any culture.

Systemic fault-line or diversifying away from a systematized conspectus. On the contrary, the subordination of potential oppositional interest groups works to delay the surfacing of cultural challengers. This is ultimately the effect of steep first-order distributions of resources, which confine the vast majority of agents to primary status.

Of equal importance in this configuration is the fact that corporate agents find themselves in a similar position as far as alternatives are concerned. Thus, the structural elite is 'trapped' in the only kind of cultural discourse which is currently in social parlance, similarly the cultural elite is enmeshed by the monolithic power structure which is the present form of social organization. It might rightly be objected that these constraints are not determinants, for both kinds of corporate agents have the means of resistance at their disposal. Thus, the concentration of resources in the hands of the structural elite means that in principle some could be diverted for the task of ransacking the CS for alternatives. On the other hand, the cultural elite enjoys a degree of social differentiation, as intellectuals, which could be directed towards the consolidation of an intelligentsia as an oppositional interest group in society – a corporate group determined to equilibrate its material rewards with its intellectual expertise. However, although both kinds of corporate groups have the means to resist mutual conditioning, both also lack the motive.

Given this conjunction, the two elites (whatever their origins) have no *immediate* alternative but to live together but what is much more important is that they have every interest in *continuing* to do so. Here, cultural morphostasis (through the stable reproduction of ideas amongst a unified population) generates an ideational environment which is highly conducive to structural maintenance. Structural morphostasis (through the control of marginality and subordination of the masses) in its turn produces an organizational environment which contributes greatly to cultural maintenance. Whatever private views the elites may entertain of one another, the opportunity costs of turning on each other (to promote a different organization or different ideas) are much too high for this to become public practice.

Quite the opposite is the case. It is in these configurations that kings and emperors readily don the insignia of the high priest – given the chance they will pocket every personal reservation in order to palm the public pay-off. Here, too, the priests ratify the divine rights of kings, the literati keep their books straight, the soothsayers arrange the entrails appropriately, and the intellectuals knuckle down to producing anything from conservative constitutions to confirmatory ceremonials. Those dominant in the structural domain do not *have* to support the culturally dominant or vice versa but in this configuration both tend to do so with gratitude.

Indeed, where there is deep mutual recognition of benefits received, the two domains may become progressively intertwined, with interlocking roles and interchangeable personnel – thus approximating to the super-imposition of structure and culture which Weber described for Ancient India and China. Thus, further exchanges are conditioned between the only corporate agents which have been differentiated out, hence reinforcing their exclusive position. Meanwhile, the mass of primary agents remain subordinate and powerless because of their relational dependency, based upon their resourcelessness.

Thus, where there is a conjunction between structural and cultural morphostasis, the consequences of each domain for the other are symmetrical and conducive to maintenance in both fields. When this state of affairs is detected it is probable that the cycle examined was preceded by anterior morphostatic cycles and succeeded by posterior ones. Indeed, the fact that many 'old and cold' societies conformed to this pattern was what got the Myth of Cultural Integration off to such a good start. But since the Myth has now been shown to rest upon the existence of this particular configuration, it can at last be put in its proper place and perspective. It is not universal to 'primitive society' but conditional there on unopposed cultural traditionalism and unchallenged structural domination – a combination not found everywhere. Nor where it is found will this configuration last for ever. For there are internal cultural dynamics which eventually engage to disrupt ideational traditionalism. These may be speeded up by structural disruption or slowed down by structural routinization.[7]

Just because the wait may be long this does not make morphostasis eternal, universal or even typical, nor does it reduce one whit its reliance on the duration of the configuration under discussion. Because of this the question of what happens when there are disjunctions between morphostasis and morphogenesis in the two fields becomes of enormous interest – for agents can then do very different things about them.

The disjunction between cultural morphostasis and structural morphogenesis

Here we are dealing with the discontinuity between, on the one hand, a single powerful cultural agent and, on the other, a number of corporate agents whose material interests have become structurally differentiated.

Basically, in this configuration culture retains the same formal features as those described above. Namely, its morphostatic character indicates

---

[7] See Archer, *Culture and Agency*, ch. 8.

that Syncretism is being made to stick or that Systematization is well protected by cultural power. For the time being the population is subject to ideational control which prevents S-C interaction from working against maintenance of the cultural status quo. In the structural field, however, for any number of reasons (e.g. possession of raw materials, war, merchantilism, political alliances, colonialism, urbanization etc.) morphogenesis has got underway quite independently. Whatever the cause, the key result for the middle element of the cycle, where the two domains intersect, is a substantial growth in the differentiation of material interest groups. Depending on the types of structural development underway, these groups are pre-occupied with self-definition, self-assertion and self-advancement through social interaction. But regardless of what kinds of structural change are being elaborated and whether some groups want to hold them back while others press them forward (and further groups act as arbitrators and yet others as opportunists), the fact remains that all this activity initially takes place in a stable cultural context. Culture provides no spur to the *group differentiation of corporate agents which is the genetic motor of structural change, but acts as a drag upon it.*

The differentiation of new collectivities (for example, the rise of the European leisured aristocracy), or more particularly their development into self-conscious promotive interest groups, is itself restrained by cultural unification and reproduction. Indeed, cultural power will be deployed against them but this is most efficacious against the weaker groups, lacking in both clout and confidence. But when change concerns those with the opposite attributes and simultaneously increases their ranks and augments their interests, the group which is already engaged in the 'brute' assertion of these interests soon recognizes that they do not gel with the prevailing form of cultural Syncretism or Systematization. Its members do so for two reasons – one at the CS level; the other operating at the S-C level.

Objectively, such a group derives no benefits from the cultural status quo. On the contrary, negative opportunity costs are associated with its support or passive acceptance. It might be argued that, all the same, in the absence of articulated cultural alternatives, this new group has no independent vantage point from which it can either know it or rebel against it. However, the notion that they must remain unaware that culture is costing them, holds no water at the S-C level. For there it receives independent indications that it is collecting cultural penalties whilst others reap cultural benefits. On the one hand, it makes comparisons with other social groups with which it interacts and can hardly fail to note that some of its competitors are beneficiaries of cultural support whereas their own promotive efforts attract cultural opprobrium. On the other hand, one of the very things which enforces awareness of this situation is the use of cultural force against the group which may take any of Lukes' three types.[8] Members of competitive groups do not have to be endowed with the qualities of good sociologists to know that they are being sanctioned, censored and coerced when their opponents are not.

Nevertheless, these new corporate agents do indeed lack ideas to counterpoise against those whose hegemony obstructs them. But they also have a structurally induced motive for acquiring them, in order to challenge the legitimacy claims of others and to establish their own. Consequently, just as their domain had been raided by the cultural controllers, so they now cross the intersection to ransack the CS for items conducive to their cause. Certainly, the nature of the CS will enmesh them in a particular form of discourse precisely because what they batten onto first are the more obvious *problems* presented by the hegemonic ideas.

Thus, where concealment or containment had cloaked a contradiction, the new interest group now rips this aside and precipitates the move towards Syncretism; if some syncretic formula is in place already this group refuses to let it stick and prompts a shift to more generous types of syncretic accommodation; when schismatic tendencies associated with accommodative Syncretism have brought the contradiction out into the full light of day, the material interest group pounces on the contradictory items and brings about their counter-actualization. The fact that a single interest group can accomplish *all* of this is indicative of the stronger influence of structure on culture, *given this conjuncture*. All the same, the fact that what the material interest group unleashes is a competitive contradiction and that its members then become embroiled in the situational logic of elimination, shows that there is always a cultural influence on structure at the intersection – even when the latter sets the former in train.

Similarly, when Systematization has enjoyed unchallenged hegemony in the cultural domain, it is the material interest groups most hindered by it who have the motivation to diagnose the problems it cannot solve and the issues with which it cannot deal. In so doing, they become nascent anti-traditionalists and traditionalism is on the skids the moment a group starts searching for its weak spots rather than viewing it as all-sufficient. Still it dominates social discourse and it is the only form of discourse the new interest group knows. Consequently, the latter is driven to interpretative adaptation and the accentuation of its more congruent elements.[9] In

---

[8] Steven Lukes, *Power: A Radical View*, Macmillan, London, 1974.
[9] Alvin Gouldner, 'Reciprocity and autonomy in functional theory', in N. J. Demerath and R. A. Peterson, *System, Change and Conflict*, Free Press, New York, 1967.

itself this neither rocks hegemony nor generates a distinctive source of self-legitimation. As a result the interest group not only remains on the alert for new compatible items which would increase its appeal without alienating potential supporters – it actually goes out looking for elements congruent to ideational diversification. What it develops is some form of contingent complementarity which buttresses its claim to a special status and special treatment, in terms which the rest of the population can still understand. To this extent its quest for a novel source of legitimation is culturally entrapped: complete novelty is not on. However, given its interests *in* sectionalism, which provides the impetus to pursue the logic of opportunity, the systematized conspectus is soon confronted with diversified ideas which complement it in one sense but are brought in from over a boundary which could no longer be maintained. The development of these ideas by corporate material interest groups eventually induces Cultural Elaboration.

Cultural Elaboration is induced at the intersection of the two domains, through the influence of Social Interaction on S-C interaction. Once new material interest groups have unleashed novel ideas and providing that they continue to hold to them, then the old unification of the population has been undermined, by definition. Henceforth, the traditional reproduction of ideas has to contend with the new options on offer. Because the material interest groups seek to legitimate their advancement in the social structure, by appeal to the newly elaborated ideas, then they necessarily promote cleavage and sectionalism in the cultural domain. Those whose quietism had been the product of containment strategies and those whose conformity had been due to lack of alternatives may well now leap to competitive opposition or flock to the new opportunities, thus augmenting Socio-Cultural conflict way beyond its original structural impetus and issuing in dramatic Cultural Elaboration. But without the structural stimulus, rooted in the disjunction between the two domains this elaborative sequence would not have got off the ground for agents with the power to promote it would have been lacking. Here, then, Structural Elaboration exerts more of an influence upon Cultural Elaboration than vice versa, through the crystallization of new corporate agents who not only are organized but have also become ideationally articulate.

The disjunction between cultural morphogenesis and structural morphostasis

This represents the reverse of the previous configuration. Here the discontinuity is between one powerful structural agent alone and a number of corporate agents who have become culturally differentiated. In this configuration the fact that cultural morphogenesis is already underway, while structure remains morphostatic, points to the fact that Pluralism or Specialization has developed from internal cultural dynamics[10] and the groups attached to them refuse to let corrective repairs stick or stable reproduction last. However, the co-existing state of affairs in the structural domain is morphostatic and continues to work through negative feedback, thus maintaining a particular form of social organization and eliminating deviations from this status quo. If such organization entails a significant degree of social differentiation, then the morphostatic process operates to reinforce the attendant social relations (based on a stable and hierarchical distribution of resources) and to prevent the crystallization of new material interest groups because of their disruptive potential.

Structural stability and the forces maintaining it will undoubtedly have acted as a brake at first on cultural change, by sanctioning the capacity of social actors for mobilization or re-grouping for, quintessentially, social control is directed against re-differentiation in society. Yet ideational diversification is totally dependent on differentiated groups who have enough power to introduce and then sustain pluralistic or specialized ideas. Structural restraints will delay their emergence. However, given the relative autonomy of the two domains, structural influences can restrain the emergence of new material interest groups but they can do no more than retard the development of new ideal interest groups.

Whatever the delays and vicissitudes involved in cultural change, the eventual elaboration of either Pluralism or Specialization has immediate effects at the S-C level. The two developments respectively entail competitive conflict between ideas and progressive diversification of ideas. As they amplify, they promote deeper cleavages or further Sectionalism in a population previously subject to ideational unification or the stable reproduction of ideas. Earlier Socio-Cultural consequences of the erosion of these morphostatic influences mean that more primary agents are drawn into cultural competition and also are drawn to cultural specialization. But, of course, these changes have repercussions on the other side of the intersection.

The most obvious of these is the withdrawal of that very cultural unity on which structural stability had partly rested. Certainly, notions about a common cultural framework which distributed similarities amongst the population and develops a community of shared meanings tend to be exaggerated as features of cultural morphostasis, but at least successful Syncretism or Systematization saved the social structure from pronounced ideational division and diversity. This is no longer the case. Cultural morphogenesis not only means that ideational uniformity ceases

[10] See Archer, *Culture and Agency*, ch. 8.

to be produced, but that what takes its place is a new fund of divisive ideas (presenting competitive advantages or new opportunities to material interest groups) which now intrudes in the structural domain. When the story is told from the structural side of the intersection this intrusion is pictured as some inexplicable 'rise of ideas', or what could be called the 'great-wave theory', in which the upsurge of the Renaissance, Enlightenment, scientific revolution, or feminism, washes over and around social institutions, reducing them to crumbling sandcastles.

The 'great wave' is, of course, no 'theory' at all, but one can respect its imagery while deploring its lack of grounding in human interaction. Yet the mechanism is there and its influence is ineluctable – though it works on people and only through them on social institutions. For what cultural morphogenesis does is to change people (or at any rate some people), from unthinking traditionalists into evaluators of alternatives and from passive conformists into potential competitors. And although this occurs in the cultural domain, its effects do not stop there because cultural actors are also structural agents. Thus, cultural change leads to the reconstitution of structural subjects. Here the 'great wave' image is pretty accurate, for the sandbags of social control cannot stem the flow of ideas.

Furthermore, it must not be assumed that the socially or institutionally dominant are *necessarily* resistant to either form of cultural change. There is no reason to assume that the social groups most responsive to the new ideas with which they come into contact, thanks to cultural morphogenesis, are always the structurally subordinate ones. This is where structure exerts its influence on culture at the intersection of the two – by determining *who* opts to pursue a novel contingent complementarity, and 'established' corporate agents are initially best placed for this, if it is advantageous to them.

Precisely the same is the case for the socially or institutionally dominant when confronted by the emergence of competitive contradictions. For the first time they are presented with cultural alternatives and the ineluctable force of Pluralism is that they must now choose to come down on one side or the other. The cultural context has shifted beneath their feet and this means that there is no longer anything 'automatic' about the ideas they endorse and work with. Certainly, they may be compromised by their past ideational commitments but on the other hand the opportunity costs for continued support of the old syncretic or systematized formula have risen and the benefits derived from them have fallen as they no longer provide a steady source of social unity. What is important here is that whichever side the socially dominant come down on, social conflict is augmented in the new context of pluralistic competition. The reason for this is that the population themselves have become pluralists, given their constant bombardment by ideal interest groups seeking support. Cleavage has been introduced across the intersection and provides a powerful impetus to the proper consolidation of what were previously latent interest groups of primary agents.

Clearly, the two sides of a competitive contradiction between ideas will not be equally or sufficiently congruent with all latent material interests to prompt complete social mobilization, but it is not necessary to presume that cultural cleavages have the effect of neatly partitioning the population in two for them to initiate a conflict which eventually introduces structural elaboration. All that is being asserted is that in some institutional areas the dominant groups will stick to the old ideas as their source of legitimation, while certain quasi-groups find the new opposing notions consonant with their nascent ambitions – the ideas not merely articulating but also shaping their ideals. Alternatively, the socially dominant group can throw in its lot with the competitive formula, in which case it faces rearguard conflict from 'old believers' defending the traditional institutional practices around which they are *already* organized, as for example in most State/Church struggles.

Thus the generic effect of cultural morphogenesis on structural morphostasis is that ideational change stimulates social regrouping. It can quietly prompt the sectional differentiation of new interest groups or can intensify conflict by bringing about the polarization of existing latent interests, as in the case of feminism. In either case subsequent social interaction changes because of the introduction of diversity or intensification of divisions between material interest groups. When this social destabilization issues in structural elaboration, it can be seen as the long-term consequence of cultural change which has exerted this influence on the social structure by precipitating group differentiation, or re-differentiation.

The conjunction between cultural morphogenesis and structural morphogenesis

This is the prime configuration for the rapid shrinkage of the category of primary agents and their transformation into new, varied and more powerful promotive interest groups. Here the distributions of resources are much flatter. In this social formation, compared with all others, more and more groups acquire the characteristics of corporate agency – namely organization *and* articulation.

The final pure case deals with instances where morphogenesis is concurrent in the two domains. It is indeed an extreme type because it is unlikely that the two cycles would manifest precise simultaneity (as represented in figure 20). Obviously, it is more probable that change gets underway in one field somewhat before the other, that interaction may be more protracted in one than the other and they do not complete the final phase at exactly the same time. The temporal discontinuities between the phases are important and it is unfortunate that their closer examination has had to be sacrificed as the price for bringing out the coarser-grained contrasts in this section in order to maintain comparability with the three preceding ones. Indeed, future work will have to devote more attention to their analysis than any other matter, for the effect of temporal precedence on *positions prises* probably explains many of the elements left open as uncertainties and possibilities here.

This last state of affairs can be seen as one possible future for cases (ii) and (iii), where the elaborated features foster further changes in *both* fields (their alternative futures being a return to (i), if the elaborated properties each then conditions maintenance; or a repetition of disjuncture if this is true of only one domain). However, the intention is not to switch analytic procedures at this stage and to start treating this case as part of a historical sequence by investigating how it is intertwined with the three configurations already discussed. It will again be examined in abstraction because, as before, the influences disengaged are intended to be sufficiently general to apply to instances where 'structure' and 'culture' do not share a common history of development, as in conquest or colonialism for example.

The basic feature of this configuration is a mêlée of competing and diverging corporate groups in both structural and cultural realms, in neither of which is domination unopposed or diversification unfamiliar. Given this high level of interaction between differentiated interest groups, seeking structural and cultural advancement respectively, the question is how material and ideal interests now intersect. Although the empirical alliances formed in reality are matters of historical contingency, this does not blur the generic reciprocity of their mutual influence across the intersection.

Let us abstract completely from history and simply picture an array of material interest groups surveying a variety of ideas, with the single thought of which will serve their structural designs best. Confronting them is a series of ideal interest groups which assesses the former purely in terms of their value as potential sponsors. Of course, real life is not like this if only because we are usually, though not necessarily (e.g. indigenous culture/foreign rulers), talking about (some of) the same people. The key point remains that it really does not matter who makes the first move or in which direction the first move is made. Whether some alliance is initiated from the cultural side (in quest of sponsorship) or from the structural side (seeking a legitimatory source), eventually all ideational options are taken up in social interaction as all interest groups become involved in Socio-Cultural interaction. The only difference in real life is that the first move has probably already been taken or at least is practically predetermined by historical complicity.

To see how this intense and reciprocal set of influences works at the interface, let us consider the two sides separately. Supposing quite baldly that one set of cultural ideas gains the sponsorship of a powerful material interest group, perhaps indeed because the protagonists of these ideas sought this support in order to break out of deadlock with their cultural opponents. Then the latter too are irresistibly drawn towards the structural domain, for if one group alone makes headway in winning support there, all others will suffer from the augmented power and resources now brought to bear against them. Consequently, they must woo *other* material interest groups to acquire their support in order to ensure the survival or the salience of their own ideas. Thus, the patterning of cultural diversification aligns itself to the pattern of structural differentiation. This alignment has further repercussions, both of which are themselves morphogenetic, namely structural mobilization and cultural accommodation.

The first material sponsor into the cultural arena probably had close social relations with the ideational group in question (overlapping membership or shared class, status, or party affiliations) which accounted for its readiness to be the first in. Simultaneously, their entry costs the cultural group very little in terms of ideational accommodation, the knowledge of which presumably made them quite so ready to issue the invitation. The same is not true of the other alliances forged between ideal and material interest groups.

Indeed, subsequent sponsorship can best be pictured as a gradient, involving more and more strenuous efforts to mobilize support from social groups who basically have less and less immediate reason for giving it. Since its acquisition is crucial because cultural survival and salience are at stake, then ironically the price of obtaining it is ideational adjustment. Ideas must be adapted, often substantially, to appeal to material interests and thus mobilize the groups associated with them. The price is rarely considered too high to pay because the alternative is that the cultural group goes under – assaulted and battered by their ideational opponents and the latter's social allies.

The consequence is, first, an intensive mobilization of material interest groups, vastly exceeding the most generous definition of their initial 'elective affinities' and eventually including some improbable forms of sponsorship. The latter have been activated through the most radical forms of cultural accommodation, for now opportunity costs attach to the *lack* of structural support. Finally, if the ideational stalemate which first prompted the quest for material supporters is not quickly broken by a substantial imbalance in the sponsorship acquired, then a variety of ideational adaptations, extensions and extrusions attempt to involve every section of the population in Socio-Cultural interaction.

Alternatively, the intersection can be examined from the other side, although of course this is purely a matter of analytical convenience since the mutual interpenetration of cultural and structural affairs is simultaneous. In the context of unfinished morphogenesis, the outcome of social interaction is unresolved at this stage. However, the fact that it is underway means that differentiated interest groups have developed divergent material interests which they now attempt to advance in the face of one another, including the opposition of any antecedent dominant group. Because interaction is intense but its outcome uncertain to participants, each attempts various ploys to gain an edge over its opponents. The one which is of concern here is the endorsement of ideas for the advancement of their cause.

Again, it matters little who makes the first move; this certainly is not the prerogative of dominant groups since frequently domination develops no well-articulated form of justification until it comes under severe challenge or pressure. The group which is the first to go in for ideational endorsement does two things: it introduces a Socio-Cultural dimension to social interaction and, in so doing, it unleashes the effects of the relevant situational logic upon itself and the rest of society. What follows is the direct counterpart of the argument about embattled ideal interest groups; let one acquire a sponsor and the others have to seek sponsorship. So here, let one material interest group present its claims as legitimate and those opposing them have to take up ideas which undermine this legitimatory source and buttress their own counter-claims.

This is where the situational logic of the cultural domain comes into play because it conditions both the fund of oppositional ideas available to be taken up and the form of the ensuing ideational battle. Structural opponents can hardly endorse the same ideas as one another if these are to play a role in legitimation and counter-legitimation. Hence, those not first in are constrained to adopt the opposing set of ideas, if necessary adapting their cause to them in the process. Thus, what is culturally on offer can make for strange bed-fellows but the opportunity costs of having no source of legitimation are usually too heavy for a group to refuse the accommodative effort (by diluting and re-defining its precise material demands). Consequently, all ideational options are taken up, and the more differentiated is social interaction, so the more the minor and extremist strands of cultural division and diversification become activated.

In sum, social interaction and S-C interaction reinforce one another, this, in turn, fosters intensified morphogenesis in both domains. Structural sponsorship means that oppositional and sectional ideas are assured of retaining salience in social life, which is a necessary though not sufficient condition for their victory. However, the very fact that Pluralism and Specialization enjoy continuing social support *is* sufficient *to prevent* the re-establishment of old-style cultural morphostasis. Reunification around the original syncretic formula or resumed reproduction of the traditional systematized conspectus are simply not on in the face of divided or sectionalized S-C groups. Similarly, the interaction of a variety of material interest groups, each of which has become articulate in its own defence and capable of detecting self-interest in the claims of others, is enough to preclude any drift back to unquestioned structural morphostasis. The groups have mobilized, ideas have helped them to do it, and assertion will not fade away because the material interests it seeks to advance do not evaporate.

Hence, social interaction and S-C interaction reinforce one another, leading to morphogenesis after intense competition, diversification, conflict and reorganization in the two domains. The process is not endless; the very fact that Structural and Cultural Elaboration takes place signals that some alliance has won out to a sufficient degree to entrench something of the change it sought – and thus to re-start a new cycle of interaction embodying this change as part and parcel of its conditional influences. Fundamentally, the outcome at the end of these two coterminous cycles is highly dependent on the resources and relations of the social groups involved in interaction; what results from it is equally dependent upon the ideas endorsed by the successful alliance. For, in turn, these will introduce their own situational logic – be it new efforts directed towards correction, elimination, protection or opportunism, depending on the nature of the victorious ideas. These will then exert their influence on subsequent interaction in the next cycle, whatever the new balance of material power turns out to be. Thus, in configurations where there is a conjunction between cultural and structural morphogenesis, the two processes are intimately intertwined but they retain their relative autonomy, not only during this cycle but also in the next and thereafter.

Through consistently adhering to analytical dualism and persistently withstanding the seduction of conflationism, it has been possible to lay the foundations of a comprehensive account of structural, cultural and agential dynamics from the morphogenetic perspective. Throughout this has depended on maintaining analytical distinctions which other approaches would readily compact together. This, of course, was our

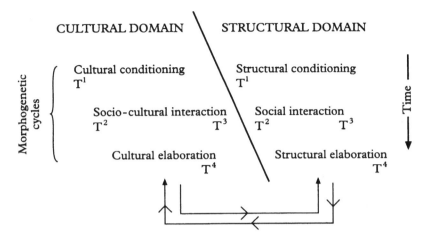

Figure 20 The structural and cultural configurations generating morphogenetic cycles in society.

starting point – a tenacious defence of the distinction between the Cultural System and Socio-Cultural interaction in opposition to every version of the Myth of Cultural Integration, and between the Social System (SS) and Social Interaction (SI), contra every kind of conflationist theory. It is also the finishing point, for the siren-call of conflationary thought persists to the end, bidding us finally to fuse structure, culture and agency into one compacted entity which once again would proscribe examination of interplay between the three by denying their relative autonomy – and so the need to resist to the end.

This last section has taken as its key premise that the structural domain and the cultural realm are analytically separable. Its object was then to utilize the fact that the two could be conceptualized in the same terms in order to examine the relationship between morphostatic and morphogenetic cycles in the two domains as mediated through agency and the power play between agents. The whole point of this exercise was to define the conditions under which structure and culture were reciprocally influential and those which resulted in one having a greater influence on the other. This point can never be reached from the predicate that the two domains exist in a state of complete fusion.

Certainly, in substantive analysis, as in everyday life, the two are indeed fused together in one sense – we often meet them and treat them as an amalgam. Thus, on entering a school, for example, one does not separately and self-consciously encounter a social organization and its cultural contents, or on taking an examination one does not engage in distinct acts of cultural communication and participation in structural allocation. Yet there is nothing in these daily experiences of fusion which warrants their extension into a methodological injunction to study their two components in this way, any more than the daily drinking of water enjoins us not to examine it as a combination of the two elements, hydrogen and oxygen.

On the contrary, social organization and cultural organization are analytically separable. Once this is done it becomes possible to assert that discursive struggles are socially organized and that social struggles are culturally conditioned. Even more importantly, it becomes possible to specify which is more influential for the other, when, where and under what conditions. Any formula which serves to compact structure and culture – like Foucault's 'power–knowledge' complex, Habermas' 'knowledge constitutive interests' or Bauman's 'culture as praxis' – merely defies and defeats analysis of different configurations. What is more, these latter are just as important experientially as they are theoretically. What we confront in daily life are, in fact, *particular* configurations and what we meet and treat as amalgams are, in fact, *specific forms of amalgamation*. To maintain otherwise is, ironically, a denial of the reality of experience, the contextual richness of which is a direct product of configurational nuances. Actors, of course, will not necessarily analyse their experiences in such terms but neither do their practices dictate to us the terms necessary in order to theorize about agents, situations and contexts.

Explaining elaboration: Analytical histories of emergence

Let us recap on the two main points in the foregoing section. *The first is that where any form of Social Elaboration is concerned, then structure, culture and agency are always involved. The investigative focus may be on one alone, but the investigation itself cannot fail to introduce the other two. Agency, of course, is indispensable by definition as the efficient (mediating) cause of elaboration. Nevertheless, as was seen in the last chapter, the number, the quality (corporate or primary) and the relations between different agents is unintelligible without reference to the structural and cultural contexts in which they develop and work.* This, after all is the corollary of conceptualizing the emergence of agency as a process of 'double morphogenesis'.

Equally, despite their relative autonomy, structure and culture cannot be addressed in total isolation from one another. This is not only because they do indeed intersect in the middle element (Phase II), since agents have ideas as well as material interests. Although that is true, it is not all, otherwise structural and cultural emergent properties would be in danger of being reduced to social interaction. It is also crucially important that as emergent properties (second order) their own interrelationships (third order), are themselves causally influential. Thus considerable attention was devoted to the disjunction or confluence between structural and cultural morphogenesis when discussing social elaboration in general – especially in the attempt to theorize about apportioning responsibility for it.

The second point to recap upon is that the manner in which power is conceptualized here, and particularly in connection with Elaboration, derives from the fact that the latter is an irreducible third order emergent property. Societal Elaboration represents the results of the results of the results of social interaction – taking place in a prior social context. Thus, most proximately, it emerges from the interplay between (second-order) SEPs, CEPs and PEPs. Yet these properties, as has been seen, are themselves emergent from more primitive forms of interplay (first-order) between distributions and collectivities advancing and defending their life chances.

Thus, to summarize, first-order emergent properties are the results of social interaction, second-order properties constitute the results of the results of necessary and internal relations amongst the former; and third-order properties, as the results of the results of the results, represent outcomes whose consequences are either societal morphogenesis or morphostasis. Hence, the initial concern of this chapter was to show how the three orders were linked together in terms of exchange and power in order to understand whether the ultimate outcome was elaborative or non-elaborative in nature – that is morphogenetic or morphostatic.

In discussing when one rather than the other would arise, the last section began at the societal level and sought to account for the conditions responsible for generating elaboration or reproduction on the largest scale. (What is of the largest scale is historically variable and non-linear: from tribalism to globalization is merely an appealingly oversimplified trajectory. For in the past, civilizations have collapsed back into tribalism, and in the present, globalism also facilitates and amplifies certain forms of localism.) Therefore 'the societal' is itself a temporal concept, whose referents vary and thus require identification, and 'the macro-' is a relational concept for each stratum is macro- in relation to the one below it. Thus what is designated as such depends upon the analytical objectives of any investigation, which directs it towards a particular stratum of emergent properties.

In what has just gone before, the societal was treated generically as those third-order properties (relations between SEPs, CEPs and PEPs) resulting from second-order properties (that is particular SEPs, particular CEPs, and particular PEPs). Although care was taken to insist that the *dynamics of the societal* were not reified, by stressing that the confluence of SEPs and CEPs was only efficacious if mediated through the power of PEPs (i.e. Corporate Agents who had themselves been elaborated as such through the double morphogenesis), equal care has to be taken to avoid any charge that the *constituents of the third order* are hypostatized entities. The only way of meeting such a challenge in advance is to show how each particular second-order property was itself elaborated – for the third order results from the confluence of the second order.

This means hanging on tenaciously to the same mediatory process which accounts for the elaboration of these emergent properties as it does for all others, namely exchange and power between agents. Thus, just as in the first section, this was the constant medium linking the second and third orders (for the results of the results of the results, it must never be forgotten are the results *of interaction*), so the same is the case now. In other words, it is again the exchange and power relations between agents which are the source of each particular second order emergent, including their own agential elaboration (in the process of attempting to transform or reproduce structural and cultural features in interaction with other agents). Here, then, they are responsible for mediating between the two strata, since the bargaining power which is lodged in the first-order distribution of resources has to be converted into negotiating strength of one set of agents in relation to others for any specific emergent property to become elaborated or to stay in being.

However, it is insufficient merely to state this: agential mediation through exchange and power has to be demonstrated. This need not simply be a defensive response to ward off potential charges of reification: it is a constructive requirement of practical social theorizing. The concern of most social analysts is to explain substantive developments, their social origins, operations and effects on subsequent interaction and change in one concrete area or another. Although they may well not express this in the terminology used here, their research objective is to account for the elaboration or reproduction of a particular SEP (e.g. multi-national transplants), CEP (e.g. gendered beliefs) or PEP (e.g. ethnic mobilization). For this, general statements about tendential powers are inadequate, whether we are dealing with questions of origins, operations or further elaboration. For in the open system which is society, the reason why things are so and not otherwise can rarely be answered by reference to the untrammelled workings of some generative mechanism. If by chance this is the case on one occasion, then the chances are very high that it will not be on the next, which is why sociology should cede claims to prediction. Nevertheless the corollary is not that our methodology then must become some version of interpretative understanding. Between prediction and *verstehen* lies a vast tract of social phenomena (including the second-order properties under discussion) which are amenable to explanation – albeit retrodictive rather than predictive in form.

The explanatory format consists in providing analytical histories of emergence. At every level the tendential powers of generative mechanisms are complemented and supplemented by a historical analysis of the concrete contingencies which intervened to produce particular outcomes. The format itself is none other than the three-phase morphogenetic/static cycle, with the phases delineated according to the problems in hand. The three parts of the analytical narrative consist of 'structural conditioning' by the prior distribution of resources, of life chances, of vested interests and of bargaining power which are mediated to agents situationally; 'social interaction' as conditioned by the former, by other structural factors which also impinge on agents, by social affinities and antagonisms between them, and ultimately by the reflexive monitoring of an inalienably innovative agency; 'structural elaboration' is quintessentially dependent upon how (or whether), in the precise combination of conditioning and contingency, bargaining power is converted into negotiating strength between corporate agents. But neither combination nor conversion are mechanical processes compelling or propelling agents: on the contrary they are the situated products of self-conscious agents which is what makes their strategic use of power and exchange that which actually mediates elaboration.

An example is presented below which is a summary analytical history of the emergence of one particular SEP in two countries since the unified analytical framework enables comparisons across space, just as the narrative format embraces space and time. Readers are referred to the full text of *Social Origins of Educational Systems*[11] for a much more thorough treatment of the exchange and power relations involved and also for the effects of culture, especially ideology, which have been left out of the present résumé for purposes of brevity. What follows is therefore a concrete illustration of the analysis of one morphogenetic cycle which culminated in the emergence of State educational systems. Through it we can exemplify the various ways in which structures conditioned social interaction, their combination with the independent powers of agency and how, when, and why different types of educational system were elaborated from this interplay. Other investigators of entirely different

---

[11] Margaret S. Archer, *Social Origins of Educational Systems*, Sage, London and Beverly Hills, 1979.

problem areas will find nothing here which will enable them to dispense with doing their own footwork (though hopefully it indicates a useful path to tread), for this is the reason why throughout this book social analysis has been held to entail *practical* social theorizing.

The elaboration of state educational systems: a brief analytical history of their emergence

Morphogenetic cycles are disengaged in relation to matters requiring explanation. In this case the problem concerned the structural elaboration and emergence of State Educational Systems defined as 'a nation wide and differentiated collection of institutions devoted to formal education, whose overall control and supervision is at least partly governmental, and whose component parts and processes are related to one another'.[12] This is the end-point of the cycle, judged to be such because their emergence then signals a completely different conditional influence upon subsequent educational interaction and change in the next cycle. In other words, the original study from which this example is taken actually examined two successive morphogenetic cycles and it is the first which is very briefly summarized here.

Obviously, as an analytical history of the emergence of State Educational Systems it is necessary to backtrack through the social interaction responsible for their elaboration and locate its own origins in a prior structural context which both contributed to the goal of transforming educational operations and conditioned who was involved and how they went about the process. In other words, it entails the historical delineation of the three phases, prior structural conditioning → social interaction → structural elaboration. As always, conditioning works through shaping the situations in which agents find themselves and what those differently situated have a vested interest in doing about them. It also influences with whom they are pre-disposed to ally and what resources can be drawn upon in their strategic action which thus defines the differential bargaining powers of participants.

Structural conditioning

In comparative terms, the most crucial *formal* similarity was that the prior structural context, which Corporate Agents were eventually to expend so much effort and so many resources to change, was one in which education was a matter of private enterprise. Because of this control of its inputs, processes and outputs accrued solely to the one institution which supplied

[12] Archer, *Social Origins*, p. 64.

education's heavy capital and labour requirements. In Europe this means that we are dealing with the necessary and internal relationship between the Church, which invested in formal education for purposes of clerical formation and popular catechization, and the schools, colleges and faculties which provided a counter-flow of services embodying the appropriate definition of instruction. This SEP therefore represented a *necessary complementarity* and correspondingly both parties were embroiled in the situational logic of protection. The Church, Catholic in France and Anglican in England, had for centuries invested substantial resources – money, personnel and buildings – to institutionalize the definition of knowledge, pedagogical practices and the type/quantity of educated outputs they required. Since initially they constituted the only part of society convinced that it had pressing educational requirements and which was also prepared to invest their own resources in order to receive them, the nature of instruction represented that which conformed to their needs alone.[13] Consequently they had every vested interest in monitoring and protecting it in that form which reinforced and reproduced its own institutional operations. Educational personnel were subject to the same situational logic of protection, for as clerics, members of religious orders or episcopal appointees, their interests were identical, their roles internally related to if not entirely embedded in the ecclesiastical hierarchy, and their knowledge and values co-extensive with those of the Magisterium. Beyond the catechetical level, pupils too had a vested interest in protecting their future; they were clergy in formation and ordination was often less a question of religious vocation than of occupational security if not social promotion.

Basically, this necessary complementarity between the Church and education served to dichotomize the population, for the simple reason that only one corporate group was assured of educational services whereas *all* the others were not. Thus it follows that the relations between education and other institutions were matters of *contingency* alone. However, this did not mean that all found themselves in the same position *vis-à-vis* education, for the nature of their own institutional operations *mediated* the objective impact of education upon them and did so via its impact upon the situations in which different corporate agents found themselves. Even by the mid eighteenth century, some corporate groups remained unaffected, being associated with institutional spheres which whilst not served by education were also unimpeded by it. This is not to say that, for example, agriculture would not have been more efficient were relevant educational outputs available. However, structural conditioning

---

[13] Technically this is an instance of asymmetrical mono-integration, with education as the dependent institution.

is never a matter of ideal operative efficiency but a practical and objective question of the objective goodness of fit between educational and other institutional practices at a given time. And at this time educational activities were still a matter of indifference to large sectors of the population, who thus had no *structural* predisposition to become either loci of support or opposition to the prevailing form of education. On the one hand, this is precisely why educational morphostasis had endured for centuries, most institutional vested interests being completely *neutral* to education and the Churches' domination of it. On the other hand, this prolonged neutrality, that is the enduring indifference of various corporate agents, accounts for that vast quasi-group, constituted by all those assured of no benefits from (religious) education, failing automatically to convert into supporters or opponents of the educational status quo.

Instead the gradual development of support and opposition was mediated through *contingent developments* in various institutional operations and interests themselves which then served to delineate two categories of corporate agents – *adventitious beneficiaries* and *obstructed parties*. The former is a matter of *contingent complementarity*: benefits are received adventitiously purely because the institutional operations in which a corporate groups has vested interests happen to be facilitated by the educational outputs available, but determined elsewhere. The benefits received can be diffuse and varied (from generalized legitimation to direct instrumental utility), but their common denominator is that they shape action contexts in a rewarding way. Recruitment and replacement, vital to institutional reproduction, will be problem-free given a pool of suitable candidates with congruent values and skills. Less tangibly, certain institutional operations, which may have endorsed and engaged in discrimination, distributive injustice, inequality or exploitation benefited by receiving the combined blessing of the Church and 'educated opinion'. Clearly adventitious beneficiaries might fail to register or may underestimate the benefits received and can also be unappreciative even if they are correctly perceived. Nevertheless, such corporate agents are in a different situation from those associated with institutions whose operations are genuinely neutral to educational outputs. For the former to oppose the educational status quo is to bite the hand that feeds them and this carries opportunity costs (which are not incurred by neutrals). Oppositional activities on the part of adventitious beneficiaries would harm their own interests if it deprived them of the current cost-free services received. This realization may not be immediate but can be learned *en route*, particularly when the education status quo is challenged and its services begin to diminish. Thus Tory support for Anglican instruction remained half-hearted until the mid nineteenth century, its contribution to social integration and popular quietism only being fully acknowledged just as protection of Anglican domination was beginning to slip.

Another way of putting this is that education is in a relation of *necessary* complementarity with the Church and will tend to receive support from corporate agents associated with other institutional operations which stand in a relation of *contingent* complementarity to the current definition of instruction. The mechanism responsible is the receipt of cost-free benefits which shape situations rewardingly for the latter and thus create a situational logic of opportunism – a motive to reproduce the structural relations which yield this free bonus. No determinism is involved, but an objective penalty is associated with opposing the source of adventitious benefits.

In complete contrast are those institutions whose operations are obstructed by current educational practices, that is, cases of *contingent* incompatibility. Again, impediments (like benefits) can be multiple. In the case of late eighteenth-century English entrepreneurs, they themselves were frequently denied educational access on religious grounds, given that many belonged to dissenting denominations, and in any case the classical curriculum was irrelevant to their concerns, whilst elementary instruction instilled deference to squire and parson but failed to socialize the workforce to respect property. Such corporate agents are in a different situation, for although some may be convinced by protective legitimatory arguments, such attitudes are maintained at a price. They suffer frustrations in their day-to-day situations and thus to support educational reproduction is to invite the penalty of continued hindrance. If this is severe it threatens operational goals and for the entrepreneurs it inflicted various injuries on their vested interests: where industrialists were concerned, those leaving elementary school did not have the right values, those leaving secondary school lacked the right skills and those leaving higher education had neither the right skills nor values. Sometimes obstructions can be evaded, by strategies like in-service training though only at a new cost, and they may be inadequate to remove all hindrances, like the restrictions imposed on entrepreneurial life chances by the University Test Acts. Not every ember of the corporate group(s) may detect the obstruction or deem it worthy of strategic action, but not all have to for opposition to develop towards the source of impediments. To hold that this contingent incompatibility conditions oppositional action is merely to argue that such corporate agents are in a situation whose logic is to *eliminate* practices which are hostile to achieving their vested interests. To maintain otherwise would involve a much more dubious assumption, namely that the existence of objective obstructions makes no difference to their actions and that the equally objective costs attaching to positive interpretations of a negative situation will have no effect upon agents' collective attitudes.

Just because only one corporate group is assured of educational services, the remainder of the population, which will include those who are elites in other parts of the system, cannot be expected to convert into a single oppositional group simply because they share the common denominator of lacking educational control. Already we have begun to examine the first conditional mechanism which divides them into potential supporters and opponents of the educational status quo according to its *actual* objective goodness of fit with their own institutional operations and how this is transmitted *experientially* to situations in which agents seek to promote their vested interests. In this structured context, agential interpretations are crucial to action, but it is not their educational situation alone which accounts for the strategies they adopt. There are further ways in which systemic relations serve to condition subsequent educational interaction.

(1) Various corporate groups may find themselves in the category of those obstructed (or enabled for that matter), but the nature of the hindrance suffered and the type of change required to eliminate it need to be congruent, though not necessarily identical, with that diagnosed by other corporate agents who also experience impediments, *if* concerted action is to ensue. Without this superimposition of congruent grievances, multiple forms of opposition tend to result whose general effect is to reduce its impact upon the dominant group and to delay and complicate transformation because of internecine struggles between oppositional agen⁹ .hemselves.

(⸢, Furthermore the conditional influence predisposing towards support or opposition to the educational status quo is modified by other institutional relationships which impinge upon these quasi-groupings: a multiplicity of shared grievances fosters alliance, whereas cross-cutting interests pre-dispose against collaborative action. In short, if the structuring of transformational or reproductive pressures under (1) concerns what the various obstructed or facilitated agents want *of education*, their further structuring under (2) concerns *what else* corporate agents seek to protect, promote in or eliminate from the social system and the alliances which are conditioned by them.

(3) The result of (1) and (2) in conjunction means that the nascent forms of reproductive or transformatory groupings which do in fact develop also stand in a particular relationship to the systemic distribution of resources, which influences both the type of strategic action in which they can engage, and the bargaining power of the various alliances at the outset of

conflict between them. In brief, the powers of corporate agents *vis-à-vis* education are not narrowly conditioned at the interface between instruction and their institutional operations, but derive from a broader web of structural relations in which they are enmeshed and whose prime influence is upon the two elements most crucial in social interaction – collaboration and resources.

(4) The ultimate state of play of these two elements will prove to be vital for the eventual outcome, even though they themselves alter in the course of interaction. However, their centrality derives from the fact that conflict rather than peaceful negotiation is itself conditioned as the *process* of change or defensive reproduction when those pursuing the situational logic of protection are confronted by a variety of incompatibilities. As has been seen, the Church in both England and France had been able to define the form and content of education which best served its exclusive purposes. If this represented a serious impediment to others then it implies that the latter required proportionately large changes in the definition of instruction which would also constitute the greatest departures from the status quo and therefore the biggest challenges to the situational logic of protection on the part of the Churches. These are thus the last things they will voluntarily concede for they would entail the largest shifts away from that which they consider appropriate for their purposes and have invested in heavily to obtain. Hence, other corporate agents, that is those seeking the furthest reaching educational changes, are the least able to obtain them through negotiation. In other words, mutual compatibility between the educational interests and requirements of the Church and those who can deal with it, set stringent limits on the (small) amount of change which can result from negotiation.

When negotiation is precluded by the sheer magnitude of educational change sought, then incompatibilities can only be resolved by obstructed agents overcoming the dominant group itself, destroying protection in order to remove the negative consequences of the impediments suffered. It thus follows that large-scale educational change will only occur if and when the existing structural relationship (the necessary compatibility between Church and education) is destroyed and replaced. Educational inputs, processes and outputs will and can only be transformed and then come to service the operational requirements of other spheres when the old necessary complementarity has been destroyed – via competitive conflict in which strategies for *protection* are overcome by deposing the protectors. The fact that all other relations with education are contingent means that they will (*ceteris paribus*) confront the unrestrained logic of elimination from those who are hindered. What makes the outcome no foregone conclusion are the other relations analysed under (1), (2), and (3) above, *plus* the outcomes of strategic interaction itself which is not merely the playing out of conditional influences.

Social interaction

Neither adventitious beneficiaries nor obstructed agents convert directly into supportive or oppositional groups, for other relations can neutralize or counteract the educationally structured predisposition towards this. As far as contingent beneficiaries are concerned, those receiving rewards must be aware of them, value them and be free of social ties, interests, or values which militate against solidarity with and defence of the dominant group i education – if they are to join it in a defensive alliance for protec on of educational reproduction.

In   ither England nor France did such factors nullify the influence of educa   onal conditioning on the formation of alliances for the maintenance of morphostasis. On the contrary, in France, conditional influences emanating from other institutional relations reinforced the educational predisposition towards an alliance between clergy and nobility twice over. On the one hand, clergy and nobility constituted the two privileged estates – they were united by social ties and similar vested interests in the retention of privilege itself – a necessary link between them which went far beyond their educational relations. On the other hand as enlightened thought permeated the bourgeois section of the Third Estate, which became simultaneously more politically radical and radically secular in its views, the nobility was not slow to recognize the rewards it received from clerical instruction. After the expulsion of the Jesuits in 1762 (on ultramontainist grounds), when the Oratorian order, with its gallican outlook and more modern curriculum stepped into the gap, then social, religious and political factors together reinforced the nobility's support of the Church in protecting its educational hegemony.

In England too, the educational alliance between Anglican Church and political elite was cemented by other internal and necessary institutional relations, (not least Establishment itself) although complicated by party politics. By the early nineteenth century, Tories and Whigs alike acknowledged the services of the Church to social control and to legitimating elitist government based on a limited franchise. Both supported the National Society for Promoting the Education of the Poor in the Principles of the Established Church. Social ties of family and class linked Anglican leaders to members of both political parties. Nevertheless, as the Whig Party increasingly received the Dissenting vote after 1832, whilst it remained a consistent supporter of *religious* instruction, it was the Tories who finally emerged as the strong and unreserved allies of Anglican education.

The formation of an assertive alliance involves exactly the same considerations, and the possibility of bringing about educational transformation requires concerted action which overrides social ties with the dominant group and its defenders. France was a striking example where the polarization of educational conflict was not restrained by other structural influences, that is by social ties and allegiances which detracted from the consolidation of bargaining power. What was especially important was that obstructed operations gave rise to *frustrations which were experienced cumulatively in one group* – the bourgeoisie. Not only was Catholic instruction irrelevant to its activities in commerce and finance but school enrolment and graduation placed its members in an anomic position when they could not gain appointments commensurate with their qualifications. These multiple penalties led to the recruitment of activists committed to educational change from all sections of the bourgeoisie. On the other hand, there were few links between the bourgeoisie and the privileged estates to restrain assertion. On the contrary, social, economic and political relations conditioned opposition to privilege itself – that is to the First and Second Estates, the clergy who were also the educational dominant group and its noble supporters. Simultaneously, the bourgeoisie could profit from the structured antagonism between privilege and the people, given the latter were subject to repression by the clergy, exploitation by the nobility and financial oppression by the state.

Thus, structured predispositions towards educational assertion were closely superimposed on further sources of social division and political opposition. Far from participation in educational conflict being restrained by other necessary or contingent relations, it was encouraged by them and assertive bargaining power was proportionately augmented. Educational conflict thus harnessed itself to social conflict structured by legal privilege. The major problem was that this polarization of alliances strictly paralleled the polarized distribution of resources in pre-revolutionary France. The bourgeoisie, as a predominantly professional and commercial group rather than an industrial middle class, was not poor but lacked capital resources to compete with those upon which the Church's control of education rested. Obviously, alliance with the popular section of the Third Estate, as the poorest group in society, did nothing to improve financial matters.

In practice, there are only two ways in which a dominant group can have educational control wrested from it: market competition which devalues its educational provisions by establishing competitive networks or legal restriction which confiscates them. Given the financial impossibility of the former, yet their exclusion from political decision-making, the bourgeoisie had a further reason for attempting to unite the Third Estate in a general assault upon privilege and a revolutionary assault upon the politics of privilege. Without a transformation of political power, bourgeois interests could not be advanced so collaboration of the Third Estate was imperative to enlarge the political bargaining power of this assertive corporate agent.

By contrast, the factors influencing the formation of educational opposition in England were complex and cross-cutting, eventually resulting in the development of two distinct assertive groups. Initially it seemed that middle-class assertion would not experience great difficulties in generating effective bargaining power since two of the major institutional activities impeded by Anglican instruction – the advancement of the industrial economy and the progress of non-conformist denominations – affected many of the same people. The entrepreneurs and dissenters were not perfectly superimposed, but there was a large overlapping sector where frustrations were doubled – where fathers were constrained to become self-taught industrialists and their children were debarred from polite education by religious affiliation and trade connections. At the same time, educational activism was tempered by the significant percentage of the middle class who did remain committed Anglicans and was considerably dampened by the high proportion of factory owners more concerned with extracting short-term profits from child-labour than with the longer-term insurance policy of educating their workforce.

Nevertheless, during the first decades of the nineteenth century it appeared that the alliance with the working class would considerably augment bargaining power. Shared opposition to the Church as the educationally dominant group, and to its defender, the political elite as the ruling class, promoted joint action. However, the non-enfranchisement of the working class in 1832, when the propertied middle classes gained the vote, accentuated the divergent political interests of the entrepreneurs and workers. In turn this triggered independent educational assertion on the part of labour for a secular instruction geared to politico-economic enlightenment. Consequently, effective action became more difficult for both forms of assertion since they had to recruit participants and resources to oppose the dominant group, but also work to ward off one another at the same time..

In terms of resources this division increased difficulties. Although the industrialists, as their economists never failed to underline, were the group making the greatest contribution to national wealth and although their political powerlessness up to 1832 (and in terms of parliamentary representation and cabinet influence for several decades beyond it), predisposed them to market competition, they made slow headway at matching school with school. Doubtless they could have inflicted much greater damage on the Anglican network were it not for the apathy which led Engels to declare, 'so stupidly narrow-minded is the English bourgeoisie in its egotism, that it does not even take the trouble to impress upon the workers the morality of the day, which the Bourgeoisie has patched together in its own interests and for its own protection'.[14] Conversely, despite the working-class's shortage of resources but given its leadership's (initial) conviction that an instructed class had a better chance of enfranchisement, Chartist schools, Halls of Science and Mechanics Institutes developed to offset *both* the National Society schools of the Anglicans *and* the British and Foreign Society schools of the entrepreneurial–dissenting alliance. The combined effect of working-class independent initiative and the industrialists' inertia was to protract an unresolved form of market competition between the two early societies and to produce an action replay among their successors in the 1870s (the assertive Education League and protective Educational Union) which lasted until the end of the nineteenth century.[15]

Structural elaboration

The changes resulting from educational interaction represent important transformations of institutional relations which in turn condition future interaction and further educational change. The aim here is not to give an exhaustive account of these new forms of structural conditioning which come into play in the next cycle, but merely to link a specific mechanism of change (the process of competitive conflict) with its effects, namely the emergence of state educational systems – which also became internally and necessarily related to a plurality of other social institutions for the first time. This is termed 'multiple integration' in contrast with the preceding form of 'mono integration'.

France, then, is a clear-cut case where a single assertive alliance succeeded in politically destroying the monopoly ownership of educational resources upon which the Church's domination rested. As such it illustrates the important point that possession of political power alone does not confer the ability to define instruction; it provides the legal means for *restricting* domination, by closure of schools, proscription of

---

[14] F. Engels, *The Condition of the Working Class in England in 1844*, London, 1892, p. 114.

[15] Struggle in the realm of ideas, although related to the structured interests of participating agents, contributes its own independent influence to determining the outcome between them. Here educational ideologies intertwined with vested interests in the recruitment of support and for and formation of assertive alliances. In France, their main role was to consolidate one assertive alliance by buttressing the wholly apparent unity of the Third Estate, whilst in England the divisions between Anglicanism, nonconformism and secularism confirmed the pluralistic nature of assertion.

teachers and state confiscation of educational property, but this is not synonymous with educational control (although it is a precondition of it), precisely because it is negative and may destroy the functioning of education altogether for a time. The second stage, where control is attained and a definition of instruction is imposed, involves the *replacement* of new educational facilities. For this to occur requires more than access to the central legislative machinery alone, but also the political ability to mobilize sufficient resources. The Revolution only gave the Third Estate the capacity to complete restriction. Replacement was prohibited by the very need to hold the Third Estate together which presented intransigent ideational and financial problems. On the one hand, bourgeois deputies in the three revolutionary Assemblies failed to thrash out a common denominator of educational reform which could serve their vested interests without alienating the people. On the other hand, there was the problem of how to finance replacement: a revolution which had been waged against the tax burden could not risk imposing new levies as one of the earliest actions of the new republic. The shift from Assembly to Consular and finally to Imperial government meant that Napoleonic militarism could coercively impose and finance educational *étatisme* which embodied the bourgeois ideology of meritocracy, nationalism, vocationalism and Gallicanism.

Thus, when the assertive alliance and the political elite are co-extensive, then use can be made of the central legal machinery to organize public educational funding which has the trebly irresistible attractions of allowing the bourgeoisie to control educational outputs in conformity with its own goals, to do so at the national level, and at public expense.

However, what takes place is not merely the integration of education to the polity, but the emergence of a national state system, for with the mobilization of public spending for educational purposes, educational ownership and educational control become separated for the first time. Control ceases to be entrepreneurial and become managerial, for although education remains subordinate, it is dependent upon resources owned and supplied by the State and not upon private ownership. The capacity to define instruction becomes firmly linked to political position and, what is completely novel, can be lost with the vacillating political fortunes of a group.

In turn, the quest for political support for large-scale public spending on education – support within the governing elite for giving it high priority, and outside it for supplementing central expenditure, means that various corporate groups can make their support conditional upon their own specific educational demands being met by government. This is purely a matter of relative negotiating strength. Ideally the assertive alliance would like to establish interdependence imperatively between education and its own institutional vested interests, yet in practice replacement is conditional upon a diversification of educational services beyond the goals designated by the political elite. Thus there are two sources of multiple integration, the intended and the unintended, which intermingle and determine the exact nature of structural relations to emerge.

The replacement phase in France (1805–33) gave steady priority to developing those forms of instruction from which political elites would gain most, whilst making shifting concessions to such corporate groups in society whose support was needed. Given strong government but limited funds, initial replacement catered for the civil and military requirements of Napoleon's empire. For him, 'to instruct is secondary, the main thing is to train and do so according to the pattern which suits the state'.[16] Thus resources were concentrated at the top to furnish military officers, numerate civil servants and a new teaching profession, thus harnessing ability to State service and creating a diploma elite from amongst the professional bourgeoisie, which hence acquired new vested interests in educational reproduction in the next cycle. Concessionary services to other corporate agents were confined to lower and inferior parts of the new system, with elementary instruction first being reconferred on the Church, to propitiate the old dominant group and to pass it the bill, though the new bourgeoisie government of the July Monarchy replaced this support base with the new industrial economic elite. The establishment of vocational schools (*primaires supérieures*) provided the skills now sought in commerce, industry and business administration, but without disturbing the connections previously established between the higher levels of instruction and state service, which proved too advantageous for any subsequent political elite to dispense with – such vested political interests meant that Napoleon had correctly forecast that 'public education is the future and the duration of my work after me'.[17] Multiple integration is thus an unintended consequence but a necessary adjunct of the emergence of a state educational system. The diversification of educational outputs to service a variety of institutional operations is the price the political elite pays for the mobilization of public resources: it is the cost of educational control without ownership.

The case of England is very different, for pluralistic assertive groups

[16] L. Liard, *L'enseignement supérieur en France*, Paris, 1888, p. 69.
[17] A. Aulard, *Napoléon 1ᵉʳ et le monopole universitaire*, Paris, 1902.

working on a substitutive basis of market competition led to the development of separate and alternative educational networks, outside the control of the Church. Its immediate effect was to stimulate Anglican efforts to retain control through the aegis of the National Society which effectively served to partition the elementary field between this reinforced network of schools belonging to the established Church and those opened by the entrepreneurial-dissenter alliance through its parallel organization, the British and Foreign Schools Society. In effect, control of the elementary level was thus left to be determined on the open educational market by competition between the two rival societies – under that misnomer the voluntary 'system'. As both sides dug deeper into their pockets, then strong, differentiated and autonomous networks of elementary schools continued to develop in parallel. The same was true at secondary level and again in higher education. Correspondingly, educational conflict did not result in a clear-cut transfer of educational control as occurred in France. Instead, deadlock developed between the corporate agents involved. The competition was fierce but since neither party could fatally injure the other or force them out of the market, their respective networks continued to develop in strength but also in parallel.

The final result was that deadlock arose between them. The resources which can be mobilized by any corporate group are not limitless and as conflict becomes protracted, each is trying to run faster in order to stay put, without making headway against the others. From this situation of stalemate, reached by the mid-nineteenth century, pressures develop which culminate in the integration of education to the State. Each of the competing parties seeks to break out of the deadlock, which can only be done by acquiring new resources or legal restraints and the state represents the great untapped source of both. It matters little which set of agents makes the first move in quest of political sponsorship and intervention (in fact it was the Anglicans turning to their old adventitious beneficiary, the Tory Party), for education is dragged irresistibly into the political arena because all competing parties are threatened if one alone makes headway in gaining the support of central government. Hence, a period of political alliance formation follows. The eventual development of a State Educational System is the unintended consequence of all competing parties seeking political intervention for their own ends simultaneously.

Ultimately, the origins of multiple integration proper and of a state educational system are found in these vigorous independent networks, each one embodying a different definition of instruction, through a process of their incorporation. However, the type of State System which emerges is not just their sum. It is the product of negotiation, conciliation, concession and coercion, all of which result in modifying the original networks – accentuating some, altering others and largely suppressing certain educational initiatives altogether.

Party sponsorship transmits educational conflict from the market place to the centre of the political arena. Conflict between government and opposition then had the effect of preserving the networks, sometimes through successive governing parties giving financial aid and legal backing to different networks (thus positively strengthening them) and sometimes through opposition preventing government from undermining a network through financial or legal sanctions (thus defending them negatively). Hence the settlement of 1870, establishing the 'dual system', which was more beneficial to the assertive alliance, reflected the balance of power with the Liberals in office. After 1875, in that quarter of a century dominated by Tory rule, the Anglicans, still enrolling some 64 per cent of elementary pupils, pressed for rate-aid and the dismantling of the Higher Grade Schools to protect their entrenchment at secondary level.

Despite considerable opposition from the Liberals, the labour movement and the free churches, these were the major components of the Tory Act passed in 1902 which created a single central authority for English education and incorporated the networks for the first time to form a national educational system. Once again the mechanism which produces both the State System and multiple integration is nothing other than the consistent pursuit of their educational interests by the conflicting corporate agents.

Thus the types of substitutive social interaction (as in England) which link education to the state are quite different from those which characterize systems with restrictive origins (as in France). There a political elite sought financial support to develop national education – here, educational entrepreneurs seek political support to consolidate their control. There educational systems developed centrifugally, by governmental initiative spreading downwards – here, they emerge from peripheric innovations which converge on government. In the former a powerful elite founds a national educational system in order to serve its various vested interests: in the latter, educational networks already serving different interests become incorporated to form a national system. Here, the emergent system is shaped by the interplay between government and opposition which determines the prominence, subordination and exclusion of the different competitive networks in and from the resulting system – and is thus decisive for who won and who lost out most in the new educational system, its definition of instruction, and its institutional dependencies.

Figure 21 summarizes the analytical framework underpinning this history of emergence.

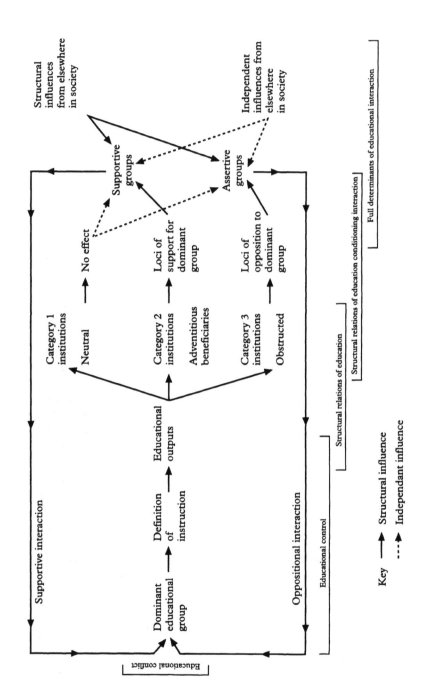

Figure 21 The structural conditioning of educational interaction.

Key   → Structural influence

         ···▶ Independant influence

Necessary narratives – sans grandeur

The whole notion of analytical histories of emergence has to transcend a fairly common tendency to regard the narrative and the analytical as standing in opposition to one another, which is exactly the opposite of what is being proposed here. On the one hand, both proponents and opponents of the *grand narrative* rightly see that the possession of, or the misguided pretension to possess (depending upon which side they are on) some master-key to historical development immediately dispenses with any need to *analyse* history: the historical becomes illustrative of a prior explanatory principle and no amount of further analysis can add anything more than local colour to explanation.[18] Yet the point here is that analytical narratives of emergence can never ever be *grand* precisely because the imperative to narrate derives from recognizing the intervention of contingency and the need to examine its effects on the exercise or suspension of the generative powers in question – since outcomes will vary accordingly but unpredictably.

On the other hand, *analytical* narratives are obviously distinct from any version of historical narration *tout court*, for although social realists in general have no difficulty in accepting the strong likelihood of uniqueness at the level of events, the endorsement of real but unobservable generative mechanisms directs analysis towards the interplay between the real, the actual and the empirical to explain precise outcomes.

Finally, analytical histories of emergence stand equally opposed to those strands of post-modernism which eschew analysis in the name of incommensurability and non-comparability yet whose vituperations against grand narratives leave them puzzlingly free to engage in Foucaldian-type rhetorical persuasion. This is after all only another non-analytic narrative form, but one which is supremely authoritarian since it works by selective perception, verificatory montage and artistic extrapolation without any context of justification. Try to expose its authoritarian jugular by suggesting alternative accounts, and rhetoric beats a quick epistemic retreat, protesting that it is *merely* rhetorical, one image in a land which invites a thousand images to bloom. Yet one has, and the hope of the story-teller is that it has scored the retina with its after-image before declaring itself only imagery. Safely back at their epistemological base,

---

[18] This recalls Marx's protest against Mikhailovsky's attempt to brush aside the importance of historical circumstances for actual social development – and thus the need to study them. Instead Marx warns, one can account for nothing 'by using as one's master key a general historico-philosophical theory, the supreme virtue of which consists in being super-historical . . .', 'Letter to Mikhailovsky', in David McLellan (ed.), *Karl Marx: Selected Writings*, Oxford University Press, Oxford, 1977, p. 572.

the postmodernist wags an admonitory finger at any generalizing ambition in social theory – such as analytical histories of emergence do indeed represent, though not of course in the grand manner.

Practical social theorizing cannot avoid the work of producing such a narrative each and every time the aim is to explain why things structural, cultural or agential are so and not otherwise, at a given moment in a given society. These analytical histories of emergence are explanatory, retrodictive and corrigible accounts. Therefore analytical narratives cannot be 'grand' since the need to narrate arises *because* contingency affects the story and its outcome; they can never be unanalytical because what is narrated is the interplay between necessity and contingency; and they cannot be purely rhetorical because they are avowedly corrigible, dependent upon the present transitive state of knowledge and revisable in the light of new scholarship.

Index

activity-dependence of structures, 72-3
actors
  and agents, 276–81
  and the triple morphogenesis, 255–6, 274–80
  under-stratified view of, 129–32
agency
  and culture, 170, 304–5, 324–5
  elaboration of, 248
  individual concept of, 36
  mediation through human agency, 195–218
  morphogenesis of, 194, 247–93
  and the ontology of praxis, 117–32
  and personal and social identity, 293
  and structure, 1, 2, 6, 7, 13, 29, 33, 324–5
    and the M/M approach, 138, 141
    and analytical dualism, 168, 170, 247
    and central conflation, 133
    double morphogenesis of, 74, 191
    and the duality of structure, 61–2
    Elisionism and Emergentism, 60–4
    interplay between, 149–54
    linking of, 58, 59–60, 64–92
    as methodologically areducible, 101–5
    as ontologically inseparable, 93–101
  structure of, 56
agential elaboration, 196
agents
  and actors, 276–81
  as collectivities, 185–6, 256, 257–8, 277
  conceptions of and social structure, 145–7
  and the double morphogenesis, 257–65
  over-active view of, 117–21
  and the position-practice system, 153
  primary, 185, 186
  and social reality, 195
  see also Corporate Agents; Primary Agents
aggregate effects, and Primary Agents, 265, 270, 272–3

Alexander, Jeffrey, 7, 9, 11–12
altruism, 210, 211–12
analytical dualism, 15–16, 62, 87, 147, 159, 165–94, 300
  and the M/M approach, 76, 81, 138, 157, 160
  and Bhaskar, 151, 157, 158
  and conflation, 151
  and the cultural context, 245
  and the morphogenetic perspective, 247, 252–3
  need for, 132–4
  time in, 66–79
  and the TMSA approach, 148–9
  see also duality
analytical histories of emergence, 324–8, 343–4
  state education systems, 328–42
areductionism, 61, 136
  structure and agency as methodologically areducible, 101–5
Asiatic societies, unchangeableness of, 220
atomism, 136
Augustine, St, 232
autonomy
  and downwards conflation, 83
  of rules and resources, 108
  of social forms, 137, 138–9
  social structure and Individualism, 43, 46
  of structure and agency, 80, 81

bargaining power, 297–300, 301, 302, 327
  and educational development, 335–6
Benedict, Ruth, 83
Bentley, A.F., 258
Benton, Ted, 143, 145, 147, 148, 149
Berger, P., 13, 63
Bhaskar, R., 20, 63, 71, 136–54, 155–9, 161
Blau, Peter, 9, 135–6, 214
Blumer, H., 197
bodies, and the identification of persons, 286–9

345